ROMANS
A SHORTER COMMENTARY

ROMANS

A SHORTER COMMENTARY

BY

C. E. B. CRANFIELD

Emeritus Professor of Theology, University of Durham

WILLIAM B. EERDMANS PUBLISHING COMPANY

GRAND RAPIDS, MICHIGAN

An abridged version of *A Critical and Exegetical Commentary on the Epistle to the Romans* by C.E.B. Cranfield: first published in two volumes by T. & T. Clark Ltd. in 1975 (volume I) and 1979 (volume II) in the *International Critical Commentary* series.

Typeset by C. R. Barber (Highlands) Ltd., Fort William, Scotland,

Printed and bound by Eerdmans Printing Co., U.S.A.
ISBN: 0-8028-0012-2

First printed 1985

Reprinted with slight corrections 1992

CONTENTS

PREFACE

The generous reception given to my two-volume commentary on Romans in the International Critical Commentary has encouraged me to think that a shorter, less detailed, Greekless, version of it might perhaps be welcomed both by some students who have no Greek and also by a wider readership. It is one encouraging feature of the present time that there are clearly very many people in many parts of the world who earnestly desire to be helped to study the Bible.

I am grateful to Messrs. T. & T. Clark, Ltd., both for allowing me to make free use of material from my larger commentary and also for themselves undertaking the publication of this volume. My grateful thanks are also due to my friend, Ian S. McCulloch, of Durham, for most valuable help and advice at an early and decisive stage of this enterprise and for continuing to encourage me to the end of it; to Gary Lee, of the Editorial Staff, Wm. Eerdmans Publishing Company, for his vigilant and expert reading of the whole typescript, which has resulted in quite numerous improvements; and to my wife, who has been, as she always is, unfailing in her help and has now compiled the index, under extreme pressure of a deadline and at a time very inconvenient to herself, without complaining.

The translation of Paul's letter which is used is virtually identical with that in the larger commentary, as printed in the 5th impression of the first volume and the 3rd impression of the second. Italics are used in the translation for words without equivalent in the Greek, added in order to complete the sense.

For detailed support of much in what follows the reader must be referred to the larger commentary. That work also contains abundant bibliographical information. Here I confine myself to mentioning just six other commentaries: C. K. Barrett, *A Commentary on the Epistle to the Romans* (Black's NT Commentaries), London, 1957, many times reprinted; K. Barth, *A Shorter Commentary on Romans* (Eng. tr. of *Kurze Erklärung des Römerbriefes*, 1956), London, 1959; M. Black, *Romans* (New Century Bible), London, 1973; F. F. Bruce, *The Epistle to the Romans* (Tyndale NT Commentaries), 2nd ed., Leicester, 1985; on a much more difficult level, E. Käsemann, *Commentary on Romans* (Eng. tr. of *An die Römer*, 1973), London, 1980, which even those, who (like myself) disagree with it in some very important matters, ought to value as a truly great commentary; and, for any who read German, U. Wilckens's magnificent *Der Brief an die Römer* (Evangelisch-Katholischer Kommentar zum Neuen Testament), 3 volumes, Zurich and Neukirchen-Vluyn, 1978, 1980 and 1982.

Having been specially seriously engaged with the Epistle to the Romans for more than a quarter of a century, I still find it always fresh and cannot read it without delight. It is my earnest hope that more and more people may become seriously engaged with it, and, hearing what it has to say, may find in the faithful, merciful, almighty God, with whom it is concerned, joy and hope and strength even in these dark and threatening and – for many – anguish-laden days, through which we are having to live.

Durham, October, 1984.   C.E.B.C.

ABBREVIATIONS

AV	The English Authorized Version
JB	The Jerusalem Bible, 1966
NEB	The New English Bible, 1970
Nestle[26]	The Nestle-Aland Novum Testamentum Graece, 26th edition, Deutsche Bibelstiftung, Stuttgart, 1979
	The 25th edition, 1963, reprint 1971, is indicated by Nestle[25]
RSV	The Revised Standard Version, 1952
RV	The English Revised Version, New Testament, 1881; Old Testament, 1884

INTRODUCTION

The outstanding importance of the Epistle to the Romans in the history of the Church is well known. Again and again it has played a decisive part in the renewal of Christian faith and life. We shall be wise to approach it with eager expectancy. It is not easy. That must be freely admitted. But, if we are willing to work at it seriously and attentively, we need have no fear at all that our labours will not be richly rewarded.

While there are but few serious scholars today who doubt that Paul is the author of the whole of Romans with the exception of 16.24–27 and, of course, 16.22 (some would further except a few very brief passages which they claim – in our view unjustifiably – are glosses), there is considerable controversy about the tangle of evidence bearing on the relation of chapters 15 and 16 to the rest of the epistle. This evidence includes, among other items, the fact that the doxology (16.25–27) is variously placed in the textual tradition, at the end of chapter 14, at the end of chapter 15, at the end of chapter 16, and also both at the end of chapter 14 and at the end of chapter 16; the fact that the 'grace' occurs twice in the great majority of manuscripts, as 16.20b and 16.24, but is omitted by some ancient authorities in the former place and by others, including some very important ones, in the latter; the omission by one Greek manuscript (with some additional support) of 'in Rome' in 1.7 and of 'who are in Rome' in 1.15, that is, of the only explicit references to Rome in the epistle; and the fact that chapter 16 consists to a large extent of greetings to particular individuals.

Of this evidence basically three explanations are offered: (i) that Paul originally composed 1.1–14.23, without the references to Rome in 1.7 and 15, as a general letter for circulation among churches not of his foundation and which he had not visited, and then subsequently adapted it for sending to the Christians in Rome by the addition of the material which now follows 14.23 as well as the insertion of the references to Rome in chapter 1; (ii) that Paul originally composed 1.1–15.33 and sent it to Rome, and then sent a copy of it supplemented by chapter 16 to another church – the church in Ephesus is usually assumed to be the church in question; and (iii) that Paul composed 1.1–16.23 to be taken to Rome.

There is little doubt that (i) should be rejected as highly improbable. For one thing, 1.8–13 contains statements (particularly vv. 8 and 13) so specific as to be hardly tolerable in a letter not intended for a particular church or at least a particular group of churches. A second, and even weightier, objection is that 14.23 is a most unsatisfying ending for the letter even with the addition of the doxology of 16.25–27. That Paul was originally content to conclude his letter at 14.23, and only later, in adapting it for Rome, felt the argument to be incomplete and so inserted 15.1–13 before adding the material with a specific relevance to the Roman Christians, is extremely improbable. The shortest form of the epistle is rather to be explained as having originated with Marcion, who, according to Origen, cut off everything after 14.23. That, with the views which he had, he should have objected to 15.1–13, with its heavy concentration of Old Testament quotations and such statements as 15.4 and 8, is easily understandable. The doxology, whatever its origin, was probably added in the first place to this short text, because some sort of conclusion was felt to be needed. The variant readings in 1.7 and 15, which are the strongest point in favour of (i), are perhaps explicable as due to a tendency to omit localizing references in liturgical use.

The contention (in support of (ii)) that chapter 16 is more suitable for Ephesus than for Rome seems to us quite unconvincing. For example, the presence of so many individual greetings, far from telling in favour of Ephesus and against Rome, points in the opposite direction; for – to judge from his other letters – Paul seems to have refrained from sending greetings to particular persons in churches he knew, probably because he felt it invidious to single out individuals where all were his friends, whereas, in writing to Rome, which he had not yet visited, the sending of greetings to individuals whom he knew would be an obvious way of establishing contact, and it is not at all surprising that many whom he had met in other places should have found their way to the imperial capital. And, had he really been sending a copy of a letter written for another church to the church in Ephesus, where he had ministered longer than anywhere else, is it conceivable that he would have had nothing more to say to them than what is said in chapter 16? The strongest point in favour of (ii) is the position of the doxology at the end of chapter 15 in one very important early Greek manuscript. But there is no great difficulty in understanding how a text-form ending at 15.33 could come into existence. If any copy of Romans was sent by Paul to another church because of the general interest and importance of its contents, it would not be at all surprising if the last chapter were omitted as not being of general interest; and at a later date someone making a copy of Romans for the use of his own church might easily have omitted it for the same reason.

Explanation (iii), according to which Paul composed 1.1–16.23 for the Christians in Rome, should surely be accepted as being capable of accounting for all the evidence most convincingly. It is not surprising that the doxology, originally added to the shortest form of Romans to provide a conclusion for a document with an obviously unsatisfactory ending, should, in view of its intrinsic attractiveness, have come to be attached to both the other text-forms.

At this point reference may be made to Tertius (see 16.22). In the ancient world secretaries were often allowed much freedom in the composition of letters; but the nature of Romans is such that we may be confident that Tertius either wrote down the epistle in long-hand directly from Paul's dictation or else took it down first in some form of shorthand, and then wrote it out.

It is virtually certain that it was during Paul's three months in the province of Achaia, to which Acts 20.2–3 refers, that Romans was written. No other period within the limits set by the indications of chapters 1 and 15 is likely to have been as suitable as this for the writing of something as substantial and as carefully thought out and composed as Romans. This period is most probably to be identified with either the last few days of AD 55 and the first few weeks of AD 56 or with the last few days of 56 and the first few weeks of 57. In view of Paul's intimate relationship with the Corinthian church it is highly likely that he and Tertius were staying in or near Corinth – a conclusion to which a number of details in the epistle may be taken as lending support.

It is highly probable that the gospel was established in Rome at a very early date, brought there through the presence of Christians in the discharge of their ordinary secular business rather than through any specially undertaken evangelistic enterprise. It is true that later tradition named Peter as the founder of the Roman church; but, since in its earliest form the tradition associated Paul with Peter, claiming both of them as co-founders, and since there can be no question of Paul's having been a founder of the Roman church in the ordinary sense of the word, it is likely that all that was meant originally was that both Peter and Paul had been in Rome, had played a significant part in the early history of the Roman church, and had finally sealed their apostolic ministries by martyrdom in Rome or its immediate neighbourhood – and so were in a special sense the Roman church's apostles, whose mortal remains were in its possession. Since the Epistle to the Romans contains no reference at all to Peter, it is virtually certain that he was not in Rome at the time that Paul was writing, and highly probable that up to that time he had never been there.

With regard to the composition of the Roman church at the time of Paul's writing, the question naturally arises whether it was predominantly Jewish-Christian or predominantly Gentile-Christian. Some have argued that Jewish Christians formed the majority. More common is the view that Paul was addressing a mainly Gentile community. But the truth would seem to be that it is impossible to decide with anything like certainty whether at the time Paul wrote to them the majority of the Roman Christians were Gentiles or Jews, and that we ought therefore to leave this question open. What is quite certain is that both the Jewish-Christian, and the Gentile-Christian, elements were considerable: it was clearly not a matter of an overwhelming majority and a tiny minority.

What organization the Roman Christians had we do not know. From the arrangement of the greetings in chapter 16 it would appear that there were a number of different groups. Did these groups meet on their own for worship? Did they ever all meet together as a single 'church of God which is' in Rome? In view of the evidence of chapter 16, of the fact that the word 'church' is never used in Romans with reference to the Christian community in Rome as a whole, and also of the size of the area covered by the city of Rome, we ought to reckon with the possibility that there may have been little, if any, central organization and that Phoebe may have had to make contact with a number of separate churches rather than just to deliver Paul's letter to a single church leadership.

The occasion of the epistle is clear enough. Paul had finished that pioneer missionary work in the east which he believed was to be done by him, and now proposed first to take the proceeds of the collection made by the churches of Macedonia and Achaia to Jerusalem and then to go to Spain, there to continue his missionary labours. He hoped to visit Rome on his way westward and to spend a short time with the Christians there, and then, refreshed by their fellowship, to journey on to his new mission field with their blessing, their interest, their support. So much is clear from 1.8–16a and 15.14–33. That at this point Paul should decide to write to the Christians in Rome was only to be expected. It was obviously appropriate to give them adequate notice of his intended visit, to tell them of his Spanish plans and to secure, or at least prepare the way for securing, their interest and active assistance in their accomplishment, and also to ask their prayers for himself. Since the great majority of the Christians in Rome had never seen him, he felt the need to introduce himself to them. It is significant that the superscription of Romans (1.1–6) is much longer than that of any other Pauline epistle. Since for Paul the most important thing about an apostle was the message he had been commissioned to proclaim, it is hardly surprising that he should have decided that the best way to introduce himself would be to incorporate in his letter an account of the gospel as he had come to understand it.

Several practical considerations probably encouraged him to make this account specially full and careful. He had now been preaching the gospel of Christ for about twenty years and may well have been conscious of having reached a certain maturity of experience, reflection and understanding, which made the time ripe for him to attempt, with God's help, such an orderly presentation of the gospel. He may well have thought that, in view of the size and importance of the Roman Christian community and its location in the imperial capital to which very many Christians from other places would be likely to come at one time or another, a setting within his letter to the Roman Christians would be a specially good setting, from the point of view of benefiting as many people as possible (both by edifying believers and also by affording guidance for the Church's missionary endeavours), for such a careful presentation of the gospel. He may possibly also have thought that the weeks before it would be time for him to set out for Jerusalem held some promise of affording him the necessary relative freedom from pressure, in which he might be able to set his thoughts in order.

ANALYSIS OF THE EPISTLE

I. SUPERSCRIPTION, ADDRESS AND SALUTATION (1.1–7)

II. PAUL AND THE ROMAN CHURCH (1.8–16a)

III. THE THEME OF THE EPISTLE IS STATED (1.16b–17)

IV. THE REVELATION OF THE RIGHTEOUSNESS WHICH IS FROM GOD BY FAITH ALONE – 'HE WHO IS RIGHTEOUS BY FAITH' EXPOUNDED (1.18–4.25)
1. In the light of the gospel there is no question of men's being righteous before God otherwise than by faith (1.18–3.20)
    (i) Man under the judgment of the gospel (1.18–32)
    (ii) Jewish man is no exception (2.1–3.20)
2. The manifestation of the righteousness which is from God in the gospel events (3.21–26)
3. All glorying is excluded (3.27–31)
4. The case of Abraham as confirmation of the statement that glorying has been excluded (4.1–25)

V. THE LIFE PROMISED FOR THOSE WHO ARE RIGHTEOUS BY FAITH – 'SHALL LIVE' EXPOUNDED (5.1–8.39)
1. A life characterized by peace with God (5.1–21)
    (i) Peace with God (5.1–11)
    (ii) Christ and Adam (5.12–21)
2. A life characterized by sanctification (6.1–23)
    (i) Dead to sin, alive to God (6.1–14)
    (ii) A choice between masters (6.15–23)
3. A life characterized by freedom from the law's condemnation (7.1–25)
    (i) Freedom from the law's condemnation (7.1–6)
    (ii) A necessary clarification of what has been said concerning the law (7.7–25)

I

THE OPENING FORMULA OF THE LETTER

(1.1-7)

[1]Paul, slave of Christ Jesus, apostle by *God's* calling, set apart for *the work of proclaiming* God's message of good news, [2]which he promised beforehand through his prophets in the holy scriptures, [3]concerning his Son, who was born of David's seed according to the flesh, [4]who was appointed Son of God in power according to the Spirit of holiness from the resurrection of the dead, even Jesus Christ our Lord, [5]through whom we received grace and apostleship in order to bring about, for his name's sake, obedience of faith among all the Gentiles, [6]among whom you also are, you who are called of Jesus Christ, [7]to all in Rome beloved of God, saints by *God's* calling: grace to you and peace from God our Father and the Lord Jesus Christ.

The first seven verses are the opening formula of an ancient Greek letter significantly modified and expanded. The first element of the formula (the superscription or indication of the sender's identity) is the most expanded, taking six verses. The reason for this is Paul's special need to introduce himself to a church to which he is not personally known and which he is hoping soon to visit. In introducing himself to the Christians in Rome he naturally refers to his mission, and this leads to a highly significant definition of the gospel which it is his mission to proclaim. This definition, which extends to the end of v. 4, is presupposed in vv. 9, 15 and 16 when the gospel is referred to. What follows in vv. 5 and 6 has an obvious and important bearing on Paul's relations with the Christians in Rome and his proposed visit. The second and third elements of the opening formula (the address and the salutation) are contained in v. 7. Each of the three elements has been made to carry a rich theological content, and the radical transformation of the opening formula from something external to the letter which follows it into what is an integral part of the letter is to be seen very clearly in Romans.

1. Paul styles himself **slave of Christ Jesus.** For a Greek in the classical tradition it was well-nigh impossible to use a word of the group to which the word here translated 'slave' belongs without some feeling of abhorrence. But in ancient Israel to call a man 'God's slave' was to accord him a title of honour. The title was used of Moses, Joshua, David and the prophets. For Paul every Christian is a slave of Christ (compare, for example, 1 Cor 7.22f; and on Paul's use of the language of slavery in connexion with the Christian life see what is said on 6.15–23). The term expresses the total belongingness, total allegiance, corresponding to the total ownership and authority denoted by 'lord' when used of Christ. But, as a self-designation, 'slave of Christ' probably carries, in addition to the personal confession of commitment, a reference to the writer's special office, in the fulfilment of which he is in a special sense Christ's slave.

The fact that Paul quite often put 'Christ' before 'Jesus' is a strong indication that he did not habitually think of 'Christ' as just a proper name, as has been suggested by some scholars, but, in using it, was conscious of its meaning ('anointed' – so the Greek equivalent of the Hebrew word we anglicize as 'Messiah'). It seems likely that he adopted this order here with the intention of giving special emphasis right at the beginning of the epistle to the fact that the One, whose slave he was, was the fulfilment of God's promises and of Israel's age-old hope.

apostle. We have no reason to doubt that Paul was sincere when he acknowledged himself the least of the apostles and unworthy to be an apostle at all because he had persecuted God's Church (1 Cor 15.9). We may be sure that he freely admitted that he was not a first-hand source of historical tradition concerning the life and teaching of Jesus but was himself dependent for his knowledge both of the details of Jesus's ministry and of the substance of His teaching on the witness of those who were apostles before him (Gal 1.17). But he also asserted the equal authority of his apostleship with theirs, basing his claim, it seems, on the facts that he too had seen the risen Lord (1 Cor 9.1), had received his commission directly from Christ Himself (Gal 1.1:

compare Acts 26.15–18), and had had his commission divinely confirmed by the signs of an apostle accompanying his labours (2 Cor 12.12). The use of the word 'apostle' here indicates that Paul claims the attention of the Roman church to what follows on the ground not of his own personal worth and wisdom but of the commission he has received from Christ. The word points away from the apostle's person to Him whose apostle he is. It is thus both a very humble word and also at the same time expressive of the most august authority.

by *God's* calling. Divine calling is opposed to human self-appointment. It is not on the basis of presumptuous human egotism but on the basis of God's call that Paul is an apostle.

set apart for *the work of proclaiming* God's message of good news. Paul knows himself as one who has been consecrated by God (compare Gal 1.15) for the task of proclaiming the gospel. Specially important for the understanding of the Greek noun represented here by 'message of good news', as it is used in the New Testament, are such Old Testament passages as Isa 40.9; 41.27; 52.7; 61.1; Nah 1.15, in which the good tidings referred to concern the intervention of God's reign, the advent of His salvation. But there is also an interesting pagan background to the New Testament use of this word *euangelion*. For the inhabitants of the Roman Empire it had special associations with the Emperor-cult, the announcements of such events as the birth of an heir to the Emperor, his coming-of-age, and his accession, being referred to as *euangelia*. There is thus in the Christian use of the word an implicit contrast between that evangel which may truly be called 'God's evangel' and these other evangels which represent the pretentious claims of self-important men. The message of good news Paul has to proclaim is God's authoritative word. Its source is none other than God Himself.

2. which he promised beforehand through his prophets in the holy scriptures. Having already defined the message of good news by 'God's', Paul now goes on to define it further, by means of a relative clause, as the fulfilment of God's promises through His prophets in the Old Testament. He thus underlines its trustworthiness. The verse is, directly, a statement about the gospel comparable with such things as the latter part of 3.21 and the repeated 'according to the scriptures' of 1 Cor 15.3f. It is also, indirectly, a statement about the Old Testament, a claim that it is to be understood as pointing forward to the gospel. So the subject of the right interpretation of the Old Testament, a subject with which Paul will be concerned throughout Romans, is introduced at its very beginning.

3–4. The fact that two of the most difficult verses in the whole epistle occur so very near its beginning is an acute embarrassment to the interpreter of Romans who is anxious that his readers should not become discouraged and give up before ever they have had a chance to get really interested. The unusual accumulation of difficulties in these verses is notorious.

The Nestle-Aland Greek Testament has no punctuation at the end of v. 2, since it assumes that vv. 3–4 are part of the relative clause introduced at the beginning of v. 2. But it is much more natural to take vv. 3-4, not as continuing the relative clause, but as a third definition of the message of good news (compare the RV, RSV, NEB, JB, and also the AV). Having defined it first by 'God's' with reference to its source, and then by the relative clause in v. 2, Paul now defines it yet further by indicating its content: it concerns God's Son, Jesus Christ our Lord.

It seems highly probable, though it is scarcely as certain as it is sometimes assumed to be, that Paul is here making use of the language of an already existing confessional formula. For him at this particular point, when he is introducing himself to the Christians in Rome, to underline his fundamental agreement with his fellow-believers in this way would make good sense. And the fact that there is no other direct reference to Christ's Davidic descent in the Pauline epistles except in 2 Tim 2.8 and the fact that the verb represented here by 'appoint' is nowhere else used by Paul may be seen as supporting this view. Whether – if it is correct – there was any tension between the theology of this formula and Paul's own thought is not clear. We do not have to assume that the original intention of the formula must have been adoptionist.[1] Our present concern is anyway with Paul's own meaning, and for this the words **concerning his Son** are decisive. The language is thoroughly characteristic of Paul (compare, for example v. 9; 5.10; 8.3, 29, 32; 1 Cor 1.9; 15.28; 2 Cor 1.19; Gal 1.16; 2.20; 4.4, 6). It is

---

[1]Adoptionism is the view that Christ is Son of God only by adoption.

clear that, as used by Paul with reference to Christ, the designation 'Son of God' expresses nothing less that a relationship to God which is 'personal, ethical and inherent' (C. A. Anderson Scott), involving a real community of nature between Christ and God. The position of the words 'his Son', placed as they are outside the bracket formed by the two relative clauses in these verses (in the Greek they are participial clauses), would seem to imply that they control the meaning of both these clauses alike and that the One who was born of the seed of David was already Son of God before, and independently of, the action denoted by the second clause ('who was appointed ... of the dead').

who was born of David's seed. Though it seems that some Jews of the New Testament period did not regard descent from David as an absolutely essential qualification of the Messiah, it is clear that the expectation that he would belong to the family of David was strongly established. These words assert the Davidic descent of Jesus, in agreement with the testimony of other parts of the New Testament (compare Mt 1.1, 2–16, 20; Lk 1.27, 32, 69; 2.4; 3.23–31; Acts 2.30; 2 Tim 2.8; Rev 5.5; 22.16). But in both Matthew and Luke it is indicated that Joseph, through whom the descent is traced (Mt 1.16, 20; Lk 1.27; 2.4; 3.23), was not the natural father of Jesus (Mt 1.18–25; Lk 1.34f). The implication of the narratives is that Jesus's Davidic descent is legal, not natural, resting on Joseph's having accepted Him as his son and thereby legitimized Him. The references to Joseph's naming Him (Mt 1.21, 25) are significant, since the giving of the name was an act of acceptance of a child as one's own. Joseph's acceptance of Jesus as his son would have conferred on Him all the legal rights of legitimate sonship. (The references to 'his parents' in Lk 2.41 and 43 may be understood in this light.) It is at least possible that Paul's use here and also in Gal 4.4 and Phil 2.7 of a Greek verb, which, while it can certainly carry the sense 'be born', more often occurs with other meanings, such as 'become', 'come to pass', rather than the more obvious Greek verb, which he does sometimes use but never in connexion with the birth of Jesus, may reflect knowledge on his part of the tradition of the birth of Jesus without natural human fatherhood.

according to the flesh is best understood both here and in 9.5 as meaning 'as a man', 'so far as his human nature is concerned'. By using it Paul implies that the fact of Christ's human nature, in respect of which what has just been said is true, is not the whole truth about Him. 'Son of David' is a valid description of Him so far as it is applicable, but the reach of its applicability is not coextensive with the fullness of His person.

who was appointed Son of God in power according to the Spirit of holiness from the resurrection of the dead. The first of the two relative clauses has just described the Son of God, whom the message of good news concerns, by reference to the event of His human birth, singling out for special mention the relationship to David into which it brought Him. And now the second relative clause describes Him by reference to another event, namely, His resurrection, though in this case the event itself as such is specified not by the verb but by a dependent phrase. The clause contains an unusual number of elements the interpretation of which is disputed. With regard to the first, there is not much doubt that the Greek verb which is used here should be taken to mean 'appoint' rather than 'declare' or 'show to be', since no clear example of its use in the latter sense either earlier than, or contemporary with, the New Testament has been adduced. With regard to the second, it seems better to connect 'in power' with 'Son of God' than with the verb. In support of this it may be said that the sense which results from taking 'in power' with 'Son of God' accords well, while the sense which results from taking it with 'was appointed', suggestive as it is of adoptionism, accords ill, not only with Paul's teaching elsewhere but also with the presence of 'his Son' at the beginning of v. 3. We understand the first part of the clause then to mean 'who was appointed Son-of-God-in-power' (that is, in contrast with His being Son of God in apparent weakness and poverty in the period of His earthly existence). Consideration of the third element ('according to the Spirit of holiness') we postpone for the moment. With regard to the fourth element, of the meanings which have been suggested for the Greek preposition rendered above by 'from', 'from' (in the sense of 'from the time of') or 'since' should surely be preferred to 'on the ground of'. Christ's resurrection was scarcely the ground of His glorification; but it was the event which was the beginning of His glorified life. With regard to the fifth, it has been variously suggested that the Greek genitive plural here has the sense 'from the dead', the preposition being omitted in order to avoid repetition of a word used just before; that the plural is used because Christ was not raised just for Himself but as the firstfruits of the dead; that the plural is to be explained as a 'generalizing' or 'allusive' plural. The last suggestion may perhaps be the simplest; but, in any case, it is clear that Christ's own resurrection is here referred to.

We now return to 'according to the Spirit of holiness', which is the most difficult element in the clause because each of the three Greek words, of which it consists, is problematic. Various meanings can be suggested for 'according to'; it is a matter of dispute whether the word 'spirit' refers to the Holy Spirit or to something inherent in Christ, His human spirit or His divinity; and 'of holiness' is variously explained as simply equivalent to the adjective 'holy'; as referring to Christ's transcendent holiness; or as referring to the sanctification which the Holy Spirit works. Widely differing interpretations of the phrase as a whole have been suggested. The explanation which seems to us most probable is that the phrase refers to the Holy Spirit whose sanctification of believers is evidence of Christ's having been appointed Son-of-God-in-power and being now exalted. Whether the Greek genitive translated above 'of holiness' was actually intended to bear the sense 'who imparts sanctification' or is simply used as the equivalent to 'Holy' (perhaps under the influence of a Hebrew expression), the thought of sanctification is, we suggest, in any case present to Paul here. We may sum up our understanding of the whole of the second relative clause by saying that Paul is affirming by it that the One who has always been God's Son ('his Son' at the beginning of v. 3) but was brought by His human birth into a relationship with David as far as His human nature is concerned, was appointed the glorious Son-of-God-in-power from the time of His resurrection – a fact which is attested by the present sanctifying work of the Holy Spirit in believers.

even Jesus Christ our Lord. Paul concludes his definition of the message of good news which he has been consecrated to proclaim by adding the full title of Him who is its content. It designates the glorified Jesus Christ who shares the majesty and authority of God and to whom those who believe in Him render adoring worship. For a full discussion of 'Lord' as applied to Christ see on

10.9. When, as here, 'our' is combined with it, or in Phil 3.8 'my', the sense of personal commitment and allegiance is brought out.

5. through whom we received grace and apostleship. Paul had special reason to acknowledge that it was through the mediation of the risen and glorified Jesus Christ that the gift had been received. Compare 1 Cor 9.1; 15.8; Gal 1.1, 12, 16; also Acts 9.3ff; 22.6ff; 26.12ff. The 'we' is probably to be explained as referring simply to Paul himself (a kind of writer's plural). It was perhaps preferred here to the first person singular (which is used in the more personal vv. 8–16a), because it suited the formal statement of authority. The suggestions that Paul used the plural because he was thinking of the fact that all Christians have received grace or because he intended to associate the other apostles with himself as recipients of both grace and apostleship are much less likely. It is possible that by 'grace and apostleship' two distinct things are meant, grace (that is, God's undeserved favour which is the very basis of the Christian life) and apostleship (that is, the office of apostle), but much more probable that we have here an example of the grammatical figure of speech by which a single idea is expressed by two words connected by a conjunction, and that the meaning is 'the grace of apostleship' or (in other words) the office of apostle as a gracious gift not deserved by any worth of Paul's. We may compare Acts 23.6 where 'the hope and resurrection of the dead' means 'the hope of the resurrection of the dead'.

in order to bring about, for his name's sake, obedience of faith among all the Gentiles. The purpose for which Paul has been given this office is that, for the glory of Christ's name, the obedience to God which consists in faith may be brought into being among all the Gentiles. We take 'of faith' to be what grammarians call a genitive of apposition. This seems more likely to be right than any of the other suggestions which have been made, as, for example, that it means 'required by faith' or that it is simply adjectival, so equivalent to 'believing'. The suggestion that the word translated 'Gentiles' should be taken in its inclusive sense of 'nations' is quite improbable. To accept it would render the following relative clause pointless. Paul is thinking of his special commission to the Gentiles (compare, for example, 11.13f; Gal 2.8f).

6. among whom you also are, you who are called of Jesus Christ is, of course, grammatically a relative clause dependent on 'Gentiles', but, as far as the thought is concerned, it is really parenthetic; for a statement about the people whom Paul is addressing is unexpected before the 'to' at the beginning of v. 7, and, placed where it is, interrupts the flow of the opening formula. The reason why it is inserted here is not difficult to guess. Paul wants to indicate as soon as possible that the Christian community in Rome, although not founded by him, is within the sphere of his apostolic commission, and that he therefore has a right to address it in the way he is doing. The words 'among whom you also are' are very often taken to be a clear indication that the Christian community in Rome was at this time predominantly Gentile; but they can quite as well simply refer to its geographical situation in the midst of the Gentile world. It would be reasonable for Paul to regard even a predominantly Jewish church, if situated at the heart of the Roman Empire, as within the sphere of his responsibility. The members are 'called of Jesus Christ', that is, called by Him (the contention of some that the meaning must be 'Jesus Christ's, called *by God*', on the ground that elsewhere in Paul's epistles it is (where the subject of the action is explicit) the Father rather than Christ who is said to call, should be rejected).

7. to all in Rome beloved of God, saints by *God's* calling is the part of the opening formula in which the people addressed are specified. The letter is to all the Christians in Rome. The 'all' is emphatic, and the emphasis is repeated by the 'all' of v. 8. God's love for them is the basis of their existence as believers. The Greek word represented here by 'saint' is simply the adjective meaning 'holy' used as a noun. It is a source of much confusion that in English we make use of words deriving from two different origins ('holy', 'holiness', 'holily', on the one hand, and 'saint', 'saintly', 'sanctify', 'sanctification', on the other hand) to correspond to a number of Greek words, all of which quite unmistakably form a single word-group. In the Bible the 'holiness' of God denotes the absolute authority with which He confronts men. But this authority is the authority of Him who has revealed Himself as merciful and righteous. Applied to Israel, the term 'holy' expressed the fact that they were God's special people. Their holiness derived from God's gracious choice of them, and it involved the obligation on their part to try to be and do what was in accordance with the revealed character of their God by

9

obedience to His law. Paul's use of 'saint' rests squarely on its Old Testament foundations. Those who have been called by the holy God are holy in virtue of His calling and are thereby claimed for holiness of life. As used by Paul, 'call' denotes God's effectual calling: the called are those who have been summoned by God and have also responded to His summons.

grace to you and peace from God our Father and the Lord Jesus Christ is the salutation which completes the threefold opening formula. It is a wish ('be to you' is to be supplied) filled with profound theological and evangelical meaning. In the New Testament 'grace' characteristically denotes – this is the meaning which it has here – God's undeserved love revealed in Christ and so may be said to sum up the whole gospel in a single word. 'Peace' was, of course, the common greeting of the Semitic world. In the New Testament, and indeed in Romans itself, the word bears various meanings in different places. It is likely that the thought which is uppermost here is that of peace with God (compare 5.1–11), though Paul may also have had in mind the blessings which result from reconciliation with God. The following words indicate the source from which Paul looks for grace and peace for the Roman Christians. The striking juxtaposition of God and Christ, while clearly not by itself a proof that Paul believed Christ to be divine in the fullest sense, is a strong pointer in that direction; and it has to be seen alongside many other pointers in the same direction to be found in Romans. The words 'our Father' anticipate the teaching of 8.14–17.

II

PAUL AND THE ROMAN CHURCH

(1.8–16a)

⁸First, I thank my God through Jesus Christ for you all, that *the news of* your faith is being published abroad in all the world. ⁹For God, whom I serve in my spirit in *the proclamation of* the gospel of his Son, is my witness, how unceasingly I make mention of you ¹⁰always in my prayers, asking if by any means now at last I may succeed in coming to you, if it be God's will. ¹¹For I long to see you, in order that I may impart to you some spiritual gift, so that you may be strengthened, ¹²or rather in your midst to be comforted together with you, each through the other's faith, both yours and mine. ¹³But I do not want you to be ignorant, brethren, of the fact that I have often purposed to come to you – but up till the present I have been prevented – in order that I might obtain some fruit among you also even as *I have done* in the rest of the Gentile world. ¹⁴I am a debtor both to the Greeks and to the barbarians, both to the wise and to the foolish: ¹⁵so my eager desire is to preach the gospel to you also who are in Rome. ¹⁶ªFor I am not ashamed of the gospel.

The first sentence of an ancient Greek letter (after the opening formula) was often of a pious nature, informing the recipient of the writer's prayer to the gods on his behalf. The prayer was sometimes a thanksgiving but more often a petition. It was usually concerned with the recipient's health. Formally the beginning of Romans conforms to the contemporary convention. But the character and content of Paul's thanksgiving are far from being conventional. He goes on to assure the Roman Christians of his unceasing prayers for them and to tell them of his eager desire to visit them – a desire which he hopes is at last about to be fulfilled.

8. First, I thank my God through Jesus Christ for you all. Quite probably Paul intended to follow up his 'First' by a further item, but then omitted to do so, or he may possibly have used it with some such sense as 'Above all' or 'From the very outset'. For an initial thanksgiving for the people addressed compare 1 Cor 1.4; Phil 1.3; Col 1.3; 1 Th 1.2; 2 Th 1.3; Philem 4: in Galatians the thanksgiving is significantly absent, while in 2 Corinthians and Ephesians it takes the form of a 'blessing' ('Blessed *be* the God and Father . . .'). The 'my' strikes a personal note reminiscent of some passages in the Psalms (for example, Ps 3.7; 5.2; 7.1, 3; 13.3; 22.1, 2, 10). Paul only rarely calls God 'my God' in this way (in Phil 1.3 and Philem 4, which are similar contexts to this, and otherwise only in 2 Cor 12.21 and Phil 4.19). He thanks God through Christ, because Christ is Mediator not only of God's approach to men but also, as the exalted Lord, of their responding approach to God in worship. Note the stress on the fact that the thanks are for them all.

that *the news of* your faith is being published abroad in all the world. The fact that they believe in Christ, that in the imperial capital also there is a church of Jesus Christ, is being published abroad far and wide. This in itself is enough to call forth Paul's thanksgiving. It is implied that he recognizes it to be God's work.

9–10. For God, whom I serve in my spirit in *the proclamation of* the gospel of his Son, is my witness, how unceasingly I make mention of you always in my prayers. Here, as seems also to be the case in the other examples of oaths in Paul's letters, the statement made is one the truth of which the readers cannot prove for themselves, since it concerns his inner life. The fact that he appeals to God as witness here is evidence of the great importance he attaches to their knowing that he prays for them continually. The phrase 'in my spirit' has been variously interpreted; but the most probable explanation is that it refers to the fact that his praying is an element of the inward part of his apostolic service contrasted with the outward part which includes such activities as preaching. On this view, the appositeness of the relative clause is apparent; for, if his prayer for them is an integral but hidden part of his service of God in the promulgation of the gospel, then his anxiety to assure them of its reality is thoroughly understandable. Some (for example, the RV) connect 'always in my prayers', not, as we have done, with what precedes, but with what follows. In favour of this it may be argued that the presence of two adverbs so similar in meaning as 'unceasingly' and 'always' in the same clause is awkward. But we think it is more probably correct to take it with what precedes (as do, for example, the AV and RSV), first, because, if 'in my prayers' is not connected with what precedes, it is not clear that 'make mention' refers to mentioning in prayer, and, secondly, because, while it is understandable that Paul should say that he always mentions the Roman Christians when he prays, it seems rather unlikely that he would actually assert that when he prays he always asks that he may succeed in visiting them. (The NEB rendering, which has 'in my prayers' connected with what precedes and 'always' with what follows, seems to be treating the Greek very cavalierly, since in the Greek 'always' comes before 'in my prayers'.)

asking if by any means now at last I may succeed in coming to you, if it be God's will. Separated by a comma from 'always in my prayers', these words indicate one particular thing which Paul asks for in his prayers for the Christians in Rome, without implying that he never prays for them without making this particular request.

11–12. For I long to see you, in order that I may impart to you some spiritual gift. The 'For' indicates that what follows in these two verses, and indeed in vv. 13–16a too, is intended as an explanation of Paul's desire to visit the Christians in Rome. A further consideration is referred to in 15.24. That it is important is not to be doubted. But to brush aside the reasons indicated in these verses of chapter 1 as merely 'reasons of a sort' and to insist that 'the basic reason' is Paul's need to use Rome as a base for his Spanish mission, as Barrett does, strikes us as arbitrary. The word represented by 'gift' here is used in 12.6 to denote a special gift or endowment bestowed on a member of the Church by God to be used in the service of God and of men. Since Paul associated this sort of gift very closely with the Spirit – so much so that in 1 Cor 14.1 the neuter plural of the adjective meaning 'spiritual' is used by itself to denote such gifts – and since in the present verse 'gift' is qualified by 'spiritual', it is natural to wonder whether Paul was thinking of a gift of this sort here. But it seems more probable that he was here using the word in a more general sense as denoting a blessing or benefit to be bestowed on the Christians in Rome by God through his presence with them and that the qualification

13

'spiritual' was added either because he thought that the blessing would be mediated through the Holy Spirit or – perhaps more probably – to indicate in a more general way (compare its use in 15.27) the sort of blessing he had in mind.

so that you may be strengthened. Paul's hope is that by the imparting of the gift they may be strengthened, that is, strengthened as Christians, strengthened in faith and obedience. But he immediately seeks to guard against a possible misunderstanding of what he has just said by re-expressing his statement of what he longs for in such a way as to combine with it the complementary truth: **or rather in your midst to be comforted together with you, each through the other's faith, both yours and mine.** His desire to see them in order to be the means of their receiving a blessing will only be rightly understood, if it is seen as part of his desire for a mutual comforting between him and them. Paul hopes to receive as well as to give. To regard v. 12 as evidence of embarrassment on Paul's part at the inconsistency between his plans to visit a church he has not himself founded and the principle which he states in 15.20 ('so to preach the good news not where Christ had already been named, that I might not build upon another man's foundation') or to see it as an attempt to curry favour with the Roman Christians is surely quite uncalled for. There seems to be no cogent reason for refusing to accept the verse at its face-value as the sincere expression of real humility. Calvin's comment is to the point: 'Note how modestly he expresses what he feels by not refusing to seek strengthening from inexperienced beginners. He means what he says, too, for there is none so void of gifts in the Church of Christ who cannot in some measure contribute to our spiritual progress. Ill will and pride, however, prevent our deriving such benefit from one another.'

13. But I do not want you to be ignorant (for the use of this formula compare 11.25; 1 Cor 10.1; 12.1; 2 Cor 1.8)**, brethren, of the fact that I have often purposed to come to you** indicates that Paul regards it as important to emphasize that his long-standing desire to see them has been so seriously felt that it has on a number of occasions led him to make definite plans to visit them. So far from being embarrassed at having to refer to his intention to visit this church which is not of his foundation, he seems to feel that his not having visited it before requires explanation. **but up till the**

present I have been prevented is a parenthesis. We may compare 15.22 ('Wherefore I have also been prevented these many times from coming to you'), in which the 'wherefore' may be taken as suggesting that it was because of the evangelistic activity referred to in the immediately preceding verses that he had been unable to visit them. **in order that I might obtain some fruit among you also even as *I have done* in the rest of the Gentile world** indicates the purpose for which he had planned to come to Rome. By 'fruit' the return hoped for from his apostolic labours is no doubt meant, the gaining of new converts and the strengthening of the faith and obedience of those already believing. The last six words probably give the right sense, though the Greek ('the rest of the Gentiles') could be taken to imply that the Roman Church was mainly Gentile.

14. The sense of **I am a debtor** is that God has laid upon him a duty in relation to the people mentioned. He is under an obligation to them, a debtor to them, as having been appointed by God to do something for them, not as having received a benefit from them which deserves to be repaid. **both to the Greeks and to the barbarians, both to the wise and to the foolish** is a good deal more difficult than one might at first be inclined to think. A variety of interpretations has been suggested. In view of Paul's reference to his Gentile mission in the preceding verse, we should probably take both pairs to refer simply to the sum of Gentile mankind and set aside the interpretations according to which both or one of the pairs includes Jews. It has still to be decided whether 'the Greeks' are identical with 'the wise', and 'the barbarians' with 'the foolish', or whether Paul's two pairs represent two different groupings of the same totality. Though the former view has had its supporters from early times down to the present, there are several considerations which incline us to regard the latter as more probable. For one thing, the division into Greeks and barbarians was so well established as to make an explanation of it in different terms superfluous. For another, 'both to the wise and to the foolish' would not be particularly illuminating as an explanation of 'both to the Greeks and to the barbarians', since it would be appropriate only if understood on a merely conventional level. While it is true that Paul quite often does use 'wise' and 'wisdom' in a more or less ironical way, there is nothing in this context to suggest that he is doing so here. But, if 'wise' and 'foolish' are intended at all seriously, they can hardly be used as synonyms for 'Greek' and 'barbarian'. The Greeks themselves knew that there were wise barbarians and foolish Greeks. How much more would Paul realize it! And, if, when he used the word 'barbarian' here, he really had in mind some of the less romanized of the Spaniards whom he hoped to evangelize (15.24), is he likely to have described the barbarians so sweepingly as 'foolish'? We take it then that by 'Greeks' are meant all those Gentiles who are possessed of Graeco-Roman culture, and by 'barbarians' all the rest of the Gentiles (the Greek word, from which our 'barbarian' is derived, was in origin onomatopoeic, being an attempt to reproduce the impression which those talking languages other than Greek made on Greek ears: as used here by Paul, it covers all non-hellenized communities (Jews excepted) whether within the Roman Empire or outside it). The other pair (as we understand it) represents a different grouping of the Gentiles, which divides them into those who are intelligent and educated, on the one hand, and, on the other hand, those who lack education and perhaps also intelligence. Here both pairs of terms seem to be used in a thoroughly objective, factual manner, without overtones of irony, complacency, prejudice or contemptuousness. While in the first grouping the thought is probably of communities, in the second it is rather of individuals.

15. **So** indicates that the fact which is about to be stated is a consequence of the fact which has just been stated in v. 14. The eagerness of which Paul speaks here has its ground in the general obligation which he recognizes as his. **my eager desire is to preach the gospel to you also who are in Rome.** The sense of the 'also' is: in addition to those to whom he has already preached it (compare the last few words of v. 13). The preaching of the gospel referred to here is not the initial proclamation to people who have not yet heard the message, but a preaching of it to those who are already believers, with a view to the deepening of their understanding and strengthening of their faith and obedience.

16a. **For I am not ashamed of the gospel** explains how it is that Paul desires eagerly to preach the good news in Rome too, and at the same time forms the transition to vv. 16b–17. The negative way in which Paul expresses himself is to be explained not as an instance of understatement (Paul meaning that he is proud of the gospel), but as reflecting his sober recognition of the fact that the gospel is something of which, in this world, Christians will constantly be tempted to be ashamed. We may compare Mk 8.38; Lk 9.26; 2 Tim 1.8. The presence of this temptation as a constant feature of the Christian life is inevitable both on account of the world's continuing hostility to God and also on account of the nature of the gospel itself, the fact that God (because He willed to leave men room in which to make a free personal decision of faith rather than to compel them) has intervened in history for men's salvation not in obvious might and majesty but in a veiled way which was bound to look to the world like abject weakness and foolishness.

III

THE THEME OF THE EPISTLE IS STATED

(1.16b–17)

16bFor it is God's saving power for every one who believes, both for the Jew first and for the Greek. 17For in it God's righteousness is being revealed from faith to faith, even as it is written: 'But he who is righteous by faith shall live'.

These one and a half verses are at the same time both an integral part of Paul's expression of his readiness to preach the gospel in Rome and also the statement of the theological theme which is going to be worked out in the main body of the epistle. They belong properly to the paragraph which began with v. 8. But we have decided in favour of presenting them as a separate main division, in order that the logical structure of the epistle may stand out more boldly.

16b. For it is God's saving power. The reason why Paul is not overcome by the temptation to be ashamed of the gospel, but glories in it and lives to proclaim it, is that he knows that it is the almighty power of God Himself directed toward the salvation of men.

In Paul's letters 'save' and 'salvation' refer primarily to God's future, to what begins with Christ's coming in glory, His Second Coming, as it is often called. This is explicit in 1 Cor 5.5 ('. . . that the spirit may be saved in the day of the Lord Jesus'), but is clear also in Rom 5.9f; 13.11; 1 Cor 3.15; Phil 1.28; 2.12; 1 Th 5.8f; 2 Th 2.13. What may be called the negative content of salvation is indicated in 5.9: it is salvation from the final manifestation of the wrath of God (on what Paul means by 'the wrath of God' see on 1.18). But there is also a positive content. It is the restoration of the glory which sinful men lack (compare 3.23). On this aspect it is illuminating to note the correspondence between salvation in 5.10

and glorification in 8.30, and also to note how the work of Christ as Saviour (Phil 3.20) is described in Phil 3.21. While salvation is characteristically spoken of with future tenses, Paul can use a past tense in connexion with it (thus in 8.24 we have the statement 'we were saved', which, however, is qualified by 'in hope'), since God's decisive act by which the believer's final salvation has been secured has already been accomplished, and also a present tense (as in 1 Cor 1.18; 2 Cor 2.15) to describe the believer's present waiting and hoping and struggling which have salvation for their goal.

What Paul is saying here, then, is that the gospel is God's effective power active in the world of men to bring about deliverance from His wrath in the final judgement and reinstatement in that glory of God which has been lost through sin – that is a future salvation which reflects its splendour back into the present of those who are to share it. The gospel, the message of good news, is this by virtue of its content, its subject, namely Jesus Christ. It is He Himself who is its effectiveness.

for every one who believes. The response which the message calls for is faith – faith in it, and so faith in Christ who is its content and in God who has acted in Him and whose power the message is. For all who respond with faith the gospel is effective to salvation. It is important here to note that the faith which is spoken of is not something existing independently of the gospel. It is not a qualification which some men already possess in themselves before the gospel meets them. It only comes into being as response to the gospel (or to its Old Testament foreshadowing). And it is not – as man's response to the gospel – a contribution from his side which, by fulfilling a condition laid down by God, enables the gospel to be saving. In that case, faith would itself be, in the last resort, a meritorious work; but it is of the very essence of faith, as Paul understands it, that it is opposed to all human deserving, all human establishing of claims on God. Faith is the openness to the gospel which God Himself creates. He not only directs the message to the hearer, but also Himself lays open the hearer's heart to the message. The 'every one' strikes a note which sounds again and again through the epistle.

both for the Jew first and for the Greek underlines and explains 'every one'. The word 'both' draws attention to the fundamental equality of Jew and Gentile ('Greek' used in contrast with 'Jew' means 'Gentile'; the use is different from that in v. 14), which the gospel reveals. The gospel is God's saving power for both alike. At the same time 'first' indicates that there is a certain priority of the Jew. How Paul understands this 'both' and this 'first' and how he holds them together should become increasingly clear as we follow him step by step through the epistle.

17. For in it God's righteousness is being revealed from faith to faith is introduced in explanation and confirmation of v. 16b: the gospel is God's saving power for every one who believes, because in it God's righteousness is being revealed. . . . The present tense is used, because the thought is of the revelation in the on-going preaching of the message. In the preaching God Himself is revealing His righteousness. That v. 17 is a most important key-verse, that it is, indeed, absolutely fundamental for the understanding of Romans, is generally agreed. But, unfortunately, its interpretation is disputed. The difficulty is the word 'righteousness'. It represents a Greek noun which belongs to a group of related words.

Very confusingly we have become accustomed to using words from two quite distinct English word-groups (on the one hand, words like 'righteous' and 'righteousness', and, on the other hand, words like 'just', 'justice', 'justify' and 'justification'), in order to cover this single Greek word-group. The natural result is that relationships which are inescapably obvious in Greek are hidden from the English reader.

A more basic complication is the fact that members of this Greek word-group had been used in the Greek version of the Old Testament to represent members of a largely, but by no means completely, corresponding Hebrew word-group, and in the process their ranges of meaning had been considerably changed. It is now generally agreed that Paul's use of them is largely influenced by the transformation thus brought about. The influence is most obvious in the case of the verb which in the RV is represented consistently throughout the New Testament by 'justify'; for none of the Pauline occurrences of this Greek verb (it occurs in Romans alone fifteen times) can be at all tolerably explained on the basis of the use of the word in non-biblical Greek. Through use in the Greek Old Testament this verb had come to have a forensic meaning, 'acquit', 'confer a status of righteousness upon'. In the case of the cognate adjective (as with the corresponding Hebrew adjective) one has to recognize that Paul may use it either in its characteristic Greek ethical sense or in a forensic sense. With the noun (which is what we have here) the situation is still more difficult, since, even when it is agreed that in a particular occurrence it has a forensic sense (as we think is the case here), we have still to ask whether what is signified is the action of acquitting (of conferring the status of righteousness upon) or the condition resulting for the object of the action, namely, the condition of having been acquitted (the conferred status of righteousness).

That question is hotly debated with reference to the phrase 'God's righteousness' in this verse. (It is quite often posed in other terms, namely, whether 'God's' is here a subjective genitive, which would mean that 'righteousness' must denote the action, or a genitive of origin, which would mean that 'righteousness' must denote the resulting condition of the object of the action.) The main arguments urged in support of the former view (that 'God's righteousness' here means God's act of justifying, acquitting, conferring a righteous status in relation to Himself) are:

(i) that the fact that 'wrath' in v. 18 refers to an activity of God suggests that 'righteousness' in v. 17a is likely, in view of the parallelism of structure between v. 17a and v. 18, to do so too;

(ii) that, in view of the connexion between v. 17a and v. 16b, the occurrence of the phrase 'God's . . . power' in v. 16b tells in favour of taking 'God's righteousness' in v. 17a to refer to an activity of God, God's saving power in action;

(iii) that in the Old Testament the corresponding Hebrew noun, when used with reference to God, refers to an activity of God, the activity of His saving power;

(iv) that the expression 'God's righteousness' had come to be a technical term in some Jewish circles for God's saving justice, which embraces His kingly and triumphant faithfulness to His covenant and to His creation, His forgiving mercy, His laying claim to men's obedience. It is claimed that Paul took over, radicalized and universalized this Jewish technical term.

At first sight these arguments seem impressive, but none of them is at all conclusive. With regard to (iii) and (iv), it may be said that, while it is of course true that Paul's expression 'God's righteousness' must be understood in the light of the righteousness language of the Old Testament and of late Judaism, there is no reason to assume that he must have used the language he took over in precisely the same way as that in which it had been used. We must allow for the possibility of his having used what he took over with freedom and originality.

We have now to consider what can be said in support of the other view, namely, that 'God's righteousness' means man's status of righteousness before God which is the result of God's act of justifying. The main arguments are:

(i) that there are several occurrences of 'righteousness' in Paul's letters which seem to afford strong support for it. One is 10.3 ('For, failing to recognize the righteousness of God, and seeking to establish their own, they did not submit to the righteousness of God'). Here it is surely natural to take the first 'the righteousness of God' to mean the status of righteousness which is made available by God as His gift, which is contrasted with 'their own', that is, a status of righteousness achieved by their own efforts, and to understand the second 'the righteousness of God' in the same sense as the first. Compare Phil 3.9, where 'a righteousness of mine own, *even* that which is of [Greek: 'from'] the law' is opposed to 'that which is through faith in Christ, the righteousness which is of [Greek: 'from'] God by faith'; and also 1 Cor 1.30; 2 Cor 5.21; Rom 5.17.

(ii) that it is extremely difficult to see how 'from faith to faith' can be a natural expression for Paul to have used here, if he meant by 'God's righteousness' an action by God, whereas it makes good sense, if 'God's righteousness' denotes the status of righteousness conferred by God.

(iii) that the Habakkuk quotation (v. 17b) tells in favour of this view, since it focuses attention on the justified man rather than on God's act of justifying him.

(iv) that to take 'God's righteousness' as referring to the righteous status given by God agrees better with the structure of the argument of the epistle, in which 1.18–4.25 expounds the words 'he who is righteous by faith' and 5.1–8.39 the promise that the man who is righteous by faith 'shall live'. If 2.13; 3.20, 28; 4.2, 13; 5.1, 9, 19, are examined carefully, it will be seen that it is on the status resulting from God's action and on the men on whom the status is conferred rather than on the actual action of God that attention is focused.

This debate will no doubt continue. The question has not been conclusively decided. But, in view of the arguments just stated, we regard the interpretation, according to which 'God's' is a genitive of origin and 'righteousness' denotes the righteous status which is given by God, as much more probable than that which takes 'God's' as a subjective genitive and 'righteousness' as denoting God's action of justifying.

The words 'from faith to faith' have been variously interpreted down the centuries; but the most probable explanation would seem to be that they are simply an emphatic way of saying 'from faith' (or 'by faith'), the added 'to faith' having much the same effect as the 'only' in the phrase 'by faith only'. Though the structure of the sentence suggests that the phrase was intended to be connected with the verb 'is being revealed', the Habakkuk quotation which follows and the comparison with 1.17a of 3.21 and 22 tell strongly, if not conclusively, in favour of connecting it with 'God's righteousness'. The sense of the whole sentence, as we understand it, may then be set out as follows: For in it (that is, in the gospel as it is being preached) a righteous status before God which is God's gift is being revealed (and so offered to men), a righteous status which is altogether by faith. The sentence explains and confirms the affirmation made in v. 16b (that the gospel 'is God's saving power for every one who believes'): by revealing and making available precisely this gift of a status of righteousness before Himself God is indeed acting mightily to save.

even as it is written: 'But he who is righteous by faith shall live'. In confirmation of what he has just said Paul cites Hab 2.4b. The sense of the original Hebrew is that the righteous shall be preserved alive because of his faithfulness (that is, his steadfast loyalty). The reference was probably to the Jewish people contrasted with their heathen oppressors, and the life referred to was probably political survival; but a tendency to understand the sentence with reference to the individual will have made itself felt quite early. The Septuagint (that is, the main Greek version of the Old Testament) has, instead of 'by his faith', 'by my faith', which could mean either 'by my [that is, 'God's'] faithfulness' or 'by faith in me [that is, 'in God']'. Paul retains neither 'my' nor 'his', and he understands the prophet's statement in the light of the gospel. As used by him, 'faith' has the same sense as it has in the earlier part of v. 17 and 'shall live' refers, not to political survival, but to the life with God, which alone is true life, the life which the believer begins to enjoy here and now, and will enjoy in its fullness hereafter. An insight into the meaning of 'shall live' can be gained from a study of 2.7; 4.17; 5.17, 18, 21; 6.4, 10, 11, 13, 22, 23; 7.10; 8.2, 6, 10, 13; 10.5; 12.1.

We have still to ask whether 'by faith' is to be connected with 'shall live', as in Habakkuk, or with 'he who is righteous', as was suggested by Calvin's successor, Beza, and has since been maintained by many interpreters. Two obvious points may be made in favour of the former alternative, namely, first, that Paul must have known that in Habakkuk 'by faith' was connected with the verb, and, secondly, that, if Paul meant 'by faith' to be taken with 'righteous', he ought, according to Greek usage, to have placed it between 'he who is' (which represents the Greek definite article) and 'righteous'. But these arguments are by no means conclusive. To the former it may be replied that Paul treats the Old Testament text with considerable freedom in other places; to the latter that it was not unnatural to adhere to the original word-order even though intending the words to be differently construed. In support of the latter alternative it may be said that it surely gives a much more satisfactory connexion between v. 17b and v. 17a; that it suits the structure of the epistle extremely well, since 1.18–4.25 may be said to be an exposition of 'he who is righteous by faith' and 5.1–8.39 an exposition of the promise that this man 'shall live'; and that the connexion between righteousness and faith is made explicit in 3.22; 4.11, 13; 5.1; 9.30; 10.6. We conclude that Paul almost certainly intended 'by faith' to be connected with 'he who is righteous' rather than with 'shall live'.

IV

THE REVELATION OF THE RIGHTEOUSNESS WHICH IS FROM GOD BY FAITH ALONE – 'HE WHO IS RIGHTEOUS BY FAITH' EXPOUNDED

(1.18–4.25)

This is Paul's first and fundamental contribution to the elucidation of the statement in 1.17 that God's righteousness is being revealed in the gospel from faith to faith and also to the exposition of the Habakkuk quotation in the same verse, 'But he who is righteous by faith shall live'. It falls into four sections.

The purpose of the first section (1.18–3.20) would seem to be to support the 'from faith to faith' of v. 17a and the qualification of 'he who is righteous' by the words 'by faith' in v. 17b by showing that there can be no question of any other righteousness of men before God than that which is by faith.

The second section (3.21–26) is the heart of the whole main division 1.18–4.25. Its purpose is to establish the truth of the 'is being revealed' of 1.17a, to establish that God's righteousness is actually being revealed now, whenever and wherever the gospel is being preached. This it does by describing the revelation which has already taken place in the past, the revelation of God's righteousness in the gospel events themselves. Without that prior revelation there could be no authentic revelation of God's righteousness in the Church's preaching; but, since God's righteousness has indeed been manifested in the gospel events, the fact of its being revealed in the preaching of the gospel is established, and so also the fact of the existence of the man 'who is righteous by faith'.

The third section (3.27–31) draws out something implicit in the second, namely, that glorying or boasting, that is the assertion of a claim on God on the ground of one's works, is altogether ruled out.

25

The fourth section (4.1–25) confirms the third by showing that, according to Scripture, not even Abraham had a right to glory.

IV.1. IN THE LIGHT OF THE GOSPEL THERE IS NO QUESTION OF MEN'S BEING RIGHTEOUS BEFORE GOD OTHERWISE THAN BY FAITH

(1.18–3.20)

The question is often asked – not unnaturally – whether the extremely dark picture of human life which is presented here is not grossly unfair. Certainly, if we read this section as an historian's assessment of the moral condition of his contemporaries made on the same sort of basis as is normally used when one is attempting a relative evaluation, and so go on to compare it with other people's moral assessments of other epochs, the result will be thoroughly unfair to Paul's contemporaries. But the truth is that Paul is not attempting to give an assessment of this sort at all. What he says must be understood as said on the basis of 1.16b–17 and 3.21–26. In other words, it is not Paul's judgment of his contemporaries that we have here, but the gospel's judgment of men, that is, of all men, the judgment the gospel itself pronounces, which Paul has heard and to which he has himself submitted. It is true that Paul has borrowed many thoughts and expressions from late Judaism; but he has transformed what he has borrowed by using it for a radically different purpose – instead of a polemic of one group of human beings against another, the testimony to a universal accusation laid against all men (Christ alone excepted) which can be recognized and submitted to only in the light of the gospel. The section depicts man as he appears in the light of the Cross. It is not a description of specially bad men only, but the innermost truth about all of us, as we are in ourselves.

(i) *Man under the judgment of the gospel*

(1.18-32)

¹⁸**For God's wrath is being revealed from heaven against every kind of ungodliness and unrighteousness of men who try to suppress**

the truth by their unrighteousness; [19]for what is knowable of God is manifest in their midst, for God has made it manifest to them. [20]For his invisible attributes are clearly seen since the creation of the world, being perceived by means of the things he has made, even both his eternal power and divinity, so that they are without excuse, [21]because, though they have known God, they have not glorified him as God or given him thanks, but have become futile in their reasonings, and their uncomprehending heart has been darkened. [22]Pretending to be wise, they have shown themselves fools, [23]and exchanged the glory of the immortal God for the likeness of the form of mortal man and of birds and fourfooted animals and reptiles. [24]Wherefore God delivered them up, in *their abandonment to* the lusts of their own hearts, to uncleanness, so that among them their bodies are dishonoured.

[25]They have actually exchanged the truth of God for the lie, and worshipped and served the creature instead of the Creator, who is blessed for ever: Amen. [26]Wherefore God has delivered them up to passions which bring dishonour: for both their females have exchanged natural intercourse for that which is contrary to nature, [27]and likewise also the males, having abandoned natural intercourse with the female, have burned in their lust for one another, males with males perpetrating shamelessness and receiving in their own persons the due wages of their deludedness.

[28]And, as they have not seen fit to take God into account, God has delivered them up to a reprobate mind, to do the things which are morally wrong, [29]filled with all manner of unrighteousness, wickedness, ruthlessness, depravity, full of envy, murder, rivalry, treachery, malice, whisperers, [30]slanderers, haters of God, insolent, arrogant, boastful, inventive of *novel* forms of evil, disobedient to parents, [31]without understanding, without loyalty, without natural affection, without pity. [32]They know God's righteous decree that those who practise such things deserve death; yet they not only do them, but actually applaud others who practise them.

That in this subsection Paul has in mind primarily the Gentiles is no doubt true. But it may be doubted whether we shall do justice to his intention, if we assume – as many interpreters do – that these verses refer exclusively to them. In v. 18 he uses the general term 'men', and nowhere in the subsection does he use either 'Gentiles' or 'Greek'. In describing men's idolatry in v. 23 he echoes the language of Ps 106.20 and Jer 2.11, the former of which refers to Israel's worship of the golden calf and the latter to Israel's forsaking the Lord for other gods at a much later date. And the main point of 2.1–3.20 is precisely that the Jew, who thinks himself entitled to sit in judgment on the Gentiles, himself does the very same things that he condemns them for doing (compare 2.3). The implication would seem to be that Paul himself reckoned that, in describing – as he certainly was doing in 1.18–32 – the obvious sinfulness of the heathen, he was also, as a matter of fact, thereby describing the basic sinfulness of fallen man as such, the inner reality of the life of Jews no less than of that of the Gentiles. And the correctness of this view is confirmed by the fact that the 'Wherefore' at the beginning of 2.1, which has proved so baffling to commentators, becomes, on this assumption, perfectly intelligible: if 1.18–32 does indeed declare the truth about *all* men, then it really does follow from it that the man who sets himself up as a judge of his fellows is without excuse. So we understand these verses as the revelation of the gospel's judgment of all men, which lays bare not only the idolatry of ancient and modern paganism but also the idolatry ensconced in Israel, in the Church, and in the life of each believer.

18. For God's wrath is being revealed. The 'For' has been variously explained. Some, feeling strongly that God's wrath and God's righteousness must be opposed to each other, have even insisted on giving to the Greek conjunction which regularly means 'for' the sense of 'but' – in certain special circumstances the Greek word can indeed acquire an adversative force, but such special circumstances do not obtain here. The most natural explanation is surely that the 'For' indicates the relation of the section 1.18–3.20 to the statement in 1.17 that God's righteousness is being revealed in the preached gospel 'from faith to faith': the fact of the revelation of God's wrath against men's sin proves that there can be no question of men's having a righteous status before God otherwise than by faith alone.

The reference to God's wrath has puzzled and troubled many. So, for example, C. H. Dodd argued that Paul did not mean to indicate a personal reaction on God's part but 'an inevitable process of cause and effect in a moral universe', on the ground that it would be objectionable to attribute to God 'the irrational passion of anger'. But even human anger is not always irrational. A man who knows, for example, about the far-reaching injustice and cruelty of *apartheid* and is not angry at such wickedness is not a good man: by his lack of anger he shows his lack of love. God would not be the truly loving God that He is, if He did not react to our evil with wrath. His wrath is not something which is inconsistent with His love: on the contrary, it is an expression of His love. It is precisely because He loves us truly and seriously and faithfully that He is wroth with us in our sinfulness. But it must of course be remembered that God's wrath is not like man's only bigger and more effective. Our wrath, even at its most righteous and purest, is always compromised and more or less distorted by our own sinfulness: only God's wrath is the wrath of perfect goodness, the altogether serious wrath. Dodd's attempt to depersonalize the reality which the Bible denotes by 'God's wrath' should surely be rejected.

The words we are considering require discussion of a third matter, the meaning of 'is being revealed'. From reading vv. 18ff one might easily get the impression that Paul is thinking of the revelation of God's wrath as taking place in the observable frustrations, futilities and disasters which result from human ungodliness and unrighteousness. But Paul has himself given a pretty clear indication by the parallelism in language and structure between vv. 17 and 18 that this is not his meaning. In v. 17 he has stated that God's righteousness is being revealed in the gospel, that is, in the on-going proclamation of the gospel. And this statement presupposes a prior revelation of God's righteousness in the gospel events themselves (a revelation to which the perfect tense 'has been manifested' in 3.21 refers). In view of the parallelism, the most natural way of taking v. 18 is to understand it to mean that God's wrath also is being revealed *in the gospel*, that is, in the on-going proclamation of the gospel, and to recognize that behind, and basic to, this revelation of the wrath of God in the preaching, is the prior revelation of the wrath of God in the gospel events. This interpretation of v. 18 which is suggested by the parallelism we have noted, is confirmed by the fact that the sense thus obtained is thoroughly Pauline and by the further fact that according to it the early chapters of Romans have a much more closely-knit character than other interpretations imply. The two revelations referred to in these two verses are then really two aspects of the same process. The preaching of the gospel is at the same time both the revelation of a status of righteousness before God for men and also the revelation of God's wrath against their sin. It is both, because the gospel events themselves, which the preaching presupposes, were both. With regard to the wrath of God, we conclude that, for Paul, its full meaning is not to be seen in the disasters befalling sinful men in the course of history: its reality is only truly known when it is seen in its revelation in Gethsemane and on Golgotha.

The purpose of the phrase **from heaven** is probably simply to emphasize the utter seriousness of 'God's wrath' as being really *God's* wrath: it amounts to an underlining of 'God's'.

against every kind of ungodliness and unrighteousness of men who try to suppress the truth by their unrighteousness indicates the object against which God's wrath is directed. In the preaching of the gospel not only is the reality of the divine wrath unveiled, but its object also is shown up in its true character. Some have understood 'ungodliness' to refer to violations of the first four, and 'unrighteousness' to violations of the last six, of the Ten Commandments; but it is more probable that the two words are used as two expressions for the same thing combined together in order to give a more rounded and complete description of it than either would have given by itself ('ungodliness' bringing out the fact that all sin is an attack on the majesty of God, and 'unrighteousness' the fact that it is a violation of God's just order). The words which follow are a most penetrating and illuminating characterization of the essential nature of sin. Sin is always an assault upon the truth, that is, the fundamental truth of God as Creator, Redeemer and Judge, which, because it is the truth, must be taken into account and come to terms with, if man is not to live in vain. It is the attempt to suppress it, bury it out of sight, obliterate it from the memory; but it is of the essence of sin that it can never be more than an *attempt* to suppress the truth, an attempt which is always bound to prove unsuccessful, futile, in the end.

19. for. The Greek word is a different one from that so translated in v. 18. It is difficult to decide whether this verse is intended to give the reason for God's wrath (so vindicating God's fairness) or to justify the language of the preceding clause (in our translation a relative, but in the original a participial clause) by showing that men do indeed have enough knowledge of the truth to warrant their being described as trying to suppress it. The latter choice would seem to yield a better articulated sequence of thought; but the general sense of the passage is not substantially affected by the decision we make on this point.

what is knowable of God. That 'knowable', rather than 'known', is the correct translation is hardly to be doubted. The phrase should not be understood as implying a belief that fallen man is capable in himself of a knowledge of God in the sense of a conscious knowledge of Him. It should rather be interpreted as meaning 'God, in so far as He is objectively knowable, that is, knowable in the sense of being experienceable' (see further on 'though they have known God' in v. 21).

is manifest. A real revelation of what is knowable of God has taken place. God (in so far as He is knowable) is truly manifest.

The next two Greek words can mean either **in their midst** or 'within them'; but the former seems more likely to be the correct translation in the context (v. 20 makes it improbable that the reference is exclusively, or even primarily, to the existence and functioning of men's inward capacities as manifestation of God, while v. 21 indicates that the revelation has not been inwardly apprehended by them). In their midst and all around them and also in their own creaturely existence (including of course what is inward as well as what is external) God is objectively manifest: His whole creation declares Him.

for God has made it manifest to them is added to make it clear that God's being manifest in His creation is a deliberate self-disclosure on God's part, not something in any way independent of His will.

20–21. For his invisible attributes are clearly seen since the creation of the world, being perceived by means of the things he has made, even both his eternal power and divinity does, as a matter of fact, afford an explanation of v. 19b; but it seems more natural to understand the initial 'For' as marking the relation of vv. 20–21 as a whole to vv. 18–19 than the relation of only v. 20a to v. 19b. The combination of 'invisible' and 'are clearly seen' is a striking, and no doubt deliberate, paradox. Ever since the beginning of God's creation God's self-revelation has continued without interruption – objectively – in what He has created. In looking upon the created universe men have all along been looking upon God's eternal power and divinity, invisible though they are in themselves; for the Creator has expressed Himself really and truly, though of course only to a limited extent, in what He has made. A person who looks at a masterpiece by Rembrandt may truly be said to be looking at Rembrandt; for the artist has expressed himself in his painting. This illustration, though inadequate, may perhaps help us towards an understanding of what Paul means.

so that they are without excuse. The result of God's self-manifestation in His creation is not a natural knowledge of God on men's part independent of God's self-revelation in His Word, a valid though limited knowledge, but simply the rendering excuseless of their ignorance. A real self-disclosure of God has indeed taken place and is always occurring, and men ought to have recognized Him, but in fact have not done so. They have been constantly surrounded on all sides by, and have possessed within their own selves, the evidences of God's eternal power and divinity, but they have not allowed themselves to be led by them to a recognition of Him.

because introduces a statement (it includes vv. 22 and 23 as well as v. 21) in explanation of 'so that they are without excuse'. It takes up the thought of the latter part of v. 18 and clarifies it. Verses 19 and 20 have already shown that the fact that God has manifested Himself to men renders them without excuse, and this thought is taken up by the next five words. But, for the rest, vv. 21–23 focus attention on the conduct for which (having had God's self-manifestation) they are without excuse, that conduct already hinted at in the last words of v. 18.

though they have known God: that is, known God in the sense that in their awareness of the created world it is of Him that all along, though unwittingly, they have been – objectively – aware. They have in fact experienced Him – His wisdom, power, generosity – in every moment of their existence, though they have not recognized Him. It has been by Him that their lives have been sustained, enriched, bounded. In this limited sense they have known Him all their lives.

they have not glorified him as God or given him thanks. Having experienced God's self-manifestation, they ought to have glorified Him as God and given Him thanks; but they have not done so. The last four words single out for special mention one particular element in the glorification owed. They ought to have recognized Him as the source of all the good things they enjoyed, and so to have been grateful to Him.

but have become futile in their reasonings. The futility to which they have succumbed is the inevitable consequence of loss of touch with reality. It is to be seen, in particular, in their thinking, which suffers from a fatal flaw, the basic disconnexion from reality involved in their failure to recognize and to glorify the true God.

and their uncomprehending heart has been darkened. Paul uses the word 'heart' to denote a man's inward self as a thinking, willing and feeling subject. The qualification of it by 'uncomprehending' suggests that it is the intellectual element of their inner lives which is particularly in mind. It is important not to misunderstand Paul's statement. It implies no contempt for reason. Those Christians who disparage the intellect and the processes of rational thought have no right to claim Paul as a supporter. But what is said here is a sober acknowledgment of the fact that man's intellect shares in the fallenness of the whole man, it is not somehow exempt from the general corruption. Even in its fallenness it should be highly valued, but it should not be regarded as an impartial arbiter capable of standing outside the influence of the ego and returning a perfectly objective judgment. The Christian should be aware not just of the more obvious evidences of the darkening of human reason, some of which are widely recognized, but also of the innumerable subtle and hidden ways in which the processes of rational thought are liable to be deflected and distorted. (See further on 'a reprobate mind' in v. 28 and on 'the renewing of your mind' in 12.2.)

22. Pretending to be wise, they have shown themselves fools drives home the contrast between human pretension and actual fact. Compare 1 Cor 1.21, and also the descriptions in Gen 3.6ff and 11.4ff of supposed wisdom which proves to be but folly.

23. and exchanged the glory of the immortal God for the likeness of the form of mortal man and of birds and fourfooted animals and reptiles. There are echoes here of the language of the Greek version of Ps 106.20 and Jer 2.11, though Paul uses 'glory' differently from the way it is used in those texts. In the present verse 'glory' is best understood as referring to the self-manifestation of the true God spoken of in vv. 19–20. That idolatry, showing itself in ever uglier and uglier forms, is the most striking characteristic of the life of all the developed nations of the modern world is perhaps too obvious to need to be said.

24. Wherefore indicates that what is related in this verse is God's response to the perverseness of men just described in vv. 22–23. **God delivered them up** sounds like a refrain through these verses (compare vv. 26 and 28). The English expression 'give up', used here by the AV, RV, RSV, and NEB, is liable to suggest a sense of finality which the Greek verb it represents certainly does not always convey. It is significant that the same Greek verb is used in 8.32 of God's delivering up His only Son to death for our sakes. While this fact in no way calls in question the seriousness of what is meant by 'deliver up' here, it ought surely to put us on our guard against lightly assuming that Paul must have meant that God gave these men up for ever. Paul's meaning is surely rather that God deliberately allowed them to go their own way in order that they might learn to hate the futility of a life turned away from the truth of God. It was an act of God's judgment and mercy, who smites in order to heal (Isa 19.22); and throughout the time of their God-forsakenness God is still concerned with them and dealing with them.

in *their abandonment to* **the lusts of their own hearts** indicates men's actual condition, describing the character of the life of those who acknowledge no criterion higher than their own wayward desires; and **to uncleanness** indicates the state into which they have been given up. **so that among them their bodies are dishonoured.** The Greek is probably best taken as consecutive, that is, as expressing the result of their having been delivered up to uncleanness.

25 is by some connected closely with v. 24: the first Greek word is then taken to mean something like 'seeing that they'. It seems better to follow those who see a break between vv. 24 and 25, and to render this first Greek word in some such way as **They ... actually.**

The words **have ... exchanged the truth of God for the lie** repeat the general sense of v. 23. We may compare 'who try to suppress the truth by their unrighteousness' in v. 18. For the use of 'lie' in connexion with idolatry see, for example, Isa 44.20. We take 'the truth of God' here to mean the reality consisting of God Himself and His self-revelation and 'the lie' to mean the whole futility of idolatry. The sentence is concluded by the words **and worshipped and served the creature instead of the Creator, who is blessed for ever: Amen.** In Jewish manner Paul attaches to his reference to God a blessing (of God).

26–27. Wherefore God has delivered them up. Compare the beginning of v. 24. These verses are connected with v. 25 in a similar way to that in which v. 24 is connected with vv. 22–23. **to passions which bring dishonour** corresponds to the 'to uncleanness' of v. 24.

for both their females have exchanged natural intercourse for that which is contrary to nature, and likewise also the males, having abandoned natural intercourse with the female, have burned in their lust for one another, males with males perpetrating shamelessness and receiving in their own persons the due wages of their deludedness. The initial 'for' indicates that vv. 26b–27 are explanation and substantiation of v. 26a. It seems probable that Paul chose to mention the women before the men, in order to give more emphasis to the male perversion by referring to it in the latter part of the sentence and dealing with it at greater length. By 'natural' and 'contrary to nature' Paul clearly means 'in accordance with the Creator's intention' and 'contrary to the Creator's intention', respectively. It is not impossible that Paul had some awareness of the great importance which 'nature' had had in Greek thought for centuries; that he was aware of its use in contemporary popular philosophy is very likely. But the decisive factor in his use of it is his biblical doctrine of creation. For him it denotes that order which is manifest in God's creation and which men have no excuse for failing to recognize and respect (compare what was said on vv. 19 and 20). It has been recognized from early times that the reference of 'the due wages of their deludedness' is more probably to their sexual perversion itself as the consequence of their abandonment of the true God than to a necessary or appropriate, but unspecified, consequence of their sexual perversion. The fact that ancient Greek and Roman society not only regarded paederasty with indulgence but was inclined to glorify it as actually superior to heterosexual love is too well known to need to be dwelt on here. Few voices were raised against it. It was common also in the Semitic world, though to the Jews it was an abomination. Paul clearly shared his fellow-Jews' abhorrence of it. But a refusal to accept that perversion is not really perversion is in no way incompatible with an understanding and compassionate attitude toward those who are in the grip of sexual perversion; and those who are at all familiar with the contents of the Bible will hardly be in any doubt of its condemnation of any inclination on the part of sinful men to judge their fellow-sinners in a hard and self-complacent spirit. Mt 10.15 and 11.23f may be cited in this connexion.

28. And, as they have not seen fit to take God into account, God has delivered them up to a reprobate mind. The first of these two clauses is more or less parallel to vv. 22–23 and 25. The first five words of the second clause repeat the statements at the beginnings of vv. 24 and 26, while 'to a reprobate mind' corresponds with 'to uncleanness' in v. 24 and 'to passions which bring dishonour' in v. 26. By 'to take God into account' is meant to know Him in the sense of acknowledging Him, reckoning with Him, taking Him into account in the practical affairs of one's life: it goes far beyond the sort of knowledge denoted by 'know' in v. 21. With 'reprobate mind' compare the last clause of v. 21. The sequel makes it clear that it is the mind in respect of its moral functions with which Paul is specially concerned. The 'reprobate mind' is one which is so corrupted as to be a quite untrustworthy guide in moral decisions. **to do the things which are morally wrong** is roughly parallel to the last clause of v. 24 ('so that among them their bodies are dishonoured'). The original here includes the negative form of an expression which in its positive form (meaning 'duty') was an ethical technical term much used by the Stoics[1] (though it had already been used before the Stoic school was founded). It is an interesting example of Paul's readiness to make use of current Gentile ethical terminology.

[1]Founded by Zeno of Citium (335-263 BC), this philosophical school had a profound influence on the thought and life of the Graeco-Roman world, extending far beyond those who formally belonged to it. One of its best-known representatives was Marcus Aurelius Antoninus, Roman Emperor AD 161–180.

29-31 comprise a list of vices arranged in three distinct groups, the end of the first being the word 'depravity', the end of the second being the word 'malice'. Lists of virtues and lists of vices occur in a number of New Testament epistles: they also appear in extra-biblical ancient literature, both Jewish and pagan. Only some of the items require comment here. **ruthlessness** represents a Greek word denoting ruthless self-assertion regardless of the rights of others or considerations of humanity. It is sometimes associated with sexual vices and sex is one of the spheres where it is often in evidence, but the word never denotes simply lust. The word translated **malice** is taken by some commentators to have the special sense of putting the worst construction on everything; but the two passages of Aristotle which are appealed to for support of this interpretation hardly justify it – it is surely more likely that Paul used the word in its ordinary general sense of malice or malignity. **whisperers, slanderers.** Both words denote people who go about to destroy others' reputations by misrepresentation; but the whisperers are the more dangerous kind, against whom there is virtually no human defence. **haters of God** is probably the right rendering here, though some take the word to mean 'hated by God' (the sense it has in classical Greek): the suggestion that it should be connected with 'slanderers' as a qualifying adjective seems improbable – even if only because it would spoil the carefully balanced structure of the list in Greek. **insolent** describes those who, confident in their own superior power, wealth, social position, physical strength, intellectual or other ability, treat fellow-men with insolent contemptuousness and so affront the majesty of God. **inventive of *novel* forms of evil** is in the original a succinct two-word phrase. One has only to think of the long, shameful history of men's ingenuity in discovering more and more hateful ways of torturing their fellow-men and of the inventiveness with which in the last half-century more and more fearful methods of mass-destruction have been developed, to realize that this phrase is far from being 'a curious expression', as it has seemed to one commentator.

32. They know God's righteous decree that those who practise such things deserve death; yet they not only do them, but actually applaud others who practise them. This has puzzled readers from early times, and the difficulty felt has caused some disturbance in the textual tradition, as may be seen from the textual apparatus of a Greek New Testament. The sentence implies that approving of others' doing evil deeds is even more depraved than doing them. This has often been judged – and still is judged by some commentators – to be untrue. But a good many have argued – surely rightly – that it is indeed true that the man who applauds and encourages those who practise something shameful, though not himself practising it, is not only as depraved as those who practise it, but very often, if not always, actually more depraved than they. For those who applaud and encourage the vicious actions of others make a deliberate contribution to the establishment of a public opinion favourable to vice and thereby promote the corruption of an unnumbered multitude; and they will not usually have been under any such powerful and violent pressure as those who commit the actions will quite often have been. So, for example, it seems reasonable to regard as even more blameworthy than the white South African supporters of *apartheid*, who have been subjected from childhood to social pressures and prejudices long and deeply established, those people who, in Britain and other countries far removed from such pressures, condone or ignore it and are ready to reap financial profits from it, so helping to cloak monstrous inhumanity with an appearance of respectability and to contribute most effectively to its firmer entrenchment.

(ii) *Jewish man is no exception*

(2.1–3.20)

¹**Wherefore thou hast no excuse, man, whoever thou art who judgest *another*; for wherein thou judgest the other thou condemnest thyself; for thou doest the same things, thou that settest thyself up as a judge. ²But we know that God's judgment is justly pronounced against those who practise such things. ³And dost thou reckon, thou man that judgest those that practise such things and yet doest them thyself, that thou shalt escape God's judgment? ⁴Or despisest thou the wealth of his kindness and forbearance and patience, refusing to see that God's kindness is meant to lead thee to repentance? ⁵But**

thou art storing up for thyself on account of thine obstinacy and unrepentant heart wrath in the day of wrath and of the revelation of the righteous judgment of God, [6]who will recompense every man according to his works, [7]to those who by steadfast perseverance in the good work seek glory and honour and immortality *he will give* eternal life, [8]but to those who are self-seeking and disobey the truth but obey unrighteousness there will be wrath and fury. [9]There will be tribulation and distress as the lot of every individual man who works what is evil, both of the Jew first and also of the Greek, [10]but glory and honour and peace for every one who works what is good, both for the Jew first and also for the Greek. [11]For there is no partiality with God.

[12]For, while all those who have sinned in ignorance of the law will also perish even though they did not have the law, all those who have sinned knowing the law will be judged on the basis of the law; [13]for it is not the hearers of the law who are righteous with God, but the doers of the law will be pronounced righteous. [14]For when Gentiles who do not possess the law by nature actually do the things which the law requires, they themselves, though not possessing the law, are a law for themselves. [15]They actually give proof of the fact that the work which the law requires is written on their hearts, and their own conscience will testify to them and their thoughts among themselves will accuse or even excuse them [16]on the day on which God judges the secrets of men through Christ Jesus according to the gospel which I preach.

[17]But, if thou hast the name of 'Jew' and reliest on the law and gloriest in God [18]and knowest his will and canst discern the things which are essential, being instructed out of the law, [19]and art confident that thou art a guide of the blind, a light of those in darkness, [20]an educator of the foolish, a teacher of the immature, having in the law the embodiment of knowledge and of truth, – [21]thou then, who teachest another, dost thou not teach thyself? thou, who preachest that one should not steal, dost thou steal? [22]thou, who sayest that one should not commit adultery, dost thou commit adultery? thou, who abhorrest idols, dost thou commit sacrilege? [23]While thou gloriest in the law, thou dishonourest God by transgressing the law. [24]For God's name is blasphemed among the Gentiles on your account, even as scripture says.

[25]For circumcision is indeed profitable, provided thou dost

practise the law; but if thou art a transgressor of the law, thy circumcision has become uncircumcision. ²⁶If then an uncircumcised man observes the righteous requirements of the law, will not his uncircumcision be reckoned as circumcision? ²⁷And the man who is by virtue of his birth an uncircumcised Gentile but who fulfils the law will judge thee, who for all thy possession of scripture and circumcision art a transgressor of the law. ²⁸For it is not the outward *Jew* who is a Jew *in the fullest sense,* nor is it the outward *circumcision* in the flesh which is circumcision *in the fullest sense;* ²⁹but *it is* the inward Jew *who is a Jew in the fullest sense,* and *it is* the circumcision of the heart (wrought by the Spirit and not merely a matter of fulfilment of the letter of the law) *which is circumcision in the fullest sense.* This man's praise is not from men but from God.

¹What advantage then does the Jew have? Or what profit is there in circumcision? ²Much in every way. First, that they were entrusted with the oracles of God. ³What then? If some have failed to respond with faith, shall their lack of faith render God's faithfulness ineffective? ⁴God forbid! We confess rather that God is true, and all men liars, even as scripture says, '. . . in order that thou mayest be acknowledged as righteous in thy words and mayest overcome when thou contendest'. ⁵But if our unrighteousness actually shows up the righteousness of God, what are we then to say? Is God unrighteous in that he inflicts his wrath *on us?* (I am giving expression to thoughts which are very human.) ⁶God forbid! For in that case how shall God judge the world? ⁷But if the truth of God has been more abundantly manifested to his glory, by means of my lie, why am I still judged as a sinner? ⁸And do we then say (as certain people slanderously allege that we say), 'Let us do evil, that good may come of it'? Those who so slander us are deservedly condemned.

⁹What then? Do we *Jews* have an advantage? Not in every respect; for we have already laid the charge against both Jews and Greeks that they are all under sin, ¹⁰even as scripture testifies:

'There is no one who is righteous, not even one,
¹¹   there is no one who has understanding,
    there is no one who seeks God.
¹²All have turned aside, together they have become useless;
    there is no one who shows kindness,
      no, not as much as one.

¹³**An open grave is their throat,**
 with their tongues they are wont to deceive,
 the poison of asps is under their lips.
¹⁴ **Their mouth is full of cursing and bitterness.**

¹⁵**Swift are their feet to shed blood,**
¹⁶ **destruction and misery mark their ways,**
¹⁷**and the way of peace they have not known.**
¹⁸ **There is no fear of God before their eyes.'**

¹⁹**But we know that whatever the law says it speaks to those who possess the law, in order that every mouth may be stopped and the whole world stand guilty before God. ²⁰For no flesh shall be justified before him on the ground of having done what the law requires; for through the law *comes* the knowledge of sin.**

That in 2.17ff Paul is apostrophizing[1] the typical Jew is clear; but there is no explicit indication before v. 17 that it is the Jews whom he has in mind. So the question arises: At what point does he turn his attention to them? Is it at v. 17? Or has he the Jews already in mind from the beginning of the chapter? Some interpreters maintain that in vv. 1ff Paul is thinking of the morally superior among the Gentiles, others that the thought is quite general, embracing all, whether Jews or Gentiles, who are inclined to judge their fellows. We agree with those who think it more probable that Paul had the Jews in mind right from 2.1.

 The subsection falls into six paragraphs. In 2.1–11 Paul, making use of apostrophe, declares those, who condemn others but themselves do the very same things, to be without excuse. They must not think to escape the judgment of God, who, as Scripture testifies, will render to each man according to his deeds, judging all men, Jew and Gentile alike, without respect of persons. The second paragraph (2.12–16) contains the first direct and explicit reference in the epistle to the law, and makes the point that knowledge of the law does not in itself constitute any defence against the judgment of God. In the third paragraph (2.17–24),

---

[1] i.e., addressing in an apostrophe, which, according to *The Shorter Oxford English Dictionary*, is a rhetorical 'figure, in which a speaker or writer suddenly stops in his discourse, and turns to address pointedly some person or thing, either present or absent'.

now apostrophizing the typical Jew by name, Paul draws attention to the disastrous contradictions by which his life is characterized.

In the fourth paragraph (2.25–29) he refers to a ground of Jewish confidence which has not been mentioned before, namely, circumcision. Circumcision profits, if one obeys the law, but, if one is a transgressor of the law, one's circumcision has become uncircumcision; and, conversely, the uncircumcised man's uncircumcision will be counted as circumcision, if he does what the law requires. Neither this nor the distinction which Paul goes on to draw between the outward Jew and the inward Jew and between outward circumcision and the circumcision of the heart, should be understood without reference to 3.1–4; 4.9–12; 9.1–11.36. The fact that Paul gives the answer which he does in 3.2 to the questions in 3.1 and the fact that in 3.4 he firmly rejects the suggestion that Israel's lack of faith will make God's faithfulness ineffective should discourage us from understanding v. 25b to mean that the circumcision of the disobedient Jew is simply annulled (though it is often so understood). Paul has not said that the transgressor's circumcision profits nothing; he has not taken away the sacramental character of circumcision, though he has certainly indicated that it does not place a man out of range of God's judgment. The point of v. 25b would seem to be that it is possible for a circumcised Jew to stand, by reason of his disobedience, in a negative relation to God's purpose in history. (On this and on the distinction between the outward and the inward Jew in v. 28f see further, in addition to the notes on the verses, what is said on chapters 9 to 11.)

The fifth paragraph is 3.1–8. Paul recognizes that what he has said in 2.25–29 is very liable to be misunderstood as implying that the Jews have after all no privilege and that there is no profit at all in circumcision. So in the first four verses of this paragraph he seeks to deal with this possible misunderstanding. But in the course of warding off this possible misunderstanding he lays himself open to another, and, recognizing that he has done so, he digresses from his argument for the last four verses of the paragraph, in order to guard against it.

With the beginning of the sixth and last paragraph of the subsection (3.9–20) Paul returns to his argument after the digression of vv. 5–8. While what was said in vv. 2–4 certainly does mean that the reality and greatness of the Jews' privilege are not to be denied, it would be wrong to infer that they are at an advantage in absolutely every respect. In one respect, in particular, they have no advantage: as far as having a claim on God in virtue of their merit is concerned, they are in exactly the same position as the Gentiles – having, equally with them, no claim at all. The fact that all men alike are under sin's power is then confirmed by the catena of Old Testament quotations in vv. 10–18. So far from imagining themselves to be excepted from God's condemnation of human sinfulness, the Jews must accept it as certainly including themselves, since what is said in the Scriptures concerns first and foremost the people of the Scriptures. And, if the Jews are no exception, then it is clear that all mankind must stand guilty before God. There is no question of the Jews' being justified by God on the ground of obedience to the law: the effect of the law is to reveal men's sinfulness.

1. Wherefore has given commentators much trouble. The difficulty has been that, on the assumption that 1.18–32 is concerned exclusively with the Gentiles, it has been impossible to explain 2.1 satisfactorily as following logically upon 1.32 (for how can it follow from the fact that *the Gentiles* fall under the condemnation declared in 1.18–32 that *the Jew* is without excuse if he judges?). But, as soon as it is recognized that 1.18–32 is not concerned exclusively with the Gentiles, the difficulty disappears. **thou hast no excuse, man, whoever thou art who judgest *another*.** Since the gospel reveals the fact of the universal sinfulness of men, the man who sets himself up to judge other men is without excuse – he has no ground at all on which to stand. That the truth thus stated has relevance to the heathen moralist, the civil magistrate, the ministers of the Church, is indeed true; but Paul himself, it is scarcely to be doubted, was thinking especially of the typical Jew. The direct address in the second person singular is used for the sake of forcefulness in this and the following verses (compare 2.17ff; 8.2; 9.19f; 11.17ff; 13.3f; 14.4, 10, 15, 20–22).

for wherein thou judgest the other, thou condemnest thyself; for thou doest the same things, thou that settest thyself up as a judge is naturally taken to mean that the man who judges his fellow-man is thereby condemning himself because he is guilty of the same sorts

43

of wrong-doing as the man he judges. Barrett has objected to this interpretation on the ground of the real moral superiority of the Jews and also of Gentile moral philosophers (he does not accept that this is addressed exclusively to the Jews), and suggested that Paul's point is rather that the act of judging is itself an attempt to put oneself in the place of God, and so the same idolatry essentially as is manifested in the sins referred to in the latter part of chapter 1. But this is over-subtle, and his objection is answered, if we recognize that 'the same things' need not imply that the judge sins in precisely the same ways. There are, for example, more ways than one of breaking the seventh commandment, as is made clear in Mt 5.27f.

2. But we know that God's judgment is justly pronounced against those who practise such things is not intended to be taken as the imagined reply of the representative Jew whom Paul is addressing, as Dodd, for example, understands it, but is Paul's own statement of what he knows to be common ground between himself and the person addressed. There are similar occurrences of 'we know' in 3.19; 7.14; 8.22, 28; 2 Cor 5.1; 1 Tim 1.8. In each of them it introduces a statement which the writer can assume will meet with general acceptance on the part of those to whom he is writing or whom he has in mind.

3. And dost thou reckon, thou man that judgest those that practise such things and yet doest them thyself, that thou shalt escape God's judgment? is closely connected with vv. 1 and 2, the language of which it echoes. It applies the truth stated in v. 2 to the person addressed in v. 1. In view of that truth does he really reckon to be a special case, to escape the judgment of God? That there were Jews who did reckon precisely this is clear from, for example, Wisd 15.2.

4. Or despisest thou the wealth of his kindness and forbearance and patience, refusing to see that God's kindness is meant to lead thee to repentance? is not an alternative interpretation of the Jew's attitude to the one put forward in v. 3 but rather a different, and heightened, statement of it. The Jew's assumption that he is going to escape God's judgment amounts to contempt for God's kindness. We have translated the Greek word, which the RV represents by 'not knowing', 'refusing to see', because the clause it introduces is clearly not intended as an extenuation of the guilt of the person addressed but as a clarification of 'despisest'. That 'God's kindness is meant to lead ... to repentance' was a well-established truth in Judaism is clear from, for example, Wisd 11.23; 12.10, 19; but its applicability to the heathen tended to be more dwelt on than its applicability to the Jew.

5. But thou art storing up for thyself on account of thine obstinacy and unrepentant heart wrath in the day of wrath and of the revelation of the righteous judgment of God. It is possible to connect the last fifteen words of the verse (as translated here) with 'thou art storing up', and so to understand them as characterizing the present time, in which the storing up is taking place, as the time of God's wrath and of the revelation of His righteous judgment. This would be consonant with the use of the present tense ('is being revealed') with reference to the wrath of God in 1.18. Paul's thought would be that even now, when God's wrath and His righteous judgment are actually being revealed as the gospel is preached, the person whom he is addressing can think of nothing better to do than to go on storing up wrath for himself by his self-righteous, impenitent attitude. But, in view of the contents of vv. 6–10, it seems more natural to connect the last fifteen words of the verse closely with 'wrath' – so to understand them as indicating when the wrath is to be experienced (namely, in the final judgment). Verses 6–10 are then explication of 'the revelation of the righteous judgment of God'.

6. who will recompense every man according to his works echoes the language of Ps 62.12; Prov 24.12. That God's judgment will be according to men's deeds is again and again affirmed in Scripture – in the New Testament no less strongly than in the Old. The question of the compatibility of this affirmation with what Paul says elsewhere (for example, in 3.20a, 21f, 28) in connexion with justification will need to be discussed in the light of vv. 6–11 as a whole, since the summary statement of this verse is spelled out in vv. 7–10 and then confirmed by v. 11. But it may be said here that we should be unwise to take it for granted that 'according to his works' must be equivalent to 'according to his deserts' or – to put it in other words – that it must be given a legalistic sense.

7-8. to those who by steadfast perseverance in the good work seek glory and honour and immortality *he will give* eternal life, but to those who are self-seeking and disobey the truth but obey

unrighteousness there will be wrath and fury explicates v. 6, breaking up its 'every man' into two opposed categories of men and indicating what recompense is in store for each. The meaning of v. 7 and, in particular, of 'the good work' will be discussed later (when we can look back over vv. 6–11 as a whole). On 'disobey the truth but obey unrighteousness' it will be sufficient commentary to compare 1.18 ('of men who try to suppress the truth by their unrighteousness'). The Greek phrase represented by 'are self-seeking' has been variously interpreted. It consists of a preposition meaning 'out of' followed by an abstract noun, which could be used in the sense 'self-seeking', 'selfishness', and is probably best so understood here. Barrett's suggestion that 'Paul intends by means of this word to describe the motives ... of those who look on their works as achievements of their own, complete in themselves, by means of which they may acquire rights' surely builds too much upon etymology (the Greek abstract noun is cognate with another noun meaning 'hired servant') to be convincing.

9-10. There will be tribulation and distress as the lot of every individual man who works what is evil, both of the Jew first and also of the Greek, but glory and honour and peace for every one who works what is good, both for the Jew first and also for the Greek is arranged to form a chiasmus or *a b b a* pattern with vv. 7 and 8, the first six words of v. 9 corresponding to the last six of v. 8, the rest of v. 9 to the earlier part of v. 8, 'glory and honour and peace' in v. 10 to 'eternal life' in v. 7, and the rest of v. 10 to the earlier part of v. 7. The general thought of the two preceding verses is repeated. For the emphasis both on the equal relevance to both Jew and Gentile of what is being said and also, at the same time, on the special precedence of the Jew, reference may be made to the notes on 1.16 and also on 3.1–2, 9.

11. For there is no partiality with God is added in confirmation of what has been said in vv. 6–10. Compare Gal 2.6; Eph 6.9; Col 3.25; also Acts 10.34.

We are now in a position to look at vv. 6–11 as a whole and to try to decide how the passage is to be understood. The difficulty which faces us here will confront us again in vv. 12–16 and 25–29; and in each of these three closely related passages it is what we may call the positive element (that is, vv. 7 and 10, 13b and 14a, and 26) which is specially problematic. Of the numerous interpretations which have been suggested it will be enough here to mention just five:

(i) that Paul is inconsistent, and, whereas elsewhere he maintains that God will justify 'on the ground of faith' or 'through faith'(3.30) and that no one will be justified on the ground of his works, he is here expressing the thought that the final judgment will be according to men's *deserts* and there will be some (both Jews and Gentiles) who will have *earned* God's approval by their goodness of life.

(ii) that Paul is here speaking hypothetically, leaving the gospel out of account and arguing from the presuppositions of the Jew, whom he is apostrophizing[1] (this is how – on the Jew's own presuppositions – the judgment will be), in order to show that his present conduct (see vv. 3 and 4) will, even on his own presuppositions, bring disaster.

(iii) that Paul means by 'works' in v. 6 faith or lack of faith and in vv. 7 and 10 is referring to Christians, meaning by 'the good work' of v. 7 and 'what is good' in v. 10 the good work consisting of faith.

(iv) that Paul is referring in vv. 7 and 10 to Christians, but means by 'the good work' and 'what is good' not their faith itself but their conduct as the expression of their faith, and similarly by 'works' in v. 6 each man's conduct as the expression either of faith or of unbelief.

(v) that Paul reckons with the existence among the heathen in some mysterious way of a faith known only to God and refers to it (or to conduct which is the expression of it) in vv. 7 and 10.

Of these (i) is surely to be rejected. While it would be rash indeed to claim that there are no inconsistencies in the Pauline epistles, the inconsistency which this explanation attributes to Paul is surely too glaring to be at all likely. In favour of (ii) it may be said that, if it is accepted (together with an interpretation of vv. 12–16 and 25–29 along similar lines), the progress of the argument up to the end of 3.20 would seem most straightforward; but the fact that there is no indication in the text that what is being said is

---

[1]For the meaning of this word see footnote on p.41.

hypothetical tells against it. On the whole, (iv) seems to us the most probable explanation.

The point which Paul wants to make after vv. 3–5 is that for the Jew to rely complacently on the fact of his knowledge of God and of God's will, as though a knowledge which stops short of obedience were enough, is folly, since God's judgment will take account of men's deeds. It is 'works' which is the operative word in v. 6, and the importance of works is further underlined in v. 13 (compare the emphatic 'do' in v. 14). So the accent in vv. 7–10 is on the negative side, on the warning these verses contain for the Jew in his complacency. This is confirmed by v. 11. Thus the intention of vv. 6–11 fits naturally into place (and the same may also be said of vv. 12–16 and of vv. 25–29) within the over-all function of 2.1–3.20 which is to show that the Jew is no exception to the verdict of the gospel that no man – apart of course from the one man, Jesus Christ – *deserves* God's favour. But in making his point in these verses Paul also sketches in the corresponding positive side, thereby anticipating the subsequent course of his argument by referring (though not explicitly) to the works of the Christian believer.

It is absolutely vital to the true understanding of these verses to recognize that the statement of v. 6 is not made in a legalistic sense – it is not an assertion of requital according to *deserts* – and that it is not implied in vv. 7 and 10 that the people referred to *earn* eternal life. The 'good work' is not regarded as constituting a claim upon God, but as the expression of faith and repentance. The good work no more earns salvation than does the evil work. The difference between them is the difference between evidence of openness to God's judgment and mercy and evidence of the persistence of a proud and stubborn self-righteousness. The insistence on the necessity of works which we have here, which should be compared with what is to be seen in such passages as Mt 7.21 and 25.31ff, has nothing to do with the idea that one can be justified on the ground of works, that is, earn one's justification by one's works. There is then nothing in these verses which is incompatible with Paul's doctrine of justification by faith.

12 begins a new paragraph within the subsection. The connexion of thought with vv. 1–11 is very close. But now there is introduced for the first time in the epistle a direct and explicit reference to the law (an indirect reference may be recognized in vv. 1 and 3, for the reader is no doubt expected to realize that it is on the basis of his knowledge of the law that the Jew presumes to judge others). The main point made in this paragraph is that knowledge of the law does not in itself constitute any defence against the judgment of God.

For, while all those who have sinned in ignorance of the law will also perish even though they did not have the law, all those who have sinned knowing the law will be judged on the basis of the law. The two halves of the verse are co-ordinate in the original, but it is clear from the following verse that the emphasis falls on the second half – hence our use of subordination ('while . . . ') in the translation. That each reference to law here is to the Old Testament law is not to be doubted.

13. for it is not the hearers of the law who are righteous with God, but the doers of the law will be pronounced righteous supports the latter half of the preceding verse, and brings to clear expression the main point of this paragraph. The fact that in this verse hearing is opposed to doing indicates that 'hear' does not have the strong sense which it often has in the Bible (for example, Deut 4.30; Jer 11.3), but denotes that hearing only which falls short of heeding and obeying (compare Jas 1.22f, 25). Those who are merely hearers of the law in this narrow sense are certainly not possessed of any status of righteousness before God. That doing what the law commands is the decisive thing, and not just hearing it and knowing about it, was a truth familiar to the Rabbis; but, though Paul takes up a Rabbinic doctrine, he is giving it fresh content. In its context in Romans this sentence can hardly be intended to imply that there are some who are doers of the law in the sense that they so fulfil it as to earn God's justification. Rather is Paul thinking of that beginning of grateful obedience to be found in those who believe in Christ, which though very weak and faltering and in no way deserving God's favour, is, as the expression of humble trust in God, well-pleasing in His sight.

14-16. The most natural explanation of the **For** at the beginning of v. 14 would seem to be that what it introduces is thought of as confirming v. 13b. Verse 13b might seem to be incompatible with 'and also for the Greek' in v. 10; but it is not really, for, if there are Gentiles who can be said to do the things which the law requires, then the use of the expression 'the doers of the law' in v. 13b does not rule out 'the Greek' of v. 10.

when Gentiles who do not possess the law by nature actually do the things which the law requires poses again both the problems common to vv. 7, 10 and 13b and also the special problem raised by 'and also for the Greek' in v. 10; and is variously interpreted. The following suggestions have to be considered: (i) that the thought is that some pagan Gentiles do in fact, on the basis of a natural law, fulfil the demands of God's law and so merit His favour; (ii) that Paul is speaking only hypothetically, his purpose being to underline the essential equality before God of Jews and Gentiles; (iii) that he refers to a secret, hidden faith, known only to God, existing mysteriously in some pagan hearts, or to the works by which it expresses itself; (iv) that the reference is to the Gentile Christians. Of this last interpretation also two forms may be distinguished: (a) that which understands 'actually do the things which the law requires' of the Gentile Christians' faith, and (b) that which takes it to refer to those works of obedience which, though but imperfect and far from deserving God's favour, are the expression of their hearts' faith. Of the interpretations we have listed (i) should be rejected as hardly compatible with 3.9, 20, 23, and (ii) on the ground that there is nothing here to suggest that Paul is speaking merely hypothetically. Interpretation (iv), which is found already in the earliest Latin commentary which has come down to us and in Augustine and also in Barth's shorter commentary, seems to us the most likely. And, as between (a) and (b), (b) should, in our view, be preferred.

The question whether 'by nature' should be connected with the preceding or with the following words has still to be considered. It has usually been connected with what follows, and Paul's meaning has commonly been understood to be that it is as a result of their possession of natural law that some Gentiles do the things required by God's law. But a comparison of other occurrences of 'nature' in the Pauline epistles suggests rather the connexion of 'by nature' here with the preceding words – so 'Gentiles which do not possess the law by nature', that is, by virtue of their birth (compare especially v. 27 of this chapter, Gal 2.15 and Eph 2.3). Moreover, if we are right in taking 'Gentiles' to refer to the Gentile Christians, there is a further point in favour of taking 'by nature' with what precedes – it would not be accurate to describe Gentile Christians as not possessing the law, since as Christians they of course would have some knowledge of the Old Testament law, whereas to describe them as not possessing the law by nature, that is, by virtue of their birth, would be appropriate.

they themselves, though not possessing the law, are a law for themselves. The words 'though not possessing the law' add nothing new, but simply pick up something already expressed in the preceding clause. 'Be a law to oneself' is a stereotyped expression used by Greek writers with reference to the man of superior virtue regarded as not needing the guidance or sanctions of external law. As used here, it must clearly be interpreted in close relation to what follows in v. 15a. Those who understand v. 14a according to the first or second interpretation listed above take these words as a statement of these particular Gentiles' knowledge of, and reverence for, that moral law which is innate in their human nature. But, on the assumption that the Gentiles referred to are Christians, the sense of these words will rather be that, although they have not been brought up by virtue of their birth in the possession of God's law (like Jews), they now know it and actually have in their hearts the earnest desire to obey it (see further on v. 15).

They actually give proof of the fact that the work which the law requires is written on their hearts. Here 'the work which the law requires' means not the required work as accomplished but the required work in the sense of the commandments contained in the law. For the use of the singular compare 8.4 ('the righteous requirement of the law'). In both cases the singular was probably intended to bring out the essential unity of the law's requirements, the fact that the plurality of commandments is no confused and confusing conglomeration but a recognizable and intelligible whole. That 'written on their hearts' is a deliberate reminiscence of Jer 31.33 is denied by many commentators, on the ground that the Jeremiah passage refers to an eschatological work of God to be wrought on Israel, while the present passage is (allegedly) concerned with a non-eschatological fact of Gentile life. The expression 'written on the heart' is accordingly explained as a specially emphatic way of indicating the inescapability of the divine requirement. But, as soon as it is recognized that the

Gentiles whom Paul has in mind are Gentile Christians, the objection to seeing here an intentional reference to Jer 31.33 disappears; for it is abundantly clear that Paul did think that God's eschatological promises were already beginning to be fulfilled through the gospel in the lives of believers, both Jews and Gentiles. And the verbal similarity between the original Greek here and the Septuagint version of Jer 31.33, which is part of a passage (Jer 31.31–34) to which Paul refers elsewhere (see 1 Cor 11.25; 2 Cor 3.2, 3, 6, 14; 6.16), is so close that it is difficult to avoid the conclusion that Paul has the Jeremiah verse in mind. We take it then that his thought is that in these Gentiles who are believers in Christ God's promise that He would establish His law by creating in His people a sincere and earnest desire to obey it is being fulfilled.

and their own conscience will testify to them and their thoughts among themselves will accuse or even excuse them on the day on which God judges the secrets of men through Christ Jesus according to the gospel which I preach. In these one and a half verses we have a number of difficulties.

There is first the use of 'conscience'. It will help us to think clearly about this, if we grasp firmly from the start the distinction between, on the one hand, the use of 'conscience' in modern English in such phrases as 'a good conscience', 'a clear conscience', 'a bad conscience', and, on the other hand, its use to denote an internal law or law-giver. C. A. Pierce made an important contribution to the study of the New Testament by demonstrating the fallacy of the commonly held assumption of the Stoic origin of Paul's use of the Greek word *suneidesis* (the word here translated 'conscience') and by his careful survey and clarification of the uses of that and related terms in classical, and in non-Christian Hellenistic, Greek.[1] He has shown that the use of this group of expressions to convey the idea of knowledge shared with oneself, so, in particular, a painful knowledge shared with oneself of having done wrong or (less frequently) a knowledge – not painful – of one's innocence, is found again and again in Greek writing, both literary and non-literary, from the sixth century BC right down to the seventh century AD. Its origin is not

[1]*Conscience in the New Testament*, London, 1955.

philosophical but popular. It is, of course, true that *suneidesis* is not by any means confined to this usage: as well as being a noun-equivalent to the verbal expression meaning 'know together with oneself', it can also, in particular, simply mean 'knowledge' (the *sun-* of the compound, in this case, not having its sense of 'with' but having simply a strengthening force). But, as far as the present occurrence is concerned, there is little doubt, in view of the rest of v. 15, that *suneidesis* is here used in its common Greek sense of knowledge shared with oneself of one's having done wrong or of one's innocence. There is, as far as we can see, no justification in Paul's sentence for identifying the Gentiles' 'conscience' with 'the work which the law requires . . . written on their hearts' or (on the basis of such an identification) seeing here the idea of conscience as an internal law or internal law-giver.

There are a number of other interrelated questions which the interpreter of the original Greek has to try to answer. To many of them our translation has already implied answers; but it is only fair to the reader to indicate them here – though we shall do so as briefly as possible. The Greek word which we have rendered by 'and . . . will testify to them' is a participle (which could refer either to the present or to the future) of a verb which can mean either 'bear witness along with' (in this case, it is implied that there is at least one other witness besides the subject of the verb and an accompanying dative, if there is one, will indicate this other witness), or simply 'bear witness', 'testify', 'assure' (in this case, an accompanying dative, if there is one, will indicate the recipient of the testimony). Since no other witness is mentioned, it is natural to take the verb in the sense 'testify' and to supply 'to them' from 'their' as the recipient of the testimony. If, as seems natural, the testimony of their conscience and their thoughts' accusing or excusing them are to be taken closely together, the latter being understood as clarification of the former, then, in view of the connexion of the latter with v. 16 (the suggestions which have been made as to how v. 16 may be disconnected from v. 15 and connected instead with v. 13 or with v. 12 strike us as counsels of despair), it would seem that both the testimony of the conscience and the accusing or excusing by their thoughts must be understood to belong to the future. While for those who take 'conscience' as an inward law or law-giver a future reference is unacceptable, on our understanding of 'conscience' it gives a satisfactory sense. At the time of the final judgment, when the all-seeing God from whom no secrets of men are hidden shall judge men – according to Paul's gospel, that is, the gospel which Paul in common with other Christian preachers proclaims – through Christ Jesus, these Gentile Christians will have the testimony of the knowledge which they share with themselves of the fact that they have (now in the present time) shown the work of the law written on their hearts. This testimony will be given through a mêlée of accusing and excusing thoughts. The fact that Paul puts 'accuse' before 'excuse' and inserts 'even' before 'excuse' suggests that he is aware that in this internal debate there will be more accusing than excusing. These Christians will know, when they appear before their Judge, that their lives fell very far short of a perfect fulfilment of God's requirement, and yet in the midst of all their painful consciousness of their sinfulness their thoughts will also be able to remind them that they did truly believe in God's forgiveness and had begun, however feebly and fitfully, to let their lives be turned in the direction of obedience.

17-20. But, if thou hast the name of 'Jew' and reliest on the law and gloriest in God and knowest his will and canst discern the things which are essential, being instructed out of the law, and art confident that thou art a guide of the blind, a light of those in darkness, an educator of the foolish, a teacher of the immature, having in the law the embodiment of knowledge and of truth, – is the beginning of the third paragraph of the subsection 2.1–3.20, and forms a conditional sentence to which there is no main clause, the structure of the sentence being broken off. The opening 'But' marks a contrast, the person whom Paul is apostrophizing[1] being contrasted with those to whom vv. 14–16 have referred. Here for the first time it is explicitly indicated that it is the typical Jew who is being addressed. In these verses Paul seems to be deliberately taking up claims which were actually being made by his fellow-Jews, echoing the very language in which they were being expressed. He should not be understood as being merely ironical. While there is an element of irony in each of the items by which the Jew is described, there is also 'a sincere acknowledgment of the

[1]For the meaning of this word see footnote on p.41.

position and the mission which the Jews have in fact been given in the Gentile metropolis and in the whole Gentile world'.[1]

The Jew is absolutely right to be seriously concerned with God's law, to follow after it (compare 9.31) with the utmost diligence, and to rely on it as God's true and righteous word. But the trouble is that he follows after it 'as on the basis of works' instead of 'on the basis of faith' (compare 9.32), and relies on it in the sense of thinking to fulfil it in such a way as to put God in his debt or of imagining complacently that the mere fact of possessing it gives him security against God's judgment. Again, to boast or glory in God is a thoroughly good thing, if it is the sort of boasting in Him which truly gives Him the glory, a truly humble boasting in His goodness and mercy; but it is an altogether different matter, if it is the sort which is a self-centred boasting in Him as a basis for one's own self-importance. (Note that 'gloriest' in v. 17 represents the first occurrence in the epistle of a member of a Greek word-group which has considerable importance in Paul's epistles: in Romans see v. 23; 3.27; 4.2; 5.2, 3, 11; 15.17; and also 11.18.) The knowledge and discernment to which Paul refers he regards as real and important, though he sees them as paradoxically compounded with a disastrous failure of comprehension (see on 10.2 and 19). And he is certainly not being merely ironical when he refers to the Jew's confidence; for it was the Jew's divine vocation to be all the things which Paul lists in vv. 19–20, and it is also true that to some extent he was in fact all these things. The real indebtedness of the Gentile to the Jew is not to be denied or glossed over. It is only when what the Jew is and does is seen in the light of God that its complete inadequacy becomes apparent.

21–22. thou then, who teachest another, dost thou not teach thyself? thou, who preachest that one should not steal, dost thou steal? thou, who sayest that one should not commit adultery, dost thou commit adultery? thou, who abhorrest idols, dost thou commit sacrilege? These four rhetorical questions (all of similar structure except that, while the first contains the negative particle and so anticipates – ironically – an affirmative answer, the others are formally open questions) draw attention to the shameful

[1]K. Barth, *A Shorter Commentary on Romans*, English translation, London, 1959, p.37.

inconsistencies of Jewish life. It is unlikely that Paul thought that any of the four implied accusations, if taken in a matter of fact conventional sense, was true of all Jews, or even of most Jews. He is thinking, rather, in terms of a radical understanding of the law (compare, for example, Mt 5.21–48). Where the full seriousness of the law's requirement is understood, there it is recognized that all are transgressors, breaking every one of the commandments. About the interpretation of the Greek word which we have translated by 'commit sacrilege' there are different views. Some take the reference to be to the use by Jews of articles stolen (whether by themselves or by others) from pagan temples and to the casuistry which invented exceptions to the categorical prohibition of Deut 7.25–26. But it is possible that what Paul is contrasting with the Jew's abhorrence of idolatry is his actually committing sacrilege against the one true God. If so, it is probably better not to assume that he must have in mind the robbing of the Jerusalem temple, but to understand him to be using the Greek verb in the more general sense of 'commit sacrilege' and to be thinking not only of behaviour which is obviously sacrilegious but also of less obvious and more subtle forms of sacrilege.

23. While thou gloriest in the law, thou dishonourest God by transgressing the law sums up vv. 21 and 22. Just as there is a right, but also a wrong, boasting or exulting in God, so too with the law. Gratefully and humbly to glory in it as the gracious revelation of God's merciful will is right, but to glory in it in the sense of thinking to use it as a means to putting God in one's debt and of regarding one's knowledge of it as conferring on one the right to look down on one's fellow-men is altogether wrong.

The Jew is right to glory in the law, but, unfortunately, his glorying in the law is to a large extent the wrong sort of glorying. The main clause sums up the situation indicated by means of the four questions of vv. 21 and 22. The Jew's conduct, which gives the lie to his doctrine and profession, is transgression of God's law, and as such it is a dishonouring of God.

24. For God's name is blasphemed among the Gentiles on your account, even as scripture says is an appeal to the Old Testament in support of what has just been said. The quotation is an adaptation of the Greek version of Isa 52.5. Isa 52.5 referred originally to the reviling of God's name by the oppressors of Israel on account of

Israel's misfortunes. The variations of the Greek version from the Hebrew made the way easier for Paul's application of the words to the reviling of God's name by the Gentiles on account of the Jews' disobedience to God's law. Israel, whose special vocation it was to sanctify God's name by its obedience and so to promote the glory of His name, is actually the cause of its being dishonoured.

25 begins the fourth paragraph of 2.1–3.20. **For circumcision is indeed profitable, provided thou dost practise the law.** The 'For' indicates the connexion between vv. 25–29 and what precedes. One of the chief grounds of Jewish confidence has so far not been mentioned – circumcision. So, in order to complete this part of his argument and meet an obvious objection from the Jewish side, and in clarification and confirmation of what he has just been saying, Paul now turns to the subject of circumcision. He freely admits that, in the case of the Jew who does what the law requires, circumcision is profitable. Of this there can be no doubt; for it is an institution appointed by the true God, a token of the covenant made by Him with Israel and a pledge of the covenant blessings.

But with the words **but if thou art a transgressor of the law, thy circumcision has become uncircumcision** Paul challenges the Jew's complacent reliance on circumcision. His words are generally taken to mean that, if a Jew is a transgressor of the law, his circumcision is annulled; and, taken by itself, this sentence could no doubt bear this meaning. But this sentence does not stand by itself. In 3.3 Paul is going to reject with emphasis the suggestion that the Jews' 'lack of faith' is going to 'render God's faithfulness ineffective', and the burden of chapter 11 is going to be that God has not cast off His people. Moreover, it is noticeable – though not often noticed – that Paul does not say here (as, in view of the first part of the verse, we might expect him to do), 'thy circumcision does not profit at all'. That would indeed have been strange in view of 3.1.

It seems therefore better to understand v. 25b to mean, not that the Jew's circumcision has been annulled in God's sight, but that he has become uncircumcised in heart (that is, one whose heart is far from God and whose life is a contradiction of his membership of the Covenant people), and now, though still a member of God's special people to whom God is still faithful, stands in his human existence in a negative, and no longer in a positive, relation to

God's purpose in history, and is outside that Israel within Israel, to which Paul refers in 9.6ff. (See further on vv. 28 and 29 below.)

26. If then an uncircumcised man observes the righteous requirements of the law, will not his uncircumcision be reckoned as circumcision? On the assumption that Paul is not putting forward merely for the sake of argument an hypothesis which he does not expect to be fulfilled, we must understand 'observes the righteous requirements of the law' to mean, not a perfect fulfilment of the law's demands (for, according to Paul, only one man, the circumcised Jesus, ever accomplished this), but a grateful and humble faith in God and the life turned in the direction of obedience which is its fruit. We take it he has in mind the Gentile Christians. The question anticipating an affirmative answer is equivalent to a positive statement that such a man's uncircumcision will be reckoned by God as circumcision, that is, that in God's sight he will count as a member of the people of Israel.

27. And the man who is by virtue of his birth an uncircumcised Gentile but who fulfils the law will judge thee, who for all thy possession of scripture and circumcision art a transgressor of the law. The meaning of 'will judge' is not that the Gentile will pronounce sentence on the Jew but probably that he will be a witness for the prosecution in the sense that his relative obedience will be evidence of what the Jew ought to have been and could have been. The words here represented by 'for all thy possession of scripture and circumcision' are difficult and have been variously interpreted. The word translated here as 'scripture' means 'letter'. It is possible to take it together with 'and circumcision' in the sense 'literal circumcision', but, in our view, the translation we have given is more likely to be correct. Paul may perhaps have used this particular Greek word not just to emphasize the Scripture's concreteness as something written, visible, tangible, but because of his awareness of the externality of the Jew's possession of Scripture (compare v. 29).

28-29. For it is not the outward _Jew_ who is a Jew _in the fullest sense_, nor is it the outward _circumcision_ in the flesh which is circumcision _in the fullest sense_; but _it is_ the inward Jew _who is a Jew in the fullest sense_, and _it is_ the circumcision of the heart (wrought by the Spirit and not merely a matter of fulfilment of the letter of the

law) *which is circumcision in the fullest sense.* **This man's praise is not from men but from God.** This forms the climax of the paragraph. Its expression is strikingly elliptic in the original Greek. Hence the numerous words in italics in the translation, which have no equivalents in the original. Paul is apparently drawing a distinction between the person who is to all outward appearance a Jew and the person who is inwardly a Jew, and claims that it is the latter, and not the former, who is a Jew – in the sense Paul here gives to the term (what precisely it is will have to be discussed below). In the light of vv. 25 and 26 it is implied both that not all outward Jews are Jews in the special sense, and also that not all Jews in the special sense are outward Jews. At the same time a similar distinction is drawn between outward circumcision in the flesh and circumcision of the heart. The idea of circumcision of the heart is one that goes back to Deuteronomy (Lev 26.41; Deut 10.16; 30.6; Jer 4.4; 9.26). Paul further defines this circumcision as (literally) 'in spirit, not in letter'. By this he most probably intends to indicate that the circumcision of the heart is not accomplished by the mere fulfilment of the letter of the law's requirement, but is a miracle, the work of God's Spirit.

The concluding sentence probably contains an intentional play on the connexion between the Hebrew for 'Jew' and the Hebrew verb meaning 'praise' and its derivatives, a word-play going back to Gen 29.35; 49.8, and well known in Judaism. For the contrast between praise from God and praise from men we may compare Jn 5.41, 44; 12.43.

It is clear that in these verses Paul is in some sense denying the name of Jew to those who are only outwardly Jews and not also secretly and inwardly, and at the same time according it to those who are secret, inward Jews but not outward Jews at all. Is he then denying that those Jews who in some sense are not Jews have any part in the promises made to Israel? Is he implying that henceforth the elect people of God consists only of those whom he describes as inward Jews, that is, of Jewish Christians together with Gentile Christians, or, in other words, that the Christian Church alone is the heir to all the promises? Taken by themselves these verses would seem to be patient of such a construction. They have certainly often been understood in this sense, and Paul has appeared as the father of those 'who have denied to the Jewish people their election privileges and promises', simply 'transferring them to Christianity as the new Israel of God'.[1] But these verses do not stand by themselves, and, if they are to be interpreted in the light of 3.1–4 and also of 9.1–11.36, they can hardly bear this meaning. The true explanation of them is rather that in them Paul is using 'Jew' in a special limited sense to denote the man who in his concrete human existence stands by virtue of his faith in a positive relation to the on-going purpose of God in history, and that, while they certainly do imply that many who are outwardly Jews are outside what may be called 'the Israel within Israel', they should not be taken as implying that those who are Jews only outwardly are excluded from the promises. (See further on 3.1–4 and especially on 9.1–11.36.)

3.1 begins the fifth paragraph of 2.1–3.20. **What advantage then does the Jew have? Or what profit is there in circumcision?** is no frivolous objection. What has just been said in the preceding chapter, and particularly in vv. 25–29, might indeed seem to imply that there is no advantage of the Jew over the Gentile and no profit in circumcision. But, if this really were the implication of Paul's argument, then it would have called in question the truthfulness of the Old Testament or the faithfulness of God Himself; for, according to the testimony of the Old Testament, God chose this nation out of all mankind to be His special people and gave them circumcision as a token of the covenant which He had made with them. If then there really is no advantage of the Jew and no profit in circumcision, this must mean either that the Old Testament is a false witness or else that God has not been faithful to His word. The question raised is nothing less than the question of the credibility of God.

2. Much in every way. According to one widely read commentary, the logical answer on the basis of Paul's own argument would have been 'None whatever!' and Paul's actual answer is to be explained as due to his deeply engrained Pharisaism and patriotism. But Paul's answer is not really incompatible with what he has been saying. 'Much in every way' is not an assertion that the Jew far outstrips the Gentile in every sort

---

[1] H. J. Schoeps, *Paul: the theology of the Apostle in the light of Jewish religious history*, English translation, London, 1961, p.234.

of advantage one might think of, but rather an assertion that the Jew has an advantage, a priority, a pre-eminence, which in every respect is great and important. What this pre-eminence is becomes clear from the reference in the latter part of the verse to one aspect of it. It is the fact of God's special choice of Israel, the fact that it is through this nation that God's covenant with mankind has been made, the fact that it is in Jewish flesh that the redemption of the world was to be, and now has been, accomplished. Of the greatness of this pre-eminence there can be – within the framework of biblical faith – no doubt. But this tremendous pre-eminence never involved exemption from God's judgment – in fact, it meant the Jews were always in a specially exposed position in relation to it (compare Amos 3.2). Those who stood nearest to the working out of God's saving purpose could be blind and deaf and uncomprehending, and, where they were rebels against God's grace, that grace could enable others who stood far off to believe. Thus they misunderstood their special position fundamentally when they thought of it as a ground for self-complacency. But to challenge the falsehood of Jewish complacency and draw attention to the fact that the Jews were for the most part excluding themselves from an active and voluntary participation in the working out of God's gracious purpose was by no means to deny the reality of their pre-eminence which rests not on the faithfulness of men but on the grace and faithfulness of God.

First, that they were entrusted with the oracles of God. It would seem that Paul was going to mention other aspects of the Jew's 'advantage' and then omitted to do so (compare 1.8 for 'First' left stranded). He does give a list of Jewish privileges in 9.4–5. The expression 'the oracles of God' has been variously understood as referring to the law, to the promises made to Israel, to both the law and the promises relating to the Messiah, to the Old Testament as a whole, to God's self-revelation in the total salvation-history both of the Old Testament and also of the New. It is perhaps best to take it in the widest sense. The Jews have been given God's authentic self-revelation in trust to treasure it and to attest it and declare it to all mankind. The gospel events and all the salvation-history which preceded them and attested them beforehand took place in the midst of this people. They have been the recipients on behalf of mankind of God's message to mankind.

3. What then? If some have failed to respond with faith, shall their lack of faith render God's faithfulness ineffective? The sense of the verse is that it is unthinkable that God's faithfulness to His covenant with Israel should be rendered ineffective even by the Jews' unbelief.

4. God forbid! is a formula of strong denial used frequently by Paul (in Romans it occurs also in vv. 6 and 31, and in 6.2, 15; 7.7, 13; 9.14; 11.1, 11), always after a question. **We confess rather that God is true.** The original means literally 'But let God be true'; but the Greek imperative has here a declaratory force, being used as a vigorous way of stating the true situation after an emphatic rejection of an altogether false suggestion. In 'true' the thought of God's faithfulness to His promises is no doubt specially prominent, though it would be wrong to exclude reference to other aspects of His truth. **and all men liars** is reminiscent of Ps 116.11. Over against the truthfulness of God stands the falsehood of men. In the light of His truth all men must be acknowledged to be liars.

even as scripture says refers forward to the quotation from Psalm 51, which follows, not to the preceding reminiscence of Psalm 116.

'**. . . in order that thou mayest be acknowledged as righteous in thy words and mayest overcome when thou contendest**' represents an almost exact quotation of the Greek version of Ps 51.4b. It is a purpose clause, which in the psalm should probably be understood as being dependent not on the preceding half-verse but on v. 3: the psalmist (according to the psalm-title, David) recognizes and confesses his sin as committed against God Himself, in order that through his confession God might be acknowledged as just in His judgment. The quotation serves as support for the general idea expressed by 'We confess rather that God is true, and all men liars', inasmuch as (understood in conjunction with the preceding half-verse of the psalm) it speaks of God's righteousness over against man's sinfulness. It is possible that Paul also had in mind, in connexion with what he had just said in v. 3, the fact that the case of David (the traditional author of the psalm) was an outstanding example of God's faithfulness in the face of grievous sin.

5. Paul has dealt in vv. 1–4 with the possible misunderstanding to which he recognized that 2.25–29 could give rise, namely, that he was implying that the Jews had no advantage at all. At this point, realizing that a false inference could be drawn from what he has said in vv. 3–4, he digresses from his argument for four verses (vv. 5–8), in order to guard against this other possible misunderstanding, to the danger of which experience has made him specially sensitive. **But if our unrighteousness actually shows up the righteousness of God, what are we then to say?** draws attention to the difficulty which presents itself, if it is really true that the unbelief of the Jews actually serves to show up the faithfulness of God (or the sinfulness of men generally to show up the righteousness of God). **Is God unrighteous in that he inflicts his wrath *on us*?** indicates the nature of the difficulty, though it does not present it (as one might have expected) in the form of an objection (if it were intended as an objector's question, it would have been in the form 'Is not God ...?'), but in the form of a rhetorical question anticipating a negative answer. The words **(I am giving expression to thoughts which are very human)** are an apology for having expressed, even though in a clearly deprecatory way, a thought all too human in its foolishness and weakness, They have the effect of underlining Paul's repudiation of the thought.

6. God forbid! For in that case how shall God judge the world? Paul rejects the notion that God is guilty of injustice as being essentially absurd, since it is tantamount to a denial of what must be held to be axiomatic, namely, that God will be the final Judge of all men. That God who shall judge the world is just is a fundamental certainty of all theological thinking. God would in fact not be God at all, if He were unjust.

7. The thought, which was expressed in v. 5b in a form which indicated that it was being repudiated, is now brought forward again – this time in the form of an objection. **But if the truth of God has been more abundantly manifested, to his glory, by means of my lie, why am I still judged as a sinner?** How can it be fair for a man to be blamed for his falsehood, when it has actually redounded to God's glory? The use of the first person singular here is simply rhetorical.

8. And do we then say (as certain people slanderously allege that we say), 'Let us do evil, that good may come of it'? Those who so

slander us are deservedly condemned. Such is the meaning of the verse, if our views with regard to the proper punctuation of it (and of the end of v. 7) and to its construction are correct. The verse, as we understand it, consists of a rhetorical question (expecting the answer 'No') which serves as a rejoinder to the objection expressed in v. 7; a parenthesis (incorporated within this rhetorical question) referring to the fact that some people allege that Paul himself teaches the attitude which he is here repudiating; and finally a condemnation of the people to whom the parenthesis refers.

9 is the beginning of the sixth and last paragraph of 2.1–3.20. Though there are textual variations, and different ways of punctuating the verse are canvassed, there is surely not very much doubt that the text and punctuation presupposed by our translation **What then? Do we *Jews* have an advantage? Not in every respect; for we have already laid the charge against both Jews and Greeks that they are all under sin** are correct. What is matter of controversy is how the verse is to be understood. The problems of interpretation are centred on the Greek word which we have represented by 'Do we *Jews* have an advantage?' and the two Greek words which we have rendered 'Not in every respect'.

To consider the former problem first – the Greek word is a verb, which can be taken in three different ways: (i) as a middle[1] with a proper middle force; (ii) as a middle with an active force; or (iii) as a passive. This verb in the active has the basic sense 'hold before', but is also used intransitively with such senses as 'jut out', 'project', 'have the start of', 'excel'. In the middle it means 'hold before oneself', as one does a shield, and so metaphorically 'put forward as a pretext or excuse'. So, according to (i), the meaning might perhaps be 'do we make excuses?' or 'Do we prevaricate?', the 'we' in the verb more probably referring to Paul himself (compare the first person plural in the latter half of the verse) than to the Jews; but against this is the fact that one would expect a direct object (the thing put forward as an excuse) to be expressed. According to (iii), the meaning would be 'Are we (Jews) excelled (by the Gentiles)?', 'Are we (Jews) worse off (than the Gentiles)?';

---

[1] In Greek, in addition to active and passive, there is a third voice, the middle, which expresses the idea that the action described has somehow special advantage or significance for the subject. In the present indicative the middle and passive are identical in form.

but this, while grammatically thoroughly unobjectionable, is surely quite unsuitable to the context. It is (ii) which should almost certainly be accepted, as it was by the Latin Vulgate: 'Have we (Jews) any advantage over them (that is, the Gentiles)?'

With regard to the latter problem of interpretation (the meaning of the two words we have translated 'Not in every respect'), the Latin Vulgate (followed by, for example, the AV, RV, RSV, NEB and JB) understood Paul to be using the Greek words (equivalent to 'not altogether') in the sense which they would naturally bear if put in the reverse order, that is, of an emphatic negative; but the fact that in both the other places where these two words are associated together in the Pauline epistles (1 Cor 5.10 and 16.12 – in the former in the order 'not altogether' and in the latter in the order 'altogether not') they are used in the order which correctly expresses his meaning strongly suggests that he is likely to have used them here also correctly. If that conclusion is right, then the interpretation 'not altogether', 'not in every respect' is to be accepted here.[1] Paul has indicated in v. 2 that the Jew has an advantage which is great and important in every respect. He now makes the point that, while this is true, it does not mean that the Jew is at an advantage in every respect. There is at least one respect in which he has no advantage – he is no less sinful before God. It is this which the latter part of the verse makes clear. It supports and explains 'Not in every respect' by the reminder that Paul has already charged both Jews and Gentiles alike with being 'under sin'. This he has indeed done in 1.18–2.29. This is the first occurrence of the noun 'sin' in Romans. Paul thinks of it as a power which has got control of men. His teaching about it will appear most fully in chapters 5–7.

10–18 may be taken together. They are a catena of Old Testament quotations in confirmation of the charge which Paul has levelled against both Jews and Gentiles. **even as scripture testifies:**

> **'There is no one who is righteous, not even one,**
> **there is no one who has understanding,**
> **there is no one who seeks God.**

---

[1] As is maintained by, for example, H. Lietzmann, M.-J. Lagrange, O. Michel, and E. Gaugler, among recent commentators.

All have turned aside, together they have become useless;
 there is no one who shows kindness,
no, not as much as one.

An open grave is their throat,
 with their tongues they are wont to deceive,
the poison of asps is under their lips.
 Their mouth is full of cursing and bitterness.

Swift are their feet to shed blood,
 destruction and misery mark their ways,
and the way of peace they have not known.
 There is no fear of God before their eyes.'

The catena has been constructed with considerable care and artistry, so as to form a real new unity out of a multiplicity of excerpts. It is arranged in three strophes, the first (vv. 10–12) consisting of two sets of three lines, the second (vv. 13–14) and third (vv. 15–18) each consisting of two sets of two lines. The first strophe is based on Ps 14.1–3, apart from the possible trace of a reminiscence of Eccles 7.20 in the first line. This psalm-passage seems to have been chosen for the sake of its testimony to the fact that all men without exception are sinners. What is said is expressed in fairly general terms – for the most part, but not exclusively, with reference to men's relation to God. In the second strophe three different sources (Ps 5.9; 140.3; and 10.7) have been used. It concentrates on men's speech, and the amount devoted to this subject in relation to the length of the whole cento is striking. We may compare the stress laid on the importance of right speaking in the Epistle of James (1.19, 26; 3.1–12). After this concentration on words the last strophe directs attention to deeds – to the fratricidal character of men's conduct. The first three lines are an abridgement of Isa 59.7–8a, while the source of the last line is Ps 36.1b. The statement 'destruction and misery mark their ways' indicates the dire results of their activities with poetic evocativeness: wherever they go, they leave behind them a trail of destruction and misery. In this context it seems natural to understand 'the way of peace they have not known' to mean that they do not know how to go about to establish real peace among themselves, though some commentators take the reference of 'peace' to be rather to salvation. Finally, the last line indicates the root of their evil deeds and also of their evil words – in fact, the very essence of their sinfulness. It is by his eyes that a man directs his steps. So to say that there is no fear of God before his eyes is a figurative way of saying that the fear of God has no part in directing his life, that God is left out of his reckoning, that he is a practical, whether or not he is a theoretical, atheist.

19. For **But we know that** see on 2.2. **whatever the law says** is naturally taken to include the quotations in vv. 10–18. Since these come from the Writings and the Prophets, and not from the Pentateuch, 'the law' must be used here, as it is also in 1 Cor 14.21; Jn 10.34; 15.25, and as the equivalent Hebrew word was quite often used by the Rabbis, to denote the Old Testament as a whole. The point of **it speaks to those who possess the law** is that the Jews, so far from imagining themselves excepted from its condemnations of human sinfulness, ought to accept them as applying first and foremost to themselves. The thought behind the final clause **in order that every mouth may be stopped and the whole world stand guilty before God** is that, if the Jews, the people who might seem to have reason to regard themselves as an exception, are in fact no exception, then without doubt the entire human race lies under God's judgment. The reference to the stopped mouth evokes the image of the defendant in court, who, when given the opportunity to speak in his own defence, remains silent, overwhelmed by the weight of the evidence against him.

20. **For no flesh shall be justified before him on the ground of having done what the law requires** is a confirmation, incorporating an echo of Ps 143.2b, of what has just been said in v. 19. Such an adequate obedience to the law as would merit justification is simply not forthcoming. **for through the law** *comes* **the knowledge of sin** is added in support of the preceding sentence. So far from its being true that there are men who so adequately fulfil the law's requirements as to earn justification for themselves, the truth is rather that the condition of all men is such that the primary effect of the law in relation to them is to show up their sin as sin and themselves as sinners.

IV.2. THE MANIFESTATION OF THE RIGHTEOUSNESS WHICH IS FROM GOD IN THE GOSPEL EVENTS

(3.21–26)

This short section is, as has already been indicated, the centre and heart of the main division to which it belongs. We may go farther and say that it is the centre and heart of the whole of Rom 1.16b–15.13. It stands out by reason of the distinctiveness of its style: it reads like a solemn proclamation. Notable, in particular, are the emphatic 'but now' followed by the perfect tense ('has been manifested'), the fewness of the finite verbs especially in the latter part of the section (in the Greek there is only one, 'purposed', in vv. 24–26), the impressive repetition of key-phrases and (in the original) the striking use in vv. 25 and 26 of prepositional phrases placed one after the other without connexion. It stands out much more, of course, by virtue of its content; for it proclaims the fact that the one decisive, once for all, redemptive act of God, the revelation both of the righteousness which is from God and also of the wrath of God against human sin, the once for all revelation which is the basis of the continuing revelation of the righteousness (1.17) and of the wrath (1.18) of God in the preaching of the gospel, has now taken place. It shows that the heart of the gospel preached by Paul is a series of events in the past (not just the crucifixion of Christ – for the Cross by itself would have been no saving act of God – but the crucifixion together with the resurrection and exaltation of the Crucified), a series of events which is *the* Event of history, an act which as the decisive act of God is altogether effective and irreversible. It attests the fact that what we have to do with in the gift of righteousness, with which Romans is concerned, is nothing less than God's costly forgiveness, which, whereas forgiveness on cheaper terms would have meant God's abandonment of His faithful love for man and the annihilation of man's real dignity as His morally accountable creature, is altogether worthy of the righteous, loving, faithful God, who does not insult or mock His creature man by pretending that his sin does not matter, but rather Himself bears the full cost of forgiving it righteously – lovingly.

²¹**But now God's righteousness, attested by the law and the prophets, has been manifested apart from the law, ²²namely, that righteousness of God which is through faith in Jesus Christ for all who believe. For there is no distinction; ²³for all have sinned and lack the glory of God, ²⁴being justified freely by his grace through the redemption *accomplished* in Christ Jesus; ²⁵whom God purposed to be by *the shedding of*his blood a propitiatory sacrifice, *the benefit to be appropriated*by faith, in order to prove his righteousness (*this was necessary* on account of the overlooking of past sins ²⁶in God's forbearance), in order, *I say*, to prove his righteousness in the present time, so that he might be righteous even in justifying the man who believes in Jesus.**

21. But now points to the decisiveness for faith of the gospel events in their objectiveness as events which took place at a particular time in the past and are quite distinct from, and independent of, the response of men to them. The 'now' is to be understood as having its full temporal significance: the contrast marked by the 'But' here is that between the situation before, and the situation after, a decisive series of events.

God's righteousness is to be understood here in the same sense as it has in 1.17, that is, as meaning a status of righteousness before God which is God's gift.

attested by the law and the prophets is formally a statement about God's righteousness, but in fact it is both this and also at the same time a statement about the Old Testament; for it affirms not only that this righteousness which is God's gift is attested by the Old Testament but also that the Old Testament, if it is to be rightly understood, must be understood to be witness to this righteousness – in other words, to the gospel of Jesus Christ. The thought expressed here is to be found again and again in Romans (compare, for example, 1.2; the whole of chapter 4; 9.25–33; 10.6–13, 16–21; 11.1–10, 26–29; 15.8–12), though Paul nowhere else uses the verb we have rendered by 'attest' (RV has 'witness') to express it. That this attestation of the gospel by the Old Testament is of very great importance for Paul is indicated by the solemn way in which he insists on it here in what is one of the great hinge-sentences on which the argument of the epistle turns.

has been manifested. In 1.17 a present tense ('is being revealed') was used, because the reference was to the revelation taking place in the on-going preaching of the gospel. Here the use of a past tense indicates that the thought is of the revelation (the Greek verb used here is different from, but more or less synonymous with, the verb used in 1.17) in the gospel events themselves. A perfect tense has been preferred to an aorist because what was made manifest in those events has ever since remained manifest.

apart from the law is an adverbial phrase modifying 'has been manifested'. In 7.8 and 9 it is used to indicate the law's absence; but it can scarcely have that meaning here, since it is clear that Paul did not think that the law was absent at the time of the manifestation referred to – on the contrary, passages like Gal 3.13 and 4.4 suggest that he thought that it was deeply involved in the gospel events. The words are most naturally understood in relation to 'on the ground of having done what the law requires' and 'through the law' in v. 20, that is, as indicating that the status of righteousness before God of which vv. 21 and 22 speak has been manifested as something which has not been earned by men's fulfilment of the law. In fact, 'apart from the law' here is equivalent in significance to 'apart from works of the law' in v. 28 and 'apart from works' in 4.6. To appeal to these words as evidence that Paul regarded the law as superseded and set aside by the gospel as something now out of date and irrelevant is surely perverse.

22. namely, that righteousness of God which is through faith in Jesus Christ for all who believe gives a closer definition of the righteousness of which Paul is speaking: it is through faith in Christ, and, further, it is for all who respond with faith. On 'faith' see on 1.5, 16, 17. Here for the first time in Romans Christ is explicitly referred to as the object of faith. (That the Greek genitive represented by 'in Jesus Christ' is objective is not to be doubted: the suggestion that it is subjective – 'Christ's faith' – is altogether unconvincing.)

For there is no distinction supports the foregoing 'all', but in its turn is explained and qualified by vv. 23 and 24.

23 and **24** indicate the scope of v. 22b. It is not to be understood as a denial of the truth affirmed in v. 2 ('much in every way' in answer to the question 'What advantage then does the Jew have? Or what profit is there in circumcision?': compare 9.4f; 11.17f, 28f;

and also the 'first' in 1.16b), but only as a denial that there is any distinction in respect of 'God's righteousness'. All alike may receive this righteousness by faith and none has any claim to it on the ground of merit; for all alike – Jews as well as Gentiles – have sinned, and receive righteousness as a free gift altogether undeserved.

for all have sinned and lack the glory of God. The 'all' continues the emphasis on universality which has already been noted (compare vv. 9, 10, 11, 12, 20, 22). Verse 23 as a whole sums up the argument of 1.18–3.20. By 'the glory of God' is probably meant that share in the divine glory, which, according to Jewish thought, man possessed before he fell away from his true relationship to God and which will be restored in the eschatological future (compare 5.2; 8.18, 21, 30). As a result of sin all men lack this illumination by the divine glory. Here both the tense of the verb and the fact that its subject is 'all' should be noted. They clearly imply that not only all other men but also all believers still lack this 'glory of God'. Attempts to soften this or to explain it away have the disastrous effect of obscuring the transcendent majesty of the glory which is yet to be ours. This is not to deny that there is a relative glory which already illumines the lives of believers – Paul can speak elsewhere of their being transformed 'from glory to glory' (2 Cor 3.18); but the decisiveness of the distinction between these two glories should not be blurred.

Verse 24 is best explained as a participial clause dependent on 'all' in v. 23 intended to indicate, in further explanation of 'For there is no distinction', the other side of the picture presented in v. 23. In **being justified freely by his grace** 'freely' and 'by his grace' support and confirm each other, the latter phrase pointing to the origin of their justification in the undeserved love of God (on the meaning of 'grace' see on 1.7). The interpretation of **through the redemption** is controversial. Some insist that the thought of a ransom paid is present here in the Greek word, which we have translated 'redemption'. Others maintain that the word means simply 'deliverance', 'emancipation', without any reference to the payment of a ransom. But the strength of the arguments which can be adduced on each side is such that an absolutely confident assertion of either view cannot – in the present state of the discussion – be justified. The question must be left open. So we have preferred the rendering 'redemption', which can, but does not necessarily, suggest the thought of a payment's being made, to such words as 'deliverance' and 'ransoming', which would foreclose the issue one way or the other. What can be said with confidence about this phrase is that it indicates that the believer's righteous status has been brought about by God by means of a definite and decisive action on God's own part. Something more of the nature and significance of that action is disclosed in the following four words and also in vv. 25 and 26. But it is already clearly implied, by the fact that 'through the redemption' is linked with 'being justified', that the slavery from which this action of God has redeemed must be the slavery of sin in the sense of subjection to sin's effects (that is, to God's condemnation, God's wrath, the condition of having an unrighteous status before Him). **accomplished in Christ Jesus** indicates that it was in and through the Messiah Jesus, that is, in and through His person and work, that God accomplished His redeeming action. The thought here is of the accomplishment of the redeeming action in the past, not of the availability of redemption in the present through union with Christ.

25–26. whom God purposed to be by *the shedding of* his blood a propitiatory sacrifice, *the benefit to be appropriated* by faith, in order to prove his righteousness (*this was necessary* on account of the overlooking of past sins in God's forbearance), in order, *I say*, to prove his righteousness in the present time, so that he might be righteous even in justifying the man who believes in Jesus. These two verses are a single relative sentence dependent on 'Christ Jesus' in v. 24. It consists of what we may regard as its main part (down to 'by faith') followed by three purpose-clauses which together serve to clarify the meaning of the key-expression 'a propitiatory sacrifice'.

The Greek verb which we have represented by 'purpose' occurs only three times in the New Testament (in 1.13, here, and in Eph 1.9). The main senses it can have, when used in the middle voice (as it is in all three New Testament occurrences), are: (i) 'propose to oneself', 'purpose'; and (ii) 'set forth publicly', 'display'. Both these possibilities have been canvassed in respect of this occurrence from early times. In favour of (ii) it has been argued that the immediate context contains a number of terms denoting publicity, and Paul's point has been assumed to be that the Cross was something accomplished in the sight of men. But the facts that in its two other New Testament occurrences the verb clearly means 'purpose' and that in eight of its twelve New Testament occurrences the cognate noun means 'purpose' tell in favour of (i), and, while it is true that the idea of publicity is present in the context, a reference to God's eternal purpose strikes us as even more apposite just here than a reference to the public character of God's deed in the passion of Christ. We take it that by the first words of v. 25 Paul means to emphasize that it is God who is the origin of the redemption which was effected in Christ and also that this redemption has its origin not in some sudden new idea or impulse on God's part but in His eternal purpose of grace.

It was 'by *the shedding of* his blood' (literally, 'in (or 'by') his blood') that God's purpose was to be accomplished. With this reference to the blood of Christ we may compare 5.9; Acts 20.28; Eph 1.7; 2.13; Col 1.20; Heb 9.11ff; 10.19, 29; 13.12, 20; I Pet 1.2, 19; 1 Jn 1.7; 5.6; Rev 1.5; 5.9; 7.14;12.11; and also, of course, Mt 26.28 = Mk 14.24 = Lk 22.20; I Cor 11.25 and 10.16. In 5.9 'by his blood' corresponds to 'through the death of his Son' in the following verse, and in the Ephesians and Colossians passages cited above the use of 'blood' could perhaps be explained as simply a way of expressing the idea of death; but in I Cor 11.25, the three Synoptic verses, and the Hebrews, I Peter and I John passages, a sacrificial significance is clearly present, and it seems probable that in the other passages cited above also a sacrificial significance attaches to the use of the word 'blood', whether felt more or less strongly. There is little doubt that this is so in the verse under consideration.

It will be convenient to postpone discussion of the next phrase ('a propitiatory sacrifice'), until after we have considered the remaining elements of vv. 25 and 26, since they contribute to its clarification.

The first of these is '*the benefit to be appropriated* by faith'. It has both a positive and a negative significance. Positively, it indicates that a response of faith on men's part is required: the benefit is to be accepted, appropriated, by faith. But it also implies, negatively, that no other way of appropriating the benefit is open to men but faith alone: every thought of their earning it is excluded.

The second of these elements is 'in order to prove his righteousness (*this was necessary* on account of the overlooking of past sins in God's forbearance)'. The word 'righteousness' here and in v. 26 must refer not to the righteous status God gives but to God's own righteousness, in spite of Nygren's arguments to the contrary. The idea of God's forbearance, His patiently holding back His wrath, is familiar in Judaism. But for God simply to pass over sins would be altogether incompatible with His righteousness. He would not be the good and merciful God which He is, had He been content to pass over sins indefinitely; for this would have been to condone evil – a denial of His own nature and a cruel betrayal of sinners. God has in fact been able to hold His hand and pass over sins, without compromising His goodness and mercy, because His intention has all along been to deal with them once and for all, decisively and finally and altogether adequately, through the Cross. Paul is saying in these two verses that God purposed (from eternity) that Christ should be a propitiatory sacrifice, in order that the reality of God's righteousness, that is, of His goodness and mercy, which would be called in question by His passing over sins committed up to the time of that decisive act, might be established.

The third of these elements is 'in order, *I say*, to prove his righteousness in the present time'. It repeats the main idea of the preceding with the addition of 'in the present time'. The time indicated is the period which embraces both the time of the gospel events themselves and also the time of their proclamation in the on-going preaching of the gospel.

The fourth and last element is 'so that he might be righteous even in justifying the man who believes in Jesus'. Two things are of very great importance here. The first is that Paul speaks of God's *being* righteous. Paul recognizes that God's proving His righteousness was necessary not only for the sake of His reputation but also for the sake of His essential integrity. God would not *be* righteous in Himself, if He failed to show Himself to be righteous: it is essential to His *being* the righteous, the loving, the merciful, God, that He prove His righteousness. The second thing is that the Greek word *kai*, which can mean either 'and' or 'even', here means 'even'. In other words, the latter purpose-clause of v. 26 does not indicate two different purposes, (i) that He might be righteous in Himself, and (ii) that He might be the justifier ... , but one single purpose, namely, that He might be righteous in the very act of justifying, that is, that He might justify righteously, without compromising His own righteousness. So interpreted, the words afford an insight into the innermost meaning of the Cross as Paul understands it. For God to have forgiven men's sin lightly – a cheap forgiveness which would have implied that moral evil does not matter very much – would have been altogether unrighteous, a violation of His truth, and profoundly unmerciful and unloving toward men, since it would have annihilated their dignity as persons morally accountable. But God does not insult His creature man by any suggestion that that, which man himself at his most human knows full well (witness, for example, the great pagan Greek tragedians) is desperately serious, is of little consequence. The forgiveness accomplished through the Cross is the costly forgiveness, worthy of God, which, so far from condoning man's evil, is, since it involves nothing less than God's bearing the intolerable burden of that evil Himself in the person of His own dear Son, the disclosure of the fullness of God's hatred of man's evil at the same time as it is its real and complete forgiveness.

We must now return to 'a propitiatory sacrifice'. Since the Greek word which we have so translated refers in twenty-one out of its twenty-seven occurrences in the Septuagint version of the Old Testament and also in its only other occurrence in the New Testament (Heb 9.5) to the mercy-seat (see Exod 25.17–22), the possibility that Paul used it in that sense here, and was thinking of Christ as the anti-type of the Old Testament mercy-seat has to be taken seriously. From early times Paul has been so understood, and this view is upheld by many recent writers. But L. Morris has shown that the arguments which have been urged in support of it are not really very strong.[1] Thus the strongest of them (that from the Septuagint usage) becomes much less formidable, as soon as it is recognized that, wherever in the Septuagint the Greek word with which we are concerned has the sense 'mercy-seat', it is used with the definite article or in another way determined and there is always something in the context to indicate which of the things

---

[1] In *New Testament Studies* 2 (1955–56), pp. 33–43.

which could be denoted by the word is intended. Here in Romans 3 there is nothing in the context which can be said to indicate at all unambiguously that the mercy-seat is in mind and there is no definite article. On the other side there are considerations which weigh heavily against this interpretation. While it is an understandable paradox to refer to Christ as being at the same time both priest and victim, to represent Him as being the place of sprinkling as well as the victim is surely excessively harsh and confusing. Moreover, there seems to be something essentially improbable in the thought of Paul's likening Christ, for whom, personally, man's redemption was so infinitely costly, and to whom he felt so tremendous a personal indebtedness (compare, for example, Gal 2.20), to something which was only an inanimate piece of temple furniture. The mercy-seat would surely be more appropriately regarded as a type of the Cross. The meaning 'mercy-seat' should therefore be rejected.

Before trying to decide between the other possibilities, it will be well to refer to Dodd's contention that to the words of the group to which the Greek word we are concerned with belongs, as they are used in the Septuagint, there attaches practically no trace of the idea of propitiation or appeasement which it is generally agreed that they express in pagan usage. Dodd argued that the thought expressed is rather, where the subject of the action is human, that of the expiation of sin, or, where the subject is God, that of God's being gracious, having mercy, forgiving.[1] But, while it is certainly true that the idea of a wrath of God which is capricious and vindictive and requires to be placated by bribery on men's part is alien to the Old Testament, it is by no means true that all ideas of divine wrath are alien. Morris has shown that in many, if not all, of the passages in which words of this group are used in the Septuagint the idea of God's wrath is present.[2] (Dodd failed to pay adequate attention to the contexts of the words' occurrences.) In view of this fact, we cannot allow that the thought of propitiation is altogether foreign to this word-group in the Septuagint. Indeed, the evidence suggests that the idea of the averting of wrath is basic to the word-group in the Old Testament no less than in extra-biblical Greek, the distinctiveness of the Old

[1] In *Journal of Theological Studies* 32 (1931), pp. 352–60.
[2] In *Expository Times* 62 (1950–51), pp. 227–33.

Testament usage being its recognition first that God's wrath, unlike all human wrath, is perfectly righteous, and therefore free from every trace of irrationality, caprice, and vindictiveness, and secondly that in the process of averting this righteous wrath from man it is God Himself who takes the initiative.

Of the meanings which have been suggested for this Greek word here other than 'mercy-seat', which we have already rejected, we may, in view of what has just been said, set aside as unlikely those which are expressly intended to exclude the idea of propitiation. The most probable suggestion would seem to be 'a propitiatory sacrifice'. We take Paul's statement that God purposed Christ as a propitiatory sacrifice to mean that God, because in His mercy He willed to forgive sinful men and, being truly merciful, willed to forgive them righteously, that is, without in any way condoning their sin, purposed to direct against His own very Self in the person of His Son the full weight of that righteous wrath which they deserved.

IV.3. ALL GLORYING IS EXCLUDED (3.27–31)

The general sense of this short section and its function in the over-all structure of the main division (its contribution to the clarification of 'from faith to faith' and 'by faith' in 1.17) are clear enough. It affirms that all glorying, that is, all thinking to establish a claim on God on the ground of one's works, has been ruled out. But precisely to define the internal articulation of the argument is not easy. Our understanding of the section is as follows: It is implied that the statement that glorying has been excluded is a conclusion which must be drawn from what precedes (whether vv. 21–26 or the whole of 1.18–3.26). At the same time it is indicated that the exclusion has been brought about through the law – not the law understood legalistically, but the law recognized as the law of faith which it is. In support of the statements that glorying has been excluded and that this has been accomplished through the law Paul appeals to the fact that believers know that men are justified by faith, apart from works of the law. To deny that they are so justified would be to imply that God is God of the Jews only, and that would be a denial of the fundamental truth that God is one. Since He is the one and only God, who is God of all men, He will assuredly justify Jews and Gentiles alike by faith and only by faith. The conclusion is that what has been said about faith, so far from contradicting the law, is thoroughly consonant with it, and is therefore confirmed.

[27]Where then is glorying? It has been excluded. By what kind of law? By a law of works? No, but by the law of faith! [28]For we reckon that it is by faith that a man is justified apart from works of the law. [29]Or is God *the God* of Jews only? Is he not *the God* of the Gentiles also? Most certainly of the Gentiles also! [30]seeing that God is one, and he will justify the circumcision on the ground of faith and the uncircumcision through faith. [31]Do we then invalidate the law through *our teaching about* faith? God forbid! Rather we uphold the law.

27. Where then is glorying? It has been excluded. It follows inevitably from what has been said (whether we think specially of vv. 21–26 or of 1.18–3.26 as a whole) that there can be no question of any man's putting God in his debt. This conclusion is stated by means of the rhetorical question. 'Where then [that is, Where, if what has been said is true] is glorying?' followed by the declaration 'It has been excluded'. The tense of 'has been excluded' (it is an aorist in Greek) indicates that the exclusion referred to has been accomplished once for all. In view of what follows it would seem that the reference is not simply to the fact that what has been said has demonstrated the absurdity of all such glorying, but to the exclusion effected by God Himself (the passive concealing a reference to a divine action), whether in the sense that God has rendered all such glorying futile and absurd by what He has done in Christ or – perhaps more probably, in view of the next few words – in the sense that He has shown it to be futile and absurd through the Old Testament scriptures.

By what kind of law? By a law of works? No, but by the law of faith! is difficult, and has been variously interpreted. Some explain 'law of faith' as a rhetorically motivated formulation due simply to the desire to match 'law of works'. Others take it to refer to a special law under which Christians stand and compare 'the law of the Spirit of life' in 8.2, 'the law of Christ' in Gal 6.2 and the expression 'under law to Christ' in 1 Cor 9.21. Others understand 'law' in this verse to have some other sense than 'law', such as 'principle', 'ethical norm', 'system'. But G. Friedrich's contention that by 'law of faith' the Old Testament law is intended[1] should probably be accepted; this interpretation seems to fit the context best. We may then understand Paul's meaning to be that the correct answer to the question 'By what kind of law (has such glorying been excluded)?' is 'By God's law (namely, the law of the Old Testament) – that is, by God's law, not misunderstood as a law which directs men to seek justification as a reward for their works, but properly understood as summoning men to faith'.

28. For we reckon that it is by faith that a man is justified apart from works of the law is best understood as intended to support v. 27 as a whole (that is, both in its basic affirmation that glorying has been excluded and also in its further affirmation that it is 'by the law of faith' that it has been excluded). The verb 'reckon' is here used to denote a faith-judgment, a conviction formed in the light of the gospel (compare 6.11; 8.18). The use of the plural ('we') while it could be explained as simply an author's plural, is more probably to be explained as indicating that this conviction is common to all believers. The words 'that it is by faith that a man is justified apart from works of the law' sum up the substance of vv. 20a, 21–22, 24, the emphasis falling now – in connexion with v. 27 – on the fact that it is not on the ground of works but only by faith that men are justified more than (as in v. 21) on the fact that such justification has actually been made available.

29–30. Or is God *the God* of Jews only? indicates what would necessarily follow, if what is stated in v. 28 were not true. If that were not true, then God would not be the God of all men in the sense that He desires and seeks the salvation of all with equal seriousness. No Jew of Paul's day would ever have thought of questioning that God is the God of all men in the sense of being their Creator and Ruler and Judge; but Paul takes it for granted that God is not the God of any man without being his gracious and merciful God. So he follows up his question with the further

[1] In *Theologische Zeitschrift* 10 (1954), pp.401–17.

question **Is he not *the God* of the Gentiles also?** to which **Most certainly of the Gentiles also!** is his own confident answer. Compare 3.22 and 10.12. Without in any way calling in question the reality of Israel's special place in God's purpose, which is attested by the 'for the Jew first' of 1.16b (compare 2.9 and 10) and by such passages as 3.2; 9.4f; 11.1, 17ff, Paul insists on the fact that the divine purpose is equally for all men gracious and merciful. In support of his affirmation that God is the God of the Gentiles also, Paul appeals with his **seeing that God is one** to the fundamental fact of the oneness of God confessed in the creed of Israel, the *Shema*, which begins with Deut 6.4. **and he will justify the circumcision on the ground of faith and the uncircumcision through faith** states what is for Paul the corollary to be drawn from the confession that God is one, namely, that He will justify Jew and Gentile alike by faith alone. (There is little doubt that the variation between 'on the ground of' and 'through' here is purely stylistic (to afford variety), as Augustine recognized many centuries ago.)

31. Do we then invalidate the law through *our teaching about faith*? God forbid! Rather we uphold the law. Some interpreters have argued that this verse should be connected with chapter 4 and understood as the beginning of the new section. We regard it as much more natural to take it as the conclusion of 3.27ff, as do many other interpreters of Romans. With regard to the sense of 'invalidate' and 'uphold' here, it is probable that Paul is reproducing in Greek a Rabbinic Hebrew usage and means that what he has been saying about faith is not in any way inconsistent with the law but rather is thoroughly consonant with it, and is therefore confirmed by it. The question introduced by 'then' in the first half of the verse indicates a false conclusion which Paul recognizes could be drawn from what he has been saying. It could be thought that what has been said of faith is inconsistent with the law and calls it in question. Such a reading of the situation Paul emphatically rejects. The truth is rather that, rightly understood, the law supports and confirms the doctrine of faith.

IV.4. THE CASE OF ABRAHAM AS CONFIRMATION OF THE STATEMENT THAT GLORYING HAS BEEN EXCLUDED (4.1–25)

The function of this section is to confirm the truth of what was said in the first part of 3.27. (At the same time it also adds an independent contribution of its own, particularly in vv. 17b–22, to the exposition of 'by faith'.) If any one has a right to glory, Abraham must have – according to Jewish assumptions. So, if it can be shown that, according to Scripture, Abraham himself has no right to glory, it will have been proved that no one has such a right – that glorying has in fact been excluded.

The first verse introduces the subject of Abraham. The rest of the chapter falls into five parts. In the first (vv. 2–8) Paul, after admitting that, if Abraham was justified on the ground of his works, he certainly would have a right to glory, goes on to argue that, rightly understood, the basic biblical text for the righteousness of Abraham (Gen 15.6) itself implies that he was justified apart from works. In the second (vv. 9–12) he makes the point that, when his faith was reckoned to him for righteousness, Abraham was not yet circumcised, and draws out its significance. In the third (vv. 13–17a) Paul argues that it was not on the condition of its being merited through fulfilment of the law that the promise that he should be heir of the world was given to Abraham and his seed, but simply on the basis of the righteousness of faith. The fourth (vv. 17b–22) – though v. 17b is grammatically part of the sentence which began with v. 16, it belongs by reason of its content to what follows – is an expanded paraphrase of Gen 15.6. Apart from v. 22, it is a drawing out of the meaning of the words 'And Abraham believed God'. It is thus a positive statement concerning the essential character of Abraham's faith. The fifth and last part (vv. 23–25) underlines the relevance to all Christians of Abraham's faith as the paradigm of their own, and at the same time makes an appropriate conclusion to the whole main division which began with 1.18.

¹What then are we to say that Abraham, our forefather according to the flesh, has found?

²For if Abraham was justified on the ground of works, then he does

indeed have a right to glory. But this is not how God sees him; ³for what does the scripture say? 'And Abraham believed God, and it was reckoned to him for righteousness.' ⁴Now if a man does have works to his credit, his wages are not reckoned as a matter of grace but as a debt; ⁵but to the man who has no work to his credit but believes in him who justifies the ungodly his faith is reckoned for righteousness, ⁶even as David also pronounces the blessing of the man to whom God reckons righteousness apart from works: ⁷'Blessed are those whose iniquities have been forgiven and whose sins have been covered; ⁸blessed is the man whose sin the Lord will in no wise reckon.'

⁹Does this blessing then apply to the circumcision *only* or also to the uncircumcision? For we say: 'To Abraham his faith was reckoned for righteousness.' ¹⁰In what circumstances then was it reckoned? When he was circumcised or when he was still uncircumcised? It was not when he was circumcised, but when he was still uncircumcised. ¹¹And he received the sign of circumcision as a seal of the righteousness by faith which he had while still uncircumcised, so that he might be the father of all those who, in a state of uncircumcision, believe, so that righteousness is reckoned to them, ¹²and also the father of the circumcision for those who not only belong to the circumcision but also* walk in the steps of the faith of our father Abraham which he had while he was still uncircumcised.

¹³For it was not on the basis of *fulfilment of* the law that the promise was made to Abraham or to his seed that he should be heir of the world, but on the basis of the righteousness of faith. ¹⁴For if it is those *who have a claim* on the basis of *their fulfilment of* the law who are heirs, then faith has been rendered vain and the promise annulled; ¹⁵for the law works wrath, but where there is no law, there there is also no transgression. ¹⁶For this reason it is on the basis of faith, namely, in order that it may be according to grace, so that the promise may be certain of fulfilment for all the seed, not only for that which is of the law, but also for that which is of Abraham's faith, who is the father of us all, ¹⁷ᵃeven as scripture says, 'Father of many nations have I made thee' –

– ¹⁷ᵇbefore God, in whom he believed, *the God* who quickens the dead and calls things which are not into being. ¹⁸He in hope against *all* hope believed, so that he became the father of many nations

---

* On the difficulty in the Greek at this point see the note on vv. 11b–12.

according to the word spoken to him, 'So shall thy seed be.' ¹⁹And without weakening in faith he considered his own body, which was *as good as* dead (for he was about a hundred years old), and the deadness of Sarah's womb, ²⁰and yet did not waver in unbelief with regard to God's promise, but was strengthened in faith, giving glory to God ²¹and being fully persuaded that he had the power to do what he had promised. ²²That is why 'it was reckoned to him for righteousness'.

²³But this statement of scripture that 'it was reckoned to him' was not written just for his sake, ²⁴but for our sakes also, to whom *our faith* is to be reckoned, who believe on him who raised Jesus our Lord from the dead, ²⁵who was delivered up for our trespasses and was raised for our justification.

1. What then are we to say that Abraham, our forefather according to the flesh, has found? raises the question of Abraham as the most obvious possible objection to the statement that glorying has been excluded (3.27), in order that the truth of that statement may be decisively confirmed by the subsequent demonstration that, according to the testimony of Scripture, even he has no ground for glorying, since he too was justified on the basis of faith. If any one has a right to glory, then – according to Jewish assumptions – Abraham must have. If it can be shown that, according to Scripture, Abraham himself has no right to glory, then glorying has indeed been excluded. The phrase 'according to the flesh' is not to be connected with 'forefather' (still less with 'found'), but with 'our'. The point is not that we have another forefather who is our forefather otherwise than according to the flesh, but that, while we (that is, the Jews) are Abraham's children according to the flesh, he has other children who are his children in a different way (compare vv. 11 and 16ff).

2. For if Abraham was justified on the ground of works, then he does indeed have a right to glory. This sentence is introduced by 'For', because it explains the relevance of the question just asked to Paul's purpose in this section to confirm the truth of the statement in 3.27 that glorying has been excluded. Paul's Jewish contemporaries were indeed accustomed to assume that Abraham was justified on the ground of his works. So, according to the *Book of Jubilees* (latter half of the second century BC) 23.10, 'Abraham was perfect in all his deeds with the Lord, and well-pleasing in righteousness all the days of his life'; and, according to the prayer of Manasses (of uncertain date, but perhaps of the first century either BC or AD) in the Apocrypha, Abraham did not sin. On such a view he clearly has ground for glorying. **But this is not how God sees him** represents four Greek words which mean literally 'but not toward God'. Paul has sometimes been understood to be intending merely to limit the scope of the statement 'then he does indeed have a right to glory': he does not have it in relation to God (acceptance of the idea that he does have it in relation to men being implicit). But, since Paul certainly rejects the supposition of the conditional clause ('if Abraham was justified on the ground of works'), it is unlikely that he would linger to limit the scope of the main clause of this conditional sentence: besides, the thought of Abraham's claim to glory in relation to men is quite irrelevant to the context. The natural interpretation of these words is rather that Paul is here rejecting the supposition of the preceding 'if' clause. Whatever men's view of the matter may be, God's view, as attested by Scripture (compare v. 3), is not that Abraham was justified on the ground of works.

3. for what does the scripture say? introduces an Old Testament quotation in support of the last part of v. 2. That in God's sight Abraham was not justified on the ground of works (and so has no right to glory) is clear from Gen 15.6. **'And Abraham believed God, and it was reckoned to him for righteousness'** is quoted according to the Septuagint, in which the active 'he counted [or 'reckoned'] it' of the Hebrew text has already been replaced by the passive 'it was counted [or 'reckoned']'. This verse, which refers to Abraham's believing God's word to him, God's promise (Gen 15.1, 4, 5), figured prominently in Jewish thought and discussion. Already in 1 Macc 2.52 ('Was not Abraham found faithful in temptation, and it was reckoned unto him for righteousness?') the faith it records is understood as a meritorious act on Abraham's part, as the use of 'deeds' (it is the same Greek word as is translated 'works' in Rom 3.20, 27, 28; 4.2, and elsewhere) in the previous verse indicates. The words attributed to Rabbi Shemaiah (about 50 BC) are more explicit: 'The faith with which their father Abraham believed in me [it is God who is represented as speaking] merits that I should divide the sea for them, as it is written: "And he believed in the

LORD, and he counted it to him for righteousness" ' (*Mekilta* on Exod 14.15). Subsequently this understanding of the verse was generally accepted in Rabbinic Judaism. Typical is the statement in *Mekilta* on Exod 14.31: 'So you find that our father Abraham became the heir of this and of the coming world simply by the merit of the faith with which he believed in the LORD, as it is written: "He believed in the LORD, and he counted it to him for righteousness" ', which contains the significant expression 'merit of faith'. That to Rabbinic Judaism Gen 15.6 was no proof at all that Abraham was not justified on the ground of works is absolutely clear. In appealing to it in support of his contention that Abraham was not justified on the ground of works and has no right to glory before God, Paul was deliberately appealing to a verse of Scripture which his fellow-Jews generally assumed to be clear support for the diametrically opposite view. That he did so is highly significant, but in no way surprising. It was clearly essential to the credibility of his argument that he should not by-pass a text which would seem to many of his fellow-Jews the conclusive disproof of the point he was trying to establish and which was on any showing a text of cardinal importance in the biblical account of Abraham, but should show that, rightly interpreted, it confirmed his contention. This he proceeds to do in vv. 4–8 by drawing out the significance of the statements contained in it.

4–5. Now if a man does have works to his credit, his wages are not reckoned as a matter of grace but as a debt; but to the man who has no work to his credit but believes in him who justifies the ungodly his faith is reckoned for righteousness has been variously explained. According to Barrett, Paul's interpretation of Gen 15.6 hinges on the use of the verb meaning 'count' or 'reckon'. So he puts 'counted' in inverted commas in his translation of v. 4, and in his comment states that Paul's first step 'is to fasten upon the verb "to count" '. He understands Paul's argument to turn on the assumption that 'count' is appropriately joined with 'believe' and 'grace', but not with 'work' and 'debt', so that 'since Abraham had righteousness *counted* to him, he cannot have done works, but must have been the recipient of grace'. But this explanation runs foul of the fact that Paul himself uses 'reckon' in v. 4 with 'as a debt' as well as with 'as a matter of grace'. Moreover, it is by no means clear that Paul's explanation of Gen 15.6 really hinges on the meaning of the word we have rendered by 'reckon'. It is very significant that in the other Pauline passage which appeals to Gen 15.6, namely, Gal 3.6ff, it is to the word 'believed' that attention is drawn. And in the present passage the emphatic contrast between 'if a man does have works to his credit' and 'to the man who has no work to his credit but believes' surely indicates that it is upon 'believed' rather than upon 'it was reckoned' that Paul is fastening. This conclusion is confirmed by the fact that the meaning of 'believed' in Gen 15.6 is further drawn out by the addition of 'in him who justifies the ungodly' after 'believes' in v. 5.

The best explanation of Paul's exposition of Gen 15.6 in these two verses is surely that which understands it to turn upon the fact that the Genesis verse makes no mention of any work of Abraham but simply refers to his faith. Had a work been referred to, then the counting of it to Abraham for righteousness would have been a matter of 'debt' and 'wages'; but that his faith was counted to him for righteousness can only be a matter of 'grace' – that is, if his faith is understood (in accordance with the context of this verse in Genesis) as his reliance upon God's promise (compare Gen 15.1, 4–5). But, when once the significance of 'believed' in Gen 15.6 is brought out, it immediately becomes clear that the verb 'reckon' or 'count' (as used in this verse) must signify a counting which is not a rewarding of merit but a free and unmerited decision of divine grace.

Paul's completion of 'believes' by 'in him who justifies the ungodly' is highly significant. To say that Abraham was one who had no claim on God on the ground of works ('to the man who has no work to his credit') is tantamount to saying that he was ungodly, a sinner (we may compare the equation of justification apart from works with the forgiveness of sins in vv. 6–8). So the faith which he had in God was necessarily faith in the God who justifies the ungodly. That God does do precisely this is the meaning of His grace (compare 'as a matter of grace' in v. 4). We may recognize in the words 'him who justifies the ungodly' an echo of the language of Exod 23.7; Prov 17.15; 24.24; Isa 5.23; but it is misleading to say, as Barrett does, that they 'describe God as doing what the Old Testament forbids'. In the Septuagint Greek version all these passages refer to human judges: they are forbidden to acquit the guilty – particularly for the sake of bribes. That the justification of the ungodly to which Paul refers is altogether different from the sort of thing against which the Old Testament warns human judges is surely obvious enough. As to the Hebrew text of Exod 23.7, the last part of which is a divine declaration, 'I will not justify the wicked', it attests a truth which is in no way contradicted by the forgiveness to which Paul refers, which is no cheap forgiveness which condones wickedness but the costly, just and truly merciful forgiveness 'through the redemption *accomplished* in Christ Jesus', to be understood in the light of 3.24–26.

6–8. It is very likely that Paul is here consciously applying a Rabbinic exegetical principle; but it is most important to recognize that his argument is not merely verbal but substantial. The validity of his appeal to Ps 32.1–2 as helping to interpret Gen 15.6 is not just a matter of the presence of a common term ('reckon' or 'count') in both places. His appeal to the psalm-passage has an inward and substantial validity, for God's reckoning righteousness to a man 'apart from works' is, in fact, equivalent to His forgiving his sins.

even as David also pronounces the blessing (not 'blessedness' which would be a different Greek word) **of the man to whom God reckons righteousness apart from works.** By means of the relative clause, which gathers up the thought of vv. 4 and 5, Paul makes the connexion between the passage he is about to quote and Gen 15.6, identifying the forgiving of sins with the reckoning of righteousness apart from works.

'Blessed are those whose iniquities have been forgiven and whose sins have been covered; blessed is the man whose sin the Lord will in no wise reckon' follows exactly the Septuagint version of Ps 32.1–2. The verb 'cover', which is used of covering sin in a bad sense (concealing instead of confessing it) in Job 31.33 and Prov 28.13, and in a good sense (with reference to a human action) in Prov 10.12 and 17.9, is here used to denote God's forgiveness, as also in Ps 85.2.

9. Does this blessing then apply to the circumcision *only* **or also to the uncircumcision?** is the beginning of the second part of 4.2–25. We may assume that it would be generally taken for granted by the Rabbis of Paul's day that the blessing pronounced in Ps 32.1–2 àpplied exclusively to the Jews. With **For we say: 'To Abraham his faith was reckoned for righteousness'** Paul begins his answer to the foregoing question, completing it in vv. 10–12. The initial 'For' may be explained as implying an unexpressed 'Also to the uncircumcision'. Paul now appeals back to Gen 15.6 as serving to interpret Ps 32.1–2.

10. In what circumstances then was it reckoned? When he was circumcised or when he was still uncircumcised? It was not when he was circumcised, but when he was still uncircumcised. Abraham's state, at the time that his faith was reckoned to him for righteousness, was that of uncircumcision; for his circumcision is not related until two chapters later (in Gen 17.1ff, where he is said to be ninety-nine years old – in 16.16 he is said to be eighty-six at the time of Ishmael's birth, which is some time after what is recorded in 15.1ff; according to the chronology of the Jews Abraham's circumcision was twenty-nine years after the promise of Gen 15.6). If then it is right to interpret Ps 32.1–2 by Gen 15.6, it follows that the blessing pronounced by the psalm cannot be limited to those who are circumcised.

11a. And he received the sign of circumcision as a seal of the righteousness by faith which he had while still uncircumcised affirms both that Abraham received circumcision and also that righteousness had already been reckoned to him before he was circumcised, and so is a basis both for v. 12 and also for v. 11b. The Greek word represented by 'sign' is the same as is used in the Septuagint version of Gen 17.11, where the RV has 'token' ('And ye shall be circumcised in the flesh of your foreskin; and it shall be a token of a covenant betwixt me and you'). Circumcision is an outward sign, a pointer to the reality of that which it signifies, namely, according to Gen 17.11, the covenant made by God with Abraham and his seed. By Paul's words here it is characterized as the seal, that is, the outward and visible authentication, ratification and guarantee, of the righteousness by faith which was already Abraham's while he was still uncircumcised. (It seems quite probable, though it is not certain, that the custom of referring to circumcision as a seal was already well established in Judaism by Paul's time.) The words imply that Abraham's circumcision, while it did not confer a status of righteousness upon him, was nevertheless precious as the outward and visible attestation of the status of righteousness which he already possessed.

11b–12. so that he might be the father of all those who, in a state of uncircumcision, believe, so that righteousness is reckoned to them, and also the father of the circumcision for those who not only belong to the circumcision but also walk in the steps of the faith of our father Abraham which he had while he was still uncircumcised. It was God's intention in causing Abraham to be circumcised that he should be the point of union between all who believe, whether circumcised or uncircumcised, being, on the one hand, by virtue of his having been justified while still uncircumcised, the father of all those who as uncircumcised believe, and, on the other hand, by virtue of the fact that he subsequently received circumcision, the father of all those who, being circumcised, are not only circumcised but are also believers. A puzzling feature of v. 12 is the presence of the definite article before the Greek word (it is a participle) represented by 'walk', which has the effect of implying that a different group of people altogether from that just mentioned is intended. But this is not only contrary to what seems to be the clear sense of the sentence; it is also ruled out grammatically by the position of the previous definite article in the Greek in relation to the words represented by 'not' and 'only'. Since the objection to the presence of this Greek word on the ground of the sense of the passage is thus confirmed by the thoroughly objective fact of its inconsistency with the grammar of the sentence (a point often not noticed), it would seem that we are justified in regarding it as a simple mistake, whether of a very early copyist or of Tertius or of Paul himself, and ignoring it in translation.[1] It should be noted that, while he is here concerned with a kinship with Abraham which depends on the sharing of his faith, Paul is not intending to deny the reality of the kinship 'according to the flesh' (v. 1) with Abraham of those Jews who do not share his faith or implying that such Jews are altogether

---

[1]Normally one should be extremely reluctant to accept a conjectural emendation, that is, a reading which has no support in the textual tradition (Greek manuscripts, ancient versions, etc.) of the New Testament, since, as far as the New Testament is concerned, there is such an enormous wealth of early witnesses to the text that, generally, one ought to assume that it is very unlikely that the original reading has not survived in any of them. But the present case – the awkward definite article has the unanimous support of the textual tradition – does seem exceptional.

excluded from the promises (compare what was said on 2.28–29).

13 is the beginning of the third part of 4.2–25. It has been very variously interpreted, but is probably best understood along the lines indicated by the translation: **For it was not on the basis of fulfilment of the law that the promise was made to Abraham or to his seed that he should be heir of the world, but on the basis of the righteousness of faith.** Paul's statement is in striking contrast to the Rabbis' assumption that all the promises were made to Abraham on the basis of his fulfilment of the law (which, according to them, was already known to him and performed in its completeness, although it had not yet been promulgated) and to their understanding of his faith as itself a meritorious work. With regard to the words 'or to his seed', the suggestion has been made that Paul may perhaps be thinking of Christ as the true seed of Abraham (compare Gal 3.16); but in view of vv. 16 and 17 this is not likely. His thought, as he takes up the expression 'thy seed' which recurs again and again in the record of God's promises to Abraham (Gen 12.7; 13.15–16; 15.5, 18; 17.8; 22.17–18) is rather of all those of whom Abraham is said in vv. 11 and 12 to be the father. Nowhere in the Old Testament is the promise to Abraham expressed in terms at all close to 'that he should be heir of the world'. What is promised in the various Genesis passages is an innumerable progeny, possession of the land of Canaan, and that all the nations of the earth shall be blessed (or shall bless themselves) in Abraham or in his seed. But Judaism came to interpret the promise to Abraham as a much more comprehensive promise. Thus, for example, Ecclus 44.21 contains the words: 'Therefore he assured him by an oath, . . . That he would . . . exalt his seed as the stars, And cause them to inherit from sea to sea, And from the River unto the utmost part of the earth'. Perhaps the best comment on the meaning of the promise as understood by Paul is provided by 1 Cor 3.21b–23 ('For all things are yours; whether Paul, or Apollos, or Cephas, or the world, or life, or death, or things present, or things to come; all are yours; and ye are Christ's; and Christ is God's'). It is the promise of the ultimate restoration to Abraham and his spiritual seed of man's inheritance (compare Gen 1.27–28) which was lost through sin. We may now explain the 'For' at the beginning of the verse as marking the introduction of a further consideration in support of what has already been said by way of proof that Abraham is no exception to the statement in 3.27 that glorying has been ruled out.

14. For if it is those *who have a claim* on the basis of *their fulfilment of* the law who are heirs, then faith has been rendered vain and the promise annulled. This verse also has been understood in a number of different ways. The simplest and most natural interpretation, especially in view of v. 15, is surely that which takes Paul's point (made in support of what he has just said in v. 13) to be that, if it were true that it is those who have a claim to the inheritance on the basis of their fulfilment of the law who are the heirs, faith would be vain and the promise a mere dead letter (since, on this condition, there could be no heirs at all, except for Christ Himself, there being none, Christ alone excepted, who actually have – as opposed to imagining that they have – a claim on God on the basis of their obedience).

If the interpretation of v. 14 given above is accepted, then the connexion between the first half of **15** and v. 14 is perfectly clear. **for the law works wrath** confirms v. 14 by drawing attention to the fact that, so far from the law's being something which a man might hope so adequately to fulfil as thereby to establish a claim on God, its actual effect, men being what they are, is to bring God's wrath upon them by turning their sin into conscious transgression and so rendering it more exceeding sinful. We may compare 3.20b; 5.20a; 7.7–13; Gal 3.19a. **but where there is no law, there there is also no transgression** is added in order to clarify the first half of v. 15. It highlights the essential characteristic of the situation which obtains in the absence of the law, in order to indicate what is the process by which the law's advent works wrath, namely, by converting sin into conscious transgression. (The law, by showing men with inescapable clarity that what they are doing is contrary to God's declared will, gives to their continuing to do it the character of conscious and wilful disobedience, of deliberate rebellion against God: 'transgression' in the Bible denotes the disobeying of definite commandments.)

16. The first two words of this verse in the original Greek (literally, 'Because of this' or 'For the sake of this') can either refer backward, whether to v. 15 or to v. 14 (if v. 15 is taken as a parenthesis) or to vv. 14 and 15 together, and so mean 'Wherefore', or they can refer forward. In view of the 'in order that' which follows almost immediately, it is surely preferable to take them as referring forward, as in the translation: **For this reason it is on the basis of faith, namely, in order that it may be according to grace, so that the promise may be certain of fulfilment for all the seed, not only for that which is of the law, but also for that which is of Abraham's faith.** The repeated 'it' can be taken as referring to 'the promise' (v. 13) or 'the inheritance' (understood from 'heirs' in v. 14), or – and this is probably best – we can understand Paul to have in mind something more comprehensive, the divine plan of salvation. God has made His plan of salvation to depend, on man's side, not on fulfilment of His law but solely on faith, in order that, on His side, it might be according to grace.

With regard to the second purpose stated in this verse, that is, 'so that the promise ... Abraham's faith', we need to decide whether the main emphasis falls on 'certain of fulfilment' or on 'for all ... Abraham's faith'. If it is on the former, then what is being stressed in the statement of the divine purpose is that the promise may be sure of fulfilment instead of being an empty promise (as it would have been, had God's plan been dependent on men's performance of the law). If, however, it is on the latter, then what is being stressed is that the promise may be so for all the seed, instead of being so only for that which is of the law. Of these alternatives the former suits the context much better, for the implication of v. 15 is not that only some of Abraham's seed would inherit but that none at all would inherit, if inheriting were really to be limited to 'those *who have a claim* on the basis of *their fulfilment of* the law'. The fact that 'for all' does indeed get considerable emphasis through being expanded in the words which follow (including the appeal to Gen 17.5, which is quoted in vv. 17 and 18) does not mean that it must be the main thought which Paul wishes to express here: rather is it a subsidiary thought, but, once mentioned, it is expanded and developed, because it is important in itself. The Greek phrase, which we have rendered by 'for that which is of the law' is sometimes taken to refer to the Jews as such: more probably it refers to the Jewish Christians, who possess the law as well as sharing Abraham's faith, while 'that which is of Abraham's faith' refers to the Gentile Christians, who share Abraham's faith without possessing the

law. The words **who is the father of us all** repeat the thought of vv.
11b and 12.

**17a. even as scripture says, 'Father of many nations have I made
thee'** provides scriptural confirmation of what has just been said.
The words quoted are in their context in Gen 17.5 an explanation
of the meaning of the name 'Abraham'. In Genesis the thought
may be simply of the Ishmaelites and Edomites and the
descendants of Abraham and Keturah, though it is possible that a
more far-reaching thought is already present.

17b. before God, in whom he believed is, by reason of its
substance, the beginning of the fourth part of 4.2–25, though
grammatically it is connected with the last clause of v. 16, v. 17a
being parenthetic. Abraham is father of us all in God's sight. This
is how God sees the matter, whatever some Jews may think. The
words lead into a positive statement about the nature of
Abraham's faith. The remainder of the verse characterizes the
God in whom Abraham believed by reference to two attributes of
the divine sovereignty exhibited in the story of Abraham and
confessed in Judaism. Abraham believed in *the God* **who quickens
the dead.** Compare the second benediction of the Eighteen
Benedictions used in the worship of the synagogue ('Blessed art
Thou, O LORD, who quickenest the dead'); also Wisd 16.13; Tob
13.2 (compare also Deut 32.39; 1 Sam 2.6; 2 Kgs 5.7). Paul has in
mind the quickening of Abraham's body and Sarah's womb,
which from the point of view of raising a family were as good as
dead (compare v. 19), conceivably also the unexpected sparing of
Isaac's life (Genesis 22: compare Heb 11.19), and certainly in the
background the raising of Jesus (compare vv. 24 and 25). **and calls
things which are not into being** completes the twofold
characterization by referring to God's creating power. 'He who
spoke and the world came into being' is a description of God used
by various Jewish teachers.

18. He in hope against *all* hope believed. Abraham's faith meant
hoping in God's promise in defiance of all human expectations
and calculations. The word 'hope' is here used in two different
senses. A good comment is provided by Charles Wesley's lines:

'In hope, against all human hope,
    Self-desperate, I believe; ...

> Faith, mighty faith, the promise sees,
>   And looks to that alone;
> Laughs at impossibilities,
>   And cries: It shall be done!'

Some prefer to place no mark of punctuation after 'believed' and to take the following Greek words to mean 'that he would become the father of many nations'; but the Greek construction which this would involve would be very surprising, and it is much better to place a comma after 'believed' and take the following words as a consecutive clause: **so that he became the father of many nations.** The effect of the addition of **according to the word spoken to him, 'So shall thy seed be'** is to connect the preceding words, including the phrase from Gen 17.5, with Gen 15.5, and so with the actual promise to which Gen 15.6, the verse which is basic to this whole chapter of Romans, refers.

19–21. And without weakening in faith he considered his own body, which was *as good as* dead (for he was about a hundred years old), and the deadness of Sarah's womb, and yet did not waver in unbelief with regard to God's promise. There is an interesting variation in the textual tradition here, some ancient witnesses having a negative particle before 'considered' (so 'did not consider': compare the AV, 'considered not'). Both readings are patient of interpretations which suit the context thoroughly well. If the negative is read, Paul's meaning may be understood to be that, because of his unweakened faith, Abraham did not concentrate all his attention on his own unpromising circumstances. If the positive reading is accepted, Paul's meaning may be taken to be that, because of his unweakened faith, Abraham considered steadily, without attempting to deceive himself, his unpromising circumstances, but, as v. 20 goes on to indicate, did not allow what he saw to make him doubt God's promise. The reading without the negative particle has strong textual support and is also to be preferred as being less obvious. There is little doubt it should be accepted. We should perhaps recognize in v. 19 Paul's attempt to do justice to Gen 17.17, understanding what is there recorded of Abraham as the expression not of unbelief but of an honest and clear-sighted acknowledgment of the facts of the situation.

The RV rendering of the first part of v. 20 ('yea, looking unto the promise of God, he wavered not') is due to failure to see that the Greek preposition, which usually means 'into' or 'unto', has here the sense 'with reference to', 'with regard to': it has introduced a reference to looking not present in the original and destroyed the close connexion between 'did not waver' and 'God's promise'. The reference to the divine promise at this point is vitally important. It makes it clear that the faith with which Paul is concerned is not a self-centred human attitude, however heroic, but is wholly based on, and controlled by, the divine promise. It is the promise on which it rests which is its power. It exists because a man has been overpowered, held and sustained by God's promise.

The combination with the negative statement, 'did not waver in unbelief', of the positive **but was strengthened in faith** serves to bring out more clearly the true nature of faith by showing it in its opposition to, and its victory over, unbelief. In a situation in which everything seems to be ranged against the promise, faith is a being enabled to rest on the promise alone, refusing to demand visible or tangible signs. Paul adds **giving glory to God.** A man gives glory to God when he acknowledges God's truthfulness and relies on it. Calvin's comment is: 'no greater honour can be given to God than by sealing His truth by our faith'. By embracing God's promise and believing it Abraham did that which the men, of whom 1.21–23 speaks, failed to do. **and being fully persuaded that he had the power to do what he had promised** completes the description of Abraham's faith, underlining the fact that it was faith in the God who had promised, not merely in what had been promised.

22. That is why 'it was reckoned to him for righteousness' concludes the fourth part of 4.2–25. The preceding verses have drawn out the meaning of the first part of Gen 15.6 according to the Septuagint ('And Abraham believed God'), and now the 'That is why', with which Paul introduces his quotation of the latter part of that verse, makes the point that it was because Abraham's faith in God, to which the former part of the verse refers, was the sort of thing that Paul has just shown it to have been, that God reckoned it to him for righteousness.

23–25 form the fifth and final part of 4.2–25. **But this statement of scripture that 'it was reckoned to him' was not written just for**

his sake, but for our sakes also makes the point that what Scripture says about Abraham was not recorded just for his sake, that is, as a memorial for him, that he might live on in men's remembrance, but for our sakes too, because his faith in God and its being reckoned to him for righteousness have a direct relevance to us.

The words **to whom *our faith* is to be reckoned** explain the relevance of Abraham's story to Paul and those to whom he is writing: to them too faith – their faith – is to be reckoned for righteousness. Some commentators insist that 'is to be reckoned' must refer to the final judgment. This interpretation is possible; but in view of the general tendency of Paul's language with regard to justification and especially of 5.1 and 9, and also in view of the past tense ('it was reckoned') in the Genesis verse which Paul has been expounding, it is surely more probable that the reference is to justification not as the eschatological hope of Christians but as the fact which they are confidently to assume as the basis of their present life. The Greek verb, which we have represented by 'is' followed by the infinitive, is probably used here in order to bring out the certainty of something already decided by God and included in His plan. The fact that those, for whose sakes – as well as for Abraham's own sake – the statement just quoted from Gen 15.6 was written, embrace Paul himself and those whom he is addressing and all Christians generally is made clear by the words **who believe on him who raised Jesus our Lord from the dead.** For the centrality of the resurrection of Jesus for Christian faith and also the close association of the reference to the Resurrection and the use of the title 'Lord' of Jesus see on 10.9. Reference to the resurrection of Jesus as God's act is characteristic of the New Testament (compare, for example, 8.11; 10.9; also Acts 3.15; 4.10; 1 Cor 6.14; 15.15; 2 Cor 4.14; 1 Pet 1.21: only in Jn 2.19, 21; 10.17, 18, is it referred to as accomplished by Jesus Himself). There is a noticeable solemnity about the latter part of v. 24, which prepares the way for v. 25, which is the solemn conclusion both of the section IV.4 and also of the whole of main division IV.

who was delivered up for our trespasses and was raised for our justification looks like a quotation of a traditional formula. That the influence of Isa 52.13–53.12 is to be seen here is hardly to be doubted. The verb translated 'deliver up' is too obvious a verb to use in this connexion for its occurrence here to prove by itself reminiscence of the Isaiah passage, in the Septuagint version of which it occurs three times (in 53.6 and twice in 53.12). But its conjunction with 'for our trespasses' is significant in the light of the Septuagint version of Isa 53.6 and 12. In addition, there is a striking parallel (though it is not generally noticed) between the association of justification with Christ's resurrection in the latter half of v. 25 and the reference in the Hebrew text of Isa 53.11 to the Servant's justifying many (the Septuagint has the verb 'justify' but differs widely from the Hebrew here), occurring, as it does, in the song's final strophe which seems to speak of the Servant's resurrection (though it does not use the term).

The two clauses are, of course, not to be understood 'woodenly' (to use Bruce's word) as though a rigid separation between the function of Christ's death and the function of His resurrection were intended (5.9 makes it clear that there is a connexion between Christ's death and our justification). At the same time, it would be a mistake to conclude that the formation of the two clauses has been controlled solely by rhetorical considerations. For what was necessitated by our sins was, in the first place, Christ's atoning death, and yet, had His death not been followed by His resurrection, it would not have been God's mighty deed for our justification. It should be noticed that 'for' (like the Greek preposition it represents) carries two different senses in this verse, in its first occurrence a causal sense ('on account of') and in its second a final ('in order to bring about').

V

THE LIFE PROMISED FOR THOSE WHO ARE RIGHTEOUS BY FAITH – 'SHALL LIVE' EXPOUNDED

(5.1–8.39)

Exactly where the new main division begins is disputed. Some see the first eleven verses, others the whole, of chapter 5 as going with what precedes, while others see the significant break as occurring between chapters 4 and 5. That there is a marked linguistic affinity between chapter 5, particularly 5.1–11, and the preceding chapters is not to be denied. But it is no proof that either part, or the whole, of chapter 5 ought to be regarded as belonging to the same main division of the epistle as 1.18–4.25. For, if the new main division is a description of the life which is promised for those who are righteous by faith, is, in fact, a drawing out of what having been justified by faith means, then it is perfectly understandable that some of the characteristic vocabulary of the previous main division should reappear in the new one, and especially in the first part of it. The chief reason for associating chapter 5 with the following, rather than with the preceding, chapters is the nature of its contents. In our view, it is parallel by virtue of its substance with the three following chapters, the chapters in this stretch of Romans coinciding exactly with the logical sections. In each of the four chapters the first subsection is a basic statement concerning the life promised for the man who is righteous by faith or concerning the meaning of justification. The four initial subsections affirm that being justified means being reconciled to God, being sanctified, being free from the law's condemnation, and being indwelt by God's Spirit; and in each case what follows the initial subsection is a necessary clarification of what has been said in it. But, in addition to the argument from the contents, two formal points may be mentioned. The first is that the occurrence of one or other of the formulae 'through our Lord Jesus Christ', 'through Jesus Christ our Lord' and 'in Christ Jesus our Lord' at the beginning, in the middle and at the end, of chapter 5, and at the end of each of the three succeeding chapters has the effect of binding the four chapters together. The second is that the solemn formula which concludes chapter 4 strongly suggests that 4.25 marks the end of a major division of the epistle.

V.1. A LIFE CHARACTERIZED BY PEACE WITH GOD
(5.1–21)

A remarkable variety of suggested titles for this section and its component subsections is to be seen in the commentaries. But the contents of vv. 1, 10 and 11 are surely sufficient warrant for claiming that Paul himself has given a fairly clear indication that his main concern in the first subsection is with the fact that those who are justified are at peace with God. And a comparison of the structures of chapters 5, 6, 7 and 8 strongly suggests the likelihood that the rest of this chapter will be in some way a clarification of the first subsection or a drawing out of what is implicit in it or to be inferred from it. That it is, in fact, at any rate formally, a conclusion from it is indicated by the Greek expression (represented by 'Wherefore' in the translation) with which v. 12 begins – if we allow that expression its natural meaning. It would seem then that the indications Paul himself has provided concerning the movement of his thought point to the conclusion that the fact of our peace with God should be regarded as the subject which gives the section as a whole its unity.[1] In our view, a detailed examination of the text bears out this conclusion.

(i) *Peace with God*
(5.1–11)

[1]Having been justified then on the basis of faith, we have peace with God through our Lord Jesus Christ, [2]through whom also we have obtained access [by faith] to this grace in which we stand, and

---

[1]Compare the title which Barth gives to this chapter in *A Shorter Commentary on Romans*: 'The Gospel as Man's Reconciliation with God'.

we exult in hope of the glory of God. ³And not only *so*, but we even exult in afflictions, knowing that affliction works endurance, ⁴and endurance provedness, and provedness hope. ⁵And this hope does not put us to shame, for God's love has been poured out in our hearts through the Holy Spirit who has been given to us. ⁶For, when we were still powerless, Christ died at the appointed time for ungodly men. ⁷For someone will scarcely die for a righteous man; for a benefactor perhaps someone might bring himself to die. ⁸But God proves his love for us by the fact that Christ died for us when we were still sinners. ⁹Since, then, we have now been justified by his blood, we shall much more be saved through him from the wrath. ¹⁰For if when we were enemies we were reconciled to God through the death of his Son, much more, having been reconciled, shall we be saved by his life. ¹¹And not only *this*; we also exult in God through our Lord Jesus Christ, through whom we have now already received reconciliation.

These verses make the point that the life promised for the man who is righteous by faith is a life characterized by peace with God ('we have peace with God' in v. 1; 'we were reconciled to God' and 'having been reconciled' in v. 10; 'we have ... received reconciliation' in v. 11). They affirm the amazing truth that God's undeserved love has through Christ transformed people from being God's enemies into being at peace with Him, being His friends. The reconciliation Paul is speaking of is not to be understood as simply identical with justification (the two terms being understood as different metaphors denoting the same thing), nor yet as a consequence of justification, a result following afterwards. The thought is rather that – in the case of the divine justification of sinners – justification necessarily involves reconciliation. Whereas between a human judge and an accused person there may be no really deep personal relationship at all, the relation between God and the sinner is altogether personal, both because God is the God He is and also because it is against God Himself that the sinner has sinned. So God's justification of sinners of necessity involves also their reconciliation, the removal of enmity, the establishment of peace. This subsection, then, is drawing out something already implicit in 3.21–26. The fact that men have been justified means that they must also have been reconciled. The fact that they are righteous by faith means that they now live as God's friends.

Verses 2b–5 are descriptive of this life at peace with God, emphasizing particularly the hope which is a characteristic feature of it. Verses 6–8 take up the reference to God's love in the latter part of v. 5 and draw out the nature of God's love for us as altogether undeserved and spontaneous. Verses 9 and 10 take up again the theme of hope, and confidently affirm in two parallel statements the certainty of our hope's fulfilment, of our final salvation, while v. 11 refers to our present jubilant exultation in God through Christ, through whom we have received reconciliation with God.

It is noteworthy that this whole subsection is in the first person plural.

1. Having been justified then on the basis of faith connects what follows with 1.18–4.25, the argument of which (summed up in the participial clause) is basic for the whole of 5.1–8.39. For the inclusion of a summary of a previous section at the beginning of a new section we may compare 3.23 (summing up 1.18–3.20) and 8.1 (summing up 7.1–6).

we have[1] peace with God states the theme of the section – that those who have been justified by God have peace with God. That 'peace' here denotes, not subjective feelings of peace (though these may indeed result) but the objective state of being at peace instead of being at enmity, is made clear by the parallel statements of vv. 10 and 11 ('when we were enemies we were reconciled', 'having been reconciled' and 'we have … received reconciliation'). The question arises: What is the significance of the combination of 'Having been justified' and 'we have peace'? or, to put it otherwise,

---

[1]There is a variation in the textual tradition between 'we have' and 'let us have' (in Greek it amounts to the difference of a single letter, between a short 'o' and a long 'o' which could easily be mistaken for each other by someone writing to dictation). The former is less strongly attested, but is almost certainly to be preferred on the ground of intrinsic probability. If the latter were accepted, it would be necessary, since vv. 10 and 11 show that Paul is here regarding the believers' peace with God as a fact, to understand it in some such sense as 'let us enjoy (or 'guard') the peace we have'; but even this would not really suit the context, which requires a statement at this point. Someone, however, who was not giving the argument quite as close attention as it demands might easily have felt that an element of exhortation would be appropriate here.

What did Paul understand to be the relation between reconciliation and justification? The correct answer would seem to be neither that reconciliation is a consequence of justification, nor that justification and reconciliation are different metaphors denoting the same thing, but that *God's* justification involves reconciliation because God is what He is. Where it is God's justification that is concerned, justification and reconciliation, though distinguishable, are inseparable. Whereas between a human judge and the person who appears before him there may be no really personal meeting at all, no personal hostility if the accused be found guilty, no establishment of friendship if the accused is acquitted, between God and the sinner there is a personal relationship, and God's justification involves a real self-engagement to the sinner on His part. (It is not surprising that this subsection contains a statement about God's love (vv. 6–8).) He does not confer the status of righteousness upon us without at the same time giving Himself to us in friendship and establishing peace between Himself and us – a work which, on account of the awful reality both of His wrath against sin and of the fierce hostility of our egotism against the God who claims our allegiance, is only accomplished at unspeakable cost to Him. Thus 'Having been justified ... , we have peace ... ' is not a mere collocation of two metaphors describing the same fact, nor does it mean that, having been justified, we were subsequently reconciled and now have peace with God; but its force is that the fact that we have been justified means that we have also been reconciled and have peace with God.

through our Lord Jesus Christ. As it is through Christ that we are justified (3.24), so it is also through Him that we are reconciled to God (compare v. 10; 2 Cor 5.18–19). It is to be noted that this formula is repeated in v. 11 (possibly without 'Christ'), and (with a slightly different word-order) in v. 21 and in 7.25, and that 'in Christ Jesus our Lord' occurs in 6.23 and 8.39. This placing of the same or similar formulae at the beginning, in the middle (that is, at the end of the first subsection), and at the end, of chapter 5, and at the ends of chapters 6, 7 and 8, in turn, is scarcely accidental. It has the double effect of marking off these four sections of the epistle and at the same time underlining the fact of their belonging together as a single main division.

2. through whom also we have obtained access [by faith] to this grace in which we stand. It is better to take 'this grace' (that is, this state of being the objects of favour) to refer to our justification than to our peace with God, since in the latter case all this part of the verse would be merely repeating what has just been said in v. 1 (from 'we have' to the end). In using the word represented by 'access' Paul may possibly have had in mind the thought of introduction into a royal presence. The question whether 'by faith' should be read or omitted is not very important, since, in any case, there is no doubt that Paul thought that the access referred to had been obtained by faith. It is possible that 'stand' here denotes no more than situation and so is equivalent to 'are'; but, in view of Pauline usage, it is more probable that it carries something of the sense 'stand firm', 'abide'.

It is better to take **and we exult in hope of the glory of God** as co-ordinate with 'we have peace with God through our Lord Jesus Christ' than as co-ordinate with 'we have obtained', etc. The Greek verb which we have rendered here (and also in vv. 3 and 11) by 'exult' is the same as that which we have elsewhere translated 'glory' (that translation seemed unsuitable here on account of the presence in the same clause of a Greek noun, quite unrelated to this verb, for which the English noun 'glory' was required). For discussion of Paul's use of the Greek verb in question the reader is referred to what was said on 2.17–20; 3.27–31, and also on 4.1–3. In the present verse it denotes a glorying or boasting, an exultant jubilation, resulting from confident expectation of the glory of God – so a good glorying. The noun 'hope', as used here and in vv. 4 and 5, denotes the confident anticipation of that which we do not yet see. By 'the glory of God' is meant here (compare 3.23; 8.17, 18, 21, 30; 9.23) that illumination of man's whole being by the radiance of the divine glory which is man's true destiny but which was lost through sin, as it will be restored (not just as it was, but immeasurably enriched through God's own personal participation in man's humanity in Jesus Christ – compare 8.17), when man's redemption is finally consummated at the parousia of Jesus Christ. Calvin's comment on this verse includes the sentence: 'Paul's meaning is that, although believers are now pilgrims on earth, yet by their confidence they surmount the heavens, so that they cherish their future inheritance in their bosoms with tranquillity'.

3–5. And not only _so_, but we even exult in afflictions. Not only do we exult in the hope of the glory of God, but we also actually exult in tribulations. For the use of 'And not only _so_ (or '_this_'), (but) . . . also (or 'even')' compare v. 11; 8.23; 9.10; 2 Cor 8.19. The expression is elliptical: with 'not only' has to be understood a repetition of what immediately precedes – here 'we exult in hope of the glory of God'. While 'in afflictions' could mean 'in the midst of afflictions', indicating the situation in which the exultation takes place, it is much more probable that it indicates the basis of the exultation (compare the 'in' after 'exult' in v. 11 and with 'glory' in 1 Cor 1.31; 3.21; 2 Cor 10.17; 12.9 (in the light of the following verse); Gal 6.13; Phil 3.3). Afflictions are actually cause for exultation. What follows indicates why.

knowing (compare 6.9; 13.11: the reference is to the knowledge which is given to faith and for which an absolute validity is claimed) **that affliction works endurance** shows that the exulting in afflictions to which this verse refers is not at all an exulting in them as in something meritorious on our part – that would of course be but a glorying in our own works! – but an exulting in them as in that to which God subjects us as part of the discipline by which He teaches us to wait patiently for His deliverance. As a general statement, 'affliction works endurance' would lack validity; for, as Calvin points out, tribulation 'provokes a great part of mankind to murmur against God, and even to curse Him'. But Paul is thinking of what it achieves, when it is met by faith in God which receives it as His fatherly discipline. Where God sustains faith, affliction produces endurance. The same Greek noun as is here translated 'endurance' occurs also in 2.7 ('steadfast perseverance'); 8.25 ('steadfast patience'); 15.4 and 5 ('patient endurance').

and endurance provedness is the second member of the climax[1] which extends to the beginning of v. 5. Such patient endurance as faith exhibits under the discipline of affliction is in its turn the source of provedness, the quality possessed by faith when it has

---

[1] 'Climax' is here used as a technical term denoting a figure of speech consisting of several members, in which the key-word of the preceding is taken up in the following.

stood up to testing, like the precious metal which is left when the base metals have all been refined away. The Greek noun which we have rendered by 'provedness' occurs also in 2 Cor 2.9; 8.2; 13.3; Phil 2.22 (in these occurrences it is represented in the RV by 'proof'), and in 2 Cor 9.13, where the RV has 'proving'. Compare also the use of a cognate word in Jas 1.3 and 1 Pet 1.7, which is translated 'proof' in the RV.

and provedness hope. To have one's faith proved by God in the fires of tribulation and sustained by Him so as to stand the test is to have one's hope in Him and in the fulfilment of His promises, one's hope of His glory (v. 2), strengthened and confirmed.

And this hope does not put us to shame completes the climax. The hope which is thus strengthened and confirmed does not put those who cherish it to shame by proving illusory. The language is reminiscent of several Old Testament passages, especially of Ps 22.5b according to the Septuagint Greek version, which has 'They hoped in thee, and were not put to shame'.

for God's love has been poured out in our hearts through the Holy Spirit who has been given to us is confirmation of the truth of the preceding statement. Grammatically, the Greek phrase represented by 'God's love' could equally well mean 'love to God' and has sometimes been so understood. But a reference to God's love for us suits the context very much better. A statement of the fact of God's love for us is a far more cogent proof of the security of our hope than a statement of the fact of our love for God would be; and it is God's love for us which vv. 6–8 go on to describe. We have no doubt that it is God's love for us that is meant. The fact that the Greek verb represented here by 'pour out' is used in the Septuagint version of Joel 2.28 and 29; Acts 2.17 and 18, 33; 10.45; Tit 3.6 of God's giving the Holy Spirit to men, together with the presence here in association with 'has been poured out' of 'in our hearts' (compare Gal 4.6) and of 'through the Holy Spirit', has led some interpreters to suggest that Paul was actually thinking of the Holy Spirit's being poured out. But the verb is used of the pouring out of God's wrath (both in the Old Testament and in the New), in Mal 3.10 of the pouring out of His blessing and in Ecclus 18.11 of the pouring out of His mercy. There is therefore nothing very strange about Paul's speaking of God's love as having been poured out. The metaphor may well have been chosen in order to express the idea of abundant generosity, as John Chrysostom suggested. The words 'in our hearts' and 'through the Holy Spirit', which on this view present a difficulty, are best explained by assuming that we have here a pregnant construction, and that the meaning is that God's love has been lavished upon us (as will be spelled out in vv. 6–8), and actually brought home to our hearts (so that we have recognized it and rejoice in it) by the Holy Spirit who has been given to us. (For Paul's assumption that the Holy Spirit has certainly been given to him and the Roman Christians, compare 8.9 and see notes there.) The proof that our hope will not disappoint us in the end is the fact of the amazing generosity of God's love for us – a fact which we have been enabled to know and understand by the gift of His Spirit to us.

6–8 describe the nature of the divine love to which v. 5 has referred. **For, when we were still powerless, Christ died at the appointed time for ungodly men.** He did not wait for us to start helping ourselves, but died for us when we were altogether helpless. And this Christ did at the time appointed by God in His sovereign freedom (compare Mk 1.15; Gal 4.4). For Christ's death on behalf of sinners compare, in this epistle, 3.25; 4.25; 6.10; 7.4; 8.32; 14.15. The 'ungodly men' referred to here are not to be distinguished from the 'we' who have just been described as 'powerless' and will be described as 'sinners' (v. 8) and 'enemies' (v. 10). What Paul is here concerned to bring out is the fact that the divine love is love for the undeserving, love which is not the result of any worth in its objects but is self-caused and in its freedom itself confers worth upon them.

That the purpose of **For someone will scarcely die for a righteous man; for a benefactor perhaps someone might bring himself to die** is to set off the 'for ungodly men' of v. 6 and so emphasize the extraordinariness of Christ's self-sacrifice is clear, but its exact interpretation is disputed. In the original Greek two adjectives are used, the meanings of which are 'righteous' or 'just' and 'good'. Both are here used as nouns, the latter being preceded by a definite article. Of those interpreters who take the two words as more or less synonymous, some regard the second sentence as a clarification of the first intended to exclude a possible misunderstanding of it (as a denial that any man at all would give his life on behalf of a just man), while others suggest that Paul may have meant v. 7b not as a complement to v. 7a but as a replacement of it, and that Tertius may have left v. 7a standing by mistake. Of those who see a distinction in meaning between the two adjectives as used here, some take both as neuter ('a just cause' and 'the public good'), others take the former as masculine ('a just man') and the latter as neuter ('the public good'), claiming that the presence of the definite article in the Greek indicates the difference. But, if 'the public good' is referred to in v. 7b, then the sentence would seem to do scant justice to the facts, for many have voluntarily died for their countries. Yet others have understood the term used in v. 7b to mean 'his benefactor' (the Greek adjective, like the English 'good', can have the sense of 'kind', and there are two cognate verbs which can mean 'do good (to some one)'); and this seems to give the best sense. We understand Paul's meaning then to be that, whereas it is a rare thing for a man deliberately and in cold blood to lay down his life for the sake of an individual just man, and not very much less rare for a man to do so for the sake of an individual who is actually his benefactor, Christ died for the sake of the ungodly.

But God proves his love for us by the fact that Christ died for us when we were still sinners. The use of the present tense is noteworthy: the event of the Cross is a past event ('died'), but the fact that it occurred remains as a present proof. In the Greek 'his' is emphatic, God's love being strongly contrasted with that shown by men (v. 7). The death of Christ is both the proof of the fact, and the revelation of the nature, of God's love for us. It is altogether undeserved, its origin not at all in its objects but wholly in Him.

9–10. Having described in vv. 6–8 the nature of God's love for us, to the reality of which (brought home to our hearts by the Holy Spirit) he had appealed in v. 5 as proof that our hope will not disappoint us, Paul now returns to the subject of our hope's not disappointing and affirms the certainty of our hope's fulfilment, of our final salvation, in two parallel statements, both having the same logical structure (compare vv. 15 and 17; Mt 6.30; 2 Cor 3.11): **Since, then, we have now been justified by his blood, we shall much more be saved through him from the wrath. For if when we were enemies we were reconciled to God through the death of his Son, much more, having been reconciled, shall we be saved by his life.** The point made in the former of these two sentences is that, since God has already done the really difficult thing, that is, justified ungodly sinners, we may be absolutely confident that He will do what is by comparison very easy, namely, save from His wrath at the last those who are already righteous in His sight. The 'now' denotes the present time in contrast both with the time before the righteousness of God was manifested and also with the future to which 'we shall ... be saved' refers. For the reference to Christ's blood in connexion with justification compare 3.24–26. The Greek preposition, the primary meaning of which is 'in', which we have translated 'by', has here the sense 'by means of' or 'by virtue of'. The verb 'save' is here used in its narrower sense of deliverance in the final judgment, and that from which we are to be saved is specified as the divine 'wrath', as in 1 Th 5.9. For the use of 'wrath' see on 1.18.

The point made in the latter sentence (v. 10) is that, since God has already done the much more difficult thing (in this case, reconciled us, when we were enemies, to Himself), we can with absolute confidence expect that He will do what by comparison is but a little thing, namely, at the last save us who are now His friends. A new term, reconciliation, is introduced here (though the thought was already present in v. 1). It expresses the quality of personal relationship which is inseparable from God's justification of men but which the word 'justification' does not as such necessarily suggest. The enmity which is removed in the act of reconciliation is both sinful man's hostility to God (compare 8.7; probably also 1.30 ('haters of God')) and also God's hostility to sinful man (this aspect of it is particularly clear in 11.28), though the removal of God's hostility is not to be thought of as involving a change of purpose in God (God's purpose with regard to man is constant, and it is an altogether merciful purpose, but the accomplishment of His merciful purpose involves both unrelenting opposition to man's sin and also His self-giving to man). The initiative in reconciliation is God's, and His too is the determinative action: Paul in fact uses the active voice of the verb only of God, the passive only of men. Yet the fact that he can in 2 Cor 5.20 represent God as calling upon men to be reconciled is a clear indication that he does not think of men's part as merely passive: indeed to have done so would have been inconsistent with that very recognition that God in redeeming man deals with him as a person which led to the use of the language of reconciliation. The close connexion that there is between reconciliation and justification – and indeed their inseparability – is shown by the parallelism between vv. 9 and 10, but to conclude that the two terms are merely synonymous would be a false inference, as we have already seen (in connexion with v. 1). It was 'through the death of his Son' that we were reconciled to God, because, on the one hand, Christ's death was the means by which God pardoned us without in any way condoning our sin and so laid aside His hostility towards us in a way that was worthy of His goodness and love and consistent with His constant purpose of mercy for us, and, on the other hand, it was the means by which He demonstrated His love for us and so broke our hostility toward Himself. But the fact that in these two sentences our justification and reconciliation are spoken of as being by Christ's blood and through His death, respectively, while our future salvation is spoken of as being 'through him' and 'by his life', should not mislead us into assuming that Paul intended any rigid distinction between what Christ's death, and what His resurrection and exaltation, accomplished. (Compare what was said on 4.25.)

11. And not only *this*. With 'not only' it is more natural to supply 'shall we be saved' (the main verb of the previous sentence) than 'having been reconciled'. In **we also exult in God through our Lord Jesus Christ, through whom we have now already received reconciliation** the tense of 'exult' is probably meant to be stressed: not only shall we be saved hereafter, but already now we exult. That this jubilant exultation in God was expressed in the churches' worship is not to be doubted; but it would be wrong to limit the reference to this cultic context. We should rather understand Paul as thinking of it as characteristic of the Christian life as a whole, though – paradoxically – in combination with the groaning to which 8.23 refers. We may compare – but must also contrast – this 'exult in God' with the glorying in God mentioned in 2.17 (where the same Greek verb is used as here), where there is a suggestion of complacency and self-righteousness, which is certainly not intended here. Note that it is through Christ, through whom we have already received the gift of reconciliation with God, that we exult. This gift which we have already received through Him is ground enough for ceaseless exultation.

(ii) *Christ and Adam*
(5.12–21)

[12]Wherefore, as through one man sin entered the world, and through sin death, and so death came to all men in turn, because all have sinned – [13]for sin was already in the world before the law was given, but, in the absence of the law, sin is not registered *with full clarity.* [14]But death reigned from Adam to Moses even over those who had not sinned in the same way as Adam, by transgression *of a definite commandment.* Now Adam is the type of him who was to come. [15]But it is not a matter of 'As is the misdeed, so also is the gracious gift'. For if by the misdeed of the one the many died, much more have the grace of God and the gift *which has come* by the grace of the one man Jesus Christ abounded unto the many. [16]And it is not a matter of 'As is the result of one man's sinning, so is the gift'; for the judgment followed one misdeed and issued in condemnation, but the gracious gift followed many misdeeds and issued in justification. [17]For if death reigned through the one man by the misdeed of the one, much more shall those who receive the abundance of grace and of the gift of righteousness reign in life through the one man, Jesus Christ. [18]So then as the result of one man's misdeed has been for all men condemnation, so also the result of one man's righteous conduct is for all men justification issuing in life. [19]For as through the disobedience of the one man the many were made sinners, so also through the obedience of the one will the many be made righteous. [20]But the law came in as a new feature of the situation in order that the misdeed might increase; but where sin increased, grace superabounded, [21]in order that, as sin reigned in death, so also grace might reign through righteousness unto eternal life through Jesus Christ our Lord.

Verses 12–21 indicate the conclusion to be drawn from the previous subsection. The fact that there are those who, being justified by faith, are also now God's friends means that something has been accomplished by Christ which does not just concern believers but is as universal in its effects as was the sin of Adam. The existence of Jesus Christ does not only determine the existence of believers: it is also the innermost secret of the life of

every man. Significantly the first person plural, used throughout
vv. 1–11, gives place to the third person plural.

Paul begins to draw his parallel between Christ and Adam in
v. 12, but breaks off at the end of the verse without having
expressed the main clause of his sentence, because, realizing the
danger of his comparison's being very seriously misunderstood,
he prefers to indicate as emphatically as possible the vast
dissimilarity between Christ and Adam before formally
completing it. Verses 13 and 14 are a necessary explanation of the
verb 'sin' at the end of v. 12; and vv. 15–17 drive home the
dissimilarity between Christ and Adam. Then in v. 18 Paul repeats
in a briefer form the substance of v. 12, and now completes it with
the long-delayed main clause. Verse 19 is explanatory of v. 18,
bringing out as it does the connecting links between Adam's
misdeed and the condemnation of all men, and between Christ's
righteous conduct and men's final justification unto life. Verses 20
and 21 refer to the part played by the law in God's purpose. The
effect of the gift of the law to Israel was to make sin abound – to
turn men's wrong-doing into conscious and wilful rebellion by
confronting them with the clear manifestation of God's will; but
at the very place where sin most fully and most outrageously
abounded (in Israel's rejection of Jesus Christ), there grace
abounded more exceedingly and triumphed gloriously. The
relevance of the reference to the law at this point lies in the fact
that it is the law which makes manifest the full magnitude of sin
and so also at the same time the full magnitude of the triumph of
grace.

12. Wherefore is best understood as indicating the connexion
between what follows and 5.1–11 as a whole. Verses 1–11 have
affirmed that those who are righteous by faith are people whom
God's undeserved love has transformed from the condition of
being God's enemies into that of being reconciled to Him, at peace
with Him. The point of the 'Wherefore' is that Paul is now going
on to indicate in vv. 12–21 the conclusion to be drawn from what
has been said in vv. 1–11. The fact that this reconciliation is a
reality in the case of believers does not stand by itself: it means that
something has been accomplished by Christ which is as universal
in its effectiveness as was the sin of the first man. Paul is no longer
speaking just about the Church: his vision now includes the whole

111

of humanity. Significantly, the first person plural of vv. 1–11 has given place to the third person plural. The existence of Jesus Christ not only determines the existence of believers: it is also the innermost secret of the life of every man. The 'Wherefore' indicates that Paul is inferring Christ's significance for all men from the reality of what He now means for believers. The connexion, then, between vv. 12–21 and 1–11 is definite and close.

That all the rest of the verse is dependent on **as** and that the sentence is broken off incomplete, no main clause having been provided, has been generally agreed from ancient times down to the present. It is the only feasible explanation of the Greek. The latter part of the verse is a continuation of the subordinate part of the sentence. Paul then breaks off his construction, in order to give a necessary explanation (vv. 13 and 14) of what he has said in that continuation of the original 'as'-clause and also to drive home with strong emphasis (vv. 15–17) the vast dissimilarity between Adam and Christ. Finally, instead of just expressing at last the main clause which he has all along intended and so completing his sentence, he now, since his parenthesis has become so unconscionably long (it is five whole verses), repeats the substance of his original 'as'-clause in v. 18a, and then immediately completes it by its proper main clause in v. 18b. The broken sentence reflects a real theological difficulty, and is a valuable clue to the right understanding of vv. 12–21 as a whole. Paul wants to draw the comparison between Christ and Adam – and indeed must draw it – in order to bring out clearly the universal significance of Christ's work, but is vividly conscious of the danger of its being misunderstood. He is therefore reluctant to complete his statement of the comparison (though in the course of his long parenthesis he certainly does give a hint – at the end of v. 14 – of the comparison he has in mind), before he has hedged it about with qualifications emphasizing that this is no comparison of like with like but a comparison of two persons who in all their effects and achievements are utterly dissimilar except in respect of the actual point of comparison. Even such a term as 'antithetical typology' is liable to be misleading in this connexion, since, while it indicates that Paul is contrasting Christ and Adam, it is liable to suggest that he sees a close correspondence between them and is balancing the one against the other. The truth is that he desires, while drawing the analogy, at the same time to deny emphatically that there is even the remotest semblance of an equilibrium between them; for, as Chrysostom observed, 'Sin and grace are not equivalents, nor yet death and life, nor yet the devil and God; but the difference between them is infinite'.

It is possible now to discuss the rest of the verse, apart from the last clause, in a preliminary way. **through one man sin entered the world** states that one man's (Adam's) transgression gave sin entrance into the world, that is, most probably, the world in the sense of 'mankind' or 'human life'. The further words **and through sin death** indicate that sin's entry meant also the entry of death, which followed sin like a shadow. **and so death came to all men in turn** states explicitly what was already implicit in the first half of the verse, namely, that the entry of sin and death into the world of men was in due course followed by its natural consequence ('and so'), death's taking hold of each individual man, as the generations succeeded one another.

because all have sinned represents four Greek words which have given rise to a vast amount of discussion. It is possible to explain the first two Greek words (a preposition and a relative pronoun) variously as meaning: (i) 'unto which' (taking 'which' to refer to 'death', the thought being that death was the end to which their sinning necessarily led); (ii) 'in whom' (taking the relative to refer to 'one man'); (iii) 'because of whom' (the relative again being referred to 'one man'); (iv) 'because' (the preposition and relative pronoun being understood together as a conjunction). Of these explanations, (i) has the undoubted advantage that the word 'death' is near to hand in the sentence, but is otherwise forced and yields a sense which cannot be said to suit the context at all well; both (ii), the explanation supported by Augustine, who took Paul to mean that all men have sinned in Adam by virtue of their seminal identity with their first forefather, and (iii) are open to the serious objection that the word 'man' is too far away to be a natural antecedent to the relative pronoun. By far the most probable explanation is (iv), and it is widely accepted today. But, even when we have decided that the first two Greek words should be translated 'because', the question has still to be asked whether 'sinned' refers to men's participation in Adam's sin (and not to their sinning in their own persons) or to men's own personal sinning. The former view is strongly supported by a good many interpreters who claim that its acceptance is required by the comparison drawn between Christ and Adam, since men's righteousness in Christ owes nothing to their own works. But the latter view should, we think, be preferred, since there is nothing in the context (if the translation 'because' is accepted for the first two words of the Greek) to suggest that the verb 'sin' is being used here in any other than its ordinary sense, and nowhere else does Paul use it otherwise than of actual personal sinning. And the argument against this view and in favour of the former from the Christ-Adam comparison is not cogent, since Paul in this passage insists on the dissimilarity as well as on the similarity between Christ and Adam, and there is no reason to assume that, because he believed Christ to be the sole source of men's righteousness, Paul must have regarded Adam equally as being alone responsible for men's ruin. We conclude that 'sinned' in this clause refers to men's sinning in their own persons but as a consequence of the corrupt nature inherited from Adam.

We must now look at v. 12 as a whole. Its first two clauses state only that through Adam sin gained entrance to mankind and that as a result death also gained entrance. So far it has not been said that death actually reached all men either as the direct result of Adam's sin or as the result of their own sinning. Thus these two clauses do not go beyond what is explicit in Gen 2.17b and 3.3, 19. The third and fourth clauses of the verse, however, say something which is not explicit in the Genesis narrative or anywhere else in the Old Testament, though it is the natural inference to be drawn from the Genesis narrative and is surely its intention, namely, that, as a result of the entrance of sin followed by death, death in time reached all men because they all sinned. What is implicit in the Old Testament account was, of course, made fully explicit in later Jewish writings (Ecclus 25.24 is the earliest passage to assert that physical death is due to the Fall and to connect all men's sinfulness with the sin of Adam and Eve), and it is significant that in these writings both the ideas expressed (if our interpretation is correct) in the third and fourth clauses of this verse, namely, that Adam's sin was the cause of the death of all men and that men did not die simply because of Adam's sin without their contributing their own sinning by their own fault, are frequently expressed.

Other ideas are also to be found. Particularly important among them is the tendency to exalt Adam as the first patriarch, the father of Israel, and to allow the imagination to run riot in extravagant descriptions of his superlative size, beauty and wisdom before his fall. In striking contrast the restraint and sobriety of Paul's references to Adam are noteworthy. Here in Rom 5.12ff his attention is firmly centred on Christ, and Adam is only mentioned in order to bring out more clearly the nature of the work of Christ. The purpose of the comparison is to make clear the universal range of what Christ has done. Though Paul does elsewhere refer by implication to the glory which was Adam's before the Fall (3.23), he is here concerned with Adam only as the man who has affected all other men disastrously but whose effectiveness for ill has been far surpassed by Christ's effectiveness for good.

According to this verse, human death is the consequence of human sin. This is stated first in the words 'and through sin death' with reference to Adam's primal sin, and then again in the second half of the verse with reference to the subsequent sinning of all individual men (if our understanding of the last clause is correct). That it is difficult for those who are in the habit of thinking of death as natural to come to terms with this doctrine of death is obvious – and it is not only in modern times that the difficulty of this doctrine has been felt.

We may perhaps tentatively suggest that, while there seems to be clear enough evidence that human death as a biological phenomenon is not consequential on sin but natural, it is not incompatible with a frank recognition of this evidence to believe that at the point (or, maybe, points) at which man first appeared as recognizably man he may have been faced with, but rejected, a God-given possibility of, and a God-given summons to, a human life such as did not need to be terminated by the death which we know, that is, a death which is for all men objectively (according to the witness of Scripture) death-as-the-wages-of-sin, whether they know it subjectively as such or not. In this connexion three truths should be steadily borne in mind: (i) that it is only in the death of Jesus Christ that we see the full reality and seriousness of human death as the death which we all objectively – but only those, who heed the witness of Scripture, subjectively – know, that is, as death-as-the-wages-of-sin; (ii) that it is in His human life alone that we see a human life which did not in itself merit the death which we know; and (iii) that in His risen and glorified humanity we see the immortality which is the life which, from all eternity, God purposed as the ultimate destiny of those of His creatures-to-be whom He would at last make to be 'conformed to the image of his Son'.

13–14 is best understood as providing a necessary explanation of the last clause of v. 12. **for sin was already in the world before the law was given** explains how it is true that 'all sinned' in spite of the fact that for a time there was no law: even during that time sin was present in mankind and men actually sinned. The sentence **but, in the absence of the law, sin is not registered** *with full clarity* is added in acknowledgment of the fact that in the absence of the law sin is not the clearly defined thing, starkly shown up in its true character, that it becomes when the law is present (compare 3.20b; 4.15). By the Greek expression which we have rendered by 'is not registered' (AV and RV: 'is not imputed') Paul does not mean that sin is not registered in the sense of being charged to men's account, reckoned against them, imputed to them; for the fact that men died because they sinned in this period of the law's absence (v. 14) shows clearly enough that in this sense their sin was indeed registered. The expression must be understood in a relative sense. It is in comparison with what takes place when the law is present that it can be said that, in the law's absence, sin is not registered. Those who lived without the law were certainly not 'innocent' sinners – they were to blame for what they were and what they did. But, in comparison with the state of affairs which has obtained since the advent of the law, sin may be said to have been, in the law's absence, 'not registered', since it was not the fully apparent, sharply defined thing, which it became in its presence. It is only in the presence of the law, only in Israel and in the Church, that the full seriousness of sin is visible and the responsibility of the sinner stripped of every extenuating circumstance.

But death reigned from Adam to Moses expresses the truth that throughout the period between Adam and the giving of the law death reigned over mankind as a result of sin's presence; and **even over those who had not sinned in the same way as Adam, by transgression** *of a definite commandment* is added in order to bring out the fact that those over whom sin reigned throughout this period were actually men who, while they had indeed sinned and were punished for their sin, had not sinned after the likeness of Adam's transgression, that is, by disobeying a clear and definite divine commandment such as Adam had had (Gen 2.17) and Israel was subsequently to have in the law.

Now Adam is the type of him who was to come is a very clear hint of the comparison, the formal statement of which will not be completed until v. 18. The word translated 'type' (it is actually the Greek word from which the English 'type' derives) denotes a mark made by striking, an impression made by something, such an impression used in its turn as a mould to shape something else, hence a form, figure, pattern, example, and – a specialized use in biblical interpretation – a type in the sense of a person or thing prefiguring (according to God's design) a person or thing pertaining to the time of eschatological fulfilment. It is in this sense that it is used here. Adam in his universal effectiveness for ruin is the type which – in God's design – prefigures Christ in His universal effectiveness for salvation. It is important to note that it is precisely his transgression (which has just been mentioned) and its results which constitute him 'the type of him who was to come'.

The purpose of **15–17** is to drive home the vast dissimilarity between Christ and Adam, before the formal comparison between them is made in v. 18f, and so to preclude possible misunderstanding of the comparison. **But it is not a matter of 'As is the misdeed, so also is the gracious gift'** is the first of two statements of this dissimilarity (the second being v. 16a), each of which is followed by supporting argument. By 'the gracious gift' Paul may possibly have meant the undeserved gift of God which is Jesus Christ and His work for men, as a whole; but, in view of the presence of 'gift' of righteousness' in v. 17 and of 'justification', 'righteous' and 'through righteousness in vv. 18, 19 and 21, respectively, it seems more probable that he had specially in mind the gracious gift of a status of righteousness before God.

The statement of the dissimilarity between Adam's sin and God's gracious gift in v. 15a is now supported in v. 15b by an appeal to the infinitely superior effectiveness of the latter. **For if by the misdeed of the one the many died, much more have the grace of God and the gift *which has come* by the grace of the one man Jesus Christ abounded unto the many.** The definite articles in the Greek before 'one', 'many', 'one man', 'many' are not otiose, and should be retained in translation. The AV's omission of them is seriously misleading. The contrast is not between any one man and many but specifically between Adam and Christ, respectively, and 'the many', that is, the rest of mankind. The word 'many' is here used inclusively, not exclusively, being opposed to 'one' or 'some', not to 'all'. The 'much more' here rests on the fact that what stands over against the sin of Adam is nothing less than the grace of *God*. How could it be supposed that God is not infinitely stronger than man, and His grace not infinitely more effective than man's sin? By 'the gift *which has come* by the grace of the one man Jesus Christ' we should probably understand God's gift of a status of righteousness before Himself.

And it is not a matter of 'As is the result of one man's sinning, so is the gift' (v. 16a) is the second statement of the dissimilarity between Christ and Adam. The gift of God given through Jesus Christ is by no means a mere equivalent of the result of Adam's sin. In confirmation of his statement Paul adds: **for the judgment followed one misdeed and issued in condemnation, but the gracious gift followed many misdeeds and issued in justification.** This draws attention to two decisive differences between the judgment which followed Adam's misdeed and the gracious gift of God by Christ. The first concerns their external circumstances or contexts: the judgment was the consequence of but one misdeed, but the gift was God's answer to a numberless multitude of misdeeds, to all the accumulated sins of the centuries. (That one single misdeed should be answered by judgment, this is perfectly understandable: that the accumulated sins and guilt of all the ages should be answered by God's free gift, this is the miracle of miracles, utterly beyond human comprehension.) The second concerns the ends to which they lead: the judgment pronounced on Adam issues in condemnation for all men, but the gift of God issues in justification.

For if death reigned through the one man by the misdeed of the one, much more shall those who receive the abundance of grace and of the gift of righteousness reign in life through the one man Jesus Christ is better understood as further support for v. 16a than as supporting v. 16b. It is reminiscent of v. 15b both in structure and substance. The phrase 'by the misdeed of the one' exactly repeats part of v. 15b; but for 'the many died' of v. 15b is substituted the more vivid and forceful 'death reigned', and 'through the one man' and the corresponding 'through the one man Jesus Christ' are added in order to give extra emphasis to what is for Paul the one really important point of likeness (beyond their both being truly human) between Christ and Adam, namely, the fact of one man's action's being determinative of the existence of the many. Particularly interesting and suggestive is the way in which the substance of the main clause of v. 15b is re-expressed in the main clause of v. 17. The structure of the main clause of v. 15b was itself an inversion of the structure of the preceding subordinate clause: instead of making 'the many' the subject of the main clause, as of the subordinate (the conditional) clause, Paul made 'the grace of God and the gift *which has come* by the grace of the one man Jesus Christ' the subject, probably because he wanted at this point to emphasize the initiative of the divine grace. In the present verse there is once again an inversion of structure between the conditional and the main clauses; for now, instead of saying 'shall life reign' in correspondence to 'death reigned' in the conditional clause, Paul says 'shall those who receive the abundance of grace and of the gift of righteousness reign in life', which is surely to say very much more. The effectiveness and the unspeakable generosity of the divine grace are such that it will not merely bring about the replacement of the reign of death by the reign of life, but it will actually make those who receive its riches to become kings themselves, that is, to live the truly kingly life purposed by God for man. It may well be that Paul has taken up an old apocalyptic tradition, the idea of the reign of the saints, but if so, he has used it because he wanted at this point to bring out as vividly as possible the measureless generosity of God's grace and the inexpressible glory of God's purpose for man. The reference of the future 'shall ... reign' is to the eschatological fulfilment. Not yet do the recipients of God's grace reign: to suppose that they do or can is the illusion of a false piety (compare 1 Cor 4.8). But to recognize this is not at all to belittle the real splendour and wonder of what is already theirs.

In vv. 15–17 Paul has sought to make clear the vast dissimilarity between Christ and Adam which has to be firmly grasped if the comparison he has to make between them is not to be altogether misunderstood. He has shown that, apart from the formal similarity between the relation of Christ to all men and the relation of Adam to all men, there is the starkest imaginable dissimilarity between the two men. Having driven that home, he can now go on to make his comparison.

18–19. So then is used to introduce the formal statement of the comparison. This is understandable, since the preceding verses have been preparing the way for it, and it may be thought of as drawing them together. Like vv. 15a and 16a, v. 18 is, in the Greek, characterized by a highly condensed style, a kind of note-form, and has no verbs expressed. **as the result of one man's misdeed has been for all men condemnation** repeats the substance of the original 'as'-half of the sentence (v. 12); and **so also the result of one man's righteous conduct is for all men justification issuing in life** is the long-awaited completion of the interrupted comparison. The Greek word which we have translated 'one man's' in both halves of the verse (compare the AV) is taken by the RV as neuter, instead of masculine, and so as qualifying the Greek neuter nouns rendered in our translation by 'misdeed' and 'righteous conduct', respectively; but it is much more likely that it is masculine, as in its three occurrences in v. 17 and also in its two occurrences in v. 19, since the whole subsection is concerned with the relation of the one man Adam and the one man Christ to the many, while, apart from v. 16b, the fact that just one misdeed was decisive for ill is not stressed, unless it is in the present verse. We take it that by Christ's 'righteous conduct' Paul means not just His atoning death but the obedience of His life as a whole, His loving God with all His heart and soul and mind and strength, and His neighbour with complete sincerity, which is the righteous conduct which God's law requires. By 'justification' here Paul probably means not only the act of justification but also the condition resulting from it, namely, the condition of possessing a status of righteousness before God.

The repetition of 'for all men' gives rise to such questions as 'How can Paul speak of both "condemnation" and "justification" as resulting for *all* men?' and 'Does he really mean "all"?'. The important thing here is to remember that vv. 15–17 have specially stressed the vast superiority of Christ to Adam, and made it abundantly clear that Adam's sin and Christ's obedience are not on an equal footing and that there is no equilibrium between their respective consequences. Condemnation does indeed result for all men from Adam's sin, but this condemnation is no absolutely irreversible, eternal fact: on the contrary, Christ has indeed already begun the process of its reversal, and therefore the 'all men' of the subordinate clause, while it really does mean 'all men', is no eternally unalterable quantity. What then of the 'all men' of the main clause? It will be wise to take it thoroughly seriously as really meaning 'all', to understand the implication to be that what Christ has done He has really done for all men, that a status of righteousness the issue of which is life is truly offered to all, and all are to be summoned urgently to accept the proffered gift, but at the same time to allow that this clause does not foreclose the question whether in the end all will actually come to share it.

For as through the disobedience of the one man the many were made sinners, so also through the obedience of the one will the many be made righteous should probably be understood not as a mere repetition of the preceding verse in somewhat different words but as affording what may properly be regarded as a necessary clarification (note the initial 'For') of it. This verse may be seen as indicating an intermediate stage both between Adam's misdeed and the condemnation of the many and also between Christ's perfect fulfilment of God's requirements and the possession by the many of that righteous status which means eternal life at the last. If what was said about the last clause of v. 12 was right, we may assume that by 'were made sinners' in the former part of v. 19 Paul means that through Adam's misdeed all other men (Jesus alone excepted) were constituted sinners in the sense that, sin having once obtained entrance into human life through it, they all in their turns lived sinful lives. The many have not been condemned for someone else's transgression, namely, Adam's sin, but because, as a result of Adam's transgression, they have themselves in their own persons been sinners. The intermediate stage between Adam's transgression and the condemnation of the many is the sinning of the many in their own persons. There seems to be no justification for the confident assumption of numerous interpreters that Paul's 'as ... , so also ...' must imply that he thought that the ways in which Adam's sin and Christ's obedience were effective for other men must correspond exactly. All that is implied surely is that in both cases what one man does affects all other men and is determinative of their existence.

By 'will . . . be made righteous' in the latter part of v. 19 Paul means, we assume, that the many will be constituted righteous through Christ's obedience in the sense that, since God has in Christ identified Himself with sinners and taken upon Himself the burden of their sin, they will receive as a free gift from Him that status of righteousness which Christ's perfect obedience alone has deserved. Here there is no reference to any righteousness of life corresponding to the personal sinning by all. The adjective 'righteous' in v. 19b refers to status before God, not to righteousness of life (though Romans 6–8 will make it abundantly clear that it is unthinkable that those who know themselves to have received the gift of a righteous status before God should fail to strive in the strength of the Holy Spirit to live righteously). But the fact that the adjective is used here in the way that it is with reference to the many suggests that the justification-resulting-in-life accomplished for all men is not just a decision concerning them made, as it were, at a distance from them, in which they are dealt with generally in the mass, but involves the gift of a righteous status to each man as an individual person. It is this personal, individual matter, which, so it seems to us, is here intended to be brought out, and which may be regarded in the light of a kind of intermediate stage between Christ's obedience and the possession by the many of the status of righteousness which promises eternal life.

The use of 'disobedience' and 'obedience' in this verse makes explicit the fact that Adam's 'misdeed' and Christ's 'righteous conduct' are both to be understood in relation to the revealed will of God, the one as disobedience to it, the other as obedience. For Christ's obedience compare Phil 2.8. The term covers His whole life, not just His passion and death. As to the future 'will . . . be made', while it could refer to the final judgment, it is probably better understood, in agreement with 5.1 and 9, as referring to the present life of believers.

20. But the law came in as a new feature of the situation. The last nine words are an attempt to render one Greek word, a verb. It has been very widely assumed that it must here have a more or less disparaging sense, conveying some such idea as that the law came in as a sort of afterthought or to take its subordinate place. But the

Greek verb, while it probably does mean something like 'insinuate oneself in' or 'intrude' in Gal 2.4 (its only other occurrence in the New Testament), need not have a depreciatory significance. It can mean simply 'enter alongside', and the most natural way of understanding it here is surely to take it as referring to the undisputed fact that the law was given at a later date than that of Adam's fall, namely, in the time of Moses. To refer to this fact is not, in itself, to say anything depreciatory or otherwise about the worth of the law.

in order that the misdeed might increase states not, of course, the whole purpose of God in giving the law but an important part of it – an intermediate object, not the ultimate goal of the divine action. If sin, which was already present and disastrously active in mankind, though as yet nowhere clearly visible and defined, were ever to be decisively defeated and sinners forgiven in a way worthy of the goodness and mercy of God and recreated in newness of life, it was first of all necessary that sin should increase somewhere among men in the sense of becoming clearly manifest. So the law was given 'in order that the misdeed might increase', in order that in one people (for their own sake and also for the sake of all others) sin might be known as sin. But 'might increase' covers more than this; for, when the advent of the law makes sin increase in the sense of becoming manifest as sin, it also makes it increase in the sense of being made more sinful, since the law by showing men that what they are doing is contrary to God's will gives to their continuing to do it the character of conscious and wilful disobedience. It is possible that Paul also had in mind here (see on 7.5) a third sense in which sin would increase as a result of the coming of the law, namely, that it would actually increase in quantity, since the response of man's egotism to the law's attack upon it would be to seek to defend itself by all sorts of feverish activity including even (indeed, above all!) the attempt to exploit in its own interest the very law of God itself. But the purpose 'that the misdeed might increase' is only rightly understood, when it is recognized as a purpose of God, an intermediate purpose within (and not outside or contrary to) His merciful purpose for the salvation of men, an intermediate object which has to be fulfilled, if the ultimate goal expressed in v. 21 is to be achieved. When this is realized, it is possible to see that the law, even in its apparently negative and disastrous effects is, for Paul, the instrument of the mercy of God; and the theological justification for insisting on a depreciatory interpretation of the main verb of the sentence disappears.

but where sin increased: that is, in Israel to which God's gracious will has been clearly revealed in His law and to which His generosity and forbearance have been most signally shown. Nowhere else does the sin of man increase to such fearful proportions, nowhere else is it so exceedingly sinful, as in Israel (and, since the days of the apostles, in the Christian Church). Oppression and torture, for example, are monstrous evils when practised by pagans and atheists, but when practised by Jews or Christians they are infinitely more evil. But Paul no doubt had in mind the climax of sin's increasing, when the people of Israel, because of their stubborn refusal to submit to their law and their insistence on trying instead to exploit it for the satisfaction of their own egotism, rejected God's Messiah and handed Him over to the pagans to be crucified, and when the Gentile world in the person of Pilate responded to Israel's challenge by the deliberate prostitution of justice to expediency. It was then and there, above all, that grace superabounded in mercy for Israel and also for all other peoples.

21. in order that, as sin reigned in death, so also grace might reign through righteousness unto eternal life through Jesus Christ our Lord. The triumph of grace described in v. 20b was not itself the end of the matter. Its goal was the dispossession of the usurper sin and the replacement of its reign by the reign of grace. In expressing the divine purpose in the triumphant overflowing of grace, Paul has for the last time in this section made use of a comparison – this time comparing the never-ending reign of the divine grace with the passing reign of sin. Once again it is a comparison of things which in almost every respect are utterly dissimilar. By 'in death' is probably meant 'with death as its result and accompaniment'. For Paul, with Gen 2.17 not far from his mind, death is the result of sin, willed not by sin but by God. Death is not sin's soldier or servant or instrument, but the sign of God's authority, appointed by God as the inseparable, inescapable accompaniment of sin. In v. 14 it was death, not sin, which was said to have reigned. To the single phrase 'in death' in the 'as'-clause, there correspond three distinct phrases in the main clause: 'through righteousness', which indicates that it is through the gift to men of a righteous status before God that grace reigns; 'unto eternal life', which indicates the result of its reign; and 'through Jesus Christ our Lord', which indicates that it is through Christ that the reign of grace is both established and sustained. On the use of the last phrase see on v. 1.

It remains to draw attention to an implication of Paul's argument in vv. 12–21, which is highly significant and, if one reflects carefully upon it, surely profoundly encouraging.[1] The fact, which these verses clearly attest, that, in spite of the vast and altogether decisive dissimilarity between Christ and Adam, there is nevertheless a real likeness between them consisting in the correspondence of structure between the Christ-and-all-men relationship and the Adam-and-all-men relationship, a likeness which makes it possible and appropriate to compare them, to refer to Adam as the 'type' of Christ (v. 14) and to argue from the one relational structure to the other with a 'much more' (vv. 15 and 17) – this fact must surely mean that human existence as such cannot avoid bearing witness to the truth of Christ and of His saving work. Because the structure of the Adam-and-all-men relationship, that is, of mankind's solidarity in sin, corresponds to the structure of that other relationship, the concrete reality of human existence cannot help being a constant pointer to that other relationship of all men with Christ; and, since not even the deepest degradation can remove a human being from the solidarity of mankind, no man whatsoever can help being, simply by virtue of his being human, a type of Christ, in the sense that – however far this may be from his intention or consciousness – his life must needs be, in spite of its sin and wretchedness, an authentic witness to the truth and grace of Jesus Christ.

[1]Cf. K. Barth, *Christ and Adam: man and humanity in Romans 5*, English translation, Edinburgh, 1956, to which this paragraph is much indebted.

V.2. A LIFE CHARACTERIZED BY SANCTIFICATION
(6.1–23)

On the main burden of this section there is widespread agreement, though there is plenty of controversy about some of the details. Paul is here concerned to insist that justification has inescapable moral implications and to think to accept it without at the same time striving to lay hold on sanctification would be a profane absurdity. The word 'sanctification' may be taken as the key-word of the section, though it does not occur until v. 19 (compare v. 22).

The importance of this section for the understanding of the theological basis of the Christian's moral obligation is apparent. But it must not be forgotten that as a general account of that basis it is incomplete, since, containing no explicit reference to the work of the Spirit (Paul's plan being to treat of the gift of the Spirit in a later section), it lacks an essential element of such an account. While Romans 6 makes the point that the life promised for the man who is righteous by faith is a life characterized by sanctification, it is not in this chapter by itself but in the whole of 6.1–8.39 that the meaning of the believer's sanctification is set forth.

(i) *Dead to sin, alive to God*
(6.1–14)

¹What then are we to say? Are we to continue in sin, in order that grace may increase? ²God forbid! Seeing that we have died to sin, how shall we still live in it? ³Or are you ignorant of the fact that all of us who have been baptized into Christ Jesus have been baptized into his death? ⁴So then we have been buried together with him through baptism into *his* death, in order that, as Christ was raised from the dead through the glory of the Father, so we also might walk in newness of life. ⁵For if we have been conformed to his death, we are certainly also to be *conformed* to his resurrection. ⁶And we know that our old self was crucified with *him*, that the body of sin might be destroyed, so that we might cease to be slaves of sin. ⁷For the man who has died has been justified from sin. ⁸But if we have died with Christ, we believe we are also to live with him: ⁹and we know that Christ, now that he has been raised from the dead, dies no more, *and* death exercises lordship over him no more. ¹⁰For the death which he

died he died to sin once for all; but the life which he lives he lives to God. ¹¹So then recognize *the truth* that you yourselves are dead to sin but alive to God in Christ Jesus. ¹²Stop, then, allowing sin to reign *unopposed* in your mortal selves in such a way that you obey the self's desires, ¹³and stop placing your members at the disposal of sin as tools of unrighteousness; instead, place yourselves at the disposal of God as being alive from the dead and your members at God's disposal as tools of righteousness. ¹⁴For sin shall no longer be lord over you; for you are not under the law, but under grace.

In v. 1 Paul refers to a false inference which he knows some people will be inclined to draw from what he has said in 5.20b, namely, that we should go on sinning so that grace may be multiplied all the more, and rejects it emphatically. Verses 2–11, the purpose of which is to justify his repudiation of this false inference, are all concerned with the Christian's death and resurrection with Christ; and the key to their right understanding is the recognition that there are different senses in which our death and resurrection with Christ may properly be spoken of, and that these require to be carefully distinguished. In more than one sense the Christian has already died and been raised with Christ; but in another sense his dying and being raised with Christ is a matter of present obligation, something which ought now to be in process of being fulfilled, and in yet another sense it lies ahead of him as eschatological promise. Paul's thought in these verses moves between these different senses of death and resurrection with Christ. Verses 12–13 indicate that the conclusion which the Roman Christians are to draw from the preceding argument and, in particular, from that fact which they have been bidden in v. 11 to recognize and take seriously, is that they are under obligation to stop allowing sin to reign unopposed over their lives and to revolt in the name of their rightful ruler, God, against sin's usurping rule. The first part of v. 14 supports the imperatives of the two preceding verses by promising that sin will no longer have absolute lordship over the Roman Christians so as to have them helpless in its power; and the latter part of the verse adds in support of the promise an assurance that they are not under the law, that is (as we understand it), not under God's condemnation pronounced by the law, but under God's gracious favour.

1. What then are we to say? introduces an indication of a false inference which Paul recognizes could be drawn from what he has said and which he wants to repudiate before stating his own understanding of the matter. **Are we to continue in sin, in order that grace may increase?** looks back to 5.20b ('but where sin increased, grace superabounded'), which Paul will not have exploited as an excuse for further sinning.

2. For **God forbid!** see on 3.4. **Seeing that we have died to sin, how shall we still live in it?** is clearly of fundamental importance in this section; but there is far from being agreement about its interpretation. In our view, we shall never do justice to Paul's meaning in this verse or to his thought in this chapter as a whole, unless we recognize that in his understanding of things there are four quite different senses in which believers die to sin and, corresponding to them, four different senses in which they are raised up, and these different senses must be carefully distinguished but at the same time understood in the closest relation to one another. They may be listed as follows:

(i) *the juridical sense.* They died to sin in God's sight, when Christ died on the cross for them. This is a matter of God's decision. His decision to take their sin upon Himself in the person of His dear Son involves the decision to see Christ's death as died for them and so to see them as having died in His death. Similarly they may be said to have been raised up in His resurrection on the third day, since His resurrection was, according to God's merciful will, for them. Compare Col 3.1ff, where Christians are exhorted to seek the things above where Christ is living His exalted life, because they have died and their life, that is, their real life, the life which God mercifully regards as their life, is hidden with Christ in God, is in ᶠact the sinless life which Christ (who according to Col 3.4 is their life) lives for them.

(ii) *the baptismal sense.* They died to sin, and were raised up, in their baptism, which was at the same time both their ratification of their own acceptance of God's decision on their behalf (to regard Christ's death for their sins as their death and His risen life as their life) and also God's bestowal of His seal and pledge of the fact that His decision really concerned them individually, personally.[1]

---

[1] Looking at an ecclesiastical situation in which the administration of baptism is commonly quite separated from the believer's own ratification of his decision of faith,

(iii) *the moral sense.* They are called, and have been given the freedom, to die daily and hourly to sin by the mortification of their sinful natures, and to rise daily and hourly to newness of life in obedience to God. Those who have learned through the gospel message the truth of God's gracious decision on their behalf are under obligation to strive now with all their heart and strength to approximate more and more in their actual concrete living to that which in God's decision of justification they already are.

(iv) *the eschatological sense.* They will die to sin finally and irreversibly when they actually die, and will – equally finally and irreversibly – at Christ's coming be raised up to the resurrection life.

In the course of the following verses Paul moves freely between these different senses, implying all the time both the distinctness of these different dyings and risings with Christ and also their real and essential relatedness. The question whether in the present verse 'we have died' was intended in sense (i) or sense (ii) is not of vital importance. That Paul was already thinking particularly of baptism is possible, but it seems to us on the whole rather more probable that the sense intended was sense (i).

3. Or are you ignorant of the fact that implies that the author thinks that the Christians in Rome are likely to know at least the truth stated in the rest of this verse – perhaps also some of the doctrine which he sets out in the following verses as following from it. The use of this formula here has special significance, since the Roman church was not founded by Paul and has not as yet even been visited by him.

It is unlikely that the choice of 'into Christ', rather than 'into the name of Christ' or 'in the name of Christ', is particularly significant either here in **all of us who have been baptized into Christ Jesus** or in Gal 3.27; for in both places the context requires a purely factual statement and this is immediately followed by a further statement which goes beyond it and offers an interpretation of the objective fact. We take it that 'be baptized into Christ Jesus' here is synonymous with 'be baptized into the name of Christ Jesus' and 'be baptized in the name of Christ

we might perhaps feel inclined to break the unity of sense (ii) into two distinct senses, one sacramental and the other relative to conversion; but, as far as the exegesis of Romans is concerned, this inclination must surely be resisted.

Jesus', and that all that Paul wishes to convey here is the simple fact that the persons concerned have received Christian baptism. But at the same time the expression which he uses implies (as do also the expressions involving the use of the word 'name') – what was no doubt generally acknowledged throughout the primitive Church – that baptism has to do with a decisive personal relationship between the individual believer and Christ.

have been baptized into his death makes the point – which Paul apparently expects the Christians in Rome to accept without demur as a truth already well known to them – that the relationship to Christ with which baptism has to do includes, in particular, a relationship to His death. How then did Paul understand baptism and the Christian's relationship to Christ and, in particular, to His death to be related to each other? The view that Paul was deeply influenced in his understanding of baptism (and indeed of the believer's relationship to Christ as a whole) by the contemporary pagan mystery cults has been fairly widely held. It was characteristic of these cults that a feature of central importance was the dying and rising again of the god worshipped and that the initiation rites were supposed to achieve the union of the person being initiated with the god. But, in spite of certain obvious resemblances, there are such significant differences between baptism as understood by Paul and the essential characteristics of these cults, as to make it extremely unlikely that Paul ever conceived baptism as a mystery of this sort. To mention just some of the differences – while the mysteries were concerned with union with a nature-deity, baptism had to do with the relationship of the believer to the historical event of God's saving deed in Christ; while the dying and rising of a nature-deity were conceived as something recurring again and again, the historical event to which baptism pointed was a once for all, unique event; while the mysteries were inclusive (one could be initiated into several without offence, since they were recognized as varying forms of the same fundamental, age-old religion), baptism was altogether exclusive; while the mystery rites were magical, setting forth symbolically the god's experiences and being thought of as effecting the union with the god which they depicted, in the case of baptism the symbolism, if it was conscious at all (and as far as Paul is concerned it is far from certain that it was), was clearly not of decisive importance, since, while Rom 6.4 and Col 2.12 might suggest the thought that the Christian's immersion in the water of baptism portrays his burial with Christ (and his emergence from it his resurrection with Christ), Paul could also write. '[we] were all made to drink of one Spirit' (1 Cor 12.13) and '[you] did put on Christ' (Gal 3.27) with reference to baptism, and a mechanically objective view of baptism is ruled out by such a passage as 1 Cor 10.1–12. Another view, in most respects altogether different from the one which we have just been considering but nevertheless agreeing with it in attributing to Paul a magical understanding of baptism as effecting mechanically what it signifies, is that put forward by Albert Schweitzer. According to him, Paul believed that 'in the moment when' a man 'receives baptism, the dying and rising again of Christ takes place in him without any co-operation, or exercise of will or thought, on his part'.[1]

What then did Paul mean by his claim that Christian baptism is essentially baptism into Christ's death? Not, surely, that it actually relates the person concerned to Christ's death, since this relationship is already an objective reality before baptism takes place, having been brought into being by God's gracious decision, which is implied by the second 'for us' of 5.8; but that it points to, and is a pledge of, that death which the person concerned has already died – in God's sight. On God's side, it is the sign and pledge that the benefits of Christ's death for all men really do apply to this individual in particular, while, on man's side, it is the outward ratification (we are thinking of course of adult baptism here) of the human decision of faith, of the response already begun to what God has done in Christ. That Paul thought of it (in its aspect of divine pledge) as an automatic, mechanical, magical guarantee is impossible in view of 1 Cor 10. But it does not therefore follow that he thought of it as a 'mere sign'. It seems likely that he thought of Christ Himself as present and active personally in freedom and in power in the visible word of baptism as well as in the spoken word of the preached message (compare, for example 10.14: ' ... And how could they believe in one whom they had not heard? And how could they hear without a preacher?' and the comment on that verse).

[1] *Paul and his Interpreters*, London 1912, p. 225f.

4. So then we have been buried together with him through baptism into *his* death draws out and clarifies the meaning of the last clause of v. 3. Through the baptism into Christ's death to which it referred we have been buried with Him. By referring to burial here Paul has expressed in the most decisive and emphatic way the truth of our having died with Christ; for burial is the seal set to the fact of death – it is when a man's relatives and friends leave his body in a grave and return home without him that the fact that he no longer shares their life is exposed with inescapable conclusiveness. So the death which we died in baptism was a death ratified and sealed by burial, an altogether unambiguous death. Baptism, according to Paul, while (as we have seen) it is no magical rite effecting mechanically that which it signifies, is no empty sign but a decisive event by which a particular man is powerfully and unequivocally claimed by God as a beneficiary of His saving deed in Christ.

in order that introduces a statement of the purpose (the reference is to God's purpose) of our burial with Christ in baptism. **as Christ was raised from the dead through the glory of the Father** serves to characterize the action denoted by the clause which follows (and which expresses the substance of the purpose) as corresponding to Christ's being raised from the dead. By 'glory' here is meant no doubt the power of God gloriously exercised. God's use of His power is always glorious, and His use of it to raise His Son from the dead is a specially clear manifestation of His glory. In **so we also might walk in newness of life** the reference is to the moral life. The use of 'walk' to denote a man's conduct occurs frequently in the New Testament: it reflects a Hebrew usage common in the Old Testament. The phrase 'in newness of life' indicates the quality of the conduct which is to be ours. The distinction between the two most common words for 'new' in Greek is by no means always observed; but, where it is, one of them means 'new' simply in the sense of not having been there before, while the other describes that which is new and fresh in comparison with other things, so different from the usual, superior to the old. There is no doubt that the proper significance of the latter word attaches to 'newness' here. The thought of the transcendent worth of the new way of life, as compared with the old, is present. The second of the two Greek words for 'new' is in the New Testament particularly associated with the hope of God's final renewal of His creation; and the newness of life, of which Paul speaks here, is a foretaste of that final renewal.

In this verse there is a movement from the thought of death (burial) in baptism (that is, in sense (ii) as listed above on v. 2) to that of resurrection in the moral sense (that is, sense (iii) in our list), the former being said to have taken place in order that the latter might take place. It is to be noted that Paul does not speak here of both death and resurrection in baptism and of both death and resurrection in the moral sense, but of death (burial) alone in the former case and of resurrection alone in the latter. Paul here (and also in v. 5) sets forth the twofold fact of our dying and being raised in baptism by means of the single term death (burial) and the twofold fact of our ethical dying to sin and being raised to newness of life by means of the single term resurrection, because – we suggest – at this point he particularly wants to bring out the positive content of the new obedience. While he thought of Christians as both dying and being raised in each of the senses which we listed in the notes on v. 2, Paul, it would seem, tended to appropriate the language of dying to senses (i) and (ii), and that of resurrection to senses (iii) and (iv).

5. For if we have been conformed to his death, we are certainly also to be *conformed* to his resurrection. This seems to us the most probable meaning of what is generally agreed to be very puzzling Greek. This interpretation involves taking the Greek noun, which the RV renders by 'likeness', in another sense which it can have, namely, 'form'; understanding the dative (this noun is in the dative case in the Greek) to be, not instrumental (as the RV understands it), but dependent on the adjective represented in the RV by 'united with' (which therefore does not require 'him' to be supplied, as it is in the RV, to depend on it); and reckoning that 'become united with (or 'assimilated to') the form of' is synonymous with 'become conformed unto' in Phil 3.10 (compare 'to be conformed to' in Rom 8.29). We thus get a sense which perfectly suits the context. The verse supports v. 4: hence its initial 'For'. If in baptism we have become conformed to Christ's death, we are certainly also to (or perhaps 'we shall certainly also') be conformed in our moral life to His resurrection.

6. And we know that introduces another fact relevant to the argument. By **our old self** is meant the whole of our fallen human nature, the whole self in its fallenness. It is the whole man, not just a part of him, that comes under God's condemnation, and that died in God's sight in Christ's death. For the expression (literally, 'our old man') compare Eph 4.22–24; Col 3.9–10. **was crucified with *him*.** The reference to crucifixion is a stark reminder – the harsh word 'cross' had not yet been rendered mellow by centuries of Christian piety! – of the vast distance separating what Paul is saying about dying and being raised with Christ from the mysticism of the contemporary mystery-cults. Our fallen human nature was crucified with Christ in our baptism in the sense that in baptism we received the sign and seal of the fact that by God's gracious decision it was, in His sight, crucified with Christ on Golgotha. It is certainly not implied that the old self no longer exists: it lingers on in the believer, who has in this life ever to be putting into effect on the moral level, by daily dying to sin, the death which in God's merciful decision and in the sacrament of baptism he has already died.

In **that the body of sin might be destroyed** 'the body of sin' must surely mean the whole man as controlled by sin. Thus 'the body of sin' and 'our old self' are identical. But does the clause as a whole refer to what happened in baptism or to the moral life of Christians? At first sight it is tempting to take it in the latter way, and so as parallel to 'in order that ... we also might walk in newness of life' in v. 4 and – as we understand it – 'we are certainly also to be *conformed* to his resurrection' in v. 5. But the reference of this clause to the moral life seems scarcely compatible with the fact that the old self remains very much alive in the Christian, and, even if this objection could be got over by giving to the Greek word which we have rendered 'might be destroyed' the weaker sense of 'might be disabled', it would still surely rob the second purpose clause (which follows) of much of its forcefulness. It is much better to take the present clause to refer to what takes place in baptism. So understood, it is by no means redundant, since a man was not immediately killed by being crucified, but was indeed crucified, in order that he might die ('be destroyed') hours, even days, later. So there is real point in saying, whether with reference to our baptism or with reference to that which lies behind it, of which it is the sign and seal, that our sinful self was crucified with

Christ in order that it might be destroyed. With **so that we might cease to be slaves of sin** we are definitely on the ethical level. In baptism our old selves were crucified that they might be destroyed (in the sense we have indicated), in order that in our practical daily living we might cease to be slaves to sin.

7. For the man who has died has been justified from sin. It is quite likely that these words are consciously reminiscent of a well-known Rabbinic legal principle, but it is not at all clear that Paul is actually appealing to it to clinch his argument. In the sense that 'death pays all debts' this principle is valid only in relation to a human court: it is certain that Paul did not think that a man's death atoned for his sins in relation to God, or that a dead man was no longer accountable to God for his sins. The Rabbinic principle is, in fact, singularly inappropriate as a confirmation of what has just been said. It is therefore much more likely that Paul, though quite probably aware of the use of similar language by the Rabbis, was using the words in his own sense, and that he meant them not as a general statement about dead men, but as a specific theological statement that the man, who has died with Christ in baptism in the sense that in his baptism he has received the sign and seal of his having died with Christ in God's decision, has been justified from his sin. To state this fact is indeed to confirm v. 6; for it is the fact that God has justified us that is the firm basis of that new freedom to resist the bondage of sin in our practical living, to which the last clause of v. 6 refers.

8. In **But if we have died with Christ, we believe that we are also to live with him** the function of 'we believe that' is not in any way to weaken the following statement by suggesting that it is made with something less than certainty but rather to emphasize it by indicating the personal and inward commitment of Paul and his fellow-Christians to its truth. The Christian firmly believes that, since (the 'if' here is used in the sense 'if, as is surely true' or 'since') he has in God's sight died with Christ, he is to live his present life with Christ in the power of His resurrection. While the reference of 'we are also to live with him' to the Christian's moral life is primary (the structure of the argument makes this clear), it is possible that the thought of the eschatological fulfilment of the life already begun is also present.

9. and we know that introduces another consideration relevant to what has just been said. This further consideration is stated in vv. 9 and 10. Being concerned with the true nature of Christ's resurrection, it throws light upon the meaning of 'we are also to live with him' in v. 8. **Christ, now that he has been raised from the dead, dies no more.** Christ was not raised, like Lazarus, to a mere extension of a natural life, only to succumb once more to death; for His resurrection was the final resurrection uniquely anticipated. Nor was His resurrection like that of a nature-deity, part of an endlessly recurring cycle of death and renewal. **and death exercises lordship over him no more** reinforces the preceding statement. For a brief period death really did exercise lordship over him (this is implied by the 'no more'), but now it has no power over Him, no hold upon Him.

10. **For the death which he died he died to sin once for all; but the life which he lives he lives to God** explains v. 9. The reason why death has no hold on Christ any more is that the death He died was death to sin once for all, an altogether decisive and unrepeatable event, while the life He lives now is life to God, and (because it is to God) eternal. The expression 'die to sin' was used in v. 2, but it is now used in a quite different sense (though in both places 'to sin' represents a Greek dative of the person affected, which may be translated 'to sin', that is, in relation to sin). What is actually meant here by 'dying to sin' has to be understood from what Paul says elsewhere about the relation of Christ's death to sin (for example, 3.24–26; 4.25; 5.6–8; 8.3; 1 Cor 15.3; 2 Cor 5.21; Gal 3.13). He died to sin, that is, He affected sin by His dying, in that, as the altogether sinless One who identified Himself with sinful men, He bore for them the full penalty of their sins and so – in the pregnant sense in which the words are used in 8.3 – 'condemned sin in the flesh'. But at this point Paul is not concerned to draw out the meaning of Christ's death as death to sin, but simply to stress its once for all character as an event which was so utterly decisive and final that there can be no question of its being repeated. For 'once for all' compare Heb 7.27; 9.12, 26, 28; 10.10; 1 Pet 3.18 (also the use of 'one' in Heb 10.12 and 14). To this once for all quality of Christ's death to sin corresponds the fact that His risen life is lived 'to God'. Once more we have a Greek dative of the person affected. His risen life belongs pre-eminently to God, and is therefore everlasting.

Verses 9 and 10, then, together do not just state the reason for our belief that we are to live with Christ: they also throw a flood of light on the character of this new life which is to be ours; for they reveal the transcendent security of its basis in the absolute finality of His death to sin and in His risen life which He lives to God, which is for ever beyond the reach of death.

With **11** there is a transition to exhortation, to the drawing of practical conclusions. **So then recognize *the truth* that you yourselves are dead to sin but alive to God in Christ Jesus.** F. F. Bruce's paraphrase, 'live as though you had already entered the resurrection life', fails to give to the verb which the AV and RV render by 'reckon' the sense which it has here. It does not denote here any sort of pretending ('as though'), but a deliberate and sober judgment on the basis of the gospel, a reasoning which accepts as its norm what God has done in Christ: recognize that the truth of the gospel means that you are . . . . Thus to see oneself as one is revealed to oneself by the gospel and to understand and take utterly seriously what one sees is a first step – and a decisively important one – on the way of obedience. The Christians in Rome are 'dead to sin but alive to God' in sense (i) of the notes on v. 2.

The formula 'in Christ', which occurs here, has been very variously explained.[1] It will suffice here to say that, in our view, where the phrase or an equivalent really is a special formula involving the idea of, in some sense, *being* in Christ (it should be remembered that there are occurrences of this phrase, where this idea is not involved, as, for example, in 3.24; 15.17 and probably 8.2), it is best explained in accordance with our understanding of Paul's references to our dying and being raised with Christ. We are in Christ in that God has graciously decided to see us in Him; we are in Christ through our baptism, in that in it we have received God's attestation of His decision to see us in Christ; we have to 'put on . . . Christ' (13.14), striving constantly to abide in Him in our daily lives; we shall one day be in Christ in the security of the final and perfect fulfilment of God's purposes. It is in the first of these senses that 'in Christ Jesus' is used here.

12. Stop, then, allowing sin to reign *unopposed* in your mortal selves. The conclusion to be drawn ('then') from the fact which

[1]For a fuller discussion see the author's ICC *Romans*, pp. 315–16, 833–5.

they have just been called upon to recognize and take seriously is not that, secure in God's gracious decision for them, they may go on contentedly living just as they always have lived, but rather that now they must fight – they must not let sin go on reigning unchallenged over their daily lives, but must revolt in the name of their rightful ruler, God, against sin's usurping rule. Some would limit the reference of the Greek word for 'body', which we have represented by 'selves', to the physical body, but it is better to understand Paul to mean by it the whole man in his fallenness (compare 'the body of sin' in v. 6). It is not only the physical body that is mortal: the whole man, as the fallen human being that he is, is subject to death. And it is over the whole of our fallen nature, not just over our bodies, that sin has established its rule. So it is in the whole field of our life as the fallen human beings we are that we are called to resist sin's dominion.

in such a way that you obey the self's desires is added as a reminder of the consequences which would result from their allowing sin to go on reigning unopposed in their mortal selves. If they do not obey the command Paul has just given, then they will be driven hither and thither in obedience to the lusts of their fallen nature, lusts which – on the view taken above concerning the meaning of the Greek word for 'body' in this verse – will include not just what we would call 'bodily lusts', but also such things as the will to dominate other people, in fact all the desires of the ego in its state of rebellion against God.

13. In **and stop placing your members at the disposal of sin as tools of unrighteousness** 'member' is used to translate a word which properly denotes a limb but came to be employed in a wider sense covering organs as well as limbs (so, for example, Paul uses it in 1 Cor 12.14ff of eyes and ears). It is here perhaps used in an even wider sense to include any natural capacity, so that there is little difference between 'your members' here and 'yourselves' later in the verse. We might perhaps say that 'members' denotes the self seen under the aspect of its capacities. Whether the word represented by 'tools' is rightly so translated here or whether it should be given its particular sense of 'weapons' is a moot question. Pauline usage favours the latter interpretation, but, in view of the references to the service of slaves in this chapter, the former is perhaps rather more appropriate to the context (in the ancient world a slave could be regarded as 'a living tool'). Paul continues: **instead, place yourselves at the disposal of God as being alive from the dead and your members at God's disposal as tools of righteousness.** In contrast with the negative command of the first half of the verse, the positive command is given a double formulation – presumably because Paul wanted to include a specific reference to the fact of the Roman Christians' new life, already mentioned in v. 11.

The first part of **14** is difficult. Not surprisingly the sentence which we have translated **For sin shall no longer be lord over you** has been variously interpreted. The view that it is a promise that those whom Paul is addressing will never again yield to sin may be set aside as altogether improbable, since Paul has elsewhere made it abundantly clear that he was under no such illusion about himself or his fellow-Christians. The suggestion that the future indicative with negative particle which the RV renders 'shall not have dominion over' was intended in an imperatival sense ('is not to . . . '), though attractive at first sight, should be rejected on the grounds that the sentence would then be a lame repetition of the substance of v. 12, which would be quite out of place at this point, and that the conjunction 'For' would be inappropriate. Unsatisfactory too is the suggestion that 'sin' refers only to that fundamental sin which consists in the attempt to use the law to establish one's own righteousness, and not material sin, that is, sinful acts, for there is no support in the context for limiting the meaning of 'sin' in this way. But we are on the way to a satisfactory explanation, when we recognize, on the one hand, that here (as often in this chapter) Paul is thinking of sin as a power, that is, personifying it, and, on the other hand, that the verb used is to be understood in its primary sense, 'be lord of'. The sentence may then be interpreted as a promise that sin will no more be their lord, because another lord has taken possession of them, namely, Christ (it is instructive to compare the use of the same verb in 14.9, where it is represented by 'become Lord of'). That does not mean that sin will have no power at all over them (Paul can state the fact of sin's continuing hold on Christians with relentless frankness, if our understanding of 7.14 is correct); but it does mean that they will never again be left helpless in sin's power – unless, of course, they wantonly turn their backs on the Lord who has redeemed them (an unconditional promise is hardly in question). Though sin will still have a hold upon them until they die (in the natural sense), they will henceforth, as subjects of Christ over whom He has decisively reasserted His authority, be free to rebel against sin's usurped power. So understood the sentence makes good sense as support ('For') for the imperatives of vv. 12 and 13.

for you are not under the law, but under grace is widely taken to mean that the Old Testament law has been superseded, its authority having been abolished for believers. This, it may be admitted, would be a plausible interpretation, if this sentence stood by itself. But, since it stands in a document which contains such things as 3.31; 7.12, 14a; 8.4; 13.8–10, and in which the law is referred to more than once as God's law (7.22, 25; 8.7) and is appealed to again and again as authoritative, such a reading of it is extremely unlikely. The fact that 'under the law' is contrasted with 'under grace' suggests the likelihood that Paul is here thinking, not of the law generally, but of the law as condemning sinners; for, since 'grace' denotes God's undeserved favour, the natural opposite to 'under grace' would seem to be 'under God's disfavour or condemnation'. And the suggestion that the meaning of the sentence is that believers are not under God's condemnation pronounced by the law but under His undeserved favour receives strong confirmation from 8.1 ('So then there is now no condemnation for those who are in Christ Jesus'), which seems to be closely connected with this half-verse through 7.1–6. Moreover, this interpretation explains the 'for' with which this part of the verse begins. The fact that we have been set free from God's condemnation and are now objects of His gracious favour confirms the truth of the promise that sin shall no more be lord over us. The man who knows that he is free from God's condemnation finds himself beginning to be free to resist the tyranny of sin with boldness and resolution.

(ii) *A choice between masters*
(6.15–23)

¹⁵**What then? Are we to sin, because we are not under the law but under grace? God forbid!** ¹⁶**Do you not know that, whoever it is at**

whose disposal you place yourselves as slaves to obey him, you are the slaves of the one whom you obey, whether it be of sin with death as the consequence or of obedience with righteousness as the consequence? [17]But thanks be to God that you, who once were slaves of sin, have from the heart become obedient to the pattern of teaching to which you were delivered, [18]and having been set free from sin you have been made slaves to righteousness. [19](I have to put this in a very human way because of the weakness of your flesh.) For just as you once placed your members as slaves at the disposal of uncleanness and lawlessness for *a life of* lawlessness, so now place your members as slaves at the disposal of righteousness for sanctification. [20]For when you were slaves of sin, you were free in relation to righteousness. [21]What fruit did you then obtain? Things of which you now are ashamed! For their end is death. [22]But now, having been set free from sin and made slaves to God, you obtain your fruit unto sanctification, and as the end eternal life. [23]For the wage which sin pays is death, but the free gift which God gives is eternal life in Christ Jesus our Lord.

This subsection underlines the fact that the question of a man's being free in the sense of having no master, of not being a slave at all, simply does not arise. Only two alternatives present themselves, to have sin for one's master or to have God (this second alternative is variously expressed in these verses); there is no third possibility. The Roman Christians have been freed from the slavery of sin and made slaves of God; and they must act accordingly and not try to combine incompatibles. Paul is aware that the figure of slavery is unworthy, inadequate and apt to be grievously misleading, as a way of indicating the believer's relation to God. Hence his apology in v. 19a. But, in spite of the fact that in so many respects it is altogether inappropriate, he cannot dispense with it, because it does express the total belongingness, total obligation and total accountability which characterize the life under grace, with a vigour and vividness which no other image seems able to equal.

15. What then? Are we to sin, because we are not under the law but under grace? God forbid! recalls v. 1. But the false conclusions dealt with in the two verses are not the same. Whereas in v. 1. the false inference from the truth stated in 5.20 was that one should continue in sin so as to make grace abound still more, here the false inference from the truth stated in v. 14b is that sinful acts do not matter any more as far as we are concerned. The pains Paul is at in the following verses to drive his point home indicate that the danger of such misunderstanding was not merely hypothetical.

16. Do you not know that, whoever it is at whose disposal you place yourselves as slaves to obey him, you are the slaves of the one whom you obey, whether it be of sin with death as the consequence or of obedience with righteousness as the consequence? By means of this somewhat cumbersome question Paul makes two main points: (i) that the Christians of Rome are slaves of that to which they yield themselves in obedience; and (ii) that they have only two alternatives from which to choose, being the slaves of sin or being the slaves of obedience. The clumsiness with which (i) is expressed is clearly due to Paul's concern to make inescapably clear the fact that obedience involves yielding oneself as a slave to that which one obeys. It is probable that by obedience here Paul means willing obedience such as that contemplated in the deliberative question 'Are we to sin . . .?' in the preceding verse and not the unwilling yielding to sin of those who are strenuously resisting it (such as is depicted in 7.14ff). Point (i) is the answer to the question in v. 15: for those who are under grace committing sinful acts does indeed matter, for to commit such acts willingly is to yield oneself as a slave to sin. With regard to (ii), two things should be noticed. First, 'with death as the consequence' and 'with righteousness as the consequence' (literally, simply 'unto death' and 'unto righteousness', respectively) amount to two subsidiary statements indicating that these slaveries lead in the end, the one to death, the other to final justification. Secondly, the use of 'obedience' as opposite to 'sin' here is surprising. In vv. 18, 19 and 20 'righteousness' is used as the opposite to 'sin' (in v. 19 'uncleanness and lawlessness'); and it is easy to understand that 'righteousness' is effectively ruled out here by Paul's decision to use it (in its sense of 'justification') as opposite to 'death'. However, in vv. 13, 22 and 23 the opposition is between 'sin' and 'God'. Why then did not Paul put 'God' here? To this the correct answer would seem to be that, while the fundamental decision for Paul was indeed between being slaves to sin and being slaves to God, he wanted at this point specially to emphasize the thought of obedience (to God), because he wanted to make his readers see that to be under God's grace is to be under obligation to obey Him.

The burden of the verse as a whole may be expressed in some such way as this: The question of a man's being free in the sense of having no master at all simply does not arise. The only alternatives open to him are to have sin, or to have God, as his master (the man who imagines he is free, because he acknowledges no god but his own ego, is deluded; for the service of one's own ego is the very essence of the slavery of sin). The one alternative has as its end death, but the other life with God.

17–18. But thanks be to God that you, who once were slaves of sin, have from the heart become obedient to the pattern of teaching to which you were delivered, and having been set free from sin you have been made slaves to righteousness. So translated, this is an intelligible thanksgiving to God, fitting the thought of the context perfectly well. Two false clues have often bedevilled the exegesis of v. 17. One is the notion that the Greek word represented by 'pattern' (it is the same word as was represented by 'type' in 5.14, in connexion with which we explained its varying senses) must mean here 'type' in the sense of one type (of Christian teaching) over against others. But the word must here denote a mould which imparts its shape to something else. What is being said is that the persons addressed have obeyed from the heart (not merely formally but with inward commitment) that mould consisting of teaching (concerning the way of life demanded by the gospel) which is to shape their lives. The other false clue is the assumption that the verb 'deliver', since it is here used in association with the word 'teaching', must bear its special sense of 'deliver' or 'transmit' tradition. But the verb must here be understood in relation to the figure of the transfer of a slave from one master to another. Those who are being addressed were delivered up to the pattern of teaching as slaves to a new master. Paul perhaps has in mind their baptism as the time when this transfer took place. What is emphatically underlined in the latter part of v. 17 is the importance of obedience in the Christian life – the fact that to be under God's grace involves the obligation to obey Him. In clarification of 'having been set free from sin' it must be said that they have already been set free from sin in the sense that they have been transferred from sin's possession to the possession of a new master, and so are now in a position to resist sin's continuing hold upon them, though that continuing hold is still real and serious. The positive relationship to the new master is forcefully expressed by the words, 'you have been made slaves to righteousness'.

19a. (I have to put this in a very human way because of the weakness of your flesh.) Paul is clearly aware of the fact that the figure of slavery is inadequate, unworthy and frighteningly liable to mislead as a way of speaking about the believer's relation to righteousness (that is, righteousness in its moral sense) – that is why he apologizes for the all too human nature of his language, as soon as he has made the statement that they have been enslaved to righteousness. (There are similar apologies in 3.5; 1 Cor 9.8; Gal 3.15.) In almost every respect the image is thoroughly inappropiate for Paul's purpose. The Christian's relation to righteousness, to obedience (v. 16), to God (v. 22), is, of course, not at all the unjust, humiliating, degrading, grievous thing which slavery has always been. On the contrary, it is 'perfect freedom' or, as John Chrysostom put it, 'better than any freedom'. But because of their human weakness Paul cannot dispense with the figure of slavery, harsh and unworthy though it is. They are prone – the whole passage reflects his consciousness of the fact – to forget the obligations involved in being under grace. But in this they are only like all other believers, so that Paul's figure seems no less necessary today; for it is doubtful whether there is any other which can so clearly express the total belongingness, the total obligation, the total commitment and the total accountability, which characterize the life under grace. It is not at all surprising that some want to ban the use of this imagery altogether from Christian speech; but the question has to be asked whether the expurgation of our exposition of the Christian life by the removal of the slave-master figure is not more likely to prove a serious impoverishment and distortion than a genuine purification. We suspect that it would be wise to retain it and at the same time always be mindful of Paul's warning of its unworthiness. The human weakness on account of which he judges it necessary to use this slave-master language is more likely to be the insensitiveness and proneness to self-deception which characterize the fallen nature even of Christians and which make the question, 'Are we to sin, because we are not under the law but under grace?', seem open, than the less serious weakness of the need to receive profound truth by human analogies.

19b–23 continues the use of the figure of slavery. **For just as you once placed your members as slaves at the disposal of uncleanness and lawlessness for *a life of* lawlessness, so now place your members at the disposal of righteousness for sanctification** largely repeats the thought of v. 13 but with significant variations. In v. 13 the yielding of their members to an evil service was the subject of a negative command: here it is spoken of as a thing of the past. The 'just as' and 'so' underline the parallel between their old self-surrender to uncleanness and lawlessness and the new self-surrender to which they are being summoned. The two phrases, 'for *a life of* lawlessness' and 'for sanctification', are parallel, indicating in each case the end in view. The noun translated 'sanctification' (compare v. 22; 1 Cor 1.30; 1 Th 4.3, 4, 7; 2 Th 2.13) denotes in the New Testament God's work in the believer, his ethical renewal. In spite of some opinions to the contrary, the word, as used by Paul, indicates a process rather than a state, and is better represented by 'sanctification' than by 'holiness' or 'consecration'.

For when you were slaves of sin, you were free in relation to righteousness. What fruit did you then obtain? Things of which you now are ashamed! For their end is death serves to support the command just given, reinforcing its urgency. The general sense of the first part (v. 20) would seem to be that one cannot be the slave of sin and the slave of righteousness at the same time. Compare Mt 6.24. There is not much doubt that the punctuation of the Greek we have adopted, which has the explicit support of the great early Church biblical scholar, Theodore of Mopsuestia, is to be preferred to that represented by the RV and RSV. The fruit which they used to have from their slavery to sin consisted of things (Paul doubtless has in mind evil deeds, evil habits, evil characters), of which they now are ashamed, since the end to which such things lead is death. The mention of their being ashamed is by no means otiose; for to be ashamed of one's past evil ways is a vital element in sanctification, as Calvin emphasized in his comment on this verse ('Only those ... who have learned well to be earnestly dissatisfied with themselves, and to be confounded with shame at their wretchedness, are imbued with the principles of Christian philosophy').

145

It is to be noted that in **But now, having been set free from sin and made slaves to God** Paul speaks directly of slavery to God, and not indirectly, as when he referred to slavery to obedience (v. 16) and to righteousness (vv. 18 and 19). What **you obtain your fruit unto sanctification** means is that they are now obtaining fruit (of their slavery to God) which is a contribution to – indeed, a beginning of – the process of their sanctification; but this is not to imply that their sanctification may simply be equated with the fruit which they are obtaining in the present (the RSV rendering, 'the return you get is sanctification', surely misrepresents the Greek). The sentence is completed by **and as the end eternal life.** As the end, the goal, of their slavery to God they will obtain eternal life, which is to be distinguished both from the fruit which they are now obtaining and also from the sanctification to which that fruit contributes.

For the wage which sin pays is death, but the free gift which God gives is eternal life in Christ Jesus our Lord provides both clarification of vv. 21–22 and also a solemn conclusion to the section as a whole. Sin is still personified, and is here represented either as a general who pays wages to his soldiers or – and this suits better the prominence of the idea of slavery in the preceding verses – as a slave-owner who pays his slaves an allowance or pocket-money (among the Romans this was normal practice). The wage which the slave of sin has to expect is death. God, by contrast, does not pay wages, since no man can put Him in his debt; but the free gift which He gives is nothing less than eternal life. The idea that Paul, in using the Greek word which we have represented here by 'free gift', was thinking of the largess given to each soldier by the emperor or by an imperial heir on his accession, introduction to public life or other extraordinary occasion, goes back to Tertullian (second and third centuries). It is perhaps possible that Paul was; but, picturesque though the suggestion may be, it is by no means as well-founded as some commentators have assumed. And, even if Paul did have this imperial largess in mind, it can only have been as a passing allusion; for it was not a particularly illuminating comparison. Paul's own use of the word elsewhere (for example, in 5.15 and 16, where we have rendered it by 'gracious gift') is a much more probable clue to his meaning here.

V.3. A LIFE CHARACTERIZED BY FREEDOM FROM THE LAW'S CONDEMNATION (7.1–25)

The life promised for the man who is righteous by faith is, in the third place, described as a life characterized by freedom from the law, that is, from the law in the limited sense of the-law-as-condemning or the law's condemnation (compare 8.1). The point is made in the first subsection (7.1–6), which takes up and elucidates the statement 'you are not under the law, but under grace' made in 6.14. The second subsection (7.7–25) is a necessary clarification of 7.1–6, intended to elucidate certain matters relating to the law and to guard against possible misunderstanding.

(i) *Freedom from the law's condemnation* (7.1–6)

¹Or are you ignorant, brethren, of the fact – it is to men who know the law that I am speaking – that the law has authority over a man so long as he lives? ²For a married woman is bound by the law to her husband as long as he is living; but, if her husband dies, she is released from the law in so far as it binds her to her husband. ³So then, while her husband is living, she will be accounted an adulteress, if she becomes another man's; but, if her husband dies, she is free from the law so that she is not an adulteress, if she becomes another man's. ⁴Therefore, my brethren, you too were made dead to the law through the body of Christ, so that you might belong to another, even to him who has been raised from the dead, in order that we might bear fruit unto God. ⁵For, when we were in the flesh, the sinful passions stimulated by the law were active in our members so that we bore fruit to death; ⁶but now we have been released from the law, having died to that by which we were held, so that we serve in newness of the Spirit, not in oldness of the letter.

Paul has told the Roman Christians in 6.14 that they are 'not under the law, but under grace', in order to encourage them to obey the imperatives of 6.12–13. Now in 7.1–6 he elucidates that statement, showing how it is true, how it has come about that they are free from the law's condemnation. They have been freed from it by their death, that is, by the death which in God's sight and by God's gracious decision they themselves have died ('you . . . were made dead' in v. 4; compare 'having died' in v. 6) in Christ's death on their behalf ('through the body of Christ' in v. 4). In this explanation what has been said in 6.2–11 and, behind that, in 3.21–26 and also in chapter 5 is of course presupposed.

Paul begins (v. 1) by appealing to the legal principle that the law's authority over a man lasts so long, but only so long, as he lives. Then in vv. 2 and 3 he gives an example which serves to clarify this principle by illustrating its corollary, namely, that the occurrence of a death effects a decisive change in respect of relationship to the law. Verse 4 is Paul's conclusion from v. 1 as clarified by vv. 2 and 3. In view of what has been said in vv. 1–3, the death which the Roman Christians have died must be understood to mean that they have been freed from the law's condemnation, so that they might henceforth belong to Christ, and, along with all other believers, render service to God. Verses 5 and 6, in which the use of the first person plural, introduced abruptly in v. 4 is continued, are added in elucidation of v. 4. While v. 5 looks back at the past from which we have been delivered, v. 6, anticipating what is to be said in chapter 8, focuses attention on the fact that, in consequence of their liberation from the law's condemnation, believers serve God not in that oldness which is the perverse way of legalism, of misunderstanding and misuse of God's law, but in the God-given newness which is the power of God's indwelling Spirit.

1. Or are you ignorant, brethren, of the fact – it is to men who know the law that I am speaking – that the law has authority over a man so long as he lives? It is widely agreed that here Paul looks back as far as 6.14b ('you are not under the law but under grace'), and this is surely right. We take it then that the thought behind the use of the 'Or are you ignorant' formula here is that, if those who are being addressed accept the conclusion which is drawn in vv. 4–6 from the principle stated in the 'that'-clause of v. 1 and then illustrated in vv. 2–3, then they must surely be able to understand and accept what was said in 6.14b and clarified by 6.15–23. But, while 7.1–6 is thus introduced as support for what has already been said in the previous chapter, it is also, as a statement in some detail of the Christian's freedom from the law's condemnation, a new paragraph of the exposition of the life which the man who is righteous by faith is to live. The 'that'-clause sounds like a legal maxim. The meaning is that the law's authority over a man lasts so long, but only so long, as he lives.

2–3. For a married woman is bound by the law to her husband as long as he is living; but, if her husband dies, she is released from the law in so far as it binds her to her husband. So then, while her husband is living, she will be accounted an adulteress, if she becomes another man's; but, if her husband dies, she is free from the law so that she is not an adulteress, if she becomes another man's. From early times it has usually been assumed that Paul's intention in these two verses was allegorical. On this assumption, the natural interpretation would seem to be to take the husband to represent the law and the woman the Christian or the company of believers as a whole set free by the removal of the law to form a new union with Christ. But this interpretation comes up against a serious difficulty in the fact that in v. 4 Paul goes on to speak not of the death of the law (as on this interpretation one would expect) but of Christians' having died to the law. Its exponents have sought to meet the difficulty by suggesting that Paul refrained from speaking of the death of the law, as the logic of his allegory demanded, and spoke instead of Christians' having died to the law, in order to avoid offending Jewish sentiment. In modern times another form of the allegorical interpretation has been proposed, according to which the husband stands not for the law but for the Christian's old self ('our old self' of 6.6), while the wife stands for the continuing self of the Christian which through the death of the old self is translated into a new condition of life. But this seems extremely complicated and forced. A less unpromising line is taken when vv. 2–3 are understood as a parable rather than as an allegory.

But the decisive clue to the right interpretation of these verses is the recognition that they were not intended to be connected directly with v. 4 but with v. 1. They are not an allegory (nor yet a parable) the interpretation of which is to be found in v. 4, but an illustration designed to elucidate v. 1. Verse 4 is the conclusion drawn from vv. 1–3 as a whole, that is, from v. 1 as clarified by vv. 2–3: it is not an interpretaion or application of vv. 2–3. The rightness of this view of the matter is confirmed by the fact that in

149

the original v. 4 is introduced by a word which (as used here) can only mark a conclusion drawn from what has been said. We take it then that these two verses are simply intended as an illustration of the principle stated in the 'that'-clause of v. 1 or – rather more accurately – of its corollary, namely, that the occurrence of a death effects a decisive change in respect of relationship to the law.

4. Therefore, my brethren, you too were made dead to the law through the body of Christ, so that you might belong to another, even to him who has been raised from the dead, in order that we might bear fruit unto God is Paul's conclusion from the principle stated in v. 1, as clarified by vv. 2 and 3. In the case of Christians and their relation to the law's condemnation also a death has occurred, not, as one might in view of the foregoing illustration be inclined to expect, the death of the law or of the law's condemnation, but the death of the Christians themselves which is to be understood in the light of 6.2ff. Paul uses here not 'die' (as in 6.2) but 'be made dead' or 'be put to death' possibly because the thought of Christ's being put to death on the cross is in his mind, more probably because he has in mind, and wants to suggest to his readers, the fact that this blessed death in the Christians' past is God's doing (compare the similar passive, 'we have been released' in v. 6). They have been made dead 'through the body of Christ', that is, through His person put to death on the cross. Christ bore the law's condemnation for them in His death; and in that He died for them, they died with Him in God's sight. They were thus set free from the condemnation pronounced by the law. And this was in order that they might henceforth belong to the risen Christ.

The clause 'in order that we might bear fruit unto God' is best taken as dependent on 'you . . . were made dead', in spite of the fact that this involves a harsh combination of the second and first persons plural. To take it as dependent on 'belong' would be no improvement, and to take it as dependent on the participle represented by 'to him who has been raised', while it would make the transition to the first person plural easier, would give a less satisfactory sense. Transitions from one person to another in successive sentences are common enough in Paul's letters: in the same sentence such a change as here is awkward, but was probably due to Paul's sense of his own personal involvement in the obligation to bear fruit to God. With regard to the sense with which 'bear fruit' is used, some commentators have maintained that Paul had in mind the image of bearing children; but, even if the suggestion that the illustration of vv. 2 and 3 is reflected in the clause 'so that you might belong to another' were accepted (it is more likely that the thought is simply of transference to another master), this explanation of 'bear fruit' should surely still be rejected on the grounds that, had Paul had this image in mind, he would have said 'unto Christ' rather than 'unto God'; that the image of Christians' bearing children to God is grotesque; and that the use of the same verb in v. 5 with 'to death' surely clinches the matter. The general sense of 'bear fruit' in the present verse is probably much the same as is expressed in v. 6 by 'serve'.

5–6. For, when we were in the flesh. The point of the 'For' is that these two verses are intended to elucidate v. 4. In 2 Cor 10.3; Gal 2.20; Phil 1.22 Paul uses 'in the flesh' of the life which Christians as well as all other men must live in this world; but here he uses it to denote the condition which for Christians belongs to the past (compare 8.8, 9). They are no longer in the flesh in the sense of having the basic direction of their living determined and controlled by their fallen nature (compare 'walk according to the flesh' in 8.4), although the flesh in the sense of fallen human nature is still a far from powerless element in their lives (see, for example, 7.14, 18, 25). When we were altogether under the domination of the flesh, then that condition prevailed in our lives which the rest of v. 5 describes.

the sinful passions stimulated by the law were active in our members. One effect which the law had then was to stimulate and intensify our sinful passions: challenged by the law which claims us for God and for our neighbour, our self-centredness, our sinful ego, recognized that it was being called in question and attacked, and so sought the more violently to defend itself. The consequence of our sinful passions' activity is indicated by the last clause of the verse: **so that we bore fruit to death.** For its general sense we may compare 'For their end is death' in 6.21.

but now we have been released from the law: that is, from the law (as condemning us), from the law's condemnation. That this is what is intended is suggested by the way in which Paul continues his argument in 8.1 (the intervening 7.7–25 is a necessary clarification of 7.1–6). The view of many interpreters that Paul means that we are freed from the law altogether falls foul of v. 25b as well as of vv. 12 and 14a, and of 3.31; 8.4; 13.8–10. Paul adds: **having died to that by which we were held.** It is natural to understand 'having died' by reference to 'you . . . were made dead' in v. 4 and so to take the here unnamed thing by which we were held, and to which we have died, to be the law's condemnation.

The last part of v. 6 is best understood as indicating the actual result of the release to which the beginning of the verse has referred: **so that we serve in newness of the Spirit, not in oldness of the letter.** While Paul is fully aware of the painful fact of the Christian's continuing sinfulness (see especially vv. 14–25) and of his need to be constantly exhorted to live according to his faith (see especially 12.1–15.13), he nevertheless maintains that, if one is a Christian at all, one has the Spirit of Christ (8.9) and walks according to the Spirit (8.4), albeit falteringly and feebly. With 'serve' here 'God' is to be supplied as object. In accordance with the insight of 6.15–23, the new life is spoken of in terms of a service, that is, a slavery. The character of this slavery is indicated by the double contrast, 'in newness of the Spirit, not in oldness of the letter', in which 'newness' and 'oldness' are used in morally positive, and negative, senses, respectively. The believer's service is characterized, not by the lifeless effeteness of the mere letter, which is what the legalist is left with by his misunderstanding and misuse of the law, but by the freshness and hopefulness which are the effect of the presence and activity of the Spirit. That Paul is not opposing the law itself to the Spirit is clear, since only a few verses later he affirms that the law is spiritual (v. 14). He does not use 'letter' as equivalent to 'law'. It is the letter of the law in separation from the Spirit. But, since 'the law is spiritual', the letter of the law in isolation from the Spirit is not the law in its true character, but the law as it were denatured. It is this which is opposed to the Spirit whose presence is the true establishment of the law (see on 8.1ff). Life in the Spirit is the newness of life which belongs to the new age: life according to 'the letter' (in the sense which we have indicated) belongs, by contrast, to this present age which is passing away.

(ii) *A necessary clarification of what has been said concerning the law*
(7.7–25)

[7]What then shall we say? Is the law sin? God forbid! but I should not have come to know sin had it not been for the law; for indeed I should not know coveting, had not the law said, 'Thou shalt not covet'; [8]but sin having obtained a base for its operations worked in me through the commandment all manner of covetousness; for in the absence of the law sin is dead. [9]But I was alive once in the absence of the law; but when the commandment came sin sprang to life, [10]and 1 died, and the commandment which was unto life proved to be, as far as I was concerned, unto death. [11]For sin having obtained a base of operations deceived me through the commandment and through it killed me. [12]So then in itself the law is holy, and the commandment holy and righteous and good.

[13]Did then that which is good become death to me? God forbid! but sin, in order that it might be manifest as sin, *was* working death for me through that which is good, in order that sin might through the commandment become sinful beyond measure. [14]For we know that the law is spiritual; but I am carnal, a slave under sin's power. [15]For that which I work I do not acknowledge; for I do not practise what I will, but I do what I hate. [16]But if I do that which I do not will, I am agreeing with the law that it is good. [17]But, this being so, it is then not I who work that which I do, but sin which dwells in me. [18]For I know that good does not dwell in me, that is, in my flesh; for, while I can will to do that which is good, to work what is good is beyond my reach. [19]For, I do not do the good which I will, but the evil which I do not will, this I practise. [20]But, if I do what I do not will, then in these circumstances it is not I who work it but sin which dwells in me, [21]So then I prove by experience the law that, though I will to do what is good, it is that which is evil which is within my reach. [22]For I, in so far as the inner man is concerned, delight in God's law, [23]but I see in my members a different law, which is waging war against the law of my mind and making me a prisoner of the law of sin which is in my members.

[24]Wretched man that I am! Who will deliver me from this body of death? [25]Thanks be to God through Jesus Christ our Lord! So then I

myself serve with my mind the law of God, but with my flesh the law of sin.

Several things which Paul has said in the course of his argument (5.20; 6.14 and 7.1–6, in particular, come to mind) could give the impression that the law is actually an evil, in some way to be identified with sin. So in the first of the three paragraphs of which this subsection is made up (vv. 7–12) Paul seeks to deal with this possible misunderstanding. In v. 7 he repudiates the suggestion that the law is sin and asserts that, far from being sin, it is that which makes him recognize his sin for what it is. (Throughout this subsection the first person singular is used. In the present summary we assume that Paul is not just speaking about his own experience, but is taking himself as representative, first (in vv. 7–13) of mankind generally, and then (in vv. 14–25) of Christians. We shall discuss the matter below). In vv. 8–11 Paul goes on to explain that, while the law certainly is not sin, it is true that sin has been able to exploit it for its own evil purpose to deadly effect. Paul seems to have in mind here the narrative of Genesis 3, in which the divine commandment which is God's good and gracious gift for man's preservation is seen to be also an opportunity which the serpent can exploit in order to ruin man. Sin has wrought man's death through the commandment. So a true understanding of the situation with regard to the law must include the recognition of the fact that it has been effectively exploited by sin for sin's purpose, but must never lose sight of the fundamental truth, which is affirmed with emphasis in v. 12, that in itself the law is God's law, holy, righteous and good.

In the second paragraph (vv. 13–23) Paul deals with the false inference which can be drawn from what has been said in vv. 9–12, namely, that the law, which is truly good, is to blame for man's death. The truth is rather that sin has made use of the good thing in order to accomplish man's death. This is stated in v. 13, which also indicates that sin's exploitation of the law actually fulfils two elements of the divine purpose in giving the law, namely, that sin might be shown to be sin and that by means of the commandment its sinfulness might be enhanced. With v. 14, which introduces evidence in confirmation of what was said in v.13, the past tenses give way to present, and, as the sequel makes clear, Paul is thinking specifically of Christians. The verses which follow depict vividly the inner conflict characteristic of the true Christian, a conflict such as is possible only in the man, in whom the Holy Spirit is active and whose mind is being renewed under the discipline of the gospel. In the man who understands the law not legalistically but in the light of Christ and so recognizes the real seriousness of its requirement, and who truly and sincerely wills to obey it, to do what is good and to avoid the evil, the man in whom the power of sin is really being seriously and resolutely challenged, in him the power of sin is clearly seen. The more he is renewed by God's Spirit, the more sensitive he becomes to the continuing power of sin over his life and the fact that even his very best activities are marred by the egotism still entrenched within him.

The third and final paragraph of the subsection (vv. 24–25), in which the real anguish of severe and relentless warfare (not despair!), the earnest longing for final deliverance, thankful confidence in God, sincere commitment to God's law, and an honest recognition of the fact of continuing sinfulness, all come to expression and are held together, forms a conclusion to the verses (14–23) describing the conflict of the Christian life; and the fact that Paul sums them up in this way is an indication that he sees them not just as being support for what he has said in v. 13 but also as contributing an indispensable element of the description of the life promised for the man who is righteous by faith. In fact, the latter part of the subsection has a dual role; on the one hand, it is an integral part of the necessary clarification of 7.1–6; on the other hand, it is to be related to chapter 8, as supplying an important insight without which what is said there would be very seriously misleading. 7.14–25 and chapter 8 are necessary to each other. Neither, if read in isolation from the other, gives a true picture of the Christian life.

It will be convenient to give some consideration to Paul's use of the first person singular in this subsection before we embark on the detailed exegesis. Between vv. 7–13 and vv. 14–25 there is the significant difference that, while past tenses are characteristic of the former passage, the use of the present tense is characteristic of the latter. In view of this difference we shall consider them separately in respect of the problem of the first person singular.

With regard to vv. 7–13, it will be enough here to mention just four of the suggestions which have been made. Two of these, that Paul is speaking autobiographically and that he is depicting by the first person singular the experience of the typical Jewish man, though both have been, and still are, popular, must, we think, be rejected on the ground that in neither case is it possible to give a credible explanation of 'I was alive once in the absence of the law'(v. 9). For the explanation which is often given, namely, that the reference is to the period before Paul (or the typical Jewish man) became a 'son of the commandment', that is, before he underwent what might roughly be termed the Jewish equivalent of confirmation, will hardly stand up. While it is true that a Jewish boy who was not yet a 'son of the commandment' was not under obligation to keep the whole law, it would not be at all accurate to describe him as living 'in the absence of the law'. The suggestion that Paul is specifically speaking in the name of Adam, which was put forward by some early Church writers and has received the support of some eminent scholars in modern times, seems to us forced – though it may certainly be said in its favour that Paul seems to have had Genesis 3 in mind when writing these verses. The most probable explanation, in our view, is that we have here a generalizing use of the first person singular intended to depict vividly the situation of man in the absence of the law and in its presence. We shall probably be right to assume that Paul's choice of this form of speech was not solely due to his desire for rhetorical vividness but also reflects his deep sense of personal involvement, his consciousness that in drawing out the general truth he is expressing the truth about himself.

With regard to vv. 14–25, in connexion with which the question of the first person singular is still very hotly disputed, we had better mention seven suggestions:

(i) that it is autobiographical, the reference being to Paul's present experience as a Christian;

(ii) that it is autobiographical, the reference being to his past experience (before his conversion) as seen by him at the time referred to;

(iii) that it is autobiographical, the reference being to his pre-conversion past but as seen by him now in the light of his Christian faith;

(iv) that it presents the experience of the non-Christian Jew, as seen by himself;

(v) that it presents the experience of the non-Christian Jew, as seen through Christian eyes;

(vi) that it presents the experience of the Christian who is living at a level of the Christian life which can be left behind, who is still trying to fight the battle in his own strength;

(vii) that it presents the experience of Christians generally, including the very best and most mature.

We may set (ii) aside at once on the ground that what is said in these verses is altogether contrary to the verdict which, according to Phil 3.6b (compare Gal 1.14), Paul before his conversion passed upon his own life. And (iv) may also be set aside, as inconsistent with the picture of Jewish self-complacency which Paul gives in chapter 2. Against (iii), and also against (ii), the use of present tenses throughout vv. 14–25 weighs heavily; for the use of the present is here sustained too consistently and for too long and contrasts too strongly with the past tenses characteristic of vv. 7–13 to be at all plausibly explained as an example of the present used for the sake of vividness in describing past events which are vividly remembered. Moreover v. 24 would be highly melodramatic, if it were not a cry for deliverance from present distress. A further objection to (iii), which also lies against (ii) and (iv) and (v) and also against (vi), is the order of the sentences in vv. 24–25. Verse 25b is an embarrassment to those who see in v. 24 the cry of an unconverted man or of a Christian living on a low level of Christian life and in v. 25a an indication that the desired deliverance has actually arrived, since, coming after the thanksgiving, it appears to imply that the condition of the speaker after deliverance is just the same as it was before it. All the attempts so far made to get over this difficulty have about them an air of desperation.

The difficulty in the way of accepting (i) or (vii), which has been felt by very many from early days on, is of course that the acceptance of either of them has seemed to involve altogether too dark a view of the Christian life and, in particular, to be incompatible with what is said of the believer's liberation from sin in 6.6, 14, 17f, 22 and 8.2. And this objection to both (i) and (vii) has seemed to a great many interpreters completely conclusive.

But we are convinced that it is only along the lines of either (i) or (vii) that we can do justice to the text. With Methodius and Augustine, Thomas Aquinas, Luther and Calvin, and a fair number of moderns, we adhere to the view that it is a Christian who is described in these verses. The man who speaks here is one who wills the good and hates the evil (vv. 15, 16, 19, 20), who as far as his inner man is concerned delights in God's law (v. 22), who serves it with his mind (v. 25b). Not so does Paul describe the unregenerate man. It is particularly instructive to set the statement in v. 25b ('So then I myself with my mind serve (as a slave) the law of God') alongside 6.17, 18, 20, according to which the Roman Christians were slaves of sin before their conversion, but have now become the slaves of righteousness, and also 8.7 which states that the mind (a different Greek word from that rendered 'mind' in 7.23 and 25b) of the flesh is not subject to God's law and indeed cannot be. In the ego which wills the good and hates the evil, in the mind of vv. 23 and 25b, in the 'inner man' of v. 22, we must surely recognize the human self which is being renewed by God's Spirit, not the self, or any part of the self, of the still unconverted man. In fact, a struggle as serious as that which is here described, can only take place where the Spirit of God is present and active (compare Gal 5.17).

With regard to the objection that it is incredible that Paul should speak of a Christian as 'a slave under sin's power', we ought to ask ourselves whether our inability to accept this expression as descriptive of a Christian is not perhaps the result of failure on our part to realize the full seriousness of the ethical demands of God's law (or of the gospel). Are we not all of us too prone still to understand them legalistically, as did the young man who could say: 'Master, all these things have I observed from my youth' (Mk 10.20)? And is it not true that the more the Christian is set free from legalistic ways of thinking about God's law and so sees more and more clearly the full splendour of the perfection towards which he is being summoned, the more conscious he becomes of his own continuing sinfulness, his stubborn all-pervasive egotism? On the question of the compatibility of interpretations (i) and (vii) with various statements in other parts of Romans the reader may be referred to the detailed commentary on this passage and on the other passages concerned (for example, on 8.2).

As to the relatively unimportant question whether (i) or (vii) is to be preferred, it seems, in view of the fact that in vv. 7–13 it is hardly possible to understand the first person singular as strictly autobiographical, rather more natural to accept the latter than the former. But again, as with regard to vv. 7–13, we may assume that Paul's use of the first person singular throughout vv. 14–25 reflects not only his desire to state in a forceful and vivid manner what is generally true – in this case, of Christians – but also his sense of his own deep personal involvement in what he is saying.

7. What then shall we say? introduces an indication of a false inference which Paul recognizes could be drawn from what has just been said. **Is the law sin?** A number of things Paul has said in the course of the epistle so far could indeed suggest that the law is actually an evil, in some way to be identified with sin. The last six verses and 5.20 and 6.14, in particular, come to mind. It is time for Paul to deal with this possible false conclusion. That the danger of misunderstanding here was not merely theoretical, subsequent Church history was to prove again and again.

God forbid! rejects the false inference. It is possible to understand **but** as indicating the relation of what follows to 'God forbid!' (the thought will then be that what follows limits its force: while the conclusion that the law is sin must be rejected, it is nevertheless true that ...); but it is probably preferable to understand it as indicating the relation of what follows to 'Is the law sin?' (the thought being of the opposition between what is about to be said and the false inference that the law is sin). **I should not have come to know sin had it not been for the law; for indeed I should not know coveting, had not the law said, 'Thou shalt not covet'.** We take Paul's meaning to be that, while men do actually sin in the absence of the law (compare 5.13), they do not fully recognize sin for what it is, apart from the law (compare 3.20), and that, while they do indeed experience covetousness even though they do not know the tenth commandment, it is only in the light of the commandment that they recognize their coveting for what it is – that coveting which God forbids, a deliberate disobeying of God's revealed will. (The suggestion that by 'know' here Paul means 'know practically', 'experience', is surely unlikely, since 2.12 and 15.12–14 show that he recognized that even in the absence of the law men do as a matter of fact sin.) Paul's choice of the tenth commandment as an example is significant, because it directs attention to the inward root of man's outward wrong-doing. Paul's omission to specify any object of 'Thou shalt not covet' both here and in 13.9, while it could be explained as simply an abbreviation (the rest of the commandment being intended to be understood), more probably reflects the consciousness, of which there is evidence in the Old Testament and in Judaism as well as elsewhere in the New Testament, of the sinfulness of all inordinate desires as the expression of man's self-centredness and self-assertion over against God.

8. but sin having obtained a base for its operations worked in me through the commandment all manner of covetousness makes a different point from that just made in v. 7 but one which has already been hinted at in v. 5 ('the sinful passions stimulated by the law'). In the divine commandment 'Thou shalt not covet' sin received its chance, its foothold in man's life, its bridgehead, of which it was able to make use, in order to produce in man all sorts of inordinate desires. How was this so? Why was the divine commandment an opportunity for sin? We shall not do justice to Paul's thought here, if we settle for a merely psychological explanation along the lines of the proverbial wisdom that speaks of forbidden fruits as sweetest. It is rather that the merciful limitation imposed on man by the commandment and intended to preserve his true freedom and dignity can be misinterpreted and misrepresented as a taking away of his freedom and an attack on his dignity, and so can be made an occasion of resentment and rebellion against the divine Creator, man's true Lord. In this way sin can make use of the commandment not to covet as a means of arousing all manner of covetousness. It is to be noted that in this verse and in the following verses sin is personified, being spoken of as an active power with a malicious purpose: Paul no doubt has the narrative of Genesis 3 in mind. In fact, these verses are best understood as exposition of the Genesis narrative. It was perhaps with that narrative in mind that Paul chose the tenth commandment as his example; for there is a specially close relationship between the tenth commandment, understood in the generalized way we have noted (which brings it into close connexion with the first commandment), and the prohibition of Gen 2.17 ('but of the tree of the knowledge of good and evil, thou shalt not eat of it'), and between the covetousness which the tenth commandment forbids and what is described in Gen 3.6 ('And when the woman saw that the tree was good for food, and that it was a delight to the eyes, and that the tree was to be desired to make one wise, she took of the fruit thereof, and did eat; and she gave also unto her husband with her, and he did eat'), when the words 'ye shall be as God' in the preceding verse are remembered in their connexion with it.

for in the absence of the law sin is dead. Even without the law sin is indeed present, but it is relatively inactive. (For the use of 'dead' in the sense of 'inactive' compare Jas 2.17, 26.) In the absence of the law sin is relatively powerless – that is why Paul can say in 1 Cor 15.56 that 'the power of sin is the law'. In the Genesis narrative the serpent was able to mount his attack because the commandment of Gen 2.17 had been given. The contrast between 'dead' here and 'sprang to life' in the next verse vividly brings out the contrast between the serpent lying motionless and hidden and the serpent stirring itself to take advantage of its opportunity. 'Nothing', observes Leenhardt suggestively, 'resembles a dead serpent more than a living serpent so long as it does not move!'

9–10. But I was alive once in the absence of the law. By far the most probable explanation of this statement is that Paul refers to man's situation before the giving of the law, along with which he probably also has in mind the state of man depicted in Gen 1.28ff and before Gen 2.16–17. In view of the contrast with 'I died' in v. 10, it seems clear that the Greek verb meaning 'live' is used in v. 9 in the strong sense of 'be alive' rather than in the weak sense of 'pass one's life'. In the primal state described in Genesis 1 man 'was alive', and in the time before the law was given through Moses, while man certainly could not be said to be alive in the full sense which this verb has for example in 1.17 or 8.13, he may be said to have been alive in the sense that his condition then was life, in comparison with his condition after the law had been received. In **but when the commandment came** we may see a double reference – to the giving of the law (represented by the tenth commandment – hence 'commandment' rather than 'law') and also to the commandment of Gen 2.16–17. **sin sprang to life, and I died, and the commandment which was unto life proved to be, as far as I was concerned, unto death.** Sin's opportunity for effective action meant man's death. Compare 5.12, 14; 6.23; Gen 2.17b. Though he continues to live, he is in a real sense already dead – being under God's sentence of death (compare v. 24b). Physical death, when it comes, is but the fulfilment of the sentence already passed. It needs scarcely be said that the death referred to here is something entirely different from what we might call 'the good death' of 6.2, 7, 8; 7.4. The true and proper purpose alike of the commandment of Gen 2.16–17 and of the tenth commandment (representing the whole law) was that man might have life. But the actual effect of the commandment, exploited by sin, has been death.

11. For sin having obtained a base of operations deceived me through the commandment and through it killed me. The use of 'deceived' is reminiscent of Gen 3.13 ('. . . The serpent beguiled me . . . '). In Genesis 3 the serpent is represented as deceiving the woman in at least three respects: first, by distorting and misrepresenting the divine commandment by drawing attention only to the negative part of the commandment and ignoring the positive (Gen 3.1b: contrast 2.16f, in which 'Of every tree of the garden thou mayest freely eat' is included in what 'the LORD God commanded the man'); secondly, by making her believe that God would not punish disobedience by death (v. 4); and thirdly, by using the very commandment itself (actually deceiving and seducing her by means of God's commandment), in order to insinuate doubts about God's good will and to suggest the possibility of man's asserting himself in opposition to God (v. 5). The case with the law of Israel is similar. Sin deceives man concerning the law, distorting it and imposing a false image of it on his understanding, and also deceives him by means of the law, in particular by making use of it in order to suggest that man is in a position so to fulfil it as to put God under an obligation to himself. Thus sin by deception succeeds in accomplishing man's death by means of that which God gave 'unto life'.

12. So then in itself the law is holy, and the commandment holy and righteous and good is Paul's definitive reply to the question raised in v. 7a. The presence of the law has actually resulted in death for man, but for this result the law is not at all to blame. (It is no more to blame for this result than is the gospel for the fact that those who reject it or try to make use of it for their own evil purposes come under a severer condemnation than would have been theirs, had they never heard the gospel.) The blame is to be laid at sin's door. The law is 'holy'. For Paul, as for Jesus, it is God's law (compare 7.22, 25; 8.7; Mt 15.3, 6; Mk 7.8), deriving from Him and bearing the unmistakable marks of its origin and authority. The use of 'the commandment' would, of course, be appropriate, if the commandment of Gen 2.16–17 were intended; but here in the definitive answer to the question, 'Is the law sin?', the reference is no doubt to the individual commandments contained in the law. God's commandments are 'righteous' (compare Deut 4.8), both in that they require righteousness of life in men and also in that, being merciful and not burdensome, they bear witness to God's own righteousness. They are 'good', in that they are intended for men's benefit. It is difficult to understand how, in the face of this verse, so many interpreters of Paul can persist in treating as axiomatic the assumption that he regarded the law as an enemy in the same class with sin and death, as does the heading of 5.12–7.25 in the Jerusalem Bible, which runs: 'Deliverance from sin and death and law'.

13. Did then that which is good become death to me? The new paragraph begins with a question parallel to that raised in v. 7. Here 'that which is good' picks up the 'good' of v. 12, and 'death' the 'I died' and 'unto death' of v. 10 and the 'killed' of v. 11. If the law is good and yet death has resulted from its presence, does this mean that that which is good has become death to me – that it is to blame for my death? To this question as to that in v. 7, the answer is the emphatic denial **God forbid!** The good thing is certainly not to blame for my death.

but sin, in order that it might be manifest as sin, *was* working death for me through that which is good, in order that sin might through the commandment become sinful beyond measure. (The Greek sentence is incomplete. The simplest way of supplementing it is to understand the equivalent of 'was' with the participle, as we have done.) The true conclusion to be drawn is not that the good thing is responsible for my death but that sin made use of the good thing in order to accomplish my death. The purposes indicated by the two final clauses, that sin might be shown to be sin (by the fact of its misusing God's good gift to men) and that by means of the commandment sin's sinfulness might actually be enhanced, are God's, though they are neither the whole, nor yet the main element, of God's intention in giving the law. But the fact that they are embraced within God's intention does not mean that God and His law are to blame for man's death, any more than the fact that it was part of His purpose in sending His Son into the world that men's sin should be revealed in its true colours as enmity to God, by the reaction which Christ's ministry of love would provoke, means that God is to blame for the rejection and crucifixion of Christ. The two final clauses are an indication that the dire results of men's encounter with the law, so far from being a proof of the triumph of sin or of the imperfection of the law, are a sign that God's purpose finally and completely to overthrow sin is being advanced.

14. For we know that the law is spiritual. For the use of 'we know' see on 2.2. The affirmation that the law is spiritual is basically an affirmation of its divine origin and authority. We should probably see here also the implication that, being spiritual, it can only be properly understood by the help of the same Spirit by whom it was given. It is only those who have the Spirit who can truly acknowledge the law and consent to it with their minds (see vv. 16, 22, 23, 25b), and also in their lives make a beginning of real obedience to it (see 8.1ff). Those who are not enlightened by the Spirit grasp only the letter (see v. 6).

but I am carnal, a slave under sin's power. The only natural way, surely, to understand this first person singular statement in the present tense is the way indicated by Calvin in his comment on the following verse: 'Paul ... is depicting in his own person the character and extent of the weakness of believers'. The faithful often refuse this natural interpretation on the ground that it involves – so they argue – a gross belittling of the victory vouchsafed to the believer, and hanker after an interpretation which regards 7.14–25 and chapter 8 as describing two successive stages, before and after conversion. Even those who see that what is depicted in 7.14–24 does not fit the pre-conversion life are liable to argue that it belongs to a stage of the Christian life which can be left behind, a stage in which the Christian is still trying to fight the battle in his own strength, and to see 8.1ff as describing a subsequent deliverance. But we are convinced that it is possible to do justice to the text of Paul – and also to the facts of Christian living wherever they are to be observed – only if we resolutely hold chapters 7 and 8 together, in spite of the obvious tension between them, and see in them not two successive stages but two different aspects, two contemporaneous realities, of the Christian life, both of which continue so long as the Christian is in this mortal life.

By describing the Christian as 'carnal' Paul is implying that in him too there is that which is radically opposed to God (compare what is said about 'the mind of the flesh' in 8.7), though in chapter 8 he will make it abundantly clear that the Christian is not, in his view, carnal in the same unqualified way that the natural man is carnal. With 'a slave under sin's power' we may compare v. 23 ('but I see in my members a different law, which is waging war against the law of my mind and making me a prisoner of the law of sin . . . '). Understood in isolation from the teaching of chapters 6 and 8 and 12ff, these words would certainly give a thoroughly wrong impression of the Christian life; but, taken closely together with it, they bring out forcefully an aspect of the Christian life which we gloss over to our undoing. When Christians fail to take account of the fact that they (and all their fellow-Christians also) are still slaves under sin's power they are specially dangerous both to others and to themselves, because they are self-deceived. The more seriously a Christian strives to live from grace and to submit to the discipline of the gospel, the more sensitive he becomes to the fact of his continuing sinfulness, the fact that even his very best acts and activities are disfigured by the egotism which is still powerful within him – and no less evil because it is often more subtly disguised than formerly. At the same time it must be said with emphasis that the realistic recognition that we are still indeed slaves under sin's power should be no encouragement to us to wallow complacently in our sins.

15. For that which I work I do not acknowledge; for I do not practise what I will, but I do what I hate. While the second 'for' in this verse simply indicates the relation of the latter part of the verse to the former, the initial 'For' indicates the relation of vv. 15–23 as a whole to v. 14 – they explain what it means to be 'a slave under sin's power'. The Greek verb represented by 'work' here and also in vv. 17, 18 and 20 probably carries the thought of the effectiveness of the action, of the fact that what is undertaken is completed. 'I do not acknowledge' here means about the same as 'I do not approve' or 'I do not condone': this is confirmed by what follows. (The Greek verb which we have translated 'acknowledge' was sometimes used of a father's acknowledging his child as his own, though its primary meaning is simply 'know' – hence RV 'know' here.)

In all of its six occurrences in this verse 'I' denotes the same subject; but in the actions denoted by 'I do not acknowledge' (the negative expression implies a positive refusal to acknowledge), 'I will' and 'I hate' there is also another subject involved, a divine Subject whose action is, so to speak, behind, under and within, these human actions. In the conflict described in this verse (and also in vv. 18b and 19) battle is joined in earnest in a way that is not possible until a man is sanctified by the Holy Spirit. In the man to whom Paul here refers there is both knowledge of the revelation of God's will for man in the divine law and also the activity of the Holy Spirit who, on the one hand, clarifies, interprets and applies the law, and, on the other hand, creates and sustains man's will to obey it. In this man there is a continual growth in understanding of God's will and in the earnest desire and commitment to obey it and also an ever-deepening perception of the extent to which he falls short of true obedience.

The fact that there is such a serious conflict in the Christian proves that there is within him that which acknowledges the goodness and rightness of the law. This is the point of **16. But if I do that which I do not will, I am agreeing with the law that it is good.** And this something within the Christian, this centre of commitment to God's law, is the work of the Holy Spirit, who, coming from without, yet works within the human personality not as an alien force but in such a way that what He does may truly be spoken of as the action of the man (hence the first person singular 'I do not will' and 'I am agreeing with').

17. But, this being so, it is then not I who work that which I do, but sin which dwells in me is not intended as an excuse, but is rather an acknowledgment of the extent to which sin, dwelling in the Christian, usurps control over his life. But, while neither what is stated in this verse nor the 'I do not will' and the 'I am agreeing with the law that it is good' of v. 16 is any excuse (the latter is no excuse, since God requires not ineffectual sentiments but obedient deeds), the fact that there is real conflict and tension is a sign of hope.

18. For I know that good does not dwell in me, that is, in my flesh; for, while I can will to do that which is good, to work what is good is beyond my reach is a confession of the self's powerlessness for good. The words 'that is, in my flesh' are a necessary qualification of 'in me', since in the Christian the Holy Spirit dwells. They are, as Aquinas pointed out, an additional indication that it is the Christian who is being spoken about, since otherwise the qualification would be superfluous. By 'flesh' here Paul means not some lower self as a part of the man, as some have suggested, but the whole fallen human nature as such – in Calvin's words, 'all the endowments of human nature, and everything that is in man, except the sanctification of the Spirit'. We take Paul to mean by the latter half of the verse not that the Christian never achieves anything beyond an ineffectual desire, but that what he actually does never fully corresponds to his will. Sometimes he may fail to carry it out at all, sometimes he may even do the very opposite of what he wills; but even his best actions, in which he comes nearest to accomplishing the good he wills, are always stained and spoiled by his egotism.

19 and **20** repeat the substance of v. 15b and the substance of vv. 16a and 17, respectively.

21. So then I prove by experience the law that, though I will to do what is good, it is that which is evil which is within my reach. One of the features which make the last five verses of this chapter specially difficult is the repeated use of the word 'law', and it is its use here which is the main problem of this verse. Many interpreters, both ancient and modern, have insisted that the reference must be to the Old Testament law, but the various explanations of the verse which have been offered on this assumption are so forced as to be incredible. Moreover, since in v. 23 a law different from the law of God is explicitly mentioned, the possibility of explaining 'the law' in v. 21 otherwise than as referring to the Old Testament law must surely be reckoned with; and the fact that in v. 22 'law' is qualified as 'God's' suggests the probability that 'law' has just been used with a different reference. Some have explained the word translated 'law' here as meaning 'principle' or 'norm'; but the simplest and most natural explanation, in our view, is that 'law' here refers to the same law as will be more clearly specified in v. 23 – the 'different law'.

22–23 is an explanation of the situation described in v. 21. **For I, in so far as the inner man is concerned, delight in God's law, but I see in my members a different law, which is waging war against the law of my mind and making me a prisoner of the law of sin which is in my members.** The clause 'in so far as the inner man is concerned' qualifies 'I': the subject of the verb 'delight' is 'I in so far as the inner man is concerned', 'I in so far as I am that inner man'. For the expression 'inner man' compare 2 Cor 4.16; Eph 3.16; and also Rom 6.6 (the thought implied by way of contrast by the reference to the old self (Greek: 'old man')); Col 3.10 and Eph 4.24. The meaning of 'the inner man' here must be much the same as that of 'my mind' in vv. 23 and 25, which must be understood in the light of that renewing of the mind which is referred to in 12.2. The mind which recognizes, and is bound to, God's law is the mind which is being renewed by God's Spirit; and the inner man of which Paul speaks is the working of God's Spirit within the Christian. The Christian, in so far as he is this new man created by God's Spirit, delights in God's law and loves it as the revelation of God's good and merciful will. Compare Ps 19.8; 119.14, 16a, 24a, 35b, 47, 70b, etc.

But he is conscious of the power of another law at work in himself (for the meaning of 'members' see on 6.13), a law which is something altogether different from 'God's law' which has just been mentioned. Since this 'different law' is spoken of as 'in my members' and 'the law of sin' mentioned later in v. 23 is also described as being 'in my members', it is natural to identify this 'different law' with 'the law of sin' (explaining 'the law of sin which is in my members' in v. 23 as substituted for the 'itself', which might have been expected, in order to clarify the indefinite 'a different law'). Moreover, it seems natural to understand 'of my mind' here as meaning 'which my mind acknowledges' and so to identify this law with 'God's law' mentioned in v. 22. Understood thus, vv. 22 and 23 depict two laws in opposition to each other. The identity of one of them, 'the law of God', is not in doubt; but the identity of the other, 'the law of sin', requires some clarification. It would seem that Paul is here using the word 'law' metaphorically, to denote exercised power, authority, control, and that he means by 'the law of sin', the power, the authority, the control exercised over us by sin. It is a forceful way of making the point that the power which sin has over us is a terrible travesty, a grotesque parody, of that authority over us which belongs by right to God's holy law. Sin's exercising such authority over us is a hideous usurpation of the prerogative of God's law.

24. Wretched man that I am! Who will deliver me from this body of death? So Paul begins the third and final paragraph of the subsection. Many commentators have stated confidently that it cannot be a Christian who speaks here. But the truth is, surely, that inability to recognize the distress reflected in this cry as characteristic of Christian existence argues a failure to grasp the full seriousness of the Christian's obligation to express his gratitude to God by obedience of life. The farther men advance in the Christian life, and the more mature their discipleship, the clearer becomes their perception of the heights to which God calls them, and the more painfully sharp their consciousness of the distance between what they ought, and want, to be, and what they are. The assertion that this cry could only come from an unconverted heart, and that the apostle must be expressing not what he feels as he writes but vividly remembered experience of the unconverted man, is, we believe, totally untrue. To make it is to indicate – with all respect be it said – that one has not yet considered how absolute are the claims of the grace of God in Jesus Christ. The man, whose cry this is, is one who, knowing himself to be righteous by faith, desires from the depths of his being to respond to the claims which the gospel makes upon him (compare v. 22). It is the very clarity of his understanding of the gospel and the very sincerity of his love to God, which make his pain at this continuing sinfulness so sharp. But, be it noted, v. 24, while it is a cry of real and deep anguish, is not at all a cry of despair. The word represented by 'wretched' can indicate distress and misery without implying hopelessness, and the question 'Who will deliver me . . .?' may be understood as expressing the speaker's earnest longing for something which he knows is surely coming (compare the expectation described in 8.23). That from which the speaker longs to be delivered ('this body of death') is the condition of life in the body as we know it under the usurping occupation of sin which has just been described, a life which, because of sin, must succumb to death.

25a. The exclamation **Thanks be to God through Jesus Christ our**

Lord! is an indirect answer to the question in v. 24. It apparently implies that the speaker knows either that God has already fulfilled for him the wish expressed by the question or that God will surely fulfil it for him in the future. Those commentators who are quite convinced that, while it is a Christian who speaks in v. 25a, v. 24 is the cry of an unconverted man, not unnaturally tend to assume that the man who thanks God in v. 25a must be conscious of having already been delivered from the body of death. But this assumption is responsible for a great deal of confusion in the exegesis of this passage and has bedevilled in particular the interpretation of v. 25b. Moreover, it is inconsistent with Paul's thought as expressed elsewhere. We may for example refer to 8.10, according to which even for the man in whom Christ dwells, while it is indeed true that the Spirit is life because of justification, it is still also true that the body is mortal because of sin. The implication of v. 25a then is not that the speaker has already been delivered 'from this body of death', but that he knows that God will surely deliver him from it in the future. Deliverance in the limited sense of separation from the body could come with death, deliverance in all its positive fullness would come with the final redemption of the body (8.23). The key to the right understanding of v. 25a is the recognition that the man who speaks in v. 24 is already a Christian; for that saves us from having to imagine a drastic change between vv. 24 and 25a.

25b. It is hardly surprising that many of those who have seen in v. 24 the cry of an unconverted man (or of a Christian on a low level of Christian life) and in v. 25a an indication that the longed for deliverance has actually been accomplished, have felt **So then I myself serve with my mind the law of God, but with my flesh the law of sin** to be an embarrassment, since, coming after the thanksgiving, it appears (on this understanding of vv. 24–25a) to imply that the condition of the speaker after his deliverance is exactly the same as it was before it. A favourite way of dealing with the difficulty has been to posit a disarrangement of the sentences at a very early stage and to re-arrange the verses in the order 23, 25b, 24, 25a. Another suggestion which has been made is that v. 25b is a secondary gloss (intended as a summary of vv. 15–23), which should therefore be omitted. But, while the possibility of a primitive corruption which has affected all the surviving witnesses to the text cannot of course be ruled out absolutely, an exegesis which rests on a re-arrangement of sentences or on the exclusion of an alleged gloss, when there is not the slightest suggestion of support in the textual tradition for either procedure, is exceedingly hazardous, and, when sense can be made of the text as it stands, has little claim to be regarded as responsible. A good many, of course, even of those who do take v. 24 as expressing the situation of the unconverted seek to explain v. 25b without recourse to such dubious expedients. Some, for example, suggest that v. 25a is only an anticipatory forward glance to what is to be made clear in chapter 8 and so does not imply that deliverance has already taken place. Others, who do take v. 25a to imply that deliverance has already occurred, explain 'I myself' as meaning 'I myself apart from Jesus Christ' and suppose that v. 25b describes not the actual condition of the person referred to but the condition which would have been his, had he been left to himself. But, when once it is recognized that the one who speaks in v. 24 is a Christian (and a mature Christian – not merely one who is still on some specially low level of Christian existence), and also that v. 25a expresses not consciousness of having already been delivered from this body of death but certainty that God will in the future deliver him from it, a straightforward and satisfying interpretation of v. 25b becomes possible. Far from being an anti-climax or an incongruous intrusion at this point, it is an altogether appropriate conclusion to the preceding verses (including vv. 24–25a). For it sums up with clear-sighted honesty – an honesty which is thoroughly consonant both with the urgency of the longing for final deliverance expressed in v. 24 and also with the confidence that God will surely accomplish that deliverance in His good time reflected in v. 25a – the tension, with all its real anguish and also all its real hopefulness, in which the Christian never ceases to be involved so long as he is living this present life. To read into this sentence any suggestion of a complacent acceptance on the part of the Christian of his continued sinfulness would be quite perverse. For – not to mention the evidence of moral earnestness in v. 24 – the words 'I ... serve with my mind the law of God' express clearly enough the Christian's engagement, in the very depths of his personality as one who is being renewed by God's Spirit, to God's holy law, his sense of being altogether bound to it. And it is fully congruous with this deep sense of commitment to God's will that this conclusion does not cloak the painful fact of continuing sinfulness, but goes on to acknowledge frankly that the Christian, so long as he remains in this present life, remains in a real, though limited, sense a slave of sin (compare v. 14b), since he still has a fallen nature.

V.4. A LIFE CHARACTERIZED BY THE INDWELLING OF GOD'S SPIRIT
(8.1–39)

The life promised for the man who is righteous by faith is, in the fourth place, described as a life characterized by the indwelling of the Spirit of God. The key-word of this section is 'spirit', which, while it is only used five times in chapters 1 to 7 and eight times in chapters 9 to 16, occurs twenty-one times in chapter 8, that is, much more often than in any other single chapter in the whole New Testament. In the majority of its occurrences in Romans 8 it quite certainly denotes the Holy Spirit, and in two of them it clearly does not. In the remaining instances it is a matter of some controversy whether the reference is, or is not, to the Holy Spirit: in all of them, in our judgment, it is.

Being characterized by the indwelling of God's Spirit, this life which is promised for the man who is righteous by faith is necessarily also a life in which God's law is being established and fulfilled (vv. 4, 12–16), a life which here and now bears the promise of resurrection and eternal life (vv. 6, 10f), a life in hope (vv. 17–30). The last subsection (vv. 31–39) is at the same time both the conclusion to this section, underlining the certainty of the believer's hope, and also the conclusion to the whole argument of the epistle up to this point.

(i) *The indwelling of the Spirit*
(8.1–11)

¹**So then there is now no condemnation for those who are in Christ Jesus. ²For the law of the Spirit of life has in Christ Jesus set thee**

free from the law of sin and of death. [3]For God, having sent his own Son in the likeness of sinful flesh and to deal with sin, condemned sin in the flesh (the thing which the law was unable to do, because it was weak through the flesh), [4]so that the righteous requirement of the law might be fulfilled in us who do not walk according to the flesh but according to the Spirit. [5]For those whose lives are determined by the flesh are on the flesh's side, but those whose lives are determined by the Spirit are on the Spirit's side. [6]For the flesh's mind is death, but the Spirit's mind is life and peace. [7]For the mind of the flesh is enmity toward God; for it is not subject to God's law – indeed, it cannot be; [8]and those who are in the flesh cannot please God. [9]But you are not in the flesh but in the Spirit, seeing that God's Spirit dwells in you. (If someone does not possess Christ's Spirit, then he does not belong to Christ.) [10]But, if Christ is in you, though your body is indeed mortal because of *your* sin, the Spirit is life because of *your* justification. [11]But, if the Spirit of him who raised Jesus from the dead dwells in you, he who raised from the dead Christ Jesus shall quicken your mortal bodies also through his Spirit who dwells in you.

The first subsection of V. 4 consists of 8.1–11. It connects not with 7.25a or 7.25b but with 7.6 (7.7–25 being, as we have seen, a necessary clarification of 7.1–6). Verse 1 draws out the significance of 7.1–6: those who are in Christ Jesus are freed from the divine condemnation pronounced by God's law. Verse 2, which takes up a point already hinted at in 7.6b (the reference to our serving in newness of the Spirit), confirms the truth of v. 1 by appealing to the fact that the further liberation which deliverance from God's condemnation makes possible, namely, the liberation of the believer by the power of God's Spirit from the power of sin and of its inevitable concomitant, death, has actually taken place as a result of the work of Christ. Verse 3 takes up and elucidates the 'in Christ Jesus' of v. 2, clarifying the basis of the freedom referred to in v. 1 and also of the resulting freedom described in v. 2. Verse 4 indicates what was God's purpose in sending His Son – a purpose which, according to v. 2, is actually being fulfilled. What God's gift of His Spirit has brought about (v. 2) is nothing less than a beginning of the fulfilment of the divine purpose of Christ's work, namely, the true establishment of God's law in the life of believers (what this means will be elucidated in the next subsection). Verses

5–8 bring out forcefully the absolute opposition existing between the Spirit of God and all that belongs to Him, on the one hand, and, on the other hand, the flesh, that is, our fallen, egocentric human nature and all that belongs to it. Verse 9 underlines the decisive fact that God has given His Spirit to indwell believers. And, finally, vv. 10 and 11, taking up the 'and of death' of v. 2, bring out the truth that the life which is characterized by the indwelling of the Spirit of God is necessarily a life which breathes the promise of resurrection and of eternal life.

The closely-knit character of the argument of this subsection, which at first sight is not at all obvious but becomes apparent when the verses are carefully analysed, should be noted.

1. So then there is now no condemnation for those who are in Christ Jesus draws out the significance ('then') of 7.1–6, in which Paul took up and elucidated his statement 'you are not under the law' in 6.14; and its content confirms our interpretation of 6.14b; 7.4 and 6.

2. For the law of the Spirit of life has in Christ Jesus set thee free from the law of sin and of death. This translation assumes several decisions about the Greek original, for example, that 'in Christ Jesus' is to be connected closely with the verb, not with 'life'; that the textual variant which gives 'me' rather than 'thee' is to be explained as assimilation to the use of the first person singular in chapter 7, and that which gives 'us' as assimilation to the first person plural in 8.4, while that which has no object of the verb expressed should be regarded as an accidental error. Having used 'law' metaphorically in 7.23 (compare 7.21 and 25b) to denote the authority or control exercised over men by sin, Paul now, it seems, goes on to use it also to denote the authority, control, constraint, exercised upon believers by the Holy Spirit. God's gift of His Spirit to believers, by which the Spirit's authority and constraint have been brought to bear upon their lives, has freed them from the authority and constraint exercised by sin and by death (sin's natural concomitant). The words 'in Christ Jesus' point to God's saving deed in Christ as the basis of the liberating work of the Spirit. The striking, and here quite unexpected, use of the second person singular 'thee' is surely to be explained as due to Paul's own consciousness that his affirmation in v. 2 is, on the surface, a contradiction of what he has just said in 7.14b and in much of what follows it, and that, if his readers are to grasp the true significance of v. 2, their committed attention must be claimed as directly and personally as possible. How can it make sense to say of the same people that they are still slaves under sin's power and also that the power of God's Holy Spirit has set them free from the power of sin and death?

It is this question which has to be honestly faced and answered, if justice is to be done to Paul's thought and to the truth of the gospel. It must surely be said, on the one hand, that no Christian escapes from the hold of sin during this life, that even the very best Christians constantly fall short of God's righteous requirements, that even the very best things they do are marred by their sinfulness, and that any impression of having attained to a perfect freedom is but an illusion, itself the expression of that very egotism which is the essence of man's sinfulness. But, on the other hand, it must surely be said that there is such a difference between the believer's and the unbeliever's relation to the power of sin as justifies Paul's use of 'has . . . set . . . free'. The believer is no longer an unresisting, or only ineffectually resisting, slave. In him a constraint even stronger than that of sin is already at work, which both gives him an inner freedom, so that he already, in so far as the inner man is concerned, delights in God's law (7.22) and already with his mind is committed to, and serves, it (7.25b), and also enables him to revolt against the usurping power of sin with a real measure of effectiveness. He has received the freedom to fight back manfully. Though the hold of his old master is not yet destroyed, his new – his rightful – Master has a firm hold upon him, and has claimed him for Himself and will not let go His claim. Having received the precious gift of the freedom to resist sin's power over us and to strike effective blows in our rightful Master's cause, though we shall not, if we heed Paul's teaching, imagine that we can be perfect in this life, we are indeed encouraged steadfastly to hope and strenuously to strive

> 'That to perfection's sacred height
>   We nearer still may rise'.

And we know that, powerful though sin still is over us and in us, and capable of worsting us again and again, the power of the Spirit is far stronger and must triumph at the end, and the power of sin and death pass away.

3–4. The initial **For** indicates the connexion between vv. 3–4 and v. 2: the presupposition and basis of the liberating bestowal of the Spirit (and of the absence of condemnation for those who are in Christ) are God's decisive deed in Christ. **God, having sent his own Son in the likeness of sinful flesh and to deal with sin, condemned sin in the flesh** states in summary fashion what the divine deed was. In the original 'his own' is specially emphatic. By 'sinful flesh' Paul no doubt meant our fallen human nature. But why did he say 'in the likeness of sinful flesh' rather than simply 'in sinful flesh'? Four suggestions must be mentioned:

(i) that he introduced 'the likeness of' in order to avoid implying that the Son of God has assumed *fallen* human nature, the sense intended being: like our fallen flesh, because really flesh, but only like, and not identical with, it, because unfallen. This, though it is the traditional solution, is open to the general theological objection that it was not unfallen, but fallen, human nature which needed redeeming.

(ii) that he inserted 'the likeness of' in order to avoid the possibility of giving the impression that Christ actually sinned, the sense intended being: like our fallen human nature, because really our fallen human nature, and yet only like ours, because not guilty of actual sin, by which everywhere else our fallen nature is characterized.

(iii) that the word represented by 'likeness' is here to be understood as meaning 'form' rather than 'likeness' – that is, without any suggestion of mere resemblance.

(iv) that the intention behind the use of 'likeness' here (compare its use in Phil 2.7, where there is no specific mention of sin) was to take account of the fact that the Son of God was not changed into a man, but rather assumed human nature while still remaining Himself. On this view the Greek word used has its sense of 'likeness'; but the intention is not in any way to water down the reality of Christ's fallen human nature, but to draw attention to the fact that, while the Son of God truly assumed fallen human nature, He never became fallen human nature and nothing more (nor fallen human nature indwelt by the Holy Spirit and nothing more – as a Christian might be described as being), but always remained Himself.

We have already indicated the serious theological objection to (i). Against (iii) it must be said that, on this view, it is difficult to see why Paul was not content simply to say 'in sinful flesh'. With regard to (ii), the use of the expression 'in the likeness of sinful flesh' hardly seems a satisfactory way of indicating that, though sharing our fallen human nature, Christ never actually sinned; for the effect of the use of 'the likeness of' is to indicate a difference between Christ's human nature and ours (that His human nature was like, but only like, ours), but the difference between Christ's freedom from actual sin and our sinfulness is not a matter of the character of His human nature (of its being not quite the same as ours), but of what He did with His human nature. And, if this suggestion is right, it may be further suggested that the natural place for Paul to refer to Christ's sinlessness was not in the participial clause which is concerned with God's sending of His Son, but in the main sentence 'God . . . condemned sin in the flesh', and that, rightly interpreted, 'condemned . . . ' does indeed include the affirmation of Christ's sinlessness. We conclude that (iv) is to be accepted as the most probable explanation of Paul's use of 'the likeness of' here, and understand Paul's thought to be that the Son of God assumed the selfsame fallen human nature that is ours, but that in His case that fallen human nature was never the whole of Him – He never ceased to be the eternal Son of God.

The words translated 'to deal with sin' could mean 'for a sin offering'; but, since the context seems to give no support for this sacrificial interpretation, it is better to take the words in a general sense as indicating that with which the mission of the Son had to do.

In connexion with 'condemned sin in the flesh', two questions have to be asked: first, how is 'in the flesh' to be understood? and, secondly, what is meant by 'condemned'? Of these the former is quite easily answered. The phrase must be connected not with 'sin' but with the verb 'condemned'. It indicates where God's 'condemnation' of sin took place. It took place in the flesh, that is, in Christ's flesh, Christ's human nature. The latter is more difficult. It must, in view of the words which we shall have next to consider, mean more than the pronouncing of sentence of condemnation, in fact, such a combination of sentence and its execution as constitutes a final and altogether decisive dealing with its object – so God's effective breaking of sin's power. That Paul had in mind Christ's death as the event in which the full weight of God's wrath against sin (see 1.18) was, in the flesh of Christ, that is, in His human nature, so effectively brought to bear upon all the sin of all mankind, as to rule out its ever having to be brought to bear upon it in any other flesh – this is scarcely to be doubted. But, if we recognize that Paul believed it was fallen human nature which the Son of God assumed, we shall probably be inclined to see here also a reference to the unintermittent warfare of His whole earthly life by which He forced our rebellious nature to render a perfect obedience to God.

(the thing which the law was unable to do, because it was weak through the flesh) refers to the action denoted by 'condemned sin'. The law could not accomplish the altogether decisive and effective action of which Paul is thinking, though it could, of course, and did, and still does, condemn sin in the sense of pronouncing God's condemnation of it. The point of the words 'because it was weak through the flesh' is to indicate that this inability of the law is not a fault in the law for which the law can be blamed but is something inherent in the situation resulting from man's fall.

so that the righteous requirement of the law might be fulfilled in us who do not walk according to the flesh but according to the Spirit expresses the purpose of God's 'condemnation' of sin. And, since God's purposes come in the end to fulfilment, we may say that these words express also its result – it leads to this. At the same time this purpose-clause clarifies the significance of the liberation spoken of in v. 2. This is the meaning of the believer's liberation from the control of sin and of death. This is what we have been set free for. The use of the singular 'righteous requirement' is significant. It brings out the fact that the law's requirements are essentially a unity, the plurality of commandments being not a confused and confusing conglomeration but a recognizable and intelligible whole, the fatherly will of God for His children. God's purpose in 'condemning' sin was that His law's requirement might be fulfilled in us, that is, that His law might be established in the sense of at last being truly and sincerely obeyed – the fulfilment of the promises of Jer 31.33 and Ezek 36.26f. But 'might be fulfilled' is not to be taken to imply that the faithful fulfil the law's requirement perfectly. Chapter 7 must not be forgotten. They fulfil it in the sense that they do have a real faith in God (which is the law's basic demand), in the sense that their lives are definitely turned in the direction of obedience, that they do sincerely desire to obey and are earnestly striving to advance ever nearer to perfection. But, so long as they remain in this present life, their faith is always in some measure mixed with unbelief, their obedience is always imperfect and incomplete. And this means of course that there can never be any question of their being able to make their new obedience a claim on God.

The relative clause is not to be understood as expressing a condition of the law's requirement's being fulfilled in us (as though the meaning were 'in order that the righteous requirement of the law might be fulfilled in us, provided we walk . . . '), nor yet as describing us as we are independently of the fulfilment of the law's requirement and independently also of the divine action described in v. 3 (as though our so walking were our own doing, our independent and meritorious work), but rather as indicating the manner of the fulfilment of the law's requirement (God's purpose in sending His Son and condemning sin was that the requirement of the law might be fulfilled by our walking not according to the flesh but according to the Spirit). Thus these words serve to clarify the meaning of 'might be fulfilled'. The law's requirement will be fulfilled by the determination of the direction, the set, of our lives by the Spirit, by our being enabled again and again to decide for the Spirit and against the flesh, to turn our backs more and more upon our own insatiable egotism and to turn our faces more and more toward the freedom which the Spirit of God has given us.

5. For those whose lives are determined by the flesh are on the flesh's side, but those whose lives are determined by the Spirit are on Spirit's side. The initial 'For' may be said to indicate the relation to v. 4 not just of v. 5 but of vv. 5–11 as a whole. They provide an explanation of the reference in v. 4 to walking not according to the flesh but according to the Spirit. In view of the widespread attestation of the Greek expression, which can be translated literally 'to mind the things of someone' (compare the RV here and in Mk 8.33), meaning 'to be of someone's mind', 'to be on someone's side', 'to be of someone's party', and the appropriateness of such a sense here, we take Paul's meaning to be that those who allow the direction of their lives to be determined by the flesh are actually taking the flesh's side in the conflict between the Spirit of God and the flesh, while those who allow the Spirit to determine the direction of their lives are taking the Spirit's side.

6. For the flesh's mind is death, but the Spirit's mind is life and peace is apparently intended as explanation of the opposition between the Spirit and the flesh presupposed in v. 5. It must be insisted (with all due deference to the AV, Barrett, and others) that the Greek expressions we have here represented by 'the flesh's mind' and 'the Spirit's mind' are not equivalents of the expressions, the literal translations of which are 'mind the things of the flesh' and 'mind the things of the Spirit', but denote, respectively, the flesh's (that is, fallen human nature's) mind, that is, its outlook, assumptions, values, desires and purposes, which those who take the side of the flesh share, and the Spirit's mind, which those who take the side of the Spirit share. The predicates 'is death' and 'is life and peace' characterize the mind of the flesh and the mind of the Spirit in terms of their respective fruits, of what in the end they amount to.

7–8. For the mind of the flesh is enmity toward God explains why the mind of the flesh has death for its fruit: it is because it is essentially enmity toward God. **for it is not subject to God's law – indeed, it cannot be** is, in its turn, explanatory of the preceding sentence. Fallen man's fierce hostility to God is the response of his egotism (which is the essence of his fallenness) to God's claim to his allegiance. Determined to assert himself, to assert his independence, to be the centre of his own life, to be his own god, he cannot help but hate the real God whose very existence gives the lie to all his self-assertion. His hatred of God and his rebellion against God's claim upon him expressed in God's law are inseparable from each other. As a rebel against God he hates God, and as one who hates God he rebels against Him. That mind of our fallen nature (its assumptions, desires, outlook, etc.) which is enmity toward God is also unsubmissive to His law, and indeed by its very nature is incapable of submitting to it. Even in the Christian this is still true, as 7.14–25 has made clear: but in the Christian fallen human nature is not left to itself. **and those who are in the flesh cannot please God** simply repeats the substance of v. 7 in a personal form, which prepares the way for the direct address to the readers in v. 9. Here and in v. 9 (as also in 7.5), 'in the flesh' is used, not simply to indicate the conditions common to all who are in this present life (including those who are walking 'according to the Spirit'), as it is, for example, in Gal 2.20, but in the sense which was expressed in v. 4 by 'according to the flesh'. Those who allow the direction of their lives to be determined by their fallen nature are, so long as they do so, unable to please God, because they are fundamentally hostile to Him and opposed to His will.

9. But you are not in the flesh but in the Spirit. Paul now addresses the Roman Christians directly. They are not 'in the flesh' in the sense in which the expression was used in v. 8 and consequently unable to please God: on the contrary, they are 'in the Spirit'. The direction of their life is determined not by the flesh but by the Spirit of God. Paul's statement is made as a statement of fact, of their actual situation which has been brought about by God. The following **seeing that God's Spirit dwells in you** is an appeal to a fact acknowledged by them, in confirmation of the statement which Paul has just made. For the use of 'dwell in', denoting what Sanday and Headlam call 'a settled permanent penetrative influence', possession by a power superior to the self, compare 7.17, 18, 20; 8.11; 1 Cor 3.16; Col 3.16. Used of the Holy Spirit, it attests the reality and at the same time the infinite grace and mystery of His presence in the lives of believers.

(If someone does not possess Christ's Spirit, then he does not belong to Christ,) The purpose of the parenthesis is the positive one of asserting that every Christian is indwelt by the Spirit, that truly to belong to Christ as a believer, however weak, carries with it possession of the Spirit. It does, however, also of course have a negative significance, namely, that the man who does not have the Spirit (whose life bears no evidences of the Spirit's sanctifying work) is no Christian, however much he may claim to be one (compare what was said above on chapter 6) – though this is not the point which Paul wishes to stress here. That the same Spirit is meant by both God's Spirit and Christ's Spirit is evident. The ease with which Paul can pass from the one expression to the other is one more indication of his recognition of the divine dignity of Christ.

10–11. But, if Christ is in you: The fact that Paul, after referring to the Spirit's dwelling in Christians in v. 9, now goes on to speak of Christ's being in them, has led some to conclude that he was unable to distinguish between the exalted Christ and the Spirit. But neither this passage nor 2 Cor 3.17f demands such an interpretation, and both passages contain phrases which are inconsistent with the identification of the Spirit and the exalted Christ ('Christ's Spirit' in v. 9 and 'The Spirit of the Lord' in 2 Cor 3.17). Paul's thought is rather that through the indwelling of the Spirit Christ Himself is present to us, the indwelling of the Spirit being – to use John Calvin's phrase – 'the manner of Christ's dwelling in us'. The sentence continues: **though your body is indeed mortal because of *your* sin, the Spirit is life because of *your* justification.** The Christian has still to submit to death as the wages of sin, because he is a sinner; but, since Christ is in them through the indwelling of the Holy Spirit, they have the presence of the Spirit (who is essentially life-giving) as the guarantee that they will finally be raised from death. The significance of 'because of *your* justification' is that, just as their having to die is due to the fact of their sin, so their being indwelt by the life-giving Spirit as the pledge of their future resurrection (that is, the Spirit's being life *for them*, not, of course, His being life *in itself*) is due to the fact of their justification.

But, if the Spirit of him who raised Jesus from the dead dwells in you, he who raised from the dead Christ Jesus shall quicken your mortal bodies also through his Spirit who dwells in you spells out more precisely the affirmation made in v. 10. Paul again refers to the Spirit's indwelling, but this time, instead of speaking simply of 'God's Spirit' or 'Christ's Spirit' (as in v. 9), he speaks of 'the Spirit of him who raised Jesus from the dead', because he wants to bring out the close connexion between the resurrection of Christians and the resurrection of Christ (compare 1 Cor 6.14; 15.20, 23; 2 Cor 4.14; Phil 3.21; 1 Th 4.14). Calvin understood 'shall quicken' to refer to the ethical renewal of the believer; but, in view of what seems to be the meaning of v. 10, of the way in which the thought of dying and living is picked up in v. 13, and also of the fact that the subject of ethics seems to be introduced in v. 12 as something which has not been referred to for some verses, it is better to understand it as referring to the final resurrection. The point which 'also' is meant to emphasize is, of course, not that their bodies will be quickened as well as their spirits, but that they will be quickened in addition to Christ.

The textual variation between 'through' and 'because of' indicated by the RV margin is a variation between a genitive case and an accusative after a Greek preposition which, when followed by a genitive, means 'through' or 'by means of', but, when followed by an accusative, means 'because of', 'on account of', or 'for the sake of'. It is hardly possible to decide the issue with certainty (both readings have strong and early attestation); but the genitive, and so the meaning 'through', seems rather more likely to be original, since an alteration of an original genitive here to an accusative is explicable as assimilation to the accusatives 'sin' and 'justification' with the same Greek preposition in v. 10, whereas an alteration in the opposite direction (whether accidental or deliberate) is not easy to explain. If the accusative were accepted, the meaning would be that the Spirit indwelling believers now will be a reason for God's raising them up hereafter; but, if the genitive is accepted, the meaning is that the Spirit who now indwells believers will hereafter be the agent of the Father in raising them up.

(ii) *The indwelling of the Spirit – the establishment of God's law* (8.12–16)

[12]**So then, brothers, we are debtors, not to the flesh to live according to the flesh.** [13]**For if you live according to the flesh, you will certainly die; but if by the Spirit you put to death the activities of the body, you shall live.** [14]**For as many as are led by the Spirit of God, these are sons of God.** [15]**For you have not received a spirit of slavery to lead you back into fear, but you have received the Spirit of adoption, by whose enabling we cry, 'Abba, Father'.** [16]**The Spirit himself assures our spirit that we are children of God.**

The subsection begins by referring to the obligation which rests on Paul and the recipients of the letter (the first person plural is used here), making the negative point that this obligation is not to the flesh to live according to it. After breaking off to warn the recipients (second person plural) of the consequence which will follow, if they do yield allegiance to the flesh, Paul then, instead of going on to speak positively of the believers' obligation to the Spirit, promises life to the Roman Christians if they mortify the flesh. Verse 14 clarifies v. 13b, repeating its substance in different terms and as a general third person plural statement: the life promised for believers is no mere not-dying, but life as sons of God. Verse 15 with its positive assertion, 'you have received the Spirit of adoption', harks back to the basic indicatives of vv. 1–11 which are the presupposition of what is said in vv. 12–16, and gives to the obligation to the Spirit to live according to the Spirit, which was implied in v. 12 but never expressed, definitive expression in the relative clause, 'by whose enabling we cry, "Abba, Father" '. The implication of this verse understood in its context is that it is in the believers' calling God 'Father' that God's holy law is established and its 'righteous requirement'(v. 4) fulfilled, and that the whole of Christian obedience is included in this calling God 'Father'. The verse, in fact, states in principle everything that there is to say in the way of Christian ethics; for there is nothing more required of us than that we should do just this – with full understanding of what it means, with full seriousness and with full sincerity. For to address the true God by the name of Father with full sincerity and seriousness will involve seeking wholeheartedly to be and think and say and do that which is pleasing to Him and to avoid everything which displeases Him. (But Paul knows, of course, that Christians continue to be sinners so long as they live this present life (compare 7.14ff), and so he knows how necessary it is also to spell out in concrete and particular exhortation what is involved in calling God 'Father' truly – a task he will attempt to fulfil for the Roman church in 12.1–15.13.) Paul speaks of this calling God 'Father' as something which is actually happening ('we cry'). Believers do this, and their doing it is God's gift given in His gift of His Spirit. The indicative, of course, contains an implicit imperative – that they must continue to do it, and do it ever more and more sincerely, consistently and resolutely. But Paul sees the imperative as being essentially God's gift, the freedom which He has given us in His gift of His Spirit on the basis of Christ's completed work, the freedom which we are permitted to enjoy. Finally, v. 16 points to our warrant for daring to call God 'Father' – the fact that He, whose testimony is in this matter the only testimony which carries weight, Himself assures us that we are God's children.

12. So then, brothers introduces a new paragraph setting out the practical conclusion to be drawn from vv. 1–11. The position of the 'not' in the following **we are debtors, not to the flesh to live according to the flesh** strongly suggests that Paul intended to continue with something like 'but to the Spirit to live according to the Spirit', but broke off in order to insert the warning of v. 13a, and then, after adding a natural complement to v. 13a, failed to complete the sentence begun in v. 12. For 'debtors' see on 1.14. It follows from what has been said in vv. 1–11 that we have no duty to the flesh to allow our lives to be determined by it. For 'according to the flesh' see on vv. 4 and 5.

13. For if you live according to the flesh, you will certainly die; but if by the Spirit you put to death the activities of the body, you shall live. The two contrasted conditional clauses indicate the choice confronting the people addressed. Compare Deut 11.26ff and 30.15ff: in the latter passage, as here, life and death are presented as the consequences of the alternative ways. The verb 'die' is used pregnantly: the meaning is not merely that they will die (those who live according to the Spirit also have to die – compare v. 10), but that they will die without hope of life with God. The Greek dative represented by 'by the Spirit' is instrumental. The Spirit of God – and only the Spirit of God – is to be the means of the destruction of the flesh's activities. But the use of the dative is certainly not to be taken to imply that the Holy Spirit is a tool in the hands of Christians, wielded and managed by them. The first eleven words of v. 14 afford a safeguard against such a misapprehension. The putting to death is an action which is continuous or again and again repeated, not one which can be done once for all. The word 'body' is here apparently used in the sense of 'flesh'. It is not the body's activities, which include such things as sleeping and walking, which are intended, but the activities and schemings (the Greek word translated 'activities' can be used pejoratively with a suggestion of intrigue and treachery) of the sinful flesh, of one's self-centredness and self-assertiveness. For the promise 'you shall live' (that is, eternally) compare 1.17 ('shall live') and the notes on it.

14. For as many as are led by the Spirit of God, these are sons of

God is explanatory of v. 13b, which it may be said to repeat in different terms. The words 'as many as are led by the Spirit of God' interpret 'if by the Spirit you put to death the activities of the body'. The daily, hourly putting to death of the schemings and enterprises of the sinful flesh by means of the Spirit is a matter of being led, directed, impelled, controlled by the Spirit. Though the active participation of the Christian is indeed involved ('you put to death'), it is fundamentally the work of the Spirit (hence the passive 'are led'). The words 'are sons of God' interpret 'you shall live'. The life which God promises is not a mere not-dying: it is to be a son of God, to live as a son of God, both now and hereafter.

15. **For you have not received a spirit of slavery to lead you back into fear, but you have received the Spirit of adoption** is best explained as meaning simply that the Holy Spirit, whom the Roman Christians have received, is not a spirit of bondage, to receive which would be to be led back into the sort of anxious fears that they had experienced in the past (whether in paganism or in Judaism), but the Spirit of adoption. The emphasis is on the positive assertion. By 'the Spirit of adoption' is meant surely the Spirit who brings about adoption, uniting men with Christ by enabling them to believe in Him, and so making them sharers in His sonship. Barrett's translation of the Greek phrase as 'the Spirit which anticipates our adoption as sons' on the ground that v. 23 'makes quite clear that our adoption . . . lies in the future' must, we think, be rejected, because it makes nonsense of the present tenses in v. 14 (the second 'are') and v. 16 ('are').

by whose enabling we cry, 'Abba, Father'. It is possible to connect this clause either with what precedes it, as we have done, placing a comma after 'of adoption' and a full stop after 'Father', or with what follows, placing a full stop after 'of adoption' and a comma after 'Father'. If the former alternative is adopted, the relative pronoun which is the second word of the clause in the original must refer to 'the Spirit' and the first two words must mean 'in whom' or 'by whom' (hence our rendering, 'by whose enabling'). If, however, the latter alternative is chosen, the first two words must mean 'When' or 'In that'. The former alternative should, we think, be preferred. In its favour and against the other punctuation, the following points may be made: (i) If this clause is connected with what follows, then the preceding part of v. 15

seems incomplete both stylistically (since there is nothing to balance 'to lead you back into fear') and also as far as the meaning is concerned (since 'Spirit of adoption' is a new, and not easy, expression, which would seem to require some explanation within the same sentence); (ii) If this clause is connected with what precedes, it not only serves to balance 'to lead you back into fear' and to clarify the meaning of 'Spirit of adoption', but it also (construed in this way) states a theological truth of great importance, namely, that it is the Spirit who enables us to call God 'Father'; (iii) If these words are taken with v. 16 and the first two of them understood as meaning 'when' (as in the RSV), the resulting sentence, consisting of these words together with v. 16, seems to suggest that the Spirit's testimony depends on our initiative. But, if these words are connected with what precedes, the Spirit's testimony is not in any way confined to the fact of our calling God 'Father', but our doing so is represented as the result of God's gift of His Spirit. That this is more consonant with Paul's thought as expressed elsewhere can scarcely be doubted.

We assume then that these words are to be taken with the rest of v. 15. The relative clause clarifies the use of 'Spirit of adoption'. He is the One in whom, that is, enabled by whom, Christians cry 'Abba'. The use of the particular Greek verb represented by 'cry' has given rise to a variety of suggestions (for example, that it is special ecstatic prayer to which Paul refers); but, in view of the fact that the verb is used again and again in the Septuagint version of the Old Testament (in Psalms alone more than forty times) of urgent prayer, it is best taken here simply as denoting an urgent and sincere prayer to God irrespective of whether it is loud or soft (or even unspoken), formal or informal, public or private.

For the use of 'Abba' compare Mk 14.36 and Gal 4.6. This Aramaic word, used by Jesus, continued for a while to be used in the Greek-speaking Church. In origin an exclamatory form used by small children, it had by the time of Jesus come to be used more extensively, being no longer confined to the speech of children. But its homely and affectionate origin was apparently not forgotten. It does not seem to have been used as a form of address to God in ancient Judaism, and its non-vocative use with reference to God is found only extremely rarely. Its use by Jesus expressed His consciousness of a unique relationship to God, and His authorizing them to address God in this way is to be understood as His giving them a share in His relationship to God. The translation 'Father' was perhaps rather more probably added for the sake of emphasis than because it was thought necessary for some of the Roman Christians. That the thought of the recital of the Lord's Prayer was present to Paul's mind, when he composed this clause, is highly likely, but there seems to be no good reason for thinking that he had it in mind exclusively.

Now that we are in a better position to see v. 15 as a whole, we must try to understand its function in the structure of the subsection. In v. 12 Paul stated the negative obligation which follows from what was said in vv. 1–11. He omitted to express the complementary positive obligation, though he expressed the negative obligation in such a way as to suggest that the positive was also in his mind. In v. 13a he gave a warning of the consequences of ignoring the negative obligation; and then in v. 13b instead of going on to state the positive obligation directly, he put it into the form of a conditional clause ('if by the Spirit you put to death the activities of the body') with a main clause stating the promise contingent on its fulfilment. Verse 14 takes up the conditional clause of v. 13b (being 'led by the Spirit of God' is equivalent to putting 'to death the activities of the body'), though by its use of the passive instead of the active bringing out the point that what is meant is in the last resort the work of God's Spirit, and asserts that those who fulfil it – or, rather, in whom it is fulfilled – are God's sons. Verse 15 (which in its turn will be confirmed by v. 16) harks back with its confident positive assertion, 'you have received the Spirit of adoption', to the fundamental indicatives of vv. 1–11 which are the context and presupposition of vv. 12ff, and gives to the obligation to live according to the Spirit, which was implied but never expressed in v. 12, its final and definitive expression in the relative clause, 'by whose enabling we cry, "Abba, Father" '. This then is what it means to live after the Spirit, to mortify by the Spirit the deeds of the body, and to be led by the Spirit of God – simply to be enabled by that same Spirit to cry, 'Abba, Father'. And it is here expressed not as an imperative but as an indicative: Christians do as a matter of fact do this. The implicit imperative is that they should continue to do just this, and do it more and more consistently, more and more sincerely, soberly and responsibly. This is all that is required of them. It is what the whole law of God is aimed at achieving. All that must be said about the Christian's obedience has been already said in principle when this has been said. Nothing more is required of us than that we should cry to the one true God 'Abba, Father' with full sincerity and with full seriousness. That this necessarily includes seeking with all our heart to be and think and say and do what is well-pleasing to Him and to avoid all that displeases Him, should go without saying. In the accomplishment of this work of obedience 'the righteous requirement of the law' is fulfilled (compare v. 4) and God's holy law established.

16. The Spirit himself assures our spirit that we are children of God. Here two interrelated questions have to be asked: (i) What is the relation of this verse to v. 15? and (ii) Does the Greek compound verb represented by 'assure' mean 'witness together with' or 'witness to', 'assure'? With regard to (i), the mistake has often been made (and it has by no means been confined to those who put a full stop after 'adoption') of turning things upside down by looking to the fact of our calling God 'Father' to explain v. 16, instead of seeing v. 16 as explanation of the use of 'Spirit of adoption' and the clause which follows it. Verse 16 is surely intended to confirm and clarify what has preceded it by indicating that our crying 'Abba, Father' rests upon something prior to it and independent of it, namely, the fact that no less an authority than God Himself in His Spirit has assured us – and continues to assure us – that we are His children. The knowledge that we are God's children (not to be confused with any merely natural desire of weak human beings to feel that there is someone greater and stronger than themselves who is kindly disposed to them) is something which we cannot impart to ourselves: it has to be given to us from outside and beyond ourselves – from God. Verse 16 is Paul's solemn and emphatic statement that this knowledge has been given to us. This knowledge is not to be identified with our calling God 'Father': it is rather the warrant for it. And the Spirit's imparting of it is not to be identified simply with His immediate inspiration of the prayer 'Abba, Father' (not even when that is understood, as we have suggested it should be, in the widest sense, as embracing all the obedience of Christians), but rather with His whole work of enabling us to believe in Jesus Christ, through whom alone we may rightly call God 'Father'.

With regard to (ii), it may be said that, if the Greek compound verb which we have rendered 'assures' is taken to mean 'witnesses together with', as it is by many interpreters both ancient and modern, and by the NEB and JB, and if at the same time 'our spirit' is given its natural meaning of 'our (own human) spirit' then the sense of the verse is that the Holy Spirit and our own human spirit are linked together as two witnesses to the fact that we are children of God. But what standing has our spirit in *this* matter? Of itself it surely has no right at all to testify to our being sons of God. To get over this very serious objection, recourse has often (from early times) been had to such suggestions as that by 'our spirit' is meant our new nature, the self renewed by Christ, or the spiritual gift that has been given to us; but explanations of this sort seem over-subtle. Even when full allowance has been made for the influence exercised by Deut 19.15 ('One witness shall not rise up against a man . . . : at the mouth of two witnesses, or at the mouth of three witnesses, shall a matter be established') in primitive Christian thought, it seems better here to follow the example of the Vulgate and take the verb in its other (well established) sense of 'testify to', 'assure'. We may then give to 'our spirit' its natural meaning.

(iii) *The indwelling of the Spirit – the gift of hope* (8.17–30)

[17]And if children, then also heirs: heirs of God and fellow-heirs of Christ, seeing that we are *now* suffering with him, in order that we may *hereafter* be glorified with him. [18]For I reckon that the sufferings of the present time are not worthy to be compared with the glory which is to be revealed in us. [19]For the eager expectation of the creation is waiting for the revelation of the sons of God. [20]For the creation was subjected to vanity, not of its own will but because of him who subjected it, in hope, [21]because the creation itself too shall be set free from the bondage of decay into the liberty of the glory of the children of God. [22]For we know that the whole creation groans and travails with one accord even until now. [23]And not only *this*, but we also ourselves who have the firstfruits of the Spirit, even ourselves, groan within ourselves, waiting for our adoption, that is,

the redemption of our bodies. [24]For it was in hope that we were saved; but when once something hoped for is seen it ceases to be the object of hope; for who hopes for what he actually sees?* [25]But since we hope for what we do not see, we wait for it with steadfast patience. [26]And in like manner the Spirit also helps our weakness; for we do not know what it is right for us to pray for, but the Spirit himself intercedes for us with unspoken groanings, [27]and he who searches the hearts knows what is the intention of the Spirit, that he is interceding for the saints according to God's will. [28]And we know that all things prove advantageous for *their true* good to those who love God, that is, to those who are called according to his purpose. [29]For whom he foreknew, he also foreordained to be conformed to the image of his Son, so that he might be the firstborn among many brothers; [30]and whom he foreordained, these he also called; and whom he called, these he also justified; and whom he justified, these he also glorified.

Verse 17 makes the transition to the subject with which this subsection is concerned – Christian hope. The life which is characterized by the indwelling of the Spirit of God, which is a life in which God's law is established, is a life characterized by hope. Verses 18, 19, 21 and the latter part of v. 23 give some indication of the content of this hope, of the transcendent worth of the glory to be hoped for, and of the fact that it touches not only believers, not even only mankind as a whole, but God's whole creation. An indication of the painfulness of the present context of this hope, of the circumstances in which it must be exercised, is given by v. 20; and this painfulness of hope's present context is emphasized by the reference to the groaning of creation (v. 22) and to the groaning of believers (vv. 23–25). In vv. 26–27, while their formal function seems to be to set alongside the groanings just mentioned a third groaning, namely, that of the Spirit (so v. 26 begins with 'And in like manner . . . also'), the thought of the Spirit's groaning ('with unspoken groanings') is mastered by the positive thought of what the Spirit's groaning accomplishes for believers. Verses 28–30 express the certainty of Christian hope.

---

*The translation of the last part of the verse presupposes the reading and punctuation adopted in Nestle[26].

This subsection will hardly be properly understood, unless the poetic quality displayed in it, particularly in vv. 19–22, is duly recognized. What is involved in these verses is not what belongs to the outward form of poetry, such things as artistic arrangement and rhythm, but rather those things which belong to its inner essence, imaginative power (to be seen, for instance, in the use of images), feeling for the richly evocative word, a deep sensitivity, catholicity of sympathy, and a true generosity of vision and conception. That the passage owes something to the Jewish apocalyptic tradition is not to be denied (various parallels to Paul's language may be adduced in apocalyptic and elsewhere); but, when such debts have been fully allowed for, the whole has certainly not been told. What is to be seen in these verses is an attempt by a poetic imagination, which is at the same time both altogether obedient to, and splendidly liberated by, the gospel, to suggest something of the glory of that future, worthy of Himself, which God has in store for His creation.

17. And if children, then also heirs: heirs of God and fellow-heirs of Christ by its movement of thought from sonship to heirship effects the transition to the subject of Christian hope (already hinted at in vv. 10–11, 13b and, of course, earlier in the epistle), with which the rest of the chapter is concerned. In the Pauline epistles there are three main places where the language of inheriting is used: Romans 4, Galatians 3–4, and this passage. There are interesting parallels between them; but the differences between them are such that it is better not to assume (as some have tended to do) that Rom 8.17 is to be explained simply on the basis of one or other or of both the other two passages, but to explain it independently of them. We shall then not be inhibited from recognizing the full import of what is being said. The term 'heirs of God' is not to be explained as meaning simply 'heirs of Abraham, who are to receive in due course the blessings which God promised to him and to his seed', nor is the paradox involved in referring to 'heirs of [the eternal] God' to be removed by appealing to the fact that the two Hebrew verbs, which were used when hereditary succession was referred to, mean primarily and most often not 'obtain by hereditary succession' but, respectively, 'possess' and 'have divided out to one as one's share'; for here in Rom 8.17 there is the closest possible relationship between heirship and sonship, and the sonship in question is quite clearly (compare v. 16) that of God's children. The imagery, of course, breaks down; for, since the eternal God does not die (the thought which is present in Heb 9.15–17 is not present here), there is no question of God's heirs' succeeding Him. But it points extraordinarily effectively to the facts that Christians are men who have great expectations; that their expectations are based upon their being sons of God; that these expectations are of sharing not just in various blessings God is able to bestow but in that which is peculiarly His own, the perfect and imperishable glory of His own life; and that the determination of the time when their expectations will be realized is outside their control (the appointment of the time by God's free personal decision answering to the determination of the time of succession by the death of the testator in the case of an ordinary inheritance). The addition of 'and fellow-heirs of Christ' expresses the certainty of our hope. Our sonship and our heirship rest on our relation to Him, on His having claimed us for His own. But He has already entered upon the inheritance for which we have still to wait, and this fact is the guarantee that we too, who are His joint-heirs, will enjoy the fulfilment of our expectations.

The words **seeing that we are *now* suffering with him, in order that we may *hereafter* be glorified with him** state a fact which confirms what has just been said. We may bring out the sense by some such paraphrase as 'for the fact that we are now suffering with Him, so far from calling in question the reality of our heirship, is a sure pledge of our being glorified with Him hereafter'. The suffering with Christ referred to is neither our having died with Him in God's sight nor our having suffered with Him (sacramentally) in baptism. Had either of these 'sufferings' been in mind, a past tense would have been natural. The reference is rather to that element of suffering which is inseparable from faithfulness to Christ in a world which does not yet know Him as Lord. We may understand the former 'with him' to include more than one meaning: for example, 'in conformity with the pattern of His earthly life' (though not implying that our sufferings are redemptive in the sense in which His were), 'for His sake', 'in union with Him', and perhaps also the thought that the exalted Christ participates in His brethren's sufferings. The 'in order that' indicates not the subjective purpose of the sufferers, but the objective connexion according to God's will between suffering now with Christ and being glorified with Him hereafter.

18. For I reckon that the sufferings of the present time are not worthy to be compared with the glory which is to be revealed in us explains how the sufferings and the glory to which the preceding verse has referred stand in relation to each other. Here, as in 3.28 and 6.11, the Greek verb translated here and in 3.28 'reckon' denotes a firm conviction reached by rational thought on the basis of the gospel. From his understanding of the gospel Paul is convinced that the sufferings of the present time are but a slight thing in comparison with the glory which is to be revealed. The 'sufferings' which Paul has in mind are no doubt, in view of v. 17b, those of Christians, though in vv. 19–22 the range of interest is much wider. By 'the present time' is meant the period which began with the gospel events and will be ended by the Parousia. The glory which is to be revealed in us (RV: 'to us-ward' – it is exceedingly hard to decide how the Greek preposition can be translated most satisfactorily) is the glory of the final consummation, which will embrace us too, which will transform our condition as well as so much else.

19. For the eager expectation of the creation is waiting for the revelation of the sons of God. This sentence is introduced as support for the statement made in v. 18, but, once introduced, it itself requires expansion and elucidation. In fact, the whole of vv. 19–30 may be said to be in one way or another support for, and elucidation of, v. 18. In the course of these verses Paul indicates more fully the content of the Christian hope (vv. 19 and 21), its present painful context (vv. 20, 22–27), and its certainty (vv. 28–30). But v. 19 and vv. 20–22 which follow it are certainly not to be understood as merely an inference from the observable and generally recognized fact of the prevalence of fear and suffering in nature. What these verses affirm is something which can only be known by faith.

A variety of explanations of what Paul meant by 'the creation' here has been suggested in the course of the centuries; but the only really probable explanation is that he meant the sum-total of sub-human nature both animate and inanimate. (Believers are almost certainly excluded, since in v. 23 they are contrasted with 'the creation'; 'not of its own will' in v. 20 seems to rule out the possibility that mankind in general was intended, for, in that case, Paul could hardly have excluded Adam, and Adam cannot be said to have been subjected otherwise than as a result of his own choice; and the suggestion that the reference is only to unbelieving mankind is quite unlikely, since it can hardly be supposed that a New Testament writer would use in this way a term which expresses a relation to God in which Christians stand equally with non-Christians and in which, morever, they above all men must rejoice.) The objection that Paul's use of personal language ('eager expectation', 'is waiting for', 'not of its own will', 'in hope', 'groans . . . with one accord') is inconsistent with his intending a reference to irrational nature is not to be sustained; for there is here a personification such as is often found in the Old Testament. The further objection that, if 'the creation' refers only to the sub-human creation, there is then no reference in this passage to unbelieving mankind, is not as weighty as it seems at first sight. It may be suggested that Paul may have omitted to mention unbelievers here as a separate class contrasted with believers, because he did not accept that human unbelief presents God with an eternal fact but saw believers as the firstfruits of mankind. We take it that Paul is here speaking with poetic language and in the boldness of faith of the earnest expectancy (the word we have rendered by 'eager expectation' suggests the stretching of the neck, craning forward to see something which is approaching) of the whole splendid theatre of the universe and of all the manifold sub-human life within it as eagerly awaiting the revelation of the sons of God.

Believers are already sons of God in this life, but their sonship is veiled and their incognito is impenetrable except to faith. Even they themselves have to believe in their sonship against the clamorous evidence of much in their circumstances and condition which seems to be altogether inconsistent with the reality of it. The 'revelation of the sons of God' is the manifestation beyond all possibility of doubt or contradiction of that sonship, concerning which, until that time, it must be said that

'Concealed as yet this honour lies,
By this dark world unknown'.

20–21. For indicates the relation of these two verses to v. 19:

they explain why the creation expects so eagerly the revealing of the sons of God. The statement that **the creation was subjected to vanity** refers to a particular event, and the use of the passive veils a reference to God's action. There is little doubt that Paul had in mind the judgment related in Gen 3.17–19, which includes (v. 17) the words 'cursed is the ground for thy sake'. In the Greek 'to vanity' is given special emphasis by being placed at the beginning of the sentence. The word 'vanity' has been variously explained. The parallelism between 'was subjected to vanity' and 'bondage of decay' later in the verse has led some to assume that 'vanity' must here be used as a simple synonym of 'decay' and encouraged others to understand 'vanity' and 'decay' to mean, respectively, the mutability and mortality which characterize creaturely existence as we know it. Others have taken 'vanity' as an example of the abstract used for the concrete, and have understood Paul's meaning to be that the creation was subjected to vain men. Others have thought to see the clue to the meaning of 'vanity' here in the use of the cognate Greek verb in 1.21 ('have become futile' – RV: 'became vain') and so have suggested that Paul was thinking of men's idolatry which exploits the sub-human creation for its own purposes. Others, noting that the word could be used actually to denote a god of the heathen, have suggested that Paul meant subjection to various celestial powers and have cited Gal 4.9 in support of this view. Yet others have interpreted 'vanity' here along the lines of its use in Ecclesiastes, where it denotes the futility, the disorder, the sheer absurdity, of things. But the simplest and most straightforward interpretation would seem to be to take it in the Greek word's basic sense as denoting the ineffectiveness of that which does not attain its goal (compare the Greek cognate adverb which means 'in vain'), and to understand Paul's meaning to be that the sub-human creation has been subjected to the frustration of not being able properly to fulfil the purpose of its existence, God having appointed that without man it should not be made perfect. We may think of the whole magnificent theatre of the universe together with all its splendid properties and all the chorus of sub-human life, created to glorify God but unable to do so fully, so long as man, the chief actor in the drama of God's praise, fails to contribute his rational part.

not of its own will. On the assumption that 'the creation' signifies the whole sub-human creation, this is naturally understood as meaning 'not through its own fault'. It was not through the sub-human creation's fault that it was subjected to frustration, but through man's sin. The words **because of him who subjected it** are best taken to mean 'because of God who subjected it (on·account of man's fall)'.

But Paul has added the richly significant phrase **in hope.** It is better connected with 'was subjected' than with the immediately preceding 'him who subjected it'. The creation was not subjected to frustration without any hope: the divine judgment included the promise of a better future, when at last the judgment would be lifted. Paul possibly had in mind the promise in Gen 3.15 that the woman's seed would bruise the serpent's head (compare Rom 16.20). Hope for the creation was included within the hope for man.

because the creation itself too shall be set free from the bondage of decay into the liberty of the glory of the children of God supports and clarifies the preceding 'in hope'. In the formulation 'the creation itself too' there is an implied contrast with 'the children of God'. That Paul's main interest in these verses is in the certainty of the coming glory of believers is doubtless true; but to state categorically, as Barrett does, that Paul 'is not concerned with creation for its own sake' is surely to do him an injustice – even when full weight is given to the existence of 1 Cor 9.9. The implication of these verses is surely that Paul sees the coming glory of believers not by itself but accompanied by the glorious liberation of the whole sub-human creation – with a noble breadth and generosity of vision and sympathy such as may be expected of one who truly, and therefore sincerely and intelligently, believes in God as Creator. The liberation which Paul foresees for the creation at the time of the revelation of the sons of God is liberation 'from the bondage of decay', that is, from the·condition of being the slaves of death and decay, of corruption and transitoriness, which is the very opposite of the condition of glory. The condition which is to replace that of servitude is one of freedom, a freedom which is defined by the three genitives which follow the word 'liberty'. The first of them has often been understood as adjectival (so the AV has 'the glorious liberty'); but it seems better to take it to have a sense roughly corresponding with 'of decay'. As 'the bondage of decay' is bondage to decay, the bondage which decay may be said to impose, so, it may be suggested, 'the liberty of the glory of the children of God' is the liberty which results from, is the necessary accompaniment of, the (revelation of the) glory of the children of God. When at last the children of God are made manifest, the sub-human creation will receive again its proper liberty, the liberty of each several part of it, whether animate or inanimate, fully and perfectly to fulfil its Creator's purpose for it – the liberty which is denied to it so long as man is unready to play his part in the great drama of God's praise.

Verses 19–21 surely imply that it is not enough for the Christian to respect and – in so far as he can – to protect and cherish the sub-human creation as the habitat, the environment, the amenities, of his fellow-men, both those who are now alive and also all those who are yet to be born. If it is indeed God's creation, if He is faithful to it too as well as to mankind, and if He is going to bring it also (as well as believing men) to a goal worthy of Himself, then it has a dignity of its own and an inalienable, since divinely appointed, right to be treated by us with reverence and sensitiveness. These verses should alert us to the fact that the Christian hope is something vastly more wonderful and more generous than our preoccupation with ourselves and the feebleness of our concern for God's glory allow us to imagine.

22. For we know that the whole creation groans and travails with one accord even until now. On the use of 'we know' see on 2.2. What is here introduced as something generally known among Christians represents an old Testament insight (compare especially Gen 3.17) reflected in the apocalyptic tradition, and confirmed and sharpened by the gospel. It serves to sum up the contents of vv. 20 and 21, and so (with those verses) to support what was said in v. 19. Two thoughts, already implicit in v. 19, are here expressed more clearly, on the one hand, the thought of the creation's present painful condition, and on the other hand, the thought that that painful condition is not to no purpose but will have a worthwhile issue (expressed by the image of travail). The words 'even until now' emphasize the long continuance of this groaning and travailing.

23. And not only *this,* **but we also ourselves who have the firstfruits of the Spirit, even ourselves, groan within ourselves.** Not only does the sub-human creation groan, but even Christians groan too. This is something which may well have been puzzling for some of the first recipients of the epistle – and may well be also for some modern readers of it. But note how emphatically Paul makes his point – 'we also ourselves ... , even ourselves'. No one is to imagine that Christians are exempt from this groaning and travailing. Christians already possess what Paul terms 'the firstfruits of the Spirit'. The word represented by 'firstfruits' is used in the Septuagint version of the Old Testament mainly in connexion with the cultus (see, for example, Exod 23.19; Num 18.12; Deut 18.4). Here in Romans 8 it is used with reference not to something offered by man to God but of something given by God to man, and the idea conveyed is that of the gift of a part as a pledge of the fuller gift yet to come. What the believer has already received is a foretaste and a guarantee of what he has still to hope for. Compare the use of 'earnest' (a commercial metaphor) in 2 Cor 5.5. The genitive, 'of the Spirit', is puzzling. It has been explained variously as (i) a partitive genitive; (ii) a genitive of apposition or definition; (iii) a possessive genitive. To accept (i) means understanding 'the Spirit' as denoting the whole, of which what is denoted by 'the firstfruits' is a part. To accept (ii) means understanding 'the Spirit' as indicating that of which the firstfruits consist. On either of these explanations, 'the Spirit' must mean, not the Holy Spirit Himself, but His work in relation to us. If (iii) is accepted, 'the Spirit' must be understood as signifying the Spirit Himself, and the thought will be that the firstfruits referred to belong to Him, being His work within us. On the whole, explanation (ii) seems most probable. Paul's thought, on this view, is that believers already enjoy the firstfruits consisting of the Spirit's present work in us, which is the pledge of all the glory which God has in store for us. Paul goes on to affirm that even we who have the inestimable privilege of such a foretaste and pledge of our inheritance have, like all the rest of the creation, to groan: we groan 'within ourselves' in contrast to the groaning outside of us of the rest of the creation.

waiting for our adoption. The clue to the right understanding of this is provided by v. 19 ('is waiting for the revelation of the sons of God'). We are already sons of God (vv. 14 and 16), but our sonship is not yet manifest. We have been adopted, but our adoption has yet to be publicly proclaimed. It is the final public manifestation of our adoption which is meant by 'our adoption' here (contrast the use of the word in v. 15). **that is, the redemption of our bodies** interprets 'our adoption'. The full manifestation of our adoption is identical with the resurrection of our bodies at the Parousia, our complete and final liberation from the effects of sin and death.

24. For it was in hope that we were saved. The fact that even we who have the firstfruits of the Spirit still have to groan is understandable when it is remembered that we were saved in hope – that is, though God's saving action has already taken place, its final effect, our enjoying salvation, still lies in the future. **but when once something hoped for is seen it ceases to be the object of hope** is complementary to the preceding sentence, drawing out its implication. Paul uses 'see' in a pregnant sense, 'see and actually have within one's grasp', for otherwise his statement would not be true (it is, of course, possible for something already seen still to be an object of hope, if it is still beyond one's grasp). **for who hopes for what he actually sees?** represents the Greek as printed in Nestle[26] (1979), which is the reading for which we argued in ICC *Romans*, p. 420. Again 'see' is used pregnantly.

25. But since we hope for what we do not see, we wait for it with steadfast patience. Paul comes back to the affirmation which was made in v. 23 and which v. 24 was intended to support; but, whereas in v. 23 the accent fell rather on the negative aspect ('we ... groan') than on the positive, in this verse it is the positive aspect which stands out, the fact that the Christian life is characterized by steadfast hope for that glory which has not yet been openly revealed.

26. And in like manner the Spirit also helps our weakness. The point of 'in like manner' is that Paul is setting alongside the groaning of the creation and the groaning of believers a third groaning, that of the Spirit, though the word 'groanings' only occurs at the end of this verse and the thought of what the Spirit accomplishes for believers becomes more important than the comparison with the other two groanings. By 'our weakness' Paul admits that even in our praying (that this is what is in mind is clear from the next sentence) we are weak.

for we do not know what it is right for us to pray for. The Greek which has been translated 'what ... to pray for' could equally correctly be rendered 'what ... to pray', as far as the grammar is concerned; but 'what ... to pray for' is perhaps rather more likely to be Paul's meaning. Käsemann has insisted that, in view of the fact that encouragement of confidence and joyfulness in prayer is characteristic of the New Testament generally and the fact that Paul himself shows no sign of being inhibited with regard to prayer, this statement is explicable only on the assumption that he had in mind a particular phenomenon, namely, the phenomenon of glossolaly in the church. As a conclusion drawn by Paul from the occurrence of glossolaly in Christian worship it is, he thinks, understandable (what many Christians were admiring as a glorious heavenly manifestation, as angelic tongues, Paul saw – paradoxically – as evidence of the Church's deep weakness and ignorance). But Käsemann's basic assumption that Paul could not possibly have had in mind in this statement Christian prayer quite generally must be firmly rejected. To assert, as he does, that to predicate this not-knowing of Christian prayer in general is simply absurd and contradicts everything which the New Testament says elsewhere on this subject, and that it would rob prayer of its meaning and assurance, is to fail to take properly into account that element of paradox which is characteristic of the Christian's life in this world (see especially 2 Cor 6.8–10). Käsemann has in fact failed to reckon with Paul's being as radical here as he actually is. We take Paul's meaning to be that all praying of Christian men, in so far as it is *their* praying, remains under the sign of this not-knowing, of real ignorance, weakness and poverty, and that even in their prayers they live only by God's justification of sinners. It would indeed be strange if the continuing sinfulness of Christians (compare 7.14–25) were altogether without effect in the matter of their knowledge of what to pray for.

but the Spirit himself intercedes for us with unspoken groanings explains the positive content of the first sentence of the verse (just as the preceding words explained the reference to our weakness). The Spirit Himself helps our weakness by interceding for us. Käsemann is quite sure that 'unspoken groanings' must refer to the ecstatic cries of glossolaly; but it is surely highly questionable whether Paul would think of the ecstatic cries or sighs of certain Christians, inspired by the Spirit though they might be, as being the Spirit's own groanings. It is surely much more probable that the reference is to groanings imperceptible to the Christians themselves. Whether by 'unspoken' Paul meant 'ineffable', 'that cannot be expressed in ordinary human speech', intending to indicate the transcendence of these groanings, or whether he meant simply 'not spoken', is a further question. Verse 27 suggests that the latter possibility is more likely. The Spirit's groanings are not spoken, because they do not need to be, since God knows the Spirit's intention without its being expressed.

27. and he who searches the hearts knows what is the intention of the Spirit, that he is interceding for the saints according to God's will. God who knows the secrets of men's hearts (compare 1 Sam 16.7; 1 Kgs 8.39; Ps 7.9; 17.3; 44.21; 139.1, 2, 23; Jer 17.10; Acts 1.24; 15.8) must surely *a fortiori* be assumed to know the unspoken desires of His own Spirit.

28. And we know that all things prove advantageous for *their true good* to those who love God. Paul's use of 'And we know' (see on 2.2) suggests that he is stating in this sentence something which he knows to be generally recognized as true. The language used and the fact that Jewish and other ancient parallels can be adduced make it likely that he is deliberately incorporating a piece of traditional teaching.

The two Greek words represented by 'all things prove advantageous' are quite extraordinarily difficult for a number of reasons. There is first of all a variant reading consisting of the addition of 'God' in the nominative immediately after them; secondly, the word translated 'all things' is a neuter plural which can be either nominative or accusative; thirdly, a neuter plural subject can, and very often does, in Greek take a singular verb; and, fourthly, the verb used can have a variety of meanings. A number of possibilities have therefore to be considered:

(i) to accept the longer reading including 'God' in the nominative and explain all things as an accusative of respect ('in all things', 'in all respects');

(ii) to accept the longer reading and explain the verb as transitive and 'all things' as its object (so perhaps 'God causes all things to work', 'God worketh all things with');

(iii) to accept the shorter reading and supply 'God' as the subject of the verb, explaining 'all things' as in (i);

(iv) to accept the shorter reading and supply 'God', explaining the verb and 'all things' as in (ii);

(v) to accept the shorter reading and take 'all things' as the subject of the verb;

(vi) to accept the shorter reading and understand the subject of the verb to be the same as that of the last verb of v. 27, namely, 'the Spirit', explaining 'all things' as in (i);

(vii) as in (vi), but explaining the verb and 'all things' as in (ii);

(viii) to accept the shorter reading with the emendation of the Greek word for 'all things' to the Greek for 'the Spirit'.

Of these, (viii) can, we think, be set aside at once, on the grounds that conjectural emendation, as far as the New Testament text is concerned for which there is so vast a wealth of textual evidence, is a drastic expedient requiring very special justification, and is here quite unnecessary. Against (vi), (vii) and (viii) alike there is the serious objection that they would involve a most awkward change of subject (without indication) between vv. 28 and 29, since the reference to 'his Son' in v. 29 necessitates taking the unspecified subject of the verbs 'foreknew', 'foreordained' (twice), 'called'(twice), 'justified'(twice) and 'glorified' to be 'God', not 'the Spirit'. (It is significant that the NEB, which takes the Spirit to be the subject of the verb in v. 28, inserts 'God' in v. 29 to smooth away the difficulty, and, since the NEB has dispensed with the use of italics to mark words without any equivalent in the original, the reader who does not consult the Greek has no intimation of what has been done.) Against both (i) and (ii) it must be said that the variant which consists of the addition of the Greek for 'God' in the nominative case looks very much like an insertion by a scribe who understood the subject to be God and felt it desirable to make the matter unambiguous or else a marginal gloss which has been incorporated by mistake in the text. The resulting Greek sentence is extremely clumsy – *so* clumsy as to be unlikely to be original.

Of the explanations listed above the two most likely would seem to be (iii) and (v). Against (iii) it may surely be objected that a sentence introduced by 'we know' and making a statement expected to command general agreement is the sort of sentence which one would expect to be unambiguously formulated and leave no doubt about the identity of the subject. The support of the Latin tradition for (v) is clear (in Latin a neuter plural subject requires a plural verb). Dodd's objection to it that it expresses an 'evolutionary optimism' alien to Paul's ways of thinking seems to us to have no cogency. What is expressed is rather a truly biblical confidence in God's sovereignty. That the sentence as a Greek sentence is most naturally taken according to (v) can hardly be doubted. In our view it is virtually certain that (v) should be accepted.

But the AV and RV rendering 'work together' makes too much of the separate meanings of the components of the Greek compound verb: it is better translated by some such expression as 'prove advantageous', 'be profitable'. Paul's meaning is that all things, even those which seem most adverse and hurtful, such as persecution and death itself, are profitable to those who truly love God. But not every sort of profit is meant. So the expression has to be made more precise. Hence the addition of 'for *their true* good'. Paul does not mean that all things serve the comfort or convenience or worldly interests of believers: it is obvious that they do not. What he means is that they assist our salvation.

We understand the first part of the verse, then, to mean that nothing can really harm – that is, harm in the deepest sense of the word – those who really love God, but that all things which may happen to them, including such grievous things as are mentioned in v. 35, must serve to help them on their way to salvation, confirming their faith and drawing them closer to their Master, Jesus Christ. But the reason why all things thus assist believers is, of course, that God is in control of all things. The faith expressed here is faith not in things but in God. Why then, it may be asked, does Paul make 'all things', and not 'God', the subject of his sentence? It is, we suggest, because he wants to draw attention to the transcendent power of Him who helps us. His power, His authority, is such that all things, even the actions of those who are disobedient and set themselves against Him, must subserve His will. To say that all things assist believers is thus – in a *biblical* context – a heightening of the statement that God assists them; for it is to assert not only that He assists them, but also that His help is completely effective.

Paul adds a further definition to 'those who love God' in **that is, to those who are called according to his purpose.** We said above that the purpose of vv. 28–30 was to underline the certainty of that hope of which vv. 17–27 had spoken. This certainty is indicated by the first part of v. 28; but, had Paul said no more, its fullness would not have been expressed. This begins to be seen only when it is realized that behind the love which those who are righteous by faith have to God is God's prior calling of them according to His purpose. The certainty of the hope, of which Paul has spoken, rests ultimately on nothing less than the eternal purpose of God.

29–30 are better understood as intended to support v. 28 as a whole than as intended to explain just the last part of it (from 'that is' onward). They consist of a fivefold chain introduced by **For**. The first link is **whom he foreknew**. Compare 11.2; 1 Pet 1.2. The '-knew' in 'foreknew' is to be understood in the light of the use of 'know' in such passages as Gen 18.19; Jer 1.5; Amos 3.2, where it denotes that special taking knowledge of a person which is God's electing grace. The thought expressed by the 'fore-' is not just that God's gracious choice of those referred to preceded their knowledge of Him, but that it took place before the world was created (compare Eph 1.4; 2 Tim 1.9). The second link is **he also foreordained to be conformed to the image of his Son.** Whereas 'he foreknew' denoted God's gracious election, 'he foreordained' denotes His gracious decision concerning the elect, the content of which is indicated by the words which follow. This divine predestination, this decision which appoints for the elect their goal, is, like their election, to be thought of as taking place before the creation of the world. Behind the words 'to be conformed to the image of his Son' there is probably the thought of man's creation 'in the image of God' (Gen 1.27) and also the thought (compare 2 Cor 4.4; Col 1.15) of Christ's being eternally the very 'image of God'. The believers' final glorification is their full conformity to the image of Christ glorified; but it seems probable that Paul is here thinking not only of their final glorification but also of their growing conformity to Christ here and now in suffering and obedience. If this is so, then these words are meant to embrace sanctification as well as final glory, sanctification being thought of as a progressive conformity to Christ, who is the image of God, and so as a progressive renewal of the believer into that being 'in the image of God' which is God's original purpose for man (compare Col 3.9f). **so that he might be the firstborn among many brothers** indicates God's purpose in foreordaining His elect

205

to be conformed to the likeness of His Son. It was in order that His only-begotten Son might not be alone in enjoying the privileges of sonship, but might be the Head of a multitude of brothers, of the company of those who in, and through, Him have been made sons of God. It is as their conformity to Christ is perfected in glory that believers finally enter into the full enjoyment of the privileges of their adoption in fellowship with Him.

and whom he foreordained, these he also called. With this third link of the chain we are in the realm of historical time. By 'call' here is meant 'call effectually'. When God does thus call effectually, a man responds with the obedience of faith. He is converted. The fourth link is **whom he called, these he also justified.** It is the divine gift of a status of righteousness before God with which so much of the epistle has been concerned. **and whom he justified, these he also glorified.** The fifth, and last, link in the chain is God's glorification of His elect. The use of a past tense here is significant and suggestive. In a real sense, of course, their glory is still in the future, still the object of hope (compare 5.2), and this 'not yet' with regard to their glory is certainly not to be explained away or glossed over. But their glorification has already been foreordained by God (compare v. 29); the divine decision has been taken, though its working out has not been consummated. Moreover, Christ, in whose destiny their destiny is included, has already been glorified, so that in Him their glorification has already been accomplished. So it can be spoken of as something concealed which has yet to be revealed (compare v. 18). We may compare the use of a past tense ('we were saved') in v. 24.

The fact that sanctification is not mentioned as an intermediate link between justification and glorification certainly does not mean that it was not important to Paul: the earlier part of this chapter – not to mention chapter 6 and 12.1–15.13 – is clear evidence to the contrary. It may be that he felt that sanctification had already been sufficiently emphasized in the course of the section for it to be unnecessary to refer to it again here explicitly – an implicit reference is of course present, since, according to what has already been said in the epistle, sanctification is both the natural sequel to justification and also the earthly road which leads to the heavenly glory. He may perhaps have felt that 'he . . . glorified' could be regarded as adequately covering sanctification, since there is a real sense in which sanctification is a beginning of glorification.

(iv) *Conclusion both to section V. 4 and also at the same time to the whole of the foregoing argument of the epistle*
(8.31–39)

[31]**What then shall we say in view of these things? Seeing that God is for us, who is against us?** [32]**He who did not spare his own Son, but gave him up for us all, how shall he not also with him give us all things?** [33]**Who shall lay a charge against God's elect? It is God who justifies:** [34]**who shall condemn? It is Christ Jesus who died, and, more than that, who was also raised from the dead, who is at the right hand of God, who also intercedes for us.** [35]**Who shall separate us from the love of Christ? Affliction or anguish or persecution or famine or nakedness or peril or sword? –** [36]**even as it is written in scripture: 'For thy sake we are being done to death all the day long, we have been reckoned as sheep to be slaughtered'.** [37]**But in all these things we are more than conquerors through him who loved us.** [38]**For I am persuaded that neither death nor life nor angels nor principalities nor things present nor things to come nor powers** [39]**nor height nor depth nor any other created thing shall be able to separate us from the love of God which is in Christ Jesus our Lord.**

While the primary reference of 'these things' in v. 31 is, no doubt, to what has just been said in the last two or three verses, it is clear from the contents of vv. 32–34 that it has also a wider reference and that this subsection serves not only as the conclusion of section V. 4 but also as a conclusion to the whole course of the theological exposition in the epistle up to this point, at which a significant stage has been reached – though what follows is, just as much as what precedes, integral to the argument.

This whole subsection has clearly been carefully constructed with an eye to rhetorical considerations. The elevated eloquence of the subsection is outstanding.

31. What then shall we say in view of these things? Here, as in 9.30, 'What then shall we say?' is used to introduce, not a false inference which is going to be rejected, but Paul's own conclusion from what he has been saying. **Seeing that God is for us, who is against us?** The statement 'God is for us' is a concise summary of the gospel. God is on our side, not of course as a subservient ally who can be mobilized for the accomplishment of our designs, but in the way indicated by the gospel events, as our Lord who has claimed us for Himself. The first clause states what Paul is altogether convinced is a fact, as the ground of the confidence expressed in the following rhetorical question, which is equivalent to an emphatic statement that there is no one whose hostility we need fear. Enemies we certainly have, who are against us and seek our ruin; but with God on our side we need not fear them. Though they may indeed cause us to suffer grievously (as Paul well knew, witness 2 Cor 11.23ff), they cannot snatch us from Him.

32. He who did not spare his own Son may be an intentional echo of Gen 22.12: like Abraham, God has not spared His own Son. For 'own' here compare v. 3 (though the idea is differently expressed in Greek). The thought of the contrast between the only-begotten Son and the adopted sons is possibly present: in any case, 'own' serves to heighten the poignancy of the clause, emphasizing the cost to the Father of delivering up for His creation's sake His dearest and most precious.

but gave him up for us all. The same Greek verb as is here represented by 'give up' was used in this connexion in the passive voice in 4.25. It occurs also in the Septuagint version of Isa 53.6, 12 (twice). It is noteworthy that it was also used in 1.24, 26, 28 of God's delivering up idolatrous men to the consequences of their sin. Isaac was rescued by divine intervention (Gen 22.11–13), but for Jesus there was no such intervention, no other lamb could take the place of the Lamb of God; and the delivering up meant making to drink to the very dregs the cup of wrath (see on 1.18). And this was 'for us all'. For the 'all' strengthening 'us' compare, for example, 10.11, 12, 13; 15.33; 1 Cor 1.2.

how shall he not also with him give us all things? The argument is similar both in form and content to that of 5.9–10: since God has done the unspeakably great and costly thing, we may be fully confident that He will do what is by comparison far less. God's delivering up His Son to death on our behalf may be thought of as a giving of His Son to us (compare Jn 3.16): the fact that 'deliver up' is in Greek a compound of the verb 'to give' makes the movement of thought the easier. God has delivered up His dear Son for us: therefore we may be confident that, together with His supreme Gift of His Son, He will also give us all things. By 'all things' is probably meant the fullness of salvation (compare 5.10) or else 'all that is necessary for our salvation'.

33–34. Who shall lay a charge against God's elect? It is God who justifies: who shall condemn? It is Christ Jesus who died, and, more than that, who was also raised from the dead, who is at the right hand of God, who also intercedes for us. There is some disagreement about the way these verses should be punctuated. There is some ancient support for a punctuation which would give us, in addition to the two questions in the above translation, five further questions: 'Shall God who justifies?', 'Shall Christ Jesus who died?', 'And, more than that, who was also raised from the dead?', 'Who is at the right hand of God?', 'Who also intercedes for us?' A modification of this, omitting the question marks after 'died', 'dead', and 'God', and so making one big question out of 'Shall Christ Jesus . . . for us', is given in the RV margin and is favoured by Barrett. But the punctuation of Nestle[25] and now of Nestle[26] (1979), which is also that presupposed by the RV text, and has the support of the two important Greek Fathers, Origen and John Chrysostom, and which we have followed, should surely be accepted. It gives the simplest and most natural development of thought; and it avoids breaking up what appears to be an echo of Isa 50.8 joining the last words of v. 33 and the first words of v. 34 (even if these words are not a conscious echo of the Isaiah passage, they still form a natural antithesis which it is perverse to demolish). Moreover, the views of Origen and Chrysostom on a question of this sort deserve special respect. The argument that because in vv. 31, 32 and 35 we have a series of rhetorical questions, it is likely that vv. 33 and 34 are also made up only of questions seems to lack force. Paul is just as likely to have varied his form as to have maintained it for so many verses without change.

'Who shall lay a charge against God's elect?' is probably better taken as a rhetorical question equivalent to an emphatic denial that any one will dare to do so, and so not requiring an answer, than as a genuine question answered by vv. 33b and 34. A judgment scene is envisaged. 'God's elect' picks up the thought of 'called according to his purpose' in v. 28 and 'whom he foreknew' in v. 29. 'It is God who justifies: who shall condemn?' is probably a conscious echo of Isa 50.8. The general sense is similar to that of v. 31b.

The elements which make up 'who died, and, more than that, who was also raised from the dead, who is at the right hand of God', form an ascending series. It is better to connect the third element ('who is at the right hand of God') with what precedes than to take it as part of the main framework of the sentence along with the last clause of the verse. This third element reflects the influence of Ps 110.1, which seems to be the Old Testament verse most frequently echoed in the New Testament. That its language is picture-language should go without saying (compare Calvin, *Institutes* 2.16.15: a 'comparison ... drawn from kings who have assessors at their side to whom they delegate the tasks of ruling and governing' and 'a question, not of the disposition of his body, but of the majesty of his authority'). In a real sense the chronological order in which the three elements are arranged represents also, for Paul, an ascending order of theological significance (note the 'and, more than that'): for him, as for the primitive Church generally, the focus-point of faith is the present glory of the One who once was crucified (compare the credal statement, 'Jesus is Lord' – see on 10.9). (For stimulating brief discussions of the Sitting at the Right Hand reference may be made to K. Barth, *Credo*, pp. 105ff, and *Dogmatics in Outline*, pp. 124ff.)

For the thought of Christ as our Intercessor in the last clause of v. 34 compare the reference to Him as our Advocate in 1 Jn 2.1 and to His intercession as High Priest in Heb 7.25. The Hebrew text of Isa 53.12, but not the Greek, has a reference to the Servant's intercession for the transgressors. The comment of Pelagius (the earliest known British commentator on Romans who lived in the fourth to fifth centuries AD) on this clause contains a striking and suggestive reference to the fact that Christ's high priestly intercession is accomplished as He continually shows and offers to His Father as our pledge that human nature which he assumed.

35. Who shall separate us from the love of Christ? is equivalent to an emphatic denial that any one or anything will ever separate us from Christ's love for us. The way in which Paul can speak here of

Christ's love, while in v. 39 and in 5.5 he speaks of God's love is another pointer to the naure of his Christology. **Affliction or anguish or persecution or famine or nakedness or peril or sword?** is a continuation of the preceding question. Paul had himself already experienced all the trials which he here lists, except the last.

36. Even as it is written in scripture: 'For thy sake we are being done to death all the day long, we have been reckoned as sheep to be slaughtered'. The main effect of the quotation of Ps 44.22 is to show that the tribulations which face Christians are nothing new or unexpected, but have all along been characteristic of the life of God's people. The Rabbis applied this verse of the psalm to the death of martyrs (for example to the martyrdom of the mother and her seven sons described in 2 Maccabees 7), but also quite generally to the life of the godly who give themselves wholeheartedly to God. Paul probably thought of it as applicable not just to the last item but to all the things listed in v. 35.

37. Paul's declaration begins with a triumphant **But.** Its force may be brought out by some such paraphrase as 'So far from its being possible for any of these things to separate us from Christ's love'. **in all these things** could be a Hebraism meaning 'in spite of all these things', but more probably means 'in the experiencing of all these things', not evading them or being spared them, but meeting them steadfastly. **we are more than conquerors through him who loved us** indicates both the utter decisiveness of our victory and the humbling fact that it is not through any courage, endurance or determination of our own, but through Christ, and not even by our hold on Him but by His hold on us, that we are victorious. The use of the Greek aorist participle ('him who loved') indicates that the reference is to a particular historic act, namely, that act by which He proved His love to us (compare 5.6–8; also Gal 2.20).

38–39. For I am persuaded that neither death nor life nor angels nor principalities nor things present nor things to come nor powers nor height nor depth nor any other created thing shall be able to separate us from the love of God which is in Christ Jesus our Lord. Paul now adds in the first person singular his own personal declaration of his firm conviction in support of v. 37. But note that, while he uses the first person singular 'I am persuaded', he significantly reverts to the first person plural 'us' later in the sentence. While there are occasions where gratitude may demand such a use of 'me' as we have in Gal 2.20, it is usually more truly Christian to emphasize that the comforting gospel truths to which we have to testify as individuals embrace our brothers and sisters as well as ourselves. 'I am persuaded', as used in the Pauline corpus (compare 14.14; 15.14; 2 Tim 1.5, 12), denotes a firm and settled conviction, a confident certainty.

The things which menace are mentioned in pairs, apart from 'powers' and 'any other created thing'. First mentioned is death, which for most of the Old Testament period had been thought even by the people of God to separate men from God's fellowship; but for Paul to die was to 'be with Christ' and therefore could be spoken of as 'gain' and something 'very far better' than life in this present world (Phil 1.21–23). With death is coupled life, life with all its trials and distresses, enticements and distractions, life in which the believer has to 'walk by faith, not by sight' (2 Cor 5.7) and in a real sense is 'absent from the Lord' (2 Cor 5.6). Whether dying or living, we are equally 'the Lord's' (14.8), since He is Lord of the living and dead alike (14.9).

With 'nor angels nor principalities' Paul is concerned to say that there is no spiritual cosmic power, whether benevolent or malevolent, which will be able to separate us from God's love in Christ. And this he can say with confidence, because he knows that Christ has once and for all won the decisive battle against the rebellious powers (compare Col 2.15: also Eph 1.21, 22a; 1 Pet 3.22), so that their effectiveness has been drastically curtailed and their final complete subjection assured.

The third pair consists of 'things present' and 'things to come', which are most naturally understood as signifying present and future (including eschatological) events and circumstances.

The word 'powers' stands by itself. It is probably another angelic designation like 'angels' and 'principalities' (it appears in angelic lists in 1 Cor 15.24; Eph 1.21 and 1 Pet 3.22, and also outside the Bible). Separated from them, it seems to come rather as an afterthought.

The words 'height' and 'depth' have been variously explained. In ancient times they were commonly explained as referring to things above the heavens and things beneath the earth, respectively. In modern times the suggestion has been made, on the basis of the use of the two Greek words as technical terms in ancient astronomy and astrology, that the reference is to sidereal spirits ruling in the sky above the horizon and in that part of the sky that is below it. But, while such an interpretation is not to be ruled out, it is surely more probable that the reference here is to places than that it is to spirit-powers associated with them, and that the meaning is simply that neither the highest height nor the deepest depth will be able to separate us from God's love. We might perhaps compare Ps 139.8 (where the context is concerned with the impossibility of getting beyond the reach of God): 'If I ascend up into heaven, thou art there: If I make my bed in Sheol, behold thou art there'. (The assumption of many that all the items of this list must refer to spiritual powers of one sort or another must be challenged. In the case of 'death' and 'life' and also of 'things present' and 'things to come' such an interpretation is far from being natural. Moreover, the fact that v. 38f is intended as confirmation (as is indicated by the initial 'For') of the statement in v. 37 that we are more than conquerors in all these things, that is, in all the trials and tribulations referred to in v. 35f, makes it unlikely (in view of the things mentioned in v. 35f) that the list in v. 38f is intended to refer to nothing but spiritual powers. The movement of thought surely requires that the list in these two verses should be *all*-embracing, and the presence of the next phrase shows that it is intended to be so.) The list is concluded by 'any other created thing', so as to make it completely comprehensive. Neither the phrase used in 5.5 nor that used in v. 35 is as precise and definitive as 'the love of God which is in Christ Jesus our Lord'; for the love of Christ is not truly known until it is recognized as being the love of the eternal God Himself, and it is only in Jesus Christ that the love of God is fully manifest as what it really is. This main division of the epistle is thus concluded with the solemn mention of the same name and title with which it began ('through our Lord Jesus Christ' in 5.1), and which were repeated at the end of its sections in 5.21; 6.23; and 7.25.

VI
THE UNBELIEF OF MEN AND THE
FAITHFULNESS OF GOD

(9.1–11.36)

A superficial reading of Romans might easily leave the impression that chapters 9 to 11 are only an excursus which Paul has included under the pressure of his own deep personal involvement in the matter of the Jews' destiny. But a closer and more attentive study reveals the fact that they are an integral part of the working out of the theme stated in 1.16b–17. The gospel which is the subject of 1.16b is the gospel which has already been defined in 1.1–4. The use in that definition of the title 'Christ' and the statement of Jesus Christ's relationship to David mean that the gospel cannot be properly understood except in relation to Israel, God's special people. Again, the claim was made in that definition that the gospel is foretold in the Old Testament, and the epistle is concerned, from the statement of its theme onwards, with the question of the true interpretation of the Old Testament. But it is clear that no serious concern with the Old Testament can ignore the phenomenon of Israel. Had Paul not, in as full and systematic a presentation of the gospel as is attempted in Romans, come to grips with the question of the Jews, the seriousness and integrity of his appeals to the Old Testament would have been open to doubt. Moreover, the words 'both for the Jew first and for the Greek' in 1.16b raise the question quite explicitly and directly. When it is taken up in 3.1ff, it is dealt with only summarily, and it is clear that a serious discussion of God's faithfulness in relation to the lack of faith of the great majority of Jews is still outstanding.

The decision to place this discussion just here is understandable. In 8.28–39 Paul has spoken of the certainty of the believer's hope. In 8.28–30 he has referred to God's purpose as the ground of our certainty. But, according to the Old Testament, Israel had a special place within God's purpose. The end of chapter 8 was therefore a natural point at which to introduce a discussion of the relation of Israel to the divine purpose. We may, in fact, go farther and say that at this point the need for such a discussion has become urgent, since the very reliability of God's purpose as the ground of Christian hope is called in question by the exclusion of the majority of Jews. If the truth is that God's purpose with Israel has been frustrated, then what sort of a basis for Christian hope is God's purpose? And, if God's love for Israel (see, for example, Deut 7.7f; Jer 31.3) has ceased, what reliance can be placed on Paul's conviction that nothing can separate us from God's love in Christ (v. 38f)? Moreover, since the ethical consequences of God's deed in Christ have already been indicated in principle in chapters 6 to 8, the particular exhortation of 12.1–15.13 can wait for a while. Indeed, since the discussion in chapters 9 to 11 makes possible a fuller and profounder understanding of the gospel, chapters 1 to 11 are a more satisfactory theological basis for the ensuing ethical exhortation than chapters 1 to 8 could have been.

With regard to the special difficulties which the contents of this main division of the epistle present, several things may usefully be said at this point.

(i) It is of the utmost importance to take these three chapters together as a whole, and not to come to conclusions about Paul's argument before one has heard it to the end; for chapter 9 will certainly be understood in an altogether un-Pauline sense, if it is understood in isolation from its sequel in chapters 10 and 11.

(ii) We shall misunderstand these chapters, if we fail to recognize that their key-word is 'mercy'. Paul is here concerned to show that the problem of Israel's unbelief, which seems to call in question the very reliability of God Himself, is connected with the nature of God's mercy as really mercy and as mercy not just for one people but for all peoples; to show that Israel's disobedience, together with the divine judgment which it merits and procures, is surrounded on all sides by the divine mercy – and at the same time to bring home to the Christian community in Rome the fact that it is by God's mercy alone that it lives.

(iii) It is only where the Church persists in refusing to learn this message, where it secretly – perhaps quite unconsciously! – believes that its own existence is based on human achievement,

215

and so fails to understand God's mercy to itself, that it is unable to believe in God's mercy for still unbelieving Israel, and so entertains the ugly and unscriptural notion that God has cast off His people Israel and simply replaced it by the Christian Church.

(iv) Mention must be made here of the magnificent section on God's election of grace in Karl Barth's *Church Dogmatics* II/2, pp.1–506, which has shed a great deal of light on these chapters of Romans. His great contribution was to insist on the truth – so entirely obvious, when once it has been clearly stated, that it is almost incredible that it had not been formulated long before – that the doctrine of election, if it is to be faithful to Scripture, must not begin in an abstract way, either from the concept of an electing God or from the concept of an elected man, but 'must begin concretely with the acknowledgment of Jesus Christ as both the electing God and elected man'.[1] The Church's doctrine of election had come to be isolated from its Christology, as though it had to do with an electing by God from which Christ was somehow absent. Barth decisively recalled the Church to a Christocentric understanding of election, and so opened the way for the recognition that the scriptural doctrine of predestination is 'not a mixed message of joy and terror', but 'is light and not darkness',[2] matter for deep thankfulness and joyful hope. Election is first of all and basically God's election of Jesus Christ, but included in His election are both the election of 'the many', that is, of individual sinful men, and, in a mediating position between this election of 'the many' and the election of the One, the election of 'the one community of God by the existence of which Jesus Christ is to be attested to the whole world and the whole world summoned to faith in Jesus Christ'.[3] The recognition of these different elections included in the election of Jesus Christ will save us from immediately attempting to refer what Paul says to the ultimate destiny of individuals, on which the traditional doctrine has tended to concentrate attention almost exclusively. It is, in fact, with the election of the community that Paul is concerned in

---

[1] op. cit., p. 76.
[2] op. cit., p. 13.
[3] op. cit., p. 195.

Romans 9 to 11, and Barth's account of the two forms of the one community illumines many of the difficulties of these chapters.[1]

VI. 1. THE SUBJECT OF THIS MAIN DIVISION OF THE EPISTLE IS INTRODUCED
(9.1–5)

[1]**I speak the truth in Christ, I do not lie – my conscience bears me witness in the Holy Spirit –** *when I declare* [2]**that I have great grief and continual anguish in my heart.** [3]**For I would pray that I might myself be accursed** *and cut off* **from Christ on behalf of my brethren, my kinsfolk according to the flesh,** [4]**who are Israelites, whose are the adoption and the glory and the covenants and the legislation and the worship and the promises,** [5]**whose are the fathers, and of whom so far as the flesh is concerned is Christ, who is over all, God blessed for ever, Amen.**

With striking emphasis and solemnity Paul declares his own sorrow at his fellow-Jews' unbelief and the strength of his desire for their conversion, thereby introducing the subject with which he will be concerned until the end of chapter 11.

1. I speak the truth in Christ. Paul claims that he is speaking in Christ, that is, in accordance with the standards which hold for one who is in Christ, with a due sense of his accountability to Christ. The phrase 'in Christ' thus strengthens 'I speak the truth': one who speaks in a way that is worthy of his union with Christ cannot but speak truth or, at any rate, attempt to do so. The use of the phrase here is thus an implicit appeal to Christ as the ultimate guarantor of the truth of what Paul is about to say. The combination of 'I speak the truth' and **I do not lie** is extremely emphatic. **my conscience bears me witness in the Holy Spirit** is parenthetic, the words which follow depending on 'I speak the truth', as the supplement *when I declare* is meant to indicate (to

---

[1] Our indebtedness throughout our exposition of these three chapters to Barth's discussion of election and the penetrating exegesis of these Romans chapters which it incorporates is most gratefully acknowledged – though we certainly hope that we have never followed him uncritically.

explain v. 2 as dependent on 'bears me witness' is unsatisfactory, since it leaves the first words of v. 1 in the air without any clear indication of what it is to which they refer). Whereas in 8.16 the Greek verb, which here is represented by 'bear witness', probably means simply 'testify to', 'assure', it is likely that here it means 'witness along with', 'testify in support of' (the preposition incorporated in the Greek compound verb having its sense of 'together with', and not just a strengthening force). Paul apparently thinks of the solemn statement which he is about to make (v. 2) as one testimony and of the support of his conscience as a second, corroborative testimony. It is possible that here the biblical law of evidence (Num 35.30; Deut 17.6; 19.15) has influenced Paul's thought. For 'conscience' the reader is again referred to the note on 2.15. Here too it means 'conscience' in the sense which the word has in the English expressions, 'a bad conscience', 'a good conscience', that is, in the sense of a knowledge shared with oneself which is either painful or not painful. In this case it is a good conscience that is meant. Paul, in asserting that he speaks the truth when he declares that he has great grief and continual anguish in his heart, shares with himself the knowledge that what he asserts is true. But Paul knows that the value of the testimony of a man's good conscience depends on the moral sensitivity of the man. Where the moral sense is dull (compare the references to the darkening of the heart in 1.21 and to the reprobate mind in 1.28), the testimony of the conscience is of little value. But, where the mind is bound to God's law (compare 7.23, 25), where it is being renewed (12.2), there the testimony of the conscience is of great worth. So Paul adds 'in the Holy Spirit'; for he knows that his conscience is that of one whose mind is being renewed and illumined by the Holy Spirit (compare 8.1–16).

2. that I have great grief and continual anguish in my heart. The fact that this statement has been introduced with so much emphasis and solemnity calls for explanation. It has sometimes been suggested as an explanation that Paul had been accused of indifference to the fate of his fellow-countrymen and was concerned to rebut such charges and to defend his loyalty to his nation. But this will scarcely do. A more likely explanation, in view of the contents of the sequel in 9.3–11.36, is that he recognized that the very integrity and authenticity of his apostleship to the Gentiles would be called in question, were he able to give up his fellow-Israelites, were he not to suffer grief so long as they continued in unbelief; and that he regarded it as of vital importance that the Christians to whom he was writing, both Jewish and Gentile, should know of this grief of his, because for them too such a grief was the only attitude with regard to the Jews' continuing unbelief that would be consistent with faith.

3–5 is offered as explanation of v. 2, throwing some light on the character of Paul's grief and anguish. **For I would pray** presents two problems: that of the sense in which the verb we have translated 'pray' is used and that of the significance of the Greek imperfect which is used. With regard to the former, the verb has often been understood here to have the sense 'wish' (as in the Latin Vulgate, AV, RV, and RSV), but the sense 'pray' should, in our judgment, probably here be preferred (as in the NEB), in view of the likelihood that the parallel with Moses in Exod 32.31f was in Paul's mind and of the evidence of the other occurrences of the verb in the New Testament. With regard to the latter problem, of the various grammatically possible explanations the most probable is surely that which takes Paul to mean that he would pray in the way indicated, were it permissible for him so to do and if the fulfilment of such a prayer could benefit his fellow-Jews, but does not do so, because he realizes that it would be wrong and fruitless. **that I might myself be accursed *and cut off* from Christ on behalf of my brethren, my kinsfolk according to the flesh** is the substance of this unprayed prayer. The reference is to the forfeiting of final salvation, the sentence of exclusion from Christ's presence. The Greek represented by 'I ... myself' is strongly emphatic, and the order of words in Greek ('I myself from Christ') brings out the poignancy of the separation contemplated. Paul calls the still unbelieving Jews his brethren. That is, he recognizes them still, in spite of their unbelief, as fellow-members of the people of God; for, apart from its primary use to denote a son of the same parents (or parent), 'brother' is in the Bible nearly always reserved for fellow-members of the elect community (Israel or the Church). The clear implication of this is that for Paul – and this must be stated with emphasis, since it has often been forgotten by Christians – unbelieving Israel is within the elect community, not outside it. But 'my brethren' by itself is not specific enough, since the Gentile Christians are also Paul's brethren. So he adds 'my kinsfolk according to the flesh'. For the use of 'kinsmen', 'kinsfolk', in Hellenistic Greek to denote fellow-countrymen, members of the same nation, we may compare 16.7, 11, 21. It would be wrong to read into the use of 'according to the flesh' here any suggestion that the bond of Jewish nationality is *merely* a fleshly matter: in view of vv. 4 and 5 it is clear that Paul cannot have intended any disparagement of the Jews by it.

Paul goes on to list the great privileges of the Jews. Their recital serves at the same time to underline the sadness of the Jews' present unbelief, to explain the depth of Paul's grief on their behalf, and also to indicate the continuing fact of their election. The list is arranged with what appears to be conscious artistry, and distributed over four relative clauses all of which are dependent on 'my kinsfolk according to the flesh'. The first relative clause is **who are Israelites.** While it is more naturally taken as the first item of the list than as standing outside it, it is a general statement of the Jews' special position as the people of God and so in a sense embraces the items which follow. 'Israel' and 'Israelite' are religious terms expressing the Jews' consciousness of being God's special chosen people. It is to be noted that here the verb 'to be', which in Greek is often left unexpressed, is expressed. This is important, because it means that the tense is explicit: Paul is affirming that his fellow-Jews who are unbelieving are, even in their unbelief, still members of the chosen people of God.

The second relative clause is **whose are the adoption and the glory and the covenants and the legislation and the worship and the promises.** Paul refers to 'the adoption', that is, both God's gracious adoption of the nation as His son (see especially Exod 4.22f; Jer 31.9; Hos 11.1) as the beginning of the long history of His fatherly dealings with it and also the continuing reality of the relationship thus begun. He refers to 'the glory', that is, God's own manifestation of His personal presence with His people (see, for example, Exod 16.7, 10; 24.16f; 40.34f; 1 Kgs 8.11; 2 Chr 5.14; 7.1–3; Ezek 1.28), which is always His presence in the freedom of His gracious condescension, never a presence under their control or at their disposal. He refers to 'the covenants', that is, most probably, the covenants made with Abraham (Gen 15.17ff; 17.1ff: cf. Exod 2.24), with Israel at Mount Sinai (Exod 19.5; 24.1ff), in the plains of Moab (Deut 29.1ff), and at Mounts Ebal and Gerizim (Josh 8.30ff), and possibly also the covenant with David (2 Sam 23.5; Ps 89.3f; 132.11f). The word represented by 'legislation' can denote either the action of making or giving laws (so the RV here: 'the giving of the law') or the made or given laws considered collectively. We consider it more probable that Paul used it in the latter sense here, so as equivalent to 'the law'. The fact that he includes a reference to the law in this list of the excellent privileges of Israel is clearly of the greatest significance for a true understanding of Paul's view of the law. There is no doubt that in referring to 'the worship' Paul had in mind primarily the sacrificial cultus, the Temple service of Israel, as the true worship of the true God, in contrast to all worship devised of men's own hearts (compare 1 Kgs 12.33) the worship appointed and ordered by God Himself, that cultus, which (as Paul understood it) had from its beginning pointed forward to Christ and His redeeming work. But it does not seem altogether unlikely that, as used by Paul here, the term embraced also the faithful non-sacrificial worship of synagogue and pious Jewish home, including such things as prayer, the reading of the Scriptures, the observation of the Sabbath, the reciting of the Shema, and, indeed, all that is meant by the phrase of Mic 6.8, 'to walk humbly with thy God'. It is natural to assume that in referring to 'the promises' Paul had in mind in the first place the promises made to Abraham (Gen 12.7; 13.14–17; 17.4–8; 22.16–18: also the related promise in 21.12 – compare Rom 9.7f) and repeated to Isaac (Gen 26.3f) and to Jacob (Gen 28.13f); but 2 Cor 1.20 and 7.1 (see also the concluding verses of the previous chapter) suggest the probability that he also had in mind many other Old Testament promises, particularly the eschatological and messianic promises. Such passages as 2 Sam 7.12, 16, 28f; Isa 9.6f; Jer 23.5; 31.31ff; Ezek 34.23f; 37.24ff spring naturally to mind.

The third relative clause is **whose are the fathers.** Compare 11.28. Paul no doubt means specially Abraham (compare, for example, 4.12, 16; Lk 1.73; 3.8; Jn 8.56), Isaac (compare 9.10), Jacob (compare Jn 4.12), and the twelve patriarchs, the sons of

Jacob (compare Acts 7.12, 15) – possibly also other outstanding figures of Old Testament history such as David (compare Mk 11.10: in Acts 2.29 he is called 'the patriarch').

The fourth and last of the relative clauses dependent on 'my kinsfolk according to the flesh' is **and of whom so far as the flesh is concerned is Christ, who is over all, God blessed for ever, Amen.** Paul completes his list of the privileges of the Jewish people by stating the fact that the Messiah Himself is, so far as His human nature is concerned, of their race – an honour which can never be taken from them: Jesus Christ was, and is, a Jew. But the Greek represented by 'who is over all, God blessed for ever, Amen' has caused a great deal of argument down the centuries. Broadly speaking, what is at issue is whether the whole or only part or none of it is to be understood as referring to Christ, but within this threefold framework of possibilities further variations have been suggested. The following fall to be considered:

(i) to understand the whole as referring to Christ and connect 'God' with 'over all' – 'who is God over all, blessed for ever, Amen'.

(ii) to understand the whole as referring to Christ but separate 'God' from 'over all' – 'who is over all, God blessed for ever, Amen'.

(iii) to understand 'who is over all' as referring to Christ and the rest as an independent doxology – 'who is over all. God be blessed for ever, Amen'.

(iv) to understand the whole as an independent doxology and connect 'God' and 'who is over all – 'God who is over all be blessed for ever, Amen'.

(v) to understand the whole as an independent doxology but take 'God' as in apposition to the subject – 'He who is over all, God, be blessed for ever, Amen'.

(vi) to accept the conjectural emendation *hon ho* for *ho on*, and so to understand the whole as stating the final privilege of the Jews – 'whose is the God who is over all, blessed for ever, Amen'.

The conjectural emendation (vi) was suggested more than three hundred years ago. It must surely be rejected, since it is very unlikely that Paul would have included the possession of God as a last item in a list of the Jews' privileges (though Scripture does of course frequently speak of God as the God of Israel) in this way;

the omission of 'and' before the last item in a list, when it is present before the last but one, would be stylistically offensive in Greek as in English; and the acceptance of a purely conjectural emendation always needs specially strong justification.

The one substantial argument which has been adduced in favour of (iii), (iv) or (v) and against (i) and (ii) – and it has been used from early times – is that in the rest of the Pauline corpus there is no clear instance of the use of 'God' with reference to Christ. On the other side, against (iii), (iv) and (v) and in favour of (i) or (ii), the following arguments may be stated:

(a) Pauline doxologies are generally either an integral part of the preceding sentence or else closely connected with it (the doxology referring to a person named in the preceding sentence), and do not stand in complete asyndeton,[1] as, according to (iii), (iv) and (v), this would do.

(b) Wherever either the Hebrew or the Greek equivalent of 'blessed' is used in the Bible in an independent doxology, it is always (apart from one verse in the Septuagint Old Testament, where there seems to be a duplicate translation) the first word of the sentence, and this rule is also regularly followed in extra-biblical Jewish usage. In this connexion it must be remembered that the 'Blessed be . . . ' formula is extremely common in Jewish worship.

(c) The use of 'so far as the flesh is concerned' suggests that something contrasting with this is going to follow, as it does according to (i) and (ii), but not according to (iii), (iv) and (v).

(d) An independent doxology would be rather surprising at this point, since, though a recital of Israel's privileges might well ordinarily be an occasion for such a doxology, in this case they have been mentioned in order to emphasize the grievousness of the Jews' disobedience. (A dependent doxology like that in 1.25 would be a different matter and would be perfectly natural.)

With regard to the one really serious argument against (i) and (ii) and in favour of taking either all or part of v. 5b as an independent doxology referring to God, it seems to us that, while it may be true that Paul has nowhere else in the extant epistles

---

[1] Asyndeton denotes the condition of an independent sentence which is not linked to its predecessor by a conjunction or other form of connective. Asyndeton, while extremely common in English, is very unusual in Greek.

explicitly referred to Christ as 'God' (much weight cannot be put on the two doubtful instances, 2 Th 1.12 and Tit 2.13), it is quite unjustifiable to conclude that he cannot have done so here. The stylistic arguments which strongly suggest that he has done so, namely, (a) and (b) above, are thoroughly objective, and (b) especially seems to us so strong as to be by itself almost conclusive. Moreover, Paul's application to Christ of Septuagint passages in which 'Lord' represents the sacred name, the consonants of which are YHWH (hence 'Yahweh' or 'Jehovah'), as for example in 10.13; his acceptance of the legitimacy of invoking Christ in prayer (for example, 10.12–14; 1 Cor 1.2); his association of Christ with God in such a way as is seen in 1.7b; his parallel references to Christ and God as in 8.35 and 39; his reference to Christ as 'being in the form of God' in Phil 2.6 – these things are surely sufficient evidence to prove that for Paul to designate Christ as 'God' would in no way be inconsistent with his thought as reflected in his epistles. It seems to us that the case for taking v. 5b to refer to Christ is so overwhelming as to warrant the assertion that it is virtually certain that it should be accepted.

As between (i) and (ii), (ii) should probably be preferred. According to this explanation, v. 5b affirms first Christ's lordship over all things (compare, for example, 14.9; Phil 2.10) and secondly His divine nature. To adopt (i), connecting together 'over all' with 'God', is less satisfactory; for a statement that Christ is 'God over all' would be open to serious misunderstanding – it could suggest a meaning which it is certain Paul would never have intended, namely, that Christ is somehow God in superiority over, or even to the exclusion of, the Father. We take it then that in v. 5 Paul is affirming that Christ, who, in so far as His human nature is concerned, is of Jewish race, is also Lord over all things and by nature God blessed for ever.

VI. 2. THE UNBELIEF AND DISOBEDIENCE OF MEN ARE SHOWN TO BE EMBRACED WITHIN THE WORK OF THE DIVINE MERCY
(9.6–29)

[6]But it is not that the word of God has failed. For not all who are of Israel are Israel, [7]nor, because they are Abraham's seed, are they all

his children; but 'It is thy descendants through Isaac that shall be called thy seed'. [8]This means that it is not the children of the flesh who are God's children, but the children of the promise are counted as seed. [9]For *a word* of promise is this word: 'At this season will I come and Sarah shall have a son'. [10]But not only this, *there is* also *the case of* Rebecca who conceived *both her sons* at one time by one and the same man, our father Isaac; [11]for, when they were still unborn and had not done anything good or bad, in order that God's electing purpose might stand, [12]being based not on *human* works but on him who calls, it was said to her, 'The elder shall serve the younger', [13]even as it is written, 'Jacob have I loved but Esau have I hated'.

[14]What then shall we say? Is there unrighteousness with God? God forbid! [15]For he says to Moses, 'I will have mercy on him on whom I have mercy and I will have pity on him on whom I have pity'. [16]So then it is not a matter of *man's* willing or running but of God's showing mercy. [17]For the scripture passage says to Pharaoh: 'For this very purpose have I raised thee up, that I might show in thee my power and that my name might be proclaimed in all the earth'. [18]So then on whom he wills he has mercy and whom he wills he hardens. [19]Thou wilt say to me then, 'Why does he still blame *men*? For who is resisting his will?' [20]Nay, rather, who art thou, O man, who art answering God back? Shall the thing moulded say to him who moulded it, 'Why didst thou make me thus?'? [21]Has not the potter a right over the clay to make from the same lump one part a vessel for honourable service and another a vessel for menial service? [22]But what if God endured vessels of wrath, prepared for destruction, with much longsuffering, because he willed to show forth his wrath and to make known his power, [23]and in order to make known the riches of his glory upon vessels of mercy, which he prepared beforehand for glory, [24]whom he also called, even us, not only from among the Jews but also from among the Gentiles? [25] – as he says in Hosea, 'I will call Not-my-people "My-people" and Unloved "Beloved"; [26]and instead of its being said to them "You are not my people", they shall be called the sons of the living God'. [27]But Isaiah cries concerning Israel: 'Though the number of the sons of Israel be as the sand of the sea, *only* a remnant shall be saved; [28]for a sentence complete and decisive will the Lord accomplish upon the earth'. [29]And as Isaiah foretold, 'Had not the Lord of Hosts left us a seed, we should have become as Sodom and been made like Gomorrah'.

The section falls into two parts, the first being vv. 6–13. In support of his categorical statement in v. 6a to the effect that what he has just said about his grief (vv. 1–5) does not imply that the revealed purpose of God, His purpose of election, has failed, Paul goes on to draw a distinction between 'Israel' and those 'who are of Israel' between Abraham's 'children' and 'Abraham's seed', and to remind his readers that God's distinguishing within the general area of election (what we have to do with here is the distinction between different levels or forms of election, not between election and non-election) between those who do, and those who do not, stand in a positive relationship to the accomplishment of God's purpose, is a characteristic feature of the biblical history. The fact that at the present time the majority of Jews stand outside the inner circle of election, which is the Israel within Israel, is, since it conforms to the pattern of the working out of God's purpose from the beginning, no proof of the failure of that purpose.

But the process of showing that the pattern of God's dealings with contemporary Israel is consistent with the pattern of His dealings with the patriarchs raises the question whether God's ways have not all along been unjust. In vv. 14–29 Paul emphatically rejects as an altogether false inference from what has been said the conclusion that there is unrighteousness with God, and proceeds to argue at some length in support of his rejection of this conclusion. Current interpretations of this paragraph differ very widely. Of crucial importance is v. 15. The interpretation given to it controls the interpretation of the verses which follow. It will be argued below that Paul understood Exod 33.19b as an assertion not of an absolute freedom of an indeterminate will of God distinct from His merciful will but of the freedom of God's *mercy*, and that the double 'he wills' of v. 18 is to be interpreted as referring not to an unqualified will moving now in one direction, now in another, capriciously, but to the merciful will of God, which, while it is indeed free in the sense of being free to fulfil its own purposes and altogether independent of men's willing and deserving, is also wholly determined in that it is the will of the merciful, righteous God. If we understand him correctly, Paul thinks of both the 'having mercy on' and the 'hardening', to which he refers in v. 18, as originating in one and the same merciful will. The section as a whole indeed bears witness to the *freedom* of

God's mercy, but the freedom to which it bears witness is the freedom of His *mercy* – and no other freedom. And the implication of the argument is that, though the roles they fulfil are so sharply contrasted, Ishmael as well as Isaac, Esau as well as Jacob, Pharaoh as well as Moses, the vessels of wrath as well as the vessels of mercy, that is, the mass of unbelieving Jews (and unbelieving Gentiles too) as well as the believing Church of Jews and Gentiles, stand within – and not without – the embrace of the divine mercy.

6a. But it is not that the word of God has failed. Paul's expression of his sorrow concerning his fellow-Jews is not to be understood as an indication that God's declared purpose of election has failed. This half-verse is the sign under which the whole of 9.6–29 stands – the sign and theme, indeed, of the whole of chapters 9 to 11.

6b–7a. For not all who are of Israel are Israel, nor, because they are Abraham's seed, are they all his children. In support of v. 6a Paul proceeds, in the first place, to draw a distinction between those 'who are of Israel' and 'Israel', and between the 'seed' and the 'children' of Abraham. This really amounts to a distinction between 'Israel' and 'children of Abraham' in a comprehensive sense, on the one hand, and 'Israel' and 'children of Abraham' in a selective or special sense, on the other. (The terms 'Israel' and 'children of Abraham' are not of course synonymous, since, even when used in its comprehensive sense, the former term excludes Ishmael and Esau and their descendants, while the latter term includes them.) It is important to notice that, while in vv. 6b–7a 'all who are of Israel' and 'Abraham's seed' are used to carry the comprehensive sense and 'Israel' and 'his [that is, Abraham's] children' the special or selective sense, in v. 7b the selective sense is carried by 'seed', and in v. 8 Abraham's children in the comprehensive sense are designated 'the children of the flesh', while with reference to the children in the selective sense the terms 'God's children', 'the children of the promise' and 'seed' are used. The point Paul is making is that not all who are included in the comprehensive Israel are included also in the selective, special Israel. But this does not mean what it has so often been taken to mean – that only part of the Jewish people is the elect people of God. Paul is not contriving to disinherit the majority of his fellow-Jews, to write a charter of Christian anti-semitism. This

227

explanation of his meaning is ruled out by vv. 1–5; for it is clear that the Jews he is referring to in those verses are the unbelieving ones (for the others he has no need to grieve), and that he recognizes these unbelieving ones as his brethren and acknowledges that they are still, even in their unbelief, Israelites to whom the privileges belong. Paul's meaning is rather that within the elect people itself there has been going on throughout its history a divine operation of distinguishing and separating, whereby the Israel within Israel has been differentiated from the rest of the chosen people. All Jews are members of God's elect people. This is an honour – and it is no small honour – of which no member of this race can be deprived. They are all members of the community, which is the environment of Jesus Christ. They are all necessarily witnesses to God's grace and truth. But not all of them are members of the Israel within Israel, which is the company of those who are willing, obedient, grateful witnesses to that grace and truth. But, if God's purpose of election has, from the very beginning, included a process of distinguishing and separating even within the elected people, then the present unbelief of many Jews is no proof that that purpose has failed, but may be understood rather as part of its working out.

7b. but 'It is thy descendants through Isaac that shall be called thy seed'. Paul now, going back to the pre-Israel history of the people of God, cites as his first example of this divine distinguishing the case of Isaac and Ishmael. The conjunction 'but' introduces, instead of a continuation of the sentence in the form in which it began, an exact quotation of the last part of the Septuagint Greek of Gen 21.12 (literally, 'in Isaac shall seed be called to thee'). According to Genesis 21, when Sarah demanded the expulsion of Hagar and the son she had borne to Abraham, 'the thing was very grievous in Abraham's sight on account of his son'. But God told Abraham not to grieve for his son and his bondwoman, but to do what Sarah asked; and He added as the reason the words which Paul quotes. The point then is this: not Ishmael but Isaac. That is, it is from Abraham's descendants by Isaac, and not from his descendants by Ishmael, that God's special people is to come. But it is to be carefully noted that the Genesis narrative indicates explicitly God's care for Ishmael (see Gen 21.13, 17–21: also 16.10–14; 17.20). So we must not read into Paul's argument any suggestion that Ishmael, because he is not chosen to play a positive part in the accomplishment of God's special purpose, is therefore excluded from the embrace of God's mercy.

8. This means that it is not the children of the flesh who are God's children, but the children of the promise are counted as seed draws out the general truth implicit in the case of Isaac and Ishmael. By the first half of this verse Paul does not mean to imply that the children of God are not also children of the flesh – Isaac was, of course, just as much a child of the flesh, a child of Abraham by natural birth, as was Ishmael – but to indicate that the mere fact of being physically children of Abraham does not by itself make men children of God. At this point the question arises of the relation of 'God's children' here to 'the adoption' in v. 4. The natural explanation would seem to be that, whereas the adoption referred to in v. 4 is one of the privileges of the Jewish nation as a whole (so that the possibility of a comprehensive use of 'children of God' or 'sons of God' with regard to all Jews is probably implied), the phrase 'children of God' is here used with a selective connotation, of those who are what we have termed 'the Israel within Israel'. In the second half of the verse 'the children of the promise' are referred to, in contrast to the children of the flesh mentioned in the first half. Contrasted with Ishmael is Isaac. Like Ishmael, he was also Abraham's 'child of the flesh'; but the decisive thing about him was not this, but the fact that he was the object of the divine promise to Abraham. It was because of the promise, as the child of the promise, that he was Abraham's seed in the special, selective sense, the one who (rather than Ishmael) should be the father of those who should be recognized as Abraham's descendants.

9. For *a word* of promise is this word: 'At this season will I come and Sarah shall have a son'. This supports the statement of v. 8b that the children of promise are counted as seed by showing that the word lying behind Isaac's birth (it is an abbreviated and slightly free quotation of the Septuagint Greek of Gen 18.10 and 14) is a word of promise.

10. But not only this, *there is* also *the case of* Rebecca who conceived *both her sons* at one time by one and the same man, our father Isaac. Since the case of Isaac and Ishmael might seem less than conclusive as evidence of the truth of v. 8 (for, while it is true that both were children of Abraham's begetting, there was still –

apart from the promise quoted in v. 9 – a significant difference between them on the human level in the fact that Isaac's mother was Abraham's wife and Ishmael's mother Sarah's handmaid, a difference which, it might be argued, would explain why Abraham's seed should be reckoned through Isaac rather than through Ishmael), Paul cites a second and clearer example. In this case there were for both children the same mother, the same father, and the same moment of conception (we take it that the Greek implies this, and not just that Rebecca had intercourse with only one man).

11–13 seems to have started as a parenthesis and then been continued so as to complete the thought, though not the grammar, of the original sentence begun in v. 10. **for, when they were still unborn and had not done anything good or bad** indicates the circumstances in which the divine distinguishing was revealed: it was revealed before the twins were born and therefore before they had had any chance to do either good or ill. The 'for' is probably to be explained as indicating a connexion with an unexpressed thought, which we may assume to have been that the present example is not only free from the weakness of the preceding but also exhibits very clearly a characteristic of the divine distinguishing which has not yet been mentioned, namely, its independence of all human merit. **in order that God's electing purpose might stand** is a final clause dependent on the 'it was said' which follows. The divine disclosure was made to Rebecca in the circumstances indicated in order that God's purpose which is characterized by election might be accomplished. **being based not on *human* works but on him who calls** is appended to the final clause somewhat loosely. It draws out the implication of the first clause of v. 11. The divine distinguishing between Jacob and Esau preceded their birth, so that God's electing purpose might be fulfilled in its complete independence of human merit and dependence on God alone, whose call, by which He gives effect to His election, is altogether His free act. The passive **it was said to her** avoids the use of the divine name, where Gen 25.23 has 'the LORD said unto her'. **'The elder shall serve the younger'** is an exact quotation of the last part of the Septuagint version of Gen 25.23. The interest of this Genesis verse as a whole is clearly in Jacob and Esau not just as individuals but also, and particularly, as the ancestors of two nations; for the part quoted is preceded by 'Two nations are in thy womb, And two peoples shall be separated even from thy bowels: And the one people shall be stronger than the other people'. It is important to stress that neither as they occur in Genesis nor as they are used by Paul do these words refer to the eternal destinies either of the two persons or of the individual members of the nations sprung from them; the reference is rather to the mutual relations of the two nations in history. What is here in question is not final salvation or damnation, but the historical functions of those concerned and their relations to the development of the salvation-history.

A scriptural quotation from Mal 1.2–3 is introduced to conclude this stage of the argument: **even as it is written, 'Jacob have I loved but Esau have I hated'.** There is no doubt that the concern of Mal 1.2–5 is with the nations of Israel and Edom, and Paul probably thought of the words quoted as expressing the same truth as the words from Genesis, but expressing it more clearly and pointedly, and therefore suitable as a further and decisive corroboration of what had just been said, and, in particular, of the words of Gen 25.23 ('the elder shall serve the younger'). The word 'hate' should probably not be explained, either in Malachi or in Romans, as an instance of the Semitic use of a direct opposite in order to express a lesser degree of comparison (as, for example in Gen 29.31; Deut 21.15): 'love' and 'hate' are rather to be understood as denoting election and rejection respectively. God has chosen Jacob and his descendants to stand in a positive relation to the fulfilment of His gracious purpose: He has left Esau and Edom outside this relationship. But, again, it must be stressed that, as in the case of Ishmael, so also with Esau, the rejected one is still, according to the testimony of Scripture, an object of God's merciful care. That he is, is eloquently hinted by such things as the setting of Gen 27.39f (Isaac's blessing of Esau) in close proximity to Gen 27.27–29 (Isaac's blessing of Jacob), the inclusion of the detailed genealogies of Edom in Genesis 36 and 1 Chronicles 1, the precept of Deut 23.7 ('Thou shalt not abhor an Edomite; for he is thy brother'), and the judgment of Amos 2.1–3, though, not surprisingly, the bitter hatred of Edom often felt by the Jews has also left its traces in the Old Testament as well as in extra-canonical Jewish literature. Paul's special interest here was focused on the latter part of the Malachi quotation; for his point was that the unbelief of the majority of his fellow-Jews followed the pattern of this exclusion of Esau. That he remained firmly convinced of the positive truth contained in the former part of the quotation goes without saying.

The argument of vv. 6–13 (as we understand it) may then be set out as follows: According to Scripture, God distinguished, in the working out of His purpose, between Isaac and Ishmael and between Jacob and Esau. But this was a distinguishing inside the general area of election, since, although they were not Israelites, offspring of Jacob, Ishmael was a son of Abraham, 'the friend of God', with whom the covenant had been established, and Esau was one of the twin sons of Isaac, that son of Abraham in whom Abraham's seed was to be reckoned. Therefore the fact that at the present time a large number of Jews, members of the elect nation, stand outside the circle of the Israel within Israel, that is, of those who actually stand in a positive relationship to God's purpose, does not mean that God's purpose has failed. On the contrary, it may even be said to confirm it, since it conforms to the pattern of the working of that purpose right from the beginning.

14. Paul uses the question **What then shall we say?** here, as in 6.1 and 7.7, to introduce a false conclusion which he recognizes might be drawn from what he has been saying, in order to reject it. **Is there unrighteousness with God?** The possible false inference is indicated by means of a question formulated in a way that shows that a negative answer is expected; but, though this conclusion is being rejected, it is recognized by Paul as something which must be taken seriously. The process of showing that there is no inconsistency between God's dealings with contemporary Israel and His dealings with Abraham's offspring in the remote past, as attested by Scripture, has indeed raised the question whether God's ways have not been unjust from the very beginning. If His distinguishing between men depends, and has all along depended, 'not on *human* works but on him who calls', is He not unjust? Paul's **God forbid!** is no mere dogmatic denial, for he goes on to offer support for it – hence the conjunction with which the next verse begins.

15. **For he says to Moses, 'I will have mercy on him on whom I have mercy and I will have pity on him on whom I have pity.'** Paul appeals to the fact that, according to Exod 33.19, God said these words to Moses. It is highly likely that Paul (no less than Barth) thought of them as parallel to, and as an explicatory paraphrase of, the 'I AM THAT I AM' of Exod 3.14, and therefore as affording a specially significant revelation of the innermost nature of God.

The question which has to be asked is: Why did God's use of these words seem to Paul to warrant his emphatic denial that there is unrighteousness in God's distinguishing between Isaac and Ishmael and between Jacob and Esau (and also between those Jews who believe in the Messiah and those who still reject Him), before, and quite independently of, their works? The answer must surely be that he recognized in them an affirmation, not of the freedom of an unqualified will of God, but of the freedom of God's mercy. These words of Exodus clearly do testify to the freedom of God's mercy, to the fact that His mercy is something which man can neither earn nor in any way control. But – and this is most significant, but has often not been recognized – they do not suggest that this freedom of God's mercy is an absolute freedom either to be merciful or to be unmerciful. They give no encouragement at all to the notion that there is behind God's mercy a will of God that is different from His merciful will. Here it is instructive to contrast with Paul's Greek, which reproduces the Septuagint exactly which in its turn follows the Hebrew closely, the Latin Vulgate rendering at Exod 33.19 (in Romans the Vulgate keeps closer to the original): 'I will have mercy on him on whom I will, and will have pity on him on whom I please', which at the same time both obliterates the emphatic double repetition of the idea of mercy and also suggests the existence of a will or pleasure of God that is distinguishable from His merciful will. That the traditional interpretation of this verse of Romans has been along the lines of the meaning given to Exod 33.19 by the Vulgate is clear enough. But this has involved, we believe, a disastrous distortion of Paul's meaning. It is our contention that Paul regarded these words from Exodus as an appropriate and cogent answer to the suggestion that there is unrighteousness with God, precisely because he understood them to be affirming emphatically the *freedom* of God's mercy (and therefore the fact that God's mercy is not something to which men can establish a claim whether on the ground of parentage or of works), and at the same time making it clear that it is the freedom of God's *mercy* that is being affirmed, and not of some unqualified will of God behind, and distinct from, His merciful will. And, understanding Paul thus, we take it that this quotation, set as it is at a key point in the argument, must be allowed to control the interpretation of what follows (including v. 18!).

16. So then it is not a matter of *man's* willing or running but of God's showing mercy is an inference from the Exodus word just quoted. God's mercy does not depend on man's willing or activity but simply on God's being merciful.

17. For the scripture passage says to Pharaoh. The 'For' is best explained as parallel to that in v. 15, that is, as indicating the connexion of this verse with v. 14 (not with v. 16). Verses 15 and 17 are then two different citations in support of Paul's 'God forbid!' in v. 14, each of which is followed by a sentence drawing out what is to be inferred from it. The Pharaoh of the Exodus, the cruel oppressor of Israel, is introduced here as the type of those who resist God – as the prefiguration of the unbelieving majority of Jews. It seems unlikely that any substantial difference is intended by the use here of 'the scripture passage says' as against 'he says' in v. 15.

'For this very purpose have I raised thee up, that I might show in thee my power and that my name might be proclaimed in all the earth'. This quotation of Exod 9.16 differs slightly in several respects from the Septuagint, the variations having the effect of bringing out rather more sharply the sovereignty of the divine purpose. The key to the interpretation lies in the phrases, 'my power' and 'my name'.

God's 'power' has already been mentioned in two earlier verses of Romans, in 1.16b and 20. It is perhaps significant that, whereas in Exod 9.16 the Septuagint uses a different Greek word, Paul uses here the same word for 'power' as in 1.16b and 20. The former of these two passages is particularly significant because it is part of the statement of the theme of the epistle and because in it the nature of the power of God to which it refers is very clearly indicated – it is 'God's saving power'. In view of this the possibility must be reckoned with that Paul understood the power of God referred to in Exod 9.16 in the sense in which he himself had spoken of it in 1.16b, that is, not as unqualified power but specifically as saving power. And this possibility appears as a strong probability, in our judgment, when other Pauline references to God's power are taken into account. The following may be mentioned: 1 Cor 1.18 ('the word of the cross . . . unto us which are being saved . . . is the power of God'); 1 Cor 1.24 ('unto them that are called . . . Christ the power of God, and the wisdom of God'); 1 Cor 6.14 and 2 Cor 13.4, which speak of God's power as that by which Christ was raised (now lives) and we shall be raised (shall live); and also 1 Cor 2.5; 4.20; 2 Cor 4.7; 6.7; Eph 1.19; 3.7, 20; 2 Tim 1.8. That Paul should understand the reference to God's power in an evangelical way would not be surprising. Moreover, in so doing he would not have been untrue to what is after all the general sense of the Exodus passage; for there too the thought is not of a mere show of unqualified power, of power for its own sake, but of power directed toward the deliverance of God's people.

The other phrase, 'my name', will no doubt have signified for Paul the character of God revealed in His words and acts, His self-manifestation and its inherent, overflowing glory. Suggestively Paul has just quoted from Exod 33.19 words which, as we have seen, may be regarded as a drawing out of the meaning of the divine name already disclosed to Moses (Exod 3.14), words which point to the free, sovereign mercy of God.

But the showing of God's saving power and the publishing abroad of His name, of His self-revelation, of His truth – this is the very purpose of God's election of Israel. The implication of v. 17, then, is that Pharaoh too, prefiguring the at present rejected in Israel, serves in his own different way the same gracious purpose of God, to the service of which Moses and the believing in Israel have been appointed. He too is a witness, albeit an unwilling, unbelieving and ungrateful witness, to the saving power and truth of God.

18. So then on whom he wills he has mercy and whom he wills he hardens. Two contrasting forms of God's determination of men corresponding to the two different ways in which men may serve the divine purpose are indicated by 'has mercy on' and 'hardens'. Some serve it consciously and (more or less) voluntarily, others unconsciously and involuntarily. And men's stances in relation to

God's purpose depend ultimately on God. He has mercy on some in the sense that He determines them for a positive role in relation to His purpose, to a conscious and voluntary service: others He hardens in the sense that He determines them for a negative role in relation to His purpose, for an unconscious, involuntary service. But the significance of the double 'he wills' is controlled by the words quoted in v. 15. We are not free to understand it in the sense in which it has very often been understood, namely, of an altogether unqualified, indeterminate, absolute will, which moves now in one direction, now in another, capriciously; but only to understand it in the light of v. 15, as the merciful will of God, which is indeed free in the sense of being wholly independent of men's deserts and men's contriving, but is wholly determined in that it is the will of the merciful and righteous God. Both the 'has mercy on' and the 'hardens', though so different in their effects, are expressions of the same merciful will (compare 11.32).

The background of Paul's use of 'harden' is to be seen in Exod 4.21; 7.3; 9.12; 10.20, 27; 11.10; 14.4, 8, 17. That there are difficulties here is not to be denied. It is obvious that for the individual concerned it is a matter of tremendous consequence whether he has been determined for a positive or a negative role in relation to the divine purpose. To miss the inestimable privilege of belonging here in this present life to the company of those who are conscious and (more or less) willing and grateful witnesses to God's grace is far indeed from being a trivial loss. But, while we certainly ought not to attempt to soften away the real difficulties of this verse, it is also important to avoid reading into it what it does not say. The assumption that Paul is here thinking of the ultimate destiny of the individual, of his final salvation or final ruin, is not justified by the text. The words 'for destruction' are indeed used in v. 22; but we have no right to read them back into v. 18.

19–20a. Thou wilt say to me then introduces two questions which state an obvious and pressing objection to what has just been said. Whereas in v. 14 it was not necessary to think of a real or imaginary opponent, here, at least formally (with the use of the second person singular both in this and in the next verse) we do have to do with an objector. But to try to identify the objector is superfluous, in view of the obviousness of the objection. **'Why**

does he still blame *men*? For who is resisting his will?' The two questions are closely connected, the latter supporting the former. If things are as v. 18 has indicated, why does God find fault with men, holding them responsible (as, according to Scripture, He certainly does)? What grounds has He for reproaching men, since no man actually resists His will? If men's resistance is predetermined by God, it is not really resistance to His will at all, since this predetermination must be assumed to be the expression of His will. Such is the objection.

Nay, rather, who art thou, O man, who art answering God back? The literal rendering 'O man' (not Barrett's 'my dear sir' or the NEB 'sir') is demanded here by the contrast with 'God'. In the original 'O man' begins the sentence and 'God' is the last word of it. By thus setting man over against God Paul is certainly putting man in his place. But to assume that his intention is to assert the absolute right of an indeterminate divine will over the creature is to ignore the tenor of the argument of chapters 9 to 11, not to mention the evidence of the rest of the epistle. By 'God' Paul does not mean a capricious demon but the God revealed in Jesus Christ, the God whose will is wholly determined and has once for all been revealed as mercy. And the address 'O man' is to be understood in the light of 5.12–21. It puts man in his place, not by contrasting creaturely weakness with arbitrary almightiness, but by reminding him of what 'man' is according to Holy Scripture – the creature created in the image of God, the sinner for whose sin Christ died and for whose justification He has been raised from the dead. It is because, whether one is Moses or Pharaoh, member of the believing Church or member of still unbelieving Israel, one is this man, the object of God's mercy, that one has no right to answer God back.

20b–21. Paul now makes use of the familiar Old Testament imagery of the potter (compare Job 10.9; Ps 2.9; Isa 29.16; 41.25; 45.9; 64.8; Jer 18.1–12; Wisd 15.7–17; Ecclus 27.5; 33.13; 38.29–30). In the Old Testament it is used to illustrate different points. **Shall the thing moulded say to him who moulded it** reproduces exactly a part of Septuagint Isa 29.16. **'Why didst thou make me thus?'** is in a general way reminiscent of parts of Isa 29.16; 45.9; Wisd 12.12; but cannot properly be called a quotation of any of these passages. The substance of this question is determined by the thought which Paul is about to express in the next verse, which is concerned with the right of the potter to use his clay for various purposes.

Has not the potter a right over the clay to make from the same lump one part a vessel for honourable service and another a vessel for menial service? The fact that the occurrence together of 'potter' and 'clay' can be paralleled in some of the Old Testament potter passages and of 'potter' and 'vessel' in others is hardly surprising. But the contact with Wisd 15.7 ('For a potter, kneading soft earth, Laboriously mouldeth each several *vessel* for our service: Nay, out of the same clay doth he fashion Both the vessels that minister to clean uses, and those of a contrary sort, All in like manner; But what shall be the use of each *vessel* of either sort, The craftsman *himself* is the judge') is much more significant, since not only do 'potter', 'clay' and 'vessel' all occur together there, but the thought of the differences in dignity among the vessels is also expressed. Paul was no doubt aware that he was using a common biblical image. It may be that it was actually Wisd 15.7 (a passage which is not metaphorical but literal) which suggested to him the suitability of this image for his present purpose. But the similitude which we have here is Paul's own construction, designed specially with the point he wanted to make in view. The point of the similitude lies in the fact that the potter – as potter – must, in order to fulfil the rational purposes of his craft, be free to make, from the same mass of clay, some vessels for noble, and some for menial, uses. The conclusion to be drawn is that God must be acknowledged to be free – as God, as the One who has ultimate authority – to appoint men to various functions in the on-going course of salvation-history for the sake of the fulfilment of His over-all purpose. And it cannot be emphasized too strongly that there is naturally not the slightest suggestion that the potter's freedom is the freedom of caprice, and that it is, therefore, perverse to suppose that what Paul wanted to assert was a freedom of the Creator to deal with His creatures according to some indeterminate, capricious, absolute will.

22–23a. But what if God endured vessels of wrath, prepared for destruction, with much longsuffering, because he willed to show forth his wrath and to make known his power, and in order to make known the riches of his glory upon vessels of mercy constitutes the basic structure of a sentence which (as we have translated it) extends to the end of v. 24. In the original the sentence is incomplete, being an 'if' clause with various clauses subordinate to it but no main clause. However, the occurrence of a conditional sentence without an expressed main clause is fairly common in classical Greek and there are several instances in the New Testament: the sense has to be understood from the context in every case. Something like 'what wilt thou say?' might be supplied here, the point being that to reckon with the truth (the conditional clause states what Paul believes to be true – it is not hypothetical) expressed in vv. 22–24 will make a big difference to our understanding of God's right to act in the way indicated in v. 18, going beyond what has already been established by vv. 20b–21.

The initial 'But' is important, because it makes the connexion between Paul's similitude and what is, in effect, his application of it. His use of 'but', rather than 'so' or 'therefore', indicates an element of opposition and implies that he regards his illustration as inadequate. What follows does indeed draw out the point of v. 21, but, in doing so, it also brings out the fact that God's ways are not just like the potter's.

There has been much discussion as to whether the Greek participle represented by 'because he willed' is to be understood as (i) causal (as we have taken it), or (ii) concessive. The choice of (i) involves bringing together the three purposes indicated by the two infinitives dependent on 'willed' and also by the final clause ('in order to ... '). The choice of (ii), which means translating the participle 'though he willed', involves coupling together 'with much longsuffering' and the 'in order to' clause. Thus, according to (i), the meaning is: 'But what if God endured vessels of wrath, prepared for destruction, with much longsuffering, because he willed to show forth his wrath and to make known his power, and in order to make known the riches of his glory upon vessels of mercy ... ?' According to (ii), the meaning is: 'What if God, although he willed to show forth his wrath and so make known his power, (nevertheless) endured vessels of wrath, prepared for destruction, with much longsuffering and in order to make known the riches of his glory upon vessels of mercy ... ?' We agree with the majority of recent commentators that (i) should be preferred. On this decision two things follow: first, the two purposes indicated in the causal clause ('to show forth his wrath' and 'to make known his power') stand in a close positive relation to the statement that God 'endured vessels of wrath ... with much longsuffering' (contrast the opposition which would be indicated, were the clause concessive); secondly, these two purposes are closely connected with the purpose expressed by the final clause, 'in order to make known the riches of his glory upon vessels of mercy', so that together with it they form an integrated whole, a threefold purpose.

We may now refer to several details we have so far passed over, and then attempt to see as a whole the truth expressed in this verse and a half, with which Paul is bidding his readers reckon and which, if reckoned with, will make a big difference to their understanding of God's right to act in the way indicated in v. 18. The details are these. We may surely assume, unless there is something in the context which quite precludes such an interpretation, that God's 'much longsuffering' is connected with His kindness and intended to give those whom He endures the opportunity to repent. The expression 'vessels of wrath', while indicating that those whom it denotes are indeed objects of God's wrath at the present time, does not at all imply that they must always remain such (in Eph 2.3 believers are spoken of as having formerly been 'children of wrath'). And the at first sight frightening expression, 'prepared for destruction', while it certainly implies that the people concerned are worthy of destruction, does not imply that they will necessarily be destroyed. A careful comparison between the Greek of this phrase and the Greek of the relative clause, 'which he prepared beforehand for glory', in v. 23b shows that the thought of the divine predetermination, while it receives extremely strong emphasis in the latter, is not clearly expressed at all in the former. It seems probable that Paul wishes here to direct attention simply to the vessels' condition of readiness, ripeness, for destruction and not to any act, whether of God or of themselves, by which the condition was brought about.

With regard to the three purposes indicated in this passage, it is clear that the last to be mentioned ('in order to make known the riches of his glory upon vessels of mercy') is dominant. It alone is formulated in a final clause ('in order to ... '); it is given special emphasis by its position in the sentence, by the fact that it is extended by means of the two relative clauses which follow, and by the fact that vv. 25–29 focus further attention on it; and, above all, its content marks it off from the other purposes mentioned, for the manifestation of the wealth of the divine glory is nothing less than the ultimate purpose of God. The first and second purposes to be mentioned ('to show forth his wrath' and 'to make known his power') must be understood as subordinate to it. It is for the sake of the accomplishment of His one ultimate gracious purpose that God also wills the fulfilment of the other two purposes.

To attempt to sum up the truth with which Paul is inviting the Christians in Rome to reckon: God endured a Pharaoh, and He now endures rebellious Israel, with much longsuffering for the sake of the ultimate manifestation of the riches of His glory on vessels of mercy, but also, in the meantime, for the sake of the showing forth of His wrath and the making known of His power (if we were right about v. 17, His saving power), since this twofold revelation is necessary for the accomplishment of His ultimate gracious purpose.

The relations between God's patient enduring of vessels of wrath, the showing forth of His wrath, the making known of His power, and the manifestation of the wealth of His glory upon vessels of mercy, will be illumined by 9.30–11.36. We shall see in those sections that the ultimate purpose of that patience of God toward rebellious Israel which is depicted in 10.21 includes the salvation of rebellious Israel itself (chapter 11); but we shall see also how the divine patience must first show up the full seriousness of Israel's sin (9.30–10.21), or, in other words, how God is patient for the sake of showing His wrath, of judging men's sin (His patience shows up the hatefulness of men's sin by showing it to be the rejection of the grace of the God who is thus patient), in order that ultimately He may have mercy. In these chapters it will also become clear that the 'vessels of wrath' and the 'vessels of mercy' are not immutable quantities, and that it is God's purpose that the 'vessels of wrath' should become 'vessels of mercy'. It will also become clear that the showing of God's wrath is necessary in order that it may be manifest to the vessels of mercy that what is revealed in their case is indeed the wealth of God's glory, of the glory of His boundless mercy, and not any glory of their own deserving.

23b–24. which he prepared beforehand for glory. In the case of the vessels of mercy the divine predetermining is asserted explicitly. For 'for glory' compare 2.7, 10; 3.23; 5.2; 8.18. For the thought of the clause as a whole and also of the following verse, 8.28–30 should be compared. **whom he also called, even us, not only from among the Jews but also from among the Gentiles?** In view of the sequel in vv. 25 and 26, we must understand Paul's point to be that God has effectually called the vessels of mercy not only from among the Jews but also from among the Gentiles. The presence of Gentiles within the Church is the sign and pledge that the realm of rejection, of Ishmael, Esau, Pharaoh, and of the unbelieving Jews themselves, is not finally shut out from the mercy of God. The presence of 'even us' has the effect of giving to this statement something of the character of personal confession of faith.

25–26. – as he says in Hosea, 'I will call Not-my-people "My-people" and Unloved "Beloved"; and instead of its being said to them, "You are not my people", they shall be called the sons of the living God' does not have the form of an independent sentence, but is loosely attached to vv. 22–24. It is the first element of a catena of confirmatory Old Testament quotations which extends to the end of v. 29. Quoted are parts of Hos 2.23 and 1.10. In the first quotation there are several variations from the Septuagint, the most significant being the replacement of 'say to' by 'call', which affords a link between vv. 24 and 25 and also between vv. 25 and 26. The original reference of the Hosea verses was to the northern kingdom of Israel: Paul applies them to the Gentiles (compare 1 Pet 2.10). The ten tribes were indeed thrust out into the dark realm of the heathen, so that there is real justification for regarding them as a type of rejection. But their restoration was promised in Hosea's prophecy, and Paul takes this promise as a proof of God's purpose to include the Gentiles in His salvation. But, in view of the sequel in chapters 10 and 11, it is most unlikely that Paul did not also have in mind the fact that the original reference was to the ten lost tribes, and did not see in those lost tribes of Israel not only a type of the Gentiles but also the type of the unbelieving majority of his Jewish contemporaries.

27–28. Having provided a scriptural confirmation of the 'also from among the Gentiles' of v. 24, Paul now takes up the 'from among the Jews'. But all that he has said so far has presupposed the fact that at present the great majority of Jews are unbelieving. Those whom God has so far called from among the Jews are but few in number. So in these verses Paul proceeds to show that a situation in which the great majority of Jews suffer exclusion is something which is foretold in Scripture. The burden of the passage quoted is that only a remnant will be saved. That Paul thought of this as a condition through which Israel must pass rather than as God's last word concerning Israel is, however, clear from the sequel in Romans 10 and 11. **But Isaiah cries concerning Israel.** Isaiah's threatening word is contrasted ('But') with Hosea's word of promise. **'Though the number of the sons of Israel be as the sand of the sea, *only* a remnant shall be saved; for a sentence complete and decisive will the Lord accomplish upon the earth'** is an abbreviation of Isa 10.22–23. The form of the first part seems to have been assimilated by Paul to the wording of Hos 1.10. The Hebrew of the latter part is difficult, and the Septuagint translators were apparently baffled by the details. But both their translation and Paul's abbreviation of it, though differing considerably from the original, give the general idea of it quite correctly. It explains how it will come about that only a remnant will be saved.

29. And as Isaiah foretold, 'Had not the Lord of Hosts left us a seed, we should have become as Sodom and been made like Gomorrah'. A second quotation from Isaiah (1.9) is added in support of the first. The idea of a remnant is present here too; but, whereas the point of the previous quotation was that only a remnant will be preserved, the point of the present quotation is that the preservation of even a remnant is a miracle of divine grace – had not God's mercy spared a remnant, Israel would have been utterly destroyed like Sodom and Gomorrah (Gen 19.24–25). Paul regarded the words of Isaiah's oracle which referred to what was happening at the time of its utterance as a foretelling of the circumstances in which, in his own time, a small number of Jews was included in the Church.

VI. 3. ISRAEL IS WITHOUT EXCUSE, BUT IN THE LIGHT OF SCRIPTURE WE MAY HOPE THAT THE FACT THAT GENTILES BELIEVE WILL PROVOKE ISRAEL TO JEALOUSY: THE OLD TESTAMENT QUOTATION IN THE LAST VERSE STRIKES A HOPEFUL NOTE IN THAT, WHILE IT INDICATES THE GRIEVOUSNESS OF ISRAEL'S SIN BY SHOWING THE GOODNESS OF HIM AGAINST WHOM THEY HAVE SINNED, IT FOCUSES ATTENTION NOT ON ISRAEL'S SIN BUT ON GOD'S GOODNESS TOWARD ISRAEL

(9.30–10.21)

[30]What then shall we say? That Gentiles, who were not pursuing righteousness, have obtained righteousness, but the righteousness of faith; [31]but Israel, which was pursuing the law of righteousness, has not attained to that law. [32]Why? *It was* because *they pursued it* not on the basis of faith but as on the basis of works. They stumbled against the stone of stumbling, [33]even as it is written: 'Behold, I lay in Zion a stone of stumbling and a rock of offence, and he who believes on him shall not be put to shame.' [1]Brethren, as for me, the desire of my heart and my prayer to God for them are that they may be saved. [2]For I bear them witness that they have zeal for God, yet not according to knowledge. [3]For, failing to recognize the righteousness of God, and seeking to establish their own, they did not submit to the righteousness of God. [4]For Christ is the end of the law, so that righteousness is available to every one who believes. [5]For Moses writes that 'the man who does' the righteousness which is of the law 'shall live in' it.* [6]But the righteousness which is of faith speaks thus; 'Say not in thine heart "Who shall ascend into heaven?"' (that is, to bring Christ down); [7]nor "Who shall descend into the abyss?"' (that is, to bring Christ up from the dead). [8]But what does it say? 'The word is near thee, in thy mouth and in thine heart'; this means the word of faith which we preach. [9]For, if thou dost confess with thy mouth Jesus as Lord and dost believe in thine heart that God has raised him from the dead, thou shalt be saved. [10]For with the heart

---

*The translation of this verse follows the text of Nestle[25]. The substantial variants preferred by Nestle[26] should surely be rejected as due to assimilation to the Septuagint.

one believes unto justification, and with the mouth confession is made unto salvation. [11]For the scripture says: 'Every one who believes on him shall escape being put to shame'. [12]For there is no distinction between Jew and Greek. For the same Lord is *Lord* of all, being rich toward all who invoke him: [13]for 'Every one who invokes the name of the Lord shall be saved'.

[14]How could they invoke one in whom they had not believed? And how could they believe in one whom they had not heard? And how could they hear without a preacher? [15]And how could people preach unless they had been sent? *Relevant here is the testimony of* the scripture *which* says, 'How beautiful are the feet of those who bring good news of good things!' [16]But not all obeyed the good news. For Isaiah says: 'Lord, who hath believed our message?' [17]It is implied that faith comes of hearing, and hearing comes about through the word of Christ. [18]But I say, did they not hear? They did indeed – 'Their voice is gone out into all the earth. And their words to the ends of the inhabited world'. [19]But I say, was Israel without knowledge? First Moses says: 'I will use a nation that is no nation to make you jealous, And a foolish nation to make you angry'. [20]And Isaiah is so bold as to say: 'I let myself be found of those who were not seeking me, I made myself manifest to those who were not inquiring after me.' [21]But concerning Israel he says: 'All the day long I stretched out my hands to a disobedient and gainsaying people'.

In the previous section Paul has spoken of the disobedience of Israel as embraced within the work of the divine mercy and has also referred (in 9.24) to the inclusion of Gentiles in the number of those called by God. But both the nature of Israel's disobedience and the nature of the Gentiles' obedience need to be defined more closely. So now in the first paragraph of the new section, that is, in vv. 30–33, Paul gives this necessary definition in summary form.

In the rest of the section, that is, in chapter 10, he proceeds to expand, develop and clarify this summary definition, concentrating more particularly on that part of it which deals with Israel (though not exclusively – see, in particular, vv. 11 and 12 and 18–20), and bringing out clearly the fact that Israel is without excuse. Paul acknowledges (v. 2) the reality of Israel's zeal for God, but refers to the disastrous failure of comprehension which distorts and perverts this zeal, their blindness to the righteousness which is God's gift and obstinate determination to establish their own righteousness on the basis of their works, which result in a refusal to accept God's proffered gift humbly as the undeserved gift of His mercy. Verse 4 explains v. 3: what Israel had failed to recognize was that Christ had been all along the goal, the meaning, the substance, of that law which they had been so earnestly pursuing. Verses 5–13 provide explication and substantiation of v. 4: Christ is the inmost meaning of the law, and, because He is, a righteous status before God is available to every one who believes, since (in accordance with the testimony borne by the law) He has by His perfect obedience maintained His own righteousness and at the same time earned righteousness for all who will believe in Him (whether Jews or Gentiles) – so that, while He is righteous in His own right, they are through Him righteous by faith.

Rom 9.30–10.13 has made the guilt of Israel abundantly clear: it is guilty because it has failed to obey its own law, that very law for which it has been so zealous. It was to faith in Christ that the law was all along leading. But the fact that the law, the inner meaning of which is Jesus Christ, has been committed to Israel does not by itself constitute such a full opportunity to call upon the Lord in the sense of vv. 12 and 13 as would render Israel without excuse. Only if the message that the promises have now been fulfilled has been proclaimed by messengers duly commissioned by God Himself is that fullness of opportunity present. In vv. 14ff Paul is concerned to show that Israel has had that fullness of opportunity and is therefore absolutely without excuse. He first indicates by a chain of related questions (vv. 14–15a) four conditions which must have been fulfilled if they are *truly* to call upon the name of the Lord. The fact that the first and second conditions (the fourth and the third in the chain of vv. 14–15a) have been fulfilled is attested by the words of prophecy quoted in v. 15b: God has commissioned messengers and they have proclaimed the message. It is the fourth condition (the first mentioned in v. 14) which is unfulfilled: Israel has not believed in Christ (the fact is stated in v. 16a in the words 'but not all obeyed the good news'). In v. 17 Paul comes back to the third condition (Christ must be heard speaking through the message), which was passed over in v. 16, and indicates by means of another Old Testament quotation (v. 18) that this condition has been fulfilled. The subject of a further condition (or a subdivision of the third) is introduced in v. 19a by the question 'was Israel without knowledge?', and the fact that Israel was not without knowledge is then indicated in vv. 19b and 20 by means of two further quotations from the Old Testament. By this point it is evident that Israel is altogether without excuse for its unbelief.

Finally the quotation of Isa 65.2 in the last verse of the section serves, on the one hand, to gather up all that has already been said concerning Israel's disobedience and, by characterizing it unmistakably as the obstinate rejection of God's patient grace, to bring out as sharply as possible its full seriousness and enormity, and, on the other hand, to point even more emphatically to the unwearying persistence of God's graciousness, and so to bring the section to an end on a note of hope.

30. What then shall we say? here introduces not a false inference but Paul's own conclusion from what he has been saying. **That Gentiles** (not 'the Gentiles', as in the AV and RV, since the reference is not to the Gentiles generally but only to some Gentiles), **who were not pursuing righteousness, have obtained righteousness, but the righteousness of faith.** In its second and third occurrences here 'righteousness' must refer to status: to take it in its first occurrence in a different sense would be extremely harsh. Paul is not concerned to deny that in their former pagan life the Gentile Christians had sought moral righteousness but that they had truly and seriously sought after a righteous status in the sight of the one true God. Barrett's translation, 'who do not make righteousness their aim', misrepresents Paul's meaning: the Greek present participle used here has an imperfect sense (Paul would hardly deny that Gentile Christians seek righteousness now that they are Christians).

31. but Israel, which was pursuing the law of righteousness, has not attained to that law. After v. 30 one is inclined to expect 'but Israel, which was pursuing righteousness, has not attained to righteousness'; but Paul has not written that. Many interpreters, determined to get out of Paul's Greek a meaning harmonious with their preconceptions about his thought, have taken extraordinary liberties with what he has written. The suggestion that 'the law of righteousness' is an instance of a rare figure of speech which involves a reversal of relations between two terms (which it would hardly be unfair to describe as expressing one's meaning upside down), though made by some highly respectable commentators, strikes us as extremely improbable. Had Paul really used this peculiar figure of speech and meant by 'law of righteousness' what the JB represents as 'a righteousness derived from law', he would surely, for the sake of some clarity, have either repeated the whole phrase in the main clause or else have put 'righteousness' there rather than 'law'. And why in the world should he indulge in such a misleading way of speaking? But it must further be said that any interpretation which assumes that by 'law of righteousness' in v. 31 Paul intended to indicate something which the Jews were wrong to aim at, falls foul of v. 32, which implies that it was not the object of their pursuit which was wrong but the way in which they had pursued it. We shall be wise to try to understand Paul's words without forcing them.

Why did he introduce the word 'law' at this point? And why did he refer to it as 'the law of righteousness'? Surely to bring out the truth that Israel had been given the law to aid it in its quest for righteousness before God. The law is the law of righteousness because it was intended and designed to show the people of Israel how they could be righteous before God, to show them that the way to this righteousness is – faith. In the law which they were pursuing so zealously they had that which was all the time pointing out the way to the possession of a status of righteousness in God's sight. It was important for Paul's argument that he should at this point make it as clear as possible that the disobedient majority of Israel had not just been seeking in a general way after righteousness before God, but had actually been pursuing specifically that very thing which was indeed the way appointed for them to lead them to that righteousness. The majority of Jews have zealously pursued the law of God which had been given to them to bring them to a status of righteousness in God's sight: their tragedy is that, though they have pursued God's law, and still are pursuing it, with so much zeal, they have somehow failed altogether really to come to grips with it, failed altogether to grasp its real meaning and to render it true obedience.

32a. Why? *It was* because *they pursued it* **not on the basis of faith but as on the basis of works** explains why Israel has not attained to the law of righteousness. The words printed above in italics are not in the Greek. A verb has to be supplied, and the only verb which it is at all natural to supply is 'pursue'. With it an object also must be supplied, and the only object which it is natural to supply is 'it', referring to 'that law', that is, the previously mentioned 'law of righteousness'. Israel has failed to attain to the law of righteousness, because they pursued it not on the basis of faith but as on the basis of works.

It is of the greatest importance to recognize something which is often completely ignored, namely, that there is not the slightest suggestion here that to *pursue* the law was wrong or useless. It is not for its pursuit of the law, not on account of the *fact that* it had pursued, and was still pursuing, the law, that Israel is condemned, but for the *way in which* it had pursued the law. The implication is that Paul thought that, had Israel pursued the law on the basis of faith, it would indeed truly have come to grips with it, and that his desire for Israel was not that it should henceforward not pursue the law, but that it should cease to pursue it as on the basis of works and henceforward pursue it on the basis of faith. The importance of this for a proper understanding of Paul's attitude to the law is obvious. What then is this pursuit of the law on the basis of faith? The answer must be, surely, that it is to respond to the claim to faith which God makes through the law, and must include accepting, without evasion or resentment, the law's criticism of one's life, recognizing that one can never so adequately fulfil its righteous requirements as to put God in one's debt, accepting God's proffered mercy and forgiveness and in return giving oneself to Him in love and gratitude and so beginning to be released from one's self-centredness and turned in the direction of a humble obedience that is free from self-righteousness; that it is to allow oneself to be turned again and again by the forgiving mercy of God in the direction of loving Him with all one's heart and soul and mind and strength and of loving one's neighbour as oneself. The tragedy of Israel was that, instead of thus responding to the law of God with faith and pursuing it on the basis of faith, they had sought to come to terms with it on the basis of their works, their deserving, cherishing the illusion that they could so fulfil its demands as to put God under an obligation to themselves. Such an illusory quest could only result in failure –

in imprisonment in one's own self-centredness, and so in failure really to get to grips with the law, failure to comprehend its true meaning. It was probably with the intention of underlining the illusory character of Israel's quest that Paul placed an 'as' before 'on the basis of works'.

32b–33. They stumbled against the stone of stumbling indicates the inward meaning of Israel's failure to come to grips with the law. Israel has failed to recognize Him who is the goal and the substance of the law, and has rejected Him. How could it really come to grips with the law, if it was not ready to believe in Him who is the law's inmost meaning? But how could it believe in Him, if it was determined to rely on its own works? So they have stumbled over Christ (compare 'unto Jews a stumbling-block' in 1 Cor 1.23). He who was given for their salvation has thus, because of their perverseness, actually proved to be the occasion of their fall. **even as it is written: 'Behold, I lay in Zion a stone of stumbling and a rock of offence, and he who believes on him shall not be put to shame'.** The basis of the quotation is Isa 28.16, the original meaning of which seems to have been that, in contrast with the false security which the rulers of Jerusalem had thought to establish for themselves, God was establishing true and lasting security in Jerusalem for those who trusted in Him. The passage came to be understood messianically. But the middle part of the Isaiah verse has been replaced by some words from Isa 8.14, which introduce a strong note of judgment and menace, though an element of promise remains in the last part, which affords Paul a statement of the theme of justification by faith to be worked out in 10.4–13. (The fact that the same two Isaiah passages are also combined in 1 Pet 2.6–8, together with Ps 118.22 – interestingly the text used in 1 Peter shows agreements with that in Romans over against both the Hebrew and the Septuagint – has been seen as support for the suggestion that a collection of 'stone' testimonies was part of the early tradition of the Church.)

Verses 32b and 33 have added to the definition of the disobedience of Israel and of the obedience of some Gentiles an explicitly Christological dimension. Both the disobedience and the obedience are essentially a matter of relationship to Christ. Israel's pursuit of the law 'as on the basis of works' was blindness to the law's witness to Christ. Its legalistic misunderstanding and perversion of the law and its rejection of Him were inextricably intertwined. Its determination to establish its own righteousness by its works naturally made it blind to the righteousness which God was making available in Christ as a free gift, while its failure to recognize Christ as the true inner substance of the law could only drive it deeper into legalistic misunderstanding and perversion of the law. And the faith which is the basis of the righteous status now possessed by some Gentiles according to v. 30 is, of course, faith in Christ – that faith which bears the promise, 'he who believes on him shall not be put to shame'.

1. Brethren, as for me, the desire of my heart and my prayer to God for them are that they may be saved. Paul's personal declaration is a pointer, often unheeded, to the Church's continuing duty seriously and wholeheartedly to desire, and earnestly and faithfully to pray for, the salvation of the still unbelieving Jews. That, as in Paul's own case, such a desire and prayer cannot fail to be accompanied by a persistent, but at the same time brotherly, witness to them concerning the Messiah Jesus should be obvious.

2. For I bear them witness that they have zeal for God is a notable tribute. Both 'zeal' and 'for God' are important. The Greek noun represented by 'zeal' can also be used in a bad sense of envy; but, as used here, it denotes a strong and persistent desire for, and concentration of the attention upon, something, and the seeking of its glory. And Paul acknowledges that his kinsmen's zeal has the right object: it is indeed zeal for the one true God. Here is no heathen fanaticism. Of how much of the churches' membership could it be asserted with equal confidence that the object of its worship is really the living God and not one or other of the various false gods of a corrupt society, and, where the churches' members are concerned with the true God, how much of their concern would be accurately described by so strong a term as 'zeal'? **yet not according to knowledge.** In spite of the earnestness of their zeal, in spite of the fact that it is truly zeal for the true God, there is a disastrous flaw in it – it is not according to knowledge. Paul certainly does not mean to deny that they know God (compare v. 19). They do indeed know God, and yet they will not know Him as He really is. There is a lack of comprehension at the most vital point. It is a matter of seeing indeed but not perceiving, of hearing indeed but not understanding (compare Mk 4.12). There is a perverse and obstinate ignorance at the very heart of their knowledge of God, and in the centre of their dedicated and meticulous obedience an obstinate disobedience.

3. For, failing to recognize the righteousness of God, and seeking to establish their own, they did not submit to the righteousness of God. The two participial clauses may be understood as defining the nature of the Jews' ignorance, and the following main clause as indicating the act of disobedience which resulted from it. Their ignorance consists in their failure to comprehend and acknowledge God's righteousness, that is, the status of righteousness before Him which He wants to give, and – what is the other side of this failure – their determination to establish their own righteousness, that is, a righteous standing of their own deserving. Such ignorance is indeed ignorance of God's own character, a failure to know Him as He has revealed Himself in His mercy and faithfulness and the real seriousness of His claim to them. The resulting disobedience is the refusal to 'submit to the righteousness of God', that is, to humble themselves to accept it as the undeserved gift of His mercy. The past tense used of this refusal ('did not submit' – we may compare 'they stumbled' in 9.32) reflects the fact that Paul had in mind the historical event of the rejection of the Messiah, in whom God's gift was offered.

4. For Christ is the end of the law, so that righteousness is available to every one who believes. This verse has been understood in very different ways, but is generally agreed to be of vital importance for the interpretation of Paul's theology, being, in one sense or another, a decisive statement about the relation of Christ and the law. The Greek word represented by 'end' is capable of bearing an extraordinarily wide variety of meanings; but, as far as its use in this verse is concerned, there are three possibilities to be considered: (i) fulfilment; (ii) goal; (iii) termination. The Fathers seem generally to have tended toward a combination of (i) and (ii). Aquinas, Luther, Calvin and Bengel all understood the verse as expressing a positive relation between Christ and the law. But in recent times (iii) has been very widely supported (so, for example, by Sanday and Headlam, Dodd, Michel, Käsemann, and also by the NEB and JB, which get rid of the ambiguity of the AV, RV and RSV 'the end'). Some have sought to combine one or other or both of the interpretations (i) and (ii) with (iii). But, in view of such passages as 3.31; 7.12, 14a; 8.4; 13.8–10, and of the fact that Paul again and again appeals to the Pentateuch in support of his arguments (specially suggestive is the fact that he does so in vv. 6–10 of this chapter), we regard (iii) and also all attempted combinations of (iii) with (i) and/or (ii) as altogether improbable.

Between (i) and (ii) it is more difficult to decide, and it is tempting to settle for the view that both meanings were intended. The statement that Christ is the fulfilment of the law and the statement that He is its goal are indeed correlatives: they express the same essential truth but describe it as seen from different angles, and each is necessary for the adequate exposition of the other. But, while the former is quite clearly a statement about Christ, a description of Him in terms of the law, the latter, though it also is formally, and indeed to some extent substantially, a statement about Christ, is in substance primarily a statement about the law, defining it by reference to Christ. And in the present context (9.30–10.13) a statement about the law seems more apposite; for in this passage Paul is concerned to show that Israel has misunderstood the law. At this point a statement that Christ is the goal to which all along the law has been directed, its true intention and meaning, is altogether apposite. Israel has misunderstood the law, because it failed to recognize what it was all about. A statement to the effect that Christ is the fulfilment of the law would be much less apposite. So we conclude that the Greek noun should be understood in sense (ii): Christ is the end of the law in the sense that He is its goal, aim, intention, real meaning and substance – apart from Him it cannot be properly understood at all.

The words 'so that righteousness is available to every one who believes' indicate the consequence. We take the meaning of the verse as a whole, then, to be: For Christ is the goal of the law, and it follows that a status of righteousness is available to every one who believes. The 'For' at the beginning of the verse indicates that it is an explanation of v. 3 – particularly of 'they did not submit to the righteousness of God'. The Jews in their legalistic quest after a righteous status of their own earning failed to recognize and accept the righteous status which God was seeking to give them; for all along, had they but known it, Christ was the goal and meaning and substance of that law which they were so earnestly pursuing, and the righteousness to which the law was summoning them was all the time nothing other than that righteousness which God offers to men in Christ.

5. For Moses writes that 'the man who does' the righteousness which is of the law 'shall live in' it. Two main interpretations of this verse have to be considered. There is, first, the usual explanation, namely, that it is intended to indicate the hopeless nature of the quest after a righteous status before God on the basis of works, which is contrasted with the way of justification by faith described in vv. 6–8. According to this interpretation, v. 5 would be related to v. 4 (as we have explained it) in some such way as the following: The fact that Christ is the goal of the law means that a righteous status is available to all who believe in Him (v. 4); for, while justification by works is the hopeless quest that Moses indicates (v. 5), Scripture has all along set forth the glorious possibility of justification by faith (vv. 6–8). Verses 5–8 as a whole would be an explanation of v. 4. The second explanation is that Paul is applying the words of Lev 18.5, not to the impossible, hopeless task which men set themselves when they think to earn a righteous status before God by their own works, but to the achievement of the one Man who has done the righteousness which is of the law in His life and, above all, in His death, in the sense of fulfilling the law's requirements perfectly and so deserving as His right a righteous status before God. We may then regard the whole of vv. 5–13 as intended to explain v. 4 (not just the former part but also the latter). In accordance with Lev 18.5 Christ has – alone among men – obeyed perfectly, and so by virtue of His obedience has actually deserved His righteous status and eternal life, but (vv. 6–13) has also won a righteous status and eternal life for all those who will believe in Him. The point of the 'But' at the beginning of v. 6 is the contrast between the righteous status altogether deserved by Christ and the righteous status which men have through faith in Him, which is altogether undeserved by them.

Of these two possible interpretations the second seems to us to have the stronger claim to acceptance, as yielding a more closely-knit sequence of thought (in Gal 3.12 also it is likely, in our view, that Paul in quoting Lev 18.5 has Christ's perfect obedience in

254

mind, since otherwise a step in his argument would seem to be missing).

6–8. But the righteousness which is of faith speaks thus. The personification of the righteousness of faith in these verses is a rhetorical device which can be paralleled in the popular philosophical preaching of Paul's time in which virtues and vices are sometimes represented as speaking. It is a lively and picturesque way of saying that the true nature of righteousness on the basis of faith is set forth in the sentences from the Old Testament which are about to be quoted. Specially noteworthy is the fact that it is in the law itself, in Deuteronomy, that Paul hears the message of justification by faith. **'Say not in thine heart** reproduces exactly the opening words of two verses of the Septuagint version of Deuteronomy (8.17 and 9.4). Both verses are warnings against a self-complacent, presumptuous boasting in one's own merit. But Paul does not go on to quote further from either of these verses. Instead he quotes (with very considerable freedom) parts of Deut 30.12–14. **"Who shall ascend into heaven?"** is part of Deut 30.12. What precedes it is: 'It is not in heaven, that thou shouldest say'. The reference is to God's commandment. The previous verse has said: 'For this commandment which I command thee this day, it is not too hard for thee; neither is it far off'. Israel does not have to climb up to heaven to discover God's will; for He has graciously shown them what is good by His law, and that law is simple and clear. They do not have to inquire after the will of a harsh or capricious tyrant. They have received the revelation of the merciful will of the God whose prior grace is the presupposition of all He requires (as, for example, in the Decalogue itself, in which Exod 20.2 and Deut 5.6 precede the commandments). Essentially what He asks is that they should give Him their hearts in humble gratitude for His goodness to them and in generous loyalty to their fellows.

(that is, to bring Christ down) is the first of the three interpretations of details of the Old Testament passage to which he is appealing, which Paul introduces in the course of these verses after the manner of Jewish biblical exposition as it is to be seen in the Qumran texts. The question naturally arises, What are we to make of Paul's treatment of Deut 30.11ff as biblical interpretation? Is it merely arbitrary, like much of the exegesis of

Qumran – a matter of forcing upon an Old Testament text a meaning quite foreign to it? So it has certainly seemed to many, including some of the most sympathetic commentators. At first sight it looks like this; for Deuteronomy is speaking about the law, and Paul refers what it says to Christ. But, if our understanding of Paul's view of the law is right, he did not think of Christ and the law as two altogether unrelated entities; on the contrary, he saw the closest inner connexion between them. Christ is the goal, the essential meaning, the real substance of the law. It is therefore only as one sets one's eyes on Christ, that one can see both the full significance of that graciousness of the law which comes to expression in this Deuteronomy passage and also the full seriousness of its imperatives. On this view of the relation of Christ and the law there is a real inward justification for what Paul is doing here. It is not arbitrary typology but true interpretation in depth. Between the fact that God's law was addressed directly to the Israelite's heart, requiring faith and obedience, and was not something esoteric to be first discovered by human searching, and the fact that the Son of God has now become incarnate, so that there can be no question of man's needing to bring Him down, there is an intimate connexion; for behind both the gift of the law and the incarnation of the Son of God is the same divine grace – that grace, the primary and basic initiative of which was God's election of man in Jesus Christ.

'nor "Who shall descend into the abyss"?'. This question is substituted for the 'Who shall go over the sea for us . . . ?' of Deut 30.13, which offered no point of contact with the history of Christ. The Greek word represented here by 'abyss' occurs upwards of thirty times in the Septuagint, usually denoting the depth of waters, but in the Septuagint version of Ps 71.20 it is used of the depths of the earth as the place of the dead, Sheol, and it is clearly in this sense that Paul understands it here. **(that is, to bring Christ up from the dead).** Just as there is no point in wanting to mount up to heaven to bring Christ down, now that the Incarnation has taken place, so neither is there any point in wanting to descend into Sheol to bring Christ up from the dead, since He has already been raised. The questions which Deut 30.12–13 sets aside indicate excuses for not responding to the law with the grateful trust in God's mercy and generous loyalty to one's fellow-men which it requires. As interpreted in Rom 10.6–7, they describe the attitude of those who, because of their failure properly to comprehend the law, fail also to recognize their Messiah when He has come to them.

But what does it say? 'The word is near thee, in thy mouth and in thine heart': this means the word of faith which we preach. The quotation from Deut 30.14 indicates the essentially gracious character of the law in which God had stooped down to reveal His will to Israel and to claim each Israelite for Himself and for his neighbour: God had drawn near to them in His word which could be taken on their lips and received in their hearts. But all along His nearness to Israel by means of His law pointed forward to His gift of Himself to men in Jesus Christ. The justification for Paul's application of the verse in the words which follow is the close relation between the law and Christ. Many commentators, who have failed to see this close relation and have insisted on reading into Paul's theology a stark opposition between Christ and the law, have made unnecessarily heavy weather of this passage. By 'of faith' is most probably meant 'which calls for (the response of) faith'.

9. For, if thou dost confess with thy mouth Jesus as Lord and dost believe in thine heart that God has raised him from the dead, thou shalt be saved explains and confirms what was said in v. 8: hence the initial 'For'. The order of the two conditional clauses, at first sight surprising since confession issues from belief, is no doubt due to the fact that 'in thy mouth' precedes 'in thy heart' in Deut 30.14: in the next verse Paul reverses the order. The content of the confession and the content of the belief are differently formulated, but in Paul's thought they amount to the same thing. He does not mean to imply that the mouth is to confess anything other than that which the heart believes. But the two formulations interpret each other, so that what is to be both believed and confessed is the more precisely defined.

In view of the evidence of this verse, in which the presence of 'confess' is suggestive, and of 1 Cor 12.3; 2 Cor 4.5; Phil 2.11, it seems clear that 'Jesus is Lord' was already an established confessional formula. It is probable that it was used in connexion with baptism, but also in Christian worship generally. Doubtless the contrast with the use of 'lord' as a designation of the Roman emperor will have given to the formula 'Jesus is Lord' a special significance, but it is not likely that it originated as a response to the 'lord Caesar'. That Christians in the Greek-speaking world were well aware of the fact that 'lord' and 'lady' were commonly used with reference to various pagan deities, especially of the oriental-Hellenistic religions, is, of course, unquestionable (Paul himself refers to these 'lords many' in 1 Cor 8.5). But the contention that the title 'Lord' was first applied to Jesus under Hellenistic influence and in a Hellenistic environment must be rejected; for – to mention one obvious objection – Paul's use of the Aramaic *marana tha* (meaning 'Our Lord, come', or possibly, if the division between the words is differently placed, 'Our Lord has come' (or 'comes')) in a Greek letter to Greek-speaking Christians (1 Cor 16.22) points unmistakably to its being a very early liturgical formula, and so to the use of 'Lord' as a title of the exalted Christ in early Aramaic-speaking Christianity. It is important to realize that in Hebrew, Aramaic and Greek alike the words in question could be used in non-religious senses like 'lord', 'owner', 'master'; and it is likely that during His ministry Jesus was sometimes addressed by His disciples as 'my lord' or 'our lord' in a sense equivalent to 'Rabbi', 'teacher' or 'revered teacher'. After the Resurrection He was still so addressed, but with the word no longer used in the sense of 'teacher' but as the title of One invoked in prayer, and He was also referred to in the third person as 'our Lord' or 'the Lord'.

What then did the confession 'Jesus is Lord' mean for Paul? The use of the Greek equivalent of 'Lord' more than six thousand times in the Septuagint to represent the divine name of four consonants, YHWH, must surely be regarded as of decisive importance here. In support of this view the following points may be made:

(i) Paul applies to Christ, without – apparently – the least sense of inappropriateness, the 'Lord' of Septuagint passages in which it is perfectly clear that the Lord referred to is God Himself (for example, 10.13; 1 Th 5.2; 2 Th 2.2).

(ii) In Phil 2.9 he describes the 'Lord' title as 'the name which is above every name', which can hardly mean anything else than the peculiar name of God Himself.

(iii) He apparently sees nothing objectionable in the invocation of Christ in prayer (the two Aramaic words in 1 Cor 16.22 are, as we have seen, probably to be understood as a prayer; and Paul approves of calling upon the name of the Lord Christ – see 10.12–14 and 1 Cor 1.2 – though 'call upon' is a technical term for invoking in prayer); but, for a Jew, to pray to anyone other than the one true God was utterly abhorred.

(iv) He associates Christ with God again and again in ways which imply nothing less than a community of nature between them. Thus without any sense of incongruity he can name together 'God our Father' and 'the Lord Jesus Christ' as the source of grace and peace (1.7; 1 Cor 1.3; 2 Cor 1.2) and can speak indifferently of the love of God and the love of Christ (for example, 8.35 and 39).

We take it that, for Paul, the confession that Jesus is Lord meant the acknowledgment that Jesus shares the name and the nature, the holiness, the authority, power, majesty and eternity of the one and only true God. And, when, as is often the case, there is joined with the title 'Lord' a personal pronoun in the genitive, there is expressed in addition the sense of His ownership of those who acknowledge Him and of their consciousness of being His property, the sense of personal commitment and allegiance, of trust and confidence.

The formulation of what is the content of the outward confession (but also of course of the inward faith, since it is unthinkable that the mouth should confess something other than that which the heart believes) in terms of Jesus's being Lord has provided a necessary clarification of the following formulation in terms of the Resurrection; for it has made it clear that His resurrection was no mere resuscitation of a corpse only for it to die again, but God's decisive, irrevocable sealing of Him who was crucified as the eternal Lord. And now the formulation of what is the content of the inward faith in terms of the Resurrection makes it clear that the Lord whom Christians confess is no mythological or symbolic figure like the 'lords many' (1 Cor 8.5) familiar to the pagan world, but one who has lived a real human life and died a shameful death under Pontius Pilate and has been raised up by God once and for all. The choice of the Resurrection for mention here is significant; for it indicates that for Paul the belief that God has raised Jesus from the dead is the distinctive and decisive belief of Christians. It is indeed the 'article by which the Church stands or falls'; for 'if Christ hath not been raised, then is our preaching vain, your faith also is vain' (1 Cor 15.14).

The promise 'thou shalt be saved' refers to future final salvation (see on 1.16 ('saving') and on 5.9 and 10), the inheriting of eternal life; but future final salvation reflects its glory back into the present for those who confidently hope for it, and who are even now 'being saved' (1 Cor 1.18).

10. For with the heart one believes unto justification, and with the mouth confession is made unto salvation supports the previous verse's reference of 'in thy mouth' and 'in thy heart' in Deut 30.14 to confession and faith, respectively. But here the order of v. 9, which was determined by that of the Deuteronomy passage, is abandoned in favour of the natural order, faith being now mentioned before confession. The distinction in this verse between 'justification' and 'salvation' (contrast the simple 'thou shalt be saved' in v. 9 answering to both 'confess' and 'believe') is not substantial, both terms referring to the same final issue.

11. For the scripture says: 'Every one who believes on him shall escape being put to shame' is introduced in support of v. 10, Paul understanding 'shall escape being put to shame' as equivalent to 'shall be justified'/'shall be saved'. 'Every' is Paul's addition which makes explicit, and emphasizes, the universal scope of the general statement of the Septuagint text, which is the aspect on which he is going to dwell in vv. 12–13. For the quotation from Isa 28.16 see on 9.33, where Paul clearly took the 'him' to refer to Christ.

12–13 consist of three sentences each of which explains or supports its predecessor (hence the threefold 'For'). With **For there is no distinction between Jew and Greek** compare 3.22. In 3.22 the point is that, since all are sinners, Gentiles and Jews alike can be justified *only* through faith: here (in view of the content of vv. 11, 12b and 13) the point is rather the *positive* one that the promise pertaining to faith applies equally to Jews and Gentiles. This promise embracing all men without distinction was all along the inner meaning of the law which was placed in the mouths and in the hearts of the Jews. And, though they have to learn the humbling lesson that righteousness with God is not theirs by right of descent or merit, they also stand under the promise that they too may share that righteousness through faith. **For the same Lord is *Lord* of all.** In 3.29 the point made was that God is God of the

Gentiles as well as of the Jews. Here, in affirming that the same Lord is Lord of all, Paul refers to Jesus, the 'Lord' of v. 9. **being rich toward all who invoke him.** The meaning of the clause must be that Christ is rich to the advantage of all who call on Him, that is, that He gives liberally of His riches (we may think of His wealth of goodness, kindness, love, glory, etc.) to them. Note the persistent emphasis in vv. 11–13 of the idea of universality: 'Every one', 'there is no distinction', 'of all', 'toward all', 'Every one' (and compare the 'to every one' of v. 4). The use of the verb represented by 'invoke' of invoking a god in prayer was well established in pagan Greek. In the Septuagint it occurs frequently with reference to calling upon God in prayer and can even be used absolutely in the sense 'pray'. In the New Testament it is used a few times of the invocation of God the Father, but more often of invoking the exalted Christ. That the word has its technical sense of 'invoke in prayer' here is confirmed by v. 13. The fact that Paul can think of prayer to the exalted Christ without the least repugnance is, in the light of the first and second commandments of the Decalogue, the decisive clarification of the significance which he attached to the title 'Lord' as applied to Christ. **for 'Every one who invokes the name of the Lord shall be saved'** brings the paragraph to an end with a scriptural quotation from Joel 2.32, Paul applying to the invocation of the exalted Christ what in its Old Testament context was a promise that in the critical period preceding 'the great and terrible day of the LORD' every one who invokes the name of the LORD, that is, Yahweh, will be saved. The 'Every' here (unlike that in v. 11) is part of the quotation.

14–15a. How could they invoke one in whom they had not believed? And how could they believe in one whom they had not heard? And how could they hear without a preacher? And how could people preach unless they had been sent? We have here four questions which are parallel in structure and together form a logical chain. The third person plural verbs of the first three questions are sometimes understood as indefinite ('How then shall men call ... '); but in view of the argument of the section 9.30–10.21 as a whole, it is more natural to assume that the subject of these verbs is the same as that of the third person plural verbs in 9.32; 10.2, 3 – namely, the Jews. At this point Paul is concerned to show that the Jews have really had full opportunity to call upon the name of the Lord in the sense of vv. 12 and 13, and are therefore without excuse. That all along the law which was constantly on their lips was pointing to Christ, that all along He had been its innermost meaning, did not by itself constitute this full opportunity. The fullness of opportunity was not present for them until the message that the promises have indeed now been fulfilled had actually been declared to them by messengers truly commissioned for the purpose by God Himself. Paul makes his point by asking the question whether this fullness of opportunity has really been present for the Jews by means of this chain of related questions, and then answering in the affirmative in v. 15b. The chain of questions does not put the essential question directly but rather indicates the impossibility of the Jews' calling upon Christ unless certain pre-conditions have been fulfilled. Its substance may be summed up in four statements thus: They can only call upon Christ in the sense of vv. 12 and 13, if they have already believed in Him; they can only believe in Him, if they have heard Him (speaking to them through the message about Him); they can only hear Him, if someone proclaims the message; the message can only be proclaimed, if God commissions someone to proclaim it. The point of the fourth question is that true Christian preaching, through which Christ Himself speaks, is not something which men can accomplish on their own initiative: it can only take place where men are authorized and commissioned by God. It is illuminating to compare what is said concerning prophetic authority in Jer 14.14; 23.21; 27.15. See further on 'apostle by *God's* calling' in 1.1.

15b. *Relevant here is the testimony of* the scripture *which* says, **'How beautiful are the feet of those who bring good news of good things!'** The quotation from Isa 52.7, so far from being a mere ornament (as it has sometimes been regarded) is an essential step in the argument, serving as a statement of the fact that the first and second conditions (that is, the last two mentioned in vv. 14–15a) have been fulfilled. Paul does not refer directly to his own apostolic ministry or the preaching of other Christian evangelists, but by appealing to Isa 52.7 he both points to it indirectly and at the same time gives the scriptural attestation of its true significance. If the apostolic preaching is truly the fulfilment of the prophecy, then it is attested as a true preaching, and this must mean that the preachers have been duly authorized and commissioned.

16. But not all obeyed the good news. For Isaiah says: 'Lord, who hath believed our message?' The former half of this is best understood as continuing the thought of v. 15: what has been lacking has been submission to the message (that is, faith) on the part of the hearers. The latter half is then a scriptural confirmation of the former: this failure to believe has been foretold by the prophet. The verse is a declaration that, as far as some of the Jews are concerned, the fourth and final condition, that is, the one mentioned first in v. 14, namely, that they should believe in Him whom they have heard, has not been fulfilled. They have not believed in Christ. Paul's 'not all' is a deliberate understatement like the 'some' in 3.3. For the use of 'obey' as equivalent to 'believe' compare 1.5. To obey the gospel is to believe it and to believe in Him who is its content; and to believe the gospel and believe in Christ involves obeying it, obeying Him.

17. It is implied that faith comes of hearing, and hearing comes about through the word of Christ. This verse has troubled commentators and has been variously interpreted. The most satisfactory explanation, in our view, is one along the following lines. In vv. 15b–16 Paul passed over the third condition (namely, hearing). This was probably due, on the one hand, to a desire to set directly over against the fulfilment on God's (Christ's) part of the basic first two conditions (namely, the commissioning of the messengers and Christ's speaking through them) the stark fact of Israel's disobedience, which is the problem with which chapters 9 to 11 as a whole are concerned, and, on the other hand, to a feeling that, as he is going to expand his treatment of the matter of the third condition (he is going to introduce knowing as a kind of subdivision of hearing), it would be more conveniently placed last. But he has to come back to the third condition, and v. 17 effects the transition from the Old Testament quotation in v. 16b to the subject of Israel's hearing. The quotation speaks of believing a message. But a message's being believed involves an intermediate occurrence between the message's being uttered and its being believed, namely, its being heard. So in v. 17 Paul draws out what is implied in his quotation, applying it to the matter in hand. Faith results from hearing the message, and the hearing of the message comes about through the word of Christ (that is, through Christ's speaking the message by the mouths of His messengers). This corroborates what was said in vv. 14–15a, but is not a mere pointless repetition, since in it hearing becomes the hinge, so that it leads naturally into v. 18.

18. But I say, did they not hear? They did indeed – 'Their voice is gone out into all the earth, And their words to the ends of the inhabited world'. Instead of stating directly that the Jews must certainly have heard the gospel preaching, Paul quotes (though without any explicit indication that he is quoting) the Septuagint version of part of Ps 19.4, applying to the Christian mission what was said of the glorification of God by the natural order. It is quite unlikely that Paul's use of this quotation means that he thinks that the preaching to all the nations (Mk 13.10) has been completed. The fact that he hopes to undertake a missionary journey to Spain (15.24, 28) itself disproves this. Probably all that he wants to assert is that the message has been publicly proclaimed in the world at large – the significant thing is that it has been quite widely preached to the Gentiles (compare v. 19f) – and therefore cannot be supposed not to have been heard by the generality of Jews.

19–21. A supplementary question (knowing did not figure as a link in the chain in vv. 14–15a) is now raised in parallel form to v. 18a, and the answer is given by means of three Old Testament quotations. **But I say, was Israel without knowledge?** The use of 'Israel', the name which expresses the fact of the Jews' election (compare what was said on 'Israelites' in 9.4), indicates the answer to the question. The excuse of ignorance cannot be sustained. But it is to be noted that Paul is not withdrawing what he has said in vv. 2–3. The truth is that in one sense they know and in another sense they do not know. They have been the recipients of God's special self-revelation, and yet they have been uncomprehending. Compare Mk 4.12 ('. . . that seeing they may see, and not perceive; and hearing they may hear, and not understand . . . '). The ignorance which is blameworthy has been characteristic of them; but the ignorance which would have constituted an excuse they cannot claim.

First Moses says: 'I will use a nation that is no nation to make you jealous, And a foolish nation to make you angry'. The first Old Testament quotation is from Deut 32.21. In their context in the

Song of Moses, the words are a warning of God's chastisement of His people Israel for their infidelity: their provoking Him to jealousy and anger by going after no-gods, vanities, He will punish by provoking them to jealousy and anger by means of no-peoples, foolish nations (that is, the various Gentile nations which God uses as His instruments in the course of history). Paul sees the words as applying to the Gentile mission. If Gentiles who, in relation to the knowledge of God, are, compared with Israel, but no-peoples, foolish nations, have come to know, then it certainly cannot be supposed that Israel has not known. It is a striking feature of the argument here that, instead of appealing directly to the actual course of the Gentile mission in which he himself had played so important a part, Paul keeps steadfastly to the Old Testament. It is a true insight which sees a connexion between the fact – so full of evangelical significance – of Paul's establishment of Israel's guilt in such a way as not to call in question but to confirm its election, and the constancy of his attention to the Old Testament throughout this chapter.

The second quotation is from the first part of Isa 65.1: **And Isaiah is so bold as to say: 'I let myself be found of those who were not seeking me, I made myself manifest to those who were not inquiring after me'.** In its context in Isaiah, Isa 65.1ff is probably to be understood (though this is disputed) as God's answer to His people's prayer in 63.7–64.12, and the sense of vv. 1 and 2 is that God has graciously and patiently made Himself accessible to His people and continually sought to welcome them into fellowship with Himself, in spite of all their rebelliousness. But Paul (as his explanatory words at the beginning of v. 21 indicate) sees a contrast between vv. 1 and 2, and applies the former to the Gentiles and only the latter to Israel. As used by him, the quotation from Isa 65.1 is parallel to the quotation in v. 19, and serves to confirm that Israel must have known, since God has actually been found by Gentiles who were not seeking Him.

The third quotation is also from Isaiah 65, but from v. 2. **But concerning Israel he says: 'All the day long I stretched out my hands to a disobedient and gainsaying people'.** The spreading out of the hands is here a gesture of appealing welcome and friendship. This last quotation confirms incidentally that Israel has known, but it has a special twofold function. It (i) looks back to what has already been said concerning Israel's disobedience and gathers it up in one comprehensive statement, which by making it clear that this disobedience is precisely rejection of God's steadfast grace brings out its full enormity; and (ii) looks forward to what is going to be said of hope for Israel, depicting vividly the steadfast patience of that divine grace against which Israel has so continually sinned.

VI. 4. GOD HAS NOT CAST OFF HIS PEOPLE
(11.1–36)

The theme of the whole section is categorically stated in v. 2a: 'God has not cast off his people whom he foreknew'. That even at the present time the disobedience of Israel is not complete (there exists 'a remnant according to the election of grace', Jews who are believers in Christ) is the burden of the first subsection (vv. 1–10), while the second (vv. 11–24) contributes the assurance that the exclusion of the majority of Jews is not going to last for ever. The third subsection (vv. 25–32) gives an insight into the mystery of the divine plan of mercy concerning both Jews and Gentiles, and finally vv. 33–36 conclude both this section and the whole of main division VI with an expression of adoring wonder and praise.

(i) *The remnant according to the election of grace*
(11.1–10)

¹I ask then, has God cast off his people? God forbid! for I myself am an Israelite, of the seed of Abraham, of the tribe of Benjamin. ²God has not cast off his people whom he foreknew. Or do you not know what the scripture says in *the section about* Elijah, how he pleads to God against Israel? ³"Lord, they have killed thy prophets, they have destroyed thine altars, and I alone am left and they seek my life.' ⁴But what does the divine answer say to him? 'I have left myself seven thousand men who have not bent their knees to Baal.' ⁵So then in the present time too there has been a remnant according to the election of grace. ⁶But if *it is* by grace, then *it is* not on the basis of works; for, if it were, grace would no more be grace. ⁷What then? What Israel is seeking it has not obtained, but the elect ones have

obtained it. And the rest were hardened, **⁸even as it is written: 'God gave them a spirit of torpor, blind eyes and deaf eyes, unto this very day'. ⁹And David says: 'Let their table become a snare and a trap and a stumbling-block and a retribution to them; ¹⁰let their eyes be darkened so that they cannot see, and do thou bow down their back continually'.**

In support of his emphatic denial of the possibility that God has cast off His people Israel Paul cites the fact of his own Jewishness (God would hardly have chosen a Jew to be His special apostle to the Gentiles, had He cast off His people, the Jews). No, God has certainly not broken His promise not to cast them off, which the Old Testament attests. In vv. 2b–4 he goes on to appeal to the story of Elijah, and to the mysterious 'seven thousand men' of God's reply to him. These seven thousand, of whom the prophet was unaware, were (according to the application in v. 5f) 'a remnant according to the election of grace', and now at the time the apostle is writing the minority of Jews who do believe in Christ is also such a remnant. And the very fact that it is a remnant according to the election of *grace*, and therefore not a remnant standing by its own deserving, makes its existence full of promise for the rest of the nation, a pledge of God's continuing interest in that 'rest' who have indeed been hardened by a divine hardening such as is spoken of in Scripture.

1. I ask then, has God cast off his people? The fact that it has just been confirmed that Israel did hear and did know, and is therefore without excuse, raises the question whether the conclusion to be drawn from Israel's stubborn disobedience is that God has cast away His people. But the terms in which the question is expressed presuppose the negative answer it must receive, for they are clearly reminiscent of Old Testament passages which declare categorically that God will not cast off His people (1 Sam 12.22: 'For the LORD will not forsake [in the Septuagint: 'cast off'] his people for his great name's sake: because it hath pleased the LORD to make you a people unto himself'; Ps 94.14: 'For the LORD will not cast off his people, Neither will he forsake his inheritance'). The question is thus tantamount to asking, 'Has God broken His explicit promise not to cast off His people?' So we may say that the first ground of the **God forbid!** which follows is the one which, though unexpressed, is implicit in the language used, namely, that Holy Scripture testifies that God will not cast off His people.

for I myself am an Israelite, of the seed of Abraham, of the tribe of Benjamin is the second ground (the first explicitly put forward as such) of the denial expressed by Paul's 'God forbid!' It is probable that Paul's point is that the fact that he, a Jew (and one who has been ferociously opposed to the gospel), is God's chosen apostle to the Gentiles, is a sure sign that God has not cast off His people. In his person the missionary vocation of Israel is at last being fulfilled and Israel is actively associated with the work of the risen Christ. This is a more cogent evidence of God's not having cast off His people than is the simple fact that one particular Jew has come to believe.

2–4 begins with a solemn and explicit denial, which is all the more emphatic for being expressed in the very words of the question asked: **God has not cast off his people.** It is the theme of chapter 11. The significance of the addition of **whom he foreknew** has been disputed. It has sometimes been understood as having a restrictive sense, limiting the reference of 'his people' to those members of the people of Israel who are the objects of God's secret election. But, in spite of the fact that vv. 4–7 do go on to differentiate between an elect remnant and the rest of the people, this interpretation is most unlikely; for it is hardly to be disputed that in v. 1 (compare 10.21) 'his people' refers to Israel as a whole, and it is unnatural to give it a different sense in v. 2. We take it then that the relative clause refers to the general election of the people as a whole, and indicates a further ground for denying that God has cast off His people. The fact that God foreknew them (that is, deliberately joined them to Himself in faithful love) excludes the possibility of His casting them off.

The passage goes on to appeal to the story of Elijah: **Or do you not know what the scripture says in *the section about* Elijah, how he pleads to God against Israel? 'Lord, they have killed thy prophets, they have destroyed thine altars, and I alone am left and they seek my life.' But what does the divine answer say to him? 'I have left myself seven thousand men who have not bent their knees to Baal.'** The speech which Paul places on Elijah's lips is constructed out of 1 Kgs 19.10 and 14, the gist of which it reproduces in abridged form. Paul was probably relying on his memory. The content of the divine answer is based on 1 Kgs 19.18. The number 7,000, occurring, as it does, not in a statement which purports to give matter of fact historical information, but in a solemn and mysterious divine utterance, is hardly to be understood either in 1 Kings or here as a mere reflection of a traditional estimate of the actual number of those who remained faithful in this time of national apostasy, but is rather to be understood in the light of the special significance attaching in the Bible and in Judaism to the number seven and to multiples of seven as a symbol of completeness, perfection. God's statement that He is preserving for Himself seven thousand men in Israel amounts to a declaration of His faithfulness to His purpose of salvation for His people, a declaration that that purpose will continue unchanged and unthwarted to its final goal.

5–6 indicates the relevance of the Elijah narrative to the question whether God has cast off his people, drawing out in particular the significance of the divine answer quoted in v. 4. **So then in the present time too there has been a remnant according to the election of grace. But if *it is* by grace, then *it is* not on the basis of works; for, if it were, grace would no more be grace.** In Elijah's time there was a remnant, but the ground of its existence was the initiative of the divine grace, God's gracious election, and not human merit. It was God, by His own decision and for the accomplishment of His own purpose, who made the remnant to stand firm; and for this very reason its existence was full of promise for the rest of the nation. The existence of a remnant, whose faithfulness was their own meritorious achievement, would have had no particularly hopeful significance for the unfaithful majority. But, precisely because this remnant was preserved in accordance with the election of grace and not on the basis of works, its existence was a pledge of God's continuing interest in, and care for, the nation, a sign of God's faithfulness to His election of Israel as a whole (though it is to be noted that there is certainly no intention in the Elijah narrative to gloss over the reality of God's punishment of Israel's sin – the biggest part of the divine answer in 1 Kgs 19.15–18 is in fact concerned with it). With this significance of 'I have left myself' (v. 4), elucidated by 'according to the election of grace' and 'not on the basis of works', the number 7,000 agrees, for it suggests a remnant which is not a closed but an open number, and so eloquent of promise for the people as a whole (compare Mt 18.22, where the point of 'Until seventy times seven' is that forgiveness of one's brother is to know no limit). The point that Paul is making is that the remnant of the present time, that is, the company of Jews who have believed in Christ, is a similar remnant, the existence of which is also based not on human deserving (he himself had been apprehended by Christ in the midst of his fierce opposition to the gospel), but on God's gracious election, and is therefore also a pledge of the continuing election of Israel as a whole.

7–10. What then? introduces a comprehensive conclusion from what has been said in vv. 1–6. **What Israel is seeking it has not obtained** repeats in different words what was said in 9.31. **but the elect ones have obtained it** gathers up the positive content of vv. 4–6, while **And the rest were hardened** sums up, and interprets, the negative element. With 'were hardened' compare 'hardens' in 9.18 (though a different Greek word is used). The passive is not to be explained away as meaning 'they hardened themselves' – a misinterpretation which can easily lead to a hard and unbrotherly attitude to the Jews on the part of Christians. Rather must a divine hardening be recognized; but, as the context makes abundantly clear, this hardening is not God's last word with regard to the persons concerned. It is important here to understand 'but the elect ones have obtained it' and 'And the rest were hardened' together, each as qualifying and interpreting the other. For the former points to the promise which concerns also 'the rest', while the latter points to the judgment from which the elect themselves are by no means exempt. The statement 'And the rest were hardened' should remind us that the elect, in so far as their human achievements and deserts are concerned, lie under God's condemnation, and their having obtained is solely by sheer grace. And the statement 'but the elect ones have obtained it' should make us aware of the provisional character of the hardening of those others. A further point may also be made, namely, that vv. 11ff will show that the hardening of the others itself belongs to salvation-history, in that it leads to the salvation of the Gentiles, which in its turn is to make those others jealous.

even as it is written: 'God gave them a spirit of torpor, blind eyes and deaf ears, unto this very day'. The former of the two Old

Testament quotations in support and elucidation of the statement that the rest were hardened is basically Deut 29.4. The phrase 'spirit of torpor' occurs in the Septuagint version of Isa 29.10: both there and here it must denote a state of spiritual insensibility. Isa 6.9–10 should also be compared. It should be noted that the context of this verse in Deuteronomy is a gracious one, speaking of God's goodness to His people, while in Isaiah 29 one does not have to read on for very many verses from the reference to 'the spirit of deep sleep' before one comes to statements strongly suggesting that the divine hardening is not God's last word for His rebellious people. And moreover Paul no doubt means these Old Testament passages to be understood in the light of the Old Testament as a whole. The phrase 'unto this very day' indicates the permanence of a name or situation or of the result of an event. It is perhaps possible that, in addition to its connotation of permanence up to the present, Paul saw in it also a suggestion of a limit set to this divine hardening (the idea of 'unto, but not beyond'), which would accord well with the tenor of vv. 11ff.

And David says: 'Let their table become a snare and a trap and a stumbling-block and a retribution to them; let their eyes be darkened so that they cannot see, and do thou bow down their back continually'. The latter of the two Old Testament quotations in these verses is Ps 69.22–23. This psalm is one which was much used in the early Church as a testimony of the ministry, and especially the passion, of Christ. Paul here applies to the unbelieving majority of Israel words which were originally the psalmist's imprecation on his persecutors but which, when the psalm is understood messianically, are naturally referred to the opponents of Christ.

The general sense of the first sentence is no doubt a wish that even the good things which these enemies enjoy may prove to be a cause of disaster to them. The original imagery has been variously explained: for example, with reference to the skin or cloth, spread out on the ground by nomads, upon which the feast was laid, which could entangle the feet of the feasters, if they sprang up suddenly at the approach of danger, or with reference to poisoned viands intended for particular individuals which those who have prepared them are themselves forced to eat. With regard to Paul's use of the words, it is probably wiser to assume that he simply understood them as in a general way suggestive of the divine hardening than to attribute to him any such interpretation of the details as those suggested by Sanday and Headlam ('So to the Jews that Law and those Scriptures wherein they trusted are to become the very cause of their fall and the snare or hunting-net in which they are caught') or by Barrett ('Their table is their table-fellowship: the unity and interrelatedness created by the law and so highly valued in Judaism were no more than a delusion since they were a union in sin (iii.20), not righteousness').

In the last sentence it is hardly possible to decide with certainty the precise significance of the image of the bent back (whether in the Septuagint version of Ps 69.23 or in Paul's use of it). The thought could be of, for example, being bowed down under oppressive slavery, being bent under a heavy burden, cowering with fear, being bowed down by grief, being too weak to stand upright, or stooping to grope on the ground because one's sight is bad or one is blind. The use of the second person singular ('do thou bow down'), addressed to God, agrees with what was said on the passive 'were hardened' in v. 7: God's action, directed by His purpose of mercy in accordance with His wisdom, is to be recognized even in the present stubborn unbelief of the majority of Paul's fellow-members of the Jewish people. The point of 'continually' is that, while God's negative action lasts, it is to be not intermittent or unsteady but sustained and steadfast. The rendering 'for ever' (Moffatt, Weymouth, RSV, NEB 1961 but not 1970, JB, Barrett) is both philologically unsound and also contrary to the whole tenor of the context, which is precisely that God has not cast off His people.

(ii) *The rejection of the greater part of Israel is not for ever* (11.11–24)

[11]**I ask then, have they stumbled so as to fall *irrevocably?* God forbid! But by their trespass salvation *has come* to the Gentiles, in order to make them jealous.** [12]**But if their trespass means riches for the world and their defeat riches for the Gentiles, how much more shall their fullness mean!** [13]**But it is to you Gentiles that I am speaking. Contrary to what you may be inclined to think, inasmuch as I am an apostle of the Gentiles I glorify my ministry** [14]**in the hope**

that I may make my kindred jealous and so save some of them. [15]For if their rejection means the reconciliation of the world, what shall their acceptance mean but life from the dead? [16]And if the firstfruit cake is holy, so also is the *whole* mixture; and if the root is holy, so also are the branches. [17]But if some of the branches have been broken off and thou, a wild olive, hast been grafted in among them and made to share the root, that is the fatness, of the olive-tree, [18]do not triumph over the branches. But if thou dost triumph over them, *remember that* it is not thou that bearest the root but the root *that bears* thee. [19]Thou wilt say then, 'Branches were broken off in order that I might be grafted in'. [20]True: they were broken off by their unbelief and thou standest by thy faith. Do not be haughty, but fear. [21]For if God has not spared the natural branches, neither shall he spare thee. [22]Consider then the kindness and the severity of God: to those who have fallen there is severity, but to thee God's kindness, if thou remainest in his kindness; for otherwise thou too shalt be cut off. [23]But they, if they do not remain in their unbelief, shall be grafted in; for God is able to graft them in again. [24]For if thou wast cut off from thy native wild olive-tree and grafted into the cultivated olive-tree to which thou by nature didst not belong, how much more shall these that are the natural branches be grafted into their own olive-tree!

The exclusion of the great majority of Jews is not permanent. It is the occasion for the coming in of the Gentiles, which, in its turn, is to have the effect of awakening the unbelieving Jews to a realization of what they are missing and so to lead to their repentance. Paul hopes that the very success of his own mission to the Gentiles may contribute in this way to the saving of some of his compatriots. And, if the present exclusion of the majority of Jews means so rich a benefit for the Gentiles, what glory shall accompany their final restoration? In the meantime the existence of those Jews who already believe in Christ serves to sanctify the unbelieving majority. What Paul says in this subsection and also in the following one is specially addressed to the Gentiles among the Christians of Rome (compare v. 13a). He is clearly concerned to warn them against adopting an unchristian attitude of superiority toward the unbelieving Jews. It seems more probable that it is for the sake of directness and forcefulness that the second person singular is used in vv. 17–24 (Paul singling out each individual Gentile Christian) than that the use is collective. The olive-tree imagery of these verses has caused a good many commentators to make heavy weather; but Paul's meaning is not in doubt. The contemplation of his situation in relation to the unbelieving Jews should lead the Gentile Christian not to haughtiness but to fear for himself; and he ought to realize that God can and will restore the unbelieving Jews.

11. I ask then, have they stumbled so as to fall *irrevocably*? God forbid! But by their trespass salvation *has come* to the Gentiles, in order to make them jealous. Contrary to the conclusion which Gentile Christian complacency might be prone to draw, the unbelief of the majority of Jews is not a spiritual ruin from which there can never be recovery. It is indeed a tragic fall, but not such a fall as precludes for ever the hope of being raised up again. By the Jews' rejection of the gospel the Gentiles have received salvation. Paul is usually understood as referring to the fact that the Jews' rejection of the message led the messengers to turn to the Gentiles (compare Acts 8.1ff; 13.45–48; 18.6; 28.24–28), and it is indeed likely that he had this in mind. But v. 15a suggests that he may well have had in mind something else, namely, that the rejection of Jesus Himself by the Jews and their delivering Him up to the Gentiles were vital elements in the process which led to His death and so to the reconciliation of the world, including Gentiles and Jews alike, to God (compare 5.10). The last clause indicates the divine intention. The coming of salvation to the Gentiles as a result of Israel's rejection of its Messiah is to make Israel jealous in accordance with the words of Deut 32.21 already quoted in 10.19. When Israel, the people whom God has made peculiarly His own, His special possession, see others the recipients of the mercy and goodness of their God, they will begin to understand what they are missing and to desire that salvation which they have rejected. Thus that hardening of which v. 7 spoke has for its ultimate purpose the salvation of those who are hardened.

12. But if their trespass means riches for the world and their defeat riches for the Gentiles, how much more shall their fullness mean! Verse 11 could give the impression that the only importance of the Gentiles' salvation is that by making the unbelieving Jews jealous it is to lead to the unbelieving Jews' salvation. Verse 12 restores the balance by its stress on the greatness of the benefits which result for the Gentiles first from the unbelief of the greater part of Israel and then, much more, from their ultimate conversion. The Greek word represented by 'defeat' is known to occur in only two other places, the Septuagint version of Isa 31.8 and 1 Cor 6.7, in both of which it may be translated 'defeat', which is the sort of meaning one would expect it to have, since it is derived from a verb which can signify 'be less', 'be weaker (than someone)', 'be defeated'; and this meaning suits the context quite well – their disobedience is indeed their spiritual and moral defeat. The habit of explaining this word here as meaning either 'diminution' or 'fewness', in order to afford a neat contrast to 'fullness', goes back a long way and is still widespread, but should surely be abandoned. There is just as much reason for expecting a word parallel in meaning to 'trespass' as for expecting a word antithetical to 'fullness'. With regard to 'their fullness', it is natural to take the reference to be to the conversion of Israel as a whole (compare 'their acceptance' in v. 15 and 'then all Israel shall be saved' in v. 26); but there is a difficulty over the word 'their'. If 'fullness' here does mean 'full and complete number', it would seem, at first sight, natural to take 'their' to refer to the whole people of Israel. In that case, we should have to assume a change of reference between the first and the last 'their' in this verse. But a different solution should perhaps be preferred, namely, to understand Paul to be thinking, not of the whole people's being brought up to its full numerical strength by the restoration of the temporarily lost majority, but of the unbelieving majority's being brought up to its full numerical strength (that is, the full strength of Israel as a whole, which is the only relevant full strength that a loyal Jew could properly be concerned with) by being reunited with the believing minority through its own (that is, the majority's) conversion.

13a. But it is to you Gentiles that I am speaking is not the beginning of a new paragraph; for the thought of vv. 11–12 is continued in vv. 15ff. It is rather that Paul recollects at this point that what he has just said in vv. 11–12 ought specially to be pondered by Gentile Christians, and so inserts vv. 13–14 parenthetically and then continues to address himself to the Gentile Christians specifically as far as v. 32. Neither this sentence nor anything else in this section indicates whether Gentile

Christians formed the majority or only a minority of the Roman church at this time. All that is clear from this passage is that the Gentile element in the church is here addressed specifically.

13b–14. Contrary to what you may be inclined to think, inasmuch as I am an apostle of the Gentiles I glorify my ministry in the hope that I may make my kindred jealous and so save some of them. It would be natural for the Gentile Christians to suppose that in turning to the Gentiles Paul was turning his back upon the unbelieving Jews. But quite the contrary is true: his very labours as apostle of the Gentiles have an Israel-ward significance – of good for Israel. He honours and reverences his ministry to the Gentiles, and so fulfils it with all his might and devotion, in the hope – though we should not, of course, draw the conclusion that this is his only, or, indeed, his primary motive – that its success may provoke the Jews to jealousy and so bring about the conversion of some of them.

15. For if their rejection means the reconciliation of the world, what shall their acceptance mean but life from the dead? This explains how it is that Paul can, not just as a Jewish Christian but precisely in his capacity of apostle of the Gentiles, be specially motivated by the desire to make his own kinsfolk jealous, since it affirms that for all (including the Gentiles) the restoration of Israel is going to bring ineffable blessing. By 'their rejection' must be meant their temporary casting away by God, which is here, it seems, thought of as identical with, rather than as consequential on, their refusal of the Messiah. Their rejection, so understood, led directly to His death at the hands of the Gentiles and so to the objective reconciliation of the world to God. By 'their acceptance' is meant God's final acceptance of what is now unbelieving Israel. The phrase 'life from the dead' here has been variously explained: the most likely interpretation is that it denotes the final resurrection itself, and that Paul means that the restoration of the mass of Israel can signify nothing less than the final consummation of all things. While the effect of this verse is then, on the one hand, to forbid all optimistic expectation of this final and complete acceptance within the course of the Church's missionary history (and how much more the folly of looking for it in any secular flowering of Jewish nationalism!), it is also, on the other hand, to join together in indissoluble union for all faithful

Gentiles the hope of the final home-coming of the Synagogue and the hope of the final fulfilment of their own existence in the Church, and to make the conversion of the individual Jew a particularly eloquent pointer to that glory ·of which even the Church has as yet but a foretaste.

16. And if the firstfruit cake is holy, so also is the *whole* mixture; and if the root is holy, so also are the branches provides confirmation of what has been clearly implied, namely, that unbelieving Israel too has a future, and at the same time by its use of the imagery of root and branches prepares the way for vv. 17–24. The former half of the verse clearly alludes to the offering of a cake from the first of the dough enjoined in Num 15.17–21. The Old Testament nowhere says that this offering hallows the rest of the dough, but a comparison of Lev 19.23–25, according to which the fruits of the trees are to be regarded as 'uncircumcised' until an offering has been made to God from them, suggests that it would be quite natural for the Jew to think of the offering of the firstfruit cake as purifying the rest of his dough. Of the various suggestions which have been made with regard to Paul's application of the figure of the firstfruit cake, the most probable in our view is that he has in mind the Jewish Christians and is thinking of them as serving to sanctify the unbelieving majority of Israel. This would be in line with the implications of what is said about the remnant in the first subsection of this chapter (especially vv. 4 and 5). In the latter half of the verse, while some take 'the root' to refer to Christ and others take it to refer to the Jewish Christians, there is a very widespread agreement among commentators that the reference is to the patriarchs, and this is supported by v. 28. This does not mean that Paul is after all establishing, in spite of what he has said in chapters 2–4, a human claim on God, or that he is now affirming, in spite of what he has said in 9.6b–29, that every Jew must have a positive role in relation to the working out in history of God's purpose, but simply that God is faithful to His own promise (compare 3.3f). The patriarchs are a holy root, not because of any innate worth or merit of their own, but by virtue of God's election of grace. But the Gentile Christians are to remember that that holiness of the fathers which results from God's gracious election reaches beyond them to all their race.

17–18a is the beginning of a passage (vv. 17–24) which has often been criticized on the ground that in actual arboricultural practice one grafts slips from cultivated into wild trees, not slips from wild into cultivated trees. According to many, Paul the town-bred man, is here guilty of an elementary blunder. Others have sought to defend him by referring to ancient technical works, which show that the practice of grafting a slip of wild olive into a cultivated tree which was unproductive in order to reinvigorate it was known in ancient times, and also to evidence of this practice in some countries in modern times. But we still have Paul's reference to the grafting in again of the cut off branches (vv. 23–24), a parallel to which in normal arboricultural practice is hardly likely to be discovered. Others have appealed to the phrase in v. 24, which we have represented by 'to which thou by nature didst not belong' but which means literally 'contrary to nature', as an indication that Paul was aware that the procedure he was describing was contrary to ordinary practice. It is more to the point to notice that he is here using metaphor neither as evidence (in the way that Jesus, for example, appeals to the conduct of the owner of sheep in Lk 15.3–7) nor as a literary ornament, but simply as a medium for the expression of his meaning, a meaning which it was not very easy to express clearly and succinctly without any recourse to metaphor. (It is to be noted that he has already referred to 'root' and 'branches' in v. 16, and that in vv. 20–23 there is a free combining of metaphorical and non-metaphorical.) In this use of metaphor – and it is surely a perfectly proper use of it – the verisimilitude of the metaphorical details is not important; the important thing is that the author's meaning should be quite clear. And about Paul's meaning here there is no doubt.

But if some of the branches have been broken off and thou, a wild olive, hast been grafted in among them and made to share the root, that is, the fatness, of the olive-tree, do not triumph over the branches. Here, as in 3.3, 'some' is an intentional understatement. The second person singular is used, the individual Gentile Christian in Rome being addressed rather than the group as a whole, for the sake of directness and forcefulness of appeal. By 'among them' must be meant 'among the remaining branches: the reference of 'them' cannot be to those of the branches which have just been mentioned, which are those which have been broken off.

Paul is aware that there is a danger that Gentile Christians may be inclined to despise Jews. Whether by 'the branches' in v. 18a are meant only the unbelieving Jews or the Jews as a whole, both unbelieving and believing, is not clear. Quite likely Paul is reckoning with the possibility (or the actual existence?) of an anti-semitic feeling within the Roman church reflecting the dislike of, and contempt for, the Jews which were common in the contemporary Roman world.

18b. But if thou dost triumph over them, *remember that* it is not thou that bearest the root but the root *that bears* thee. No amount of Gentile Christian boasting over those who are the natural branches can ever alter the fact that it is from their incorporation into the stock of Israel that Gentile Christians derive their spiritual blessings.

19–21. Thou wilt say then, 'Branches were broken off in order that I might be grafted in' exposes the self-complacent egotism of Gentile Christian contemptuousness. **True** admits the truth in the statement just put into the mouth of the Gentile Christian. But **they were broken off by their unbelief and thou standest by thy faith** brings out the fact that the contrast is simply between unbelief and faith: the thought of merit is altogether excluded. The Gentile Christian who understands this will understand the rightness of the double command which follows: **Do not be haughty, but fear.** In support of the preceding command Paul adds: **For if God has not spared the natural branches, neither shall he spare thee.**

22. Consider then the kindness and the severity of God: to those who have fallen there is severity, but to thee God's kindness, if thou remainest in his kindness; for otherwise thou too shalt be cut off. In the grafting in of Gentiles and the breaking off of unbelieving Jews are to be recognized the kindness and the severity of God, both of which are the expression of God's holy and faithful love.

23. But they, if they do not remain in their unbelief, shall be grafted in; for God is able to graft them in again. The Gentile Christians are not to imagine that, once cast away, the unbelieving Jews cannot ever be restored, but must learn to reckon with the freedom and omnipotence of God.

24 adds in support of what has just been said a direct appeal to the individual Gentile Christian in Rome. **For if thou wast cut off from thy native wild olive-tree and grafted into the cultivated olive-**

tree to which thou by nature didst not belong, how much more shall
these that are the natural branches be grafted into their own olive-
tree! If the Gentile Christian can believe that God has actually
grafted him into that holy stem to which he does not naturally
belong, how much more readily ought he to believe that God is
able and willing to do what is less wonderful – to restore to their
own native stock the unbelieving Jews, when they repent and
believe!

(iii) *The mystery of God's merciful plan*
(11.25–32)

[25]For, so that you may not be wise in your own eyes, I want you to
know this mystery, brethren, that hardening has affected part of
Israel *and will last* until the fullness of the Gentiles comes in, [26]and
thus all Israel shall be saved, as it is written: 'Out of Zion shall come
the Deliverer, he shall turn away iniquities from Jacob. [27]And this is
the covenant I will make with them, when I take away their sins.'
[28]As regards *the progress of* the gospel they are enemies for your
sake, but as regards the election they are beloved for the sake of the
fathers; [29]for the gifts and the call of God are irrevocable. [30]For as
you once were disobedient to God but now have received mercy by
their disobedience, [31]so also these now have been disobedient in order
that they too may now receive mercy by the mercy shown to you.
[32]For God has imprisoned all men in disobedience, in order that he
may have mercy upon all men.

Paul proceeds to impart a 'mystery', in order that the Gentiles
among the Christians of Rome, whom he is still specially
addressing, may not be wise in their own eyes. Its substance is in
vv. 25b–26a, and has to do with three successive stages of the
fulfilment of the divine plan of salvation: first the unbelief of the
greater part of Israel (the way it is referred to indicates that this
unbelief is not just a matter of human disobedience – a divine
hardening is involved), then the completion of the coming in of the
Gentiles, and finally the salvation of 'all Israel'. The order of
salvation thus described marks significantly an inversion of the
order in which the good news is preached according to 1.16 ('both
for the Jew first and for the Greek'). Verses 26b and 27 provide

scriptural confirmation of 'and thus all Israel shall be saved': the concentration on the forgiveness of sins in the composite Old Testament quotation is striking. The following five verses draw out the implications of vv. 25–27, and sum them up with evocative succinctness. First with a few rapid strokes vv. 28 and 29 depict Israel subjected to the wrath of God for the good of the Gentiles, yet all the time beloved by God according to election for the patriarchs' sake, since God is faithful. Then follow the carefully balanced sentence of v. 30f with its temporal framework and the bold conclusion which is v. 32. In these human disobedience is firmly and decisively related to the triumphant, all-embracing mercy of God. The subsection may be said to gather together the substance of the whole argument of 9.1–11.24.

25–26a. For, so that you may not be wise in your own eyes, I want you to know this mystery, brethren, that hardening has affected part of Israel *and will last* until the fullness of the Gentiles comes in, and thus all Israel shall be saved. Paul wants the Gentile Christians in Rome to know the mystery which he is about to state, because it is the solemn confirmation of what he has just said, which at the same time goes beyond anything which he has already said. He believes that, if they know this mystery, they will be less likely to succumb to the temptation to be conceited about their supposed superior wisdom. The Greek word represented by 'mystery' is the word from which the English word is derived. Whereas in pagan Greek, when used in a religious connexion, it denotes something revealed to initiates but not to be disclosed to the uninitiated, in the New Testament it characteristically denotes what, though formerly hidden, has now been revealed by God and is to be openly proclaimed so that all, whose ears and hearts God opens, may hear it and understand. But it is also used to denote a special revelation (note its use in association with 'prophecy' in 1 Cor 13.2: compare also Eph 3.3), and it is thought by many that Paul is here imparting a new special revelation which he himself has received. This is possible; but it is to be noted that he does not state that what he is imparting is a new revelation or that it has been specially revealed to him. It can be maintained that the contents of this mystery are to be discerned in the Old Testament seen in the light of the gospel events. In any case, the mystery is something knowable only because God has revealed it.

The words which follow 'that' indicate the content of the mystery. That the last clause, 'and thus all Israel shall be saved', is stressed seems clear from the fact that it alone is supported by the Old Testament quotation in vv. 26b–27. But rather different interpretations of the mystery result according to where, if anywhere, in the first and second clauses ('hardening has affected part of Israel *and will last* until the fullness of the Gentiles comes in') one sees special stress falling. Thus it is possible to see the emphasis falling on 'hardening' and so to understand the main point to be that Israel's unbelief is not just a matter of human disobedience but is due to a divine hardening – and this would be a compelling reason why Gentile Christians should not give way to feelings of superiority. Or one may see the emphasis falling on 'part of': it is only part of Israel, not the whole, which is unbelieving. Or, again, one may see 'until the fullness of the Gentiles comes in' as having special emphasis: Israel's hardening will last until the fullness of the Gentiles comes in, and is, in fact, for the benefit of the Gentiles – which would be a good reason for the Gentile Christians' not feeling superior; or, alternatively, the point could be that it will only last till the fullness of the Gentiles comes in, that is, that it is temporally limited and therefore the Gentiles must not be puffed up by the notion that the unbelieving Jews have been cast off for ever. But it seems more likely that the three clauses should be understood as simply indicating three successive stages in the divine plan of salvation, and that it is a mistake to try to single out any one particular word or phrase as having special emphasis, apart from recognizing that the last clause is the high point of the whole.

With regard to this last clause three things need to be mentioned. First, 'thus' is emphatic: it will be in the circumstances obtaining when the first two stages have been fulfilled, and only so and then, that 'all Israel shall be saved'. Secondly, the most likely explanation of 'all Israel' is that it means the nation Israel as a whole, though not necessarily including every individual member. Thirdly, we understand 'shall be saved' to refer to a restoration of the nation of Israel to God at the end of history, an eschatological event in the strict sense. (Could it be that this half-verse and Mt 10.23b may shed some light on each other? Could the statement, 'Ye shall not have gone through the cities of Israel, till the Son of man be come', bear the meaning (whether its authenticity as a saying of Jesus is accepted or rejected) that the conversion of 'all Israel' will not be accomplished before the Parousia?) Some light on the meaning of this 'shall be saved' in Paul's mind may be expected from the Old Testament quotation which follows.

26b–27. as it is written: 'Out of Zion shall come the Deliverer, he shall turn away iniquities from Jacob. And this is the covenant I will make with them, when I take away their sins.' The quotation is composite, representing almost exactly the Septuagint version of Isa 59.20–21a, followed by a clause from Isa 27.9. The original reference of Isa 59.20 may be to God Himself, but there is some Rabbinic evidence that it came to be interpreted of the Messiah, and it is likely that Paul so understood it. The coming he probably understood of the Parousia, and 'Zion' he probably interpreted as denoting heaven or the heavenly sanctuary. The words 'he shall turn away iniquities from Jacob' (here the Septuagint differs considerably from the Hebrew) indicate the nature of the deliverance which this Deliverer will accomplish; it will consist in turning back ungodlinesses from the nation of Israel. Such a characterization of the work of the Messiah affords a striking contrast to the Jewish expectation of a political messiah. In Isa 59.21 'this' anticipates the content of the covenant as set forth in the latter part of the verse. The effect of the substitution of a clause from the Septuagint version of Isa 27.9 for the latter part of the verse is to bring out forcefully the fact that the essence of the new covenant which God will establish with Israel is His gracious forgiveness of their sins. This composite quotation thus makes clear the nature of the deliverance indicated by 'shall be saved' in v. 26a by its relentless concentration on God's forgiveness and on Israel's need of it. It dashes Israel's self-centred hopes of establishing a claim upon God, of putting Him under an obligation by its merits, making it clear that the nation's final salvation will be a matter of the forgiveness of its sins by the sheer mercy of its God. It is also to be noted that there is here no trace of encouragement for any hopes entertained by Paul's Jewish contemporaries for the re-establishment of a national state in independence and political power, nor – incidentally – anything which could feasibly be interpreted as a scriptural endorsement of the modern nation-state of Israel.

28. As regards *the progress of* the gospel they are enemies for your sake, but as regards the election they are beloved for the sake of the fathers consists of two contrasted parallel statements. That these are not in equilibrium is clear both from the substance of the latter statement and from the fact that it alone is supported by the following verse: in fact, the addition of the latter statement limits the validity of the former. Under '*the progress of* the gospel' are included, surely, the actual accomplishment in the ministry, passion and resurrection of Jesus of the events which are the basis of the gospel message, the subsequent preaching by the Church, the acceptance or rejection of the message by men. In relation to all of these unbelieving Israel has been disobedient and has thereby come under the wrath of God. The carefully worked out parallelism between the two parts of the verse requires us to take 'enemies' in its passive sense in correspondence with 'beloved'. The point of 'for your sake' is that Israel's subjection to the divine hostility on account of its disobedience, its temporary rejection by God, was, in the divine providence, all along intended to benefit the Gentiles. But all the time that they are 'enemies', they are also – and this is the permanent thing, while the other is temporary – with regard to God's election 'beloved' of God. The election referred to here is, of course, the election of the people as a whole (compare v. 2), not that election which distinguishes within Israel (compare vv. 5 and 7). While 'for the sake of' in the former part of the verse ('for your sake') was used in the sense 'with a view to the advantage of', it is used in the latter part in the sense 'by reason of'. Paul's meaning in 'beloved for the sake of the fathers' is that Israel is beloved because God is faithful to His own love, which in His sovereign freedom He bestowed upon the fathers on no other ground than His love, which knows no cause outside itself (compare Deut 7.7f).

29. for the gifts and the call of God are irrevocable is added in support of v. 28b. While many things which are involved in this particular people's existence as the special people of God may be described equally truly as God's gracious gifts to them or as His calling of them, we should perhaps understand by 'gifts' here the precious privileges of the Jewish people seen as God's undeserved gifts to them and by 'call' God's calling of them to be His special people, to stand in a special relation to Him, and so to perform a

special task and fulfil a special function in history. In the original
the word represented by 'irrevocable' is put first in the sentence in
order to give it special emphasis. For the general sense we may
compare 3.3f; 15.8. The ground of Paul's certainty that the Jews
are still beloved of God, though under His wrath because of their
unbelief and opposition to the gospel, is the faithfulness of God,
that faithfulness, steadfastness, reliability, without which God
would not be the righteous God He is.

**30–31. For as you once were disobedient to God but now have
received mercy by their disobedience, so also these now have been
disobedient in order that they too may now receive mercy by the
mercy shown to you.** These verses are a very carefully constructed
sentence explanatory (hence the initial 'For') of vv. 28–29. The
correspondences between them may be set out as follows:

v. 30	v. 31
you	these
once	now (the first 'now' in v. 31)
were disobedient to God	have been disobedient
now	now (the second 'now' in v. 31)
have received mercy	may receive mercy
by their disobedience	by the mercy shown to you

With regard to the recognition of these correspondences there is
widespread agreement among recent interpreters. But the
question whether the Greek dative represented by 'by the mercy
shown to you', which in the original actually precedes 'in order
that', should be connected with 'these now have been disobedient'
(we call this explanation (i)) or with 'they too may now receive
mercy' (this we call explanation (ii)) has long been, and still is,
disputed; and there is also disagreement about the sense of both
this dative and also 'by their disobedience'.

Those who accept explanation (i) interpret the first clause of
v. 31 variously according to the way they understand the dative we
have translated 'by the mercy shown to you': for example, 'so also
these now have been disobedient as a result of the mercy shown to
you'; 'so also these now have been disobedient for the sake of the
mercy to be shown to you'; 'so now, when you receive mercy, these
have proved disobedient'. If, however, explanation (ii) is accepted,

the translation given at the head of this note may be adopted, and the point of 'by the mercy shown to you' will probably be either (a) that the Jews are to receive mercy by means of the mercy which has been shown to the Gentiles, or (b) that they are to receive mercy by the same sort of mercy as that which the Gentiles have received.

The fact that explanation (ii) involves taking as part of the final clause a phrase which precedes the final conjunction represented by 'in order that' is sometimes regarded as a decisive objection to it; but this objection cannot be allowed, since such a placing of a word or phrase before the word which is the natural beginning of the clause to which it belongs can be paralleled elsewhere both in the New Testament and in classical Greek. An important consideration against (i) and in favour of (ii) concerns the correspondence between the two verses. Since there is such a careful balance between six elements of v. 30 and six elements of v. 31, as set out above, it seems to us highly significant that, according to explanation (ii), the distribution of the six elements between the two clauses of v. 31 exactly matches that of the six corresponding elements between the two clauses of v. 30 (in both verses three and three), whereas, according to (i), the balance is destroyed (in v. 30 three and three, but in v. 31 four and two). A further consideration which seems to us strongly to favour (ii) is its consonance with v. 11. In view of the carefully worked out parallelism between vv. 30 and 31, it seems extremely probable that 'by their disobedience' and 'by the mercy shown to you' were intended to bear closely corresponding senses. If explanation (ii) is accepted, and the latter phrase interpreted according to (a) above, then the two phrases can indeed be given strictly parallel meanings, both confirmed by what is said in v. 11. The phrase 'by their disobedience' will mean 'through, or by means of, their disobedience' (the disobedience of the Jews has been the means of the Gentiles' receiving mercy: compare 'by their trespass salvation *has come* to the Gentiles'); and the phrase 'by the mercy shown to you' will mean 'through, or by means of, the mercy shown to you' (the mercy shown to the Gentiles is to be the means by which the Jews are brought to realize what they are missing and so the means of their eventually receiving mercy too: compare 'in order to make them jealous').

Two further points need to be made with regard to these two

verses. The first is that the 'in order that' is to be understood as referring to the divine purpose. Behind the present disobedience of the majority of Jews is to be discerned the merciful purpose of God. The second is that the second 'now' of v. 31 is to be understood as temporal, but not as evidence (as some have regarded it) that Paul was certain that the end of the world would occur within a very short time. The truth is rather that Paul sees the time which begins with the gospel events and extends to the Parousia as a unity. It is all the 'now' of the last days, the end-time.

32. For God has imprisoned all men in disobedience, in order that he may have mercy upon all men. The verse supplies a necessary explanation of vv. 30–31, and at the same time serves to draw together and conclude the argument of chapters 9 to 11 as a whole. It picks up the two leading themes of the last two verses, the themes of human disobedience and of divine mercy, and relates them together in terms of the divine action ('God has imprisoned ... in order that he may have mercy ... '). But these two themes have run right through the three chapters, and the thought reflected here in the use of 'imprison', the stress on the sovereign action of God, and the contrast between the whole and the part presupposed by the double use of 'all' here, have also been thematic in these chapters. Paul's 'imprison' here must surely, in view of 1.24, 26, 28; 9.18; 11.7, 25, be understood as referring to God's providential ordering, which, by allowing men to exercise their freedom and also by that judicial hardening to which such passages as 11.7b point, brings it about that men are imprisoned in their disobedience in such a way that they have no possibility of escape except as God's mercy releases them.

With regard to the double 'all men', since the former would seem to denote all without exception, it would seem natural to assume that the meaning of the latter is the same. But it should be noted that, while the former part of the verse is a statement of fact, the latter is a statement of purpose. It would seem wise to resist both the temptation to try to base on this verse (or on this verse together with other verses like 5.18 and 1 Tim 2.4) a dogma of universalism and also the temptation to regard the solemn and urgent warnings, of which the New Testament assuredly contains an abundance, as clear warrant for proclaiming the certainty of the final exclusion of some from the embrace of God's mercy.

(iv) *Conclusion to this main division*
(11.33–36)

[33]**O the depth of God's riches and wisdom and knowledge! How unsearchable are his judgments and incomprehensible his ways! [34]For who has known the Lord's mind? Or who has been his counsellor? [35]Or who has anticipated him in giving, so as to receive from him a payment earned?' [36]For from him and through him and unto him are all things: to him be the glory for ever. Amen.**

Verses 33–36 conclude not only section 4 but also main division VI as a whole. They are an eloquent expression of wonder and adoration before the mystery of God's ways, the majesty of His mercy and wisdom. For Paul at any rate the unflinching contemplation of the mystery of divine election cannot lead to gloom or fatalism, but must lead rather to a hymn of wondering praise, because, for him, election is a matter of the freedom and faithfulness of the merciful God. That it is not inappropriate to call these verses a hymn is clear enough. Their poetic character is apparent. That this hymn was composed by Paul as a conclusion to this division of his epistle is far more probable than that he was taking over an already existing hymn; but in composing it he has freely borrowed from several sources, from the Old Testament, perhaps also from extra-biblical apocalyptic, from Hellenistic Judaism, from Stoicism as mediated through Hellenistic Judaism, and from the language of Christian worship.

33. O the depth of God's riches and wisdom and knowledge! For the metaphorical use of 'depth' compare 1 Cor 2.10: the thought expressed is of profundity and immensity. For the idea of God's riches compare 2.4; 9.23; also 10.12. In view of these passages, while it is possible that Paul had in mind here God's infinite resources generally, it is rather more likely that he was thinking specially of the abundance of His mercy and kindness (compare vv. 31 and 32). Wisdom is associated with riches in the doxology to the Lamb in Rev. 5.12, and wisdom and knowledge are natural associates (compare Col 2.3). By 'wisdom' is perhaps especially meant the wisdom which informs God's purposes and His accomplishment of them (compare 1 Cor 1.21, 24; Eph 3.10), by 'knowledge' perhaps especially God's electing love and the loving concern and care which it involves (compare the use of 'know' in 1 Cor 8.3; Gal 4.9; 2 Tim 2.19; also 1 Cor 13.12, where in the original a compound verb is used, and the use of 'know' in the Old Testament in, for example, Ps 1.6; 31.7; Hos 5.3; 13.5; Amos 3.2).

How unsearchable are his judgments and incomprehensible his ways! directs attention to the mysteriousness of God's judgments (that is, His carrying out His judgments) and the ways He takes in the accomplishment of His purposes. As the judgments and ways of the merciful God, they do not conform to men's, even believing men's, preconceptions and they defeat their efforts to keep track of them. We have to recognize them from below; we have no vantage-point from which we can look down on them from above.

34–35. 'For who has known the Lord's mind? Or who has been his counsellor? Or who has anticipated him in giving, so as to receive from him a payment earned?' The first two questions are a quotation of the Septuagint version of Isa 40.13 (which is also quoted in 1 Cor 2.16). The third question is not to be found in the Septuagint version (except as a variant reading at Isa 40.14 – almost certainly an addition derived from this passage in Romans), but is quite close to the Hebrew of Job 41.11a. The purpose of this third question is to underline the impossibility of a man's putting God in his debt. All three questions express the transcendent wisdom and self-sufficiency of God.

36. For from him and through him and unto him are all things probably reflects Hellenistic Jewish borrowing from Stoic sources, which in turn reflect the influence of earlier Greek philosophy. But the sense of the formula as used by Paul is far removed from the pantheism of the Stoic use of similar language. He is affirming that God, the God who has acted redemptively in Jesus Christ, is the Creator, the Sustainer and Ruler, and the Goal, of all things.

The discussion of chapters 9–11 comes to its natural and fitting conclusion in a doxology: **to him be the glory for ever. Amen.**

Paul has certainly not provided neat answers to the baffling questions which arise in connexion with the subject matter of these three chapters. He has certainly not swept away all the difficulties. But, if we have followed him through these chapters with serious and open-minded attentiveness, we may well feel that he has given us enough to enable us to repeat the 'Amen' of his doxology in joyful confidence that the deep mystery which surrounds us is neither a nightmare mystery of meaninglessness nor a dark mystery of arbitrary omnipotence but the mystery which will never turn out to be anything other than the mystery of the altogether good and merciful and faithful God.

VII

THE OBEDIENCE TO WHICH THOSE WHO ARE RIGHTEOUS BY FAITH ARE CALLED

(12.1–15.13)

The first eleven chapters of Romans have already made it very clear that the life which is promised for the man who is righteous by faith must be a life of obedience to God. Implied already in chapters 1–5, this becomes explicit in chapter 6. Those who know that God has graciously decided to see them as having died to sin can hardly go on living in it complacently. It is an inescapable implication of their baptism that, far from continuing to allow sin to reign over them as the undisputed master of their lives, they must – and can – rebel against the usurping tyrant and present themselves to Him to whom they by right belong. They have been decisively claimed for obedience to God, for sanctification. While the tension, with all its real anguish, in which the Christian is involved and from which he cannot escape in this life, was brought out in chapter 7 with impressive realism and frankness, the strength of the hold of sin upon the believer being honestly acknowledged, Paul was nevertheless able to affirm confidently in chapter 8 that a liberation has been effected. The bestowal of the Spirit means the freedom to begin to fulfil the righteous requirement of God's law, to begin to obey God. And all that needs to be said about Christian obedience was said in principle in 8.15 ('you have received the Spirit of adoption, by whose enabling we cry "Abba, Father"'); for to address the true God by the name of 'Father' with understanding, seriousness and sincerity is indeed the whole of what is required of us. For to call Him 'Father' with true understanding, seriousness and sincerity, necessarily involves striving wholeheartedly to be and think and speak and do what is well-pleasing to Him and to avoid everything which is displeasing to Him. But, since this obedience of thought and attitude, of word and deed, is to be wrought out in the difficult and dangerous concrete situations of human existence by believers who are, all of them, far from being fully understanding, fully serious, fully sincere, Paul – after he has in chapters 9–11 sought to lead the Roman Christians into a deeper perception of the reality and the mystery of God's mercy – goes on in 12.1–15.13 to an exhortation which is practical and particular.

It is widely agreed that Paul has in this division of the epistle made considerable use of traditional material of various sorts. From time to time we shall notice his probable sources. But our main concern will properly be with the significance which such material has in its context in Romans.

VII. 1. THE THEME OF THIS MAIN DIVISION OF THE EPISTLE IS SET FORTH
(12.1–2)

These two verses serve as an introduction to the rest of the main division 12.1–15.13, the theme of which they set forth.

¹I exhort you, therefore, brethren, by the mercies of God to present yourselves as a sacrifice living, holy and well-pleasing to God, which is your understanding worship. ²And stop allowing yourselves to be conformed to this age, but continue to let yourselves be transformed by the renewing of your mind, so that you may prove what is the will of God, that which is good and well-pleasing and perfect.

1. I exhort you, therefore, brethren, by the mercies of God. Supported as it is by the following 'by the mercies of God', which looks back to what Paul has been writing about, 'therefore' probably has its full force and indicates that what is about to be said is based upon, follows from, what has already been said. The Christian's obedience is his response to what God has done for him and for all men in Jesus Christ. Its basic motive is gratitude for God's goodness in Christ. This means that all truly Christian moral endeavour is theocentric, having its origin not in a humanistic desire for the enhancement of the self by the attainment of a moral superiority nor in the legalist's illusory hope of putting God under an obligation to himself but simply in the gracious action of God. The choice of 'Thankfulness' as the heading of the third division of the Heidelberg Catechism which deals with Christian obedience and J. A. Bengel's comment on this verse, 'The Christian ... understands his duty from the kindness of the merciful God', reflect a true perception of the significance of the present verse.

The words 'by the mercies of God' indicate Paul's ground of appeal. The use of the plural is probably due to the influence of the Septuagint, which regularly represents the Hebrew word for 'pity', which is a plural noun, by a Greek plural, and an English singular may be preferred. Paul is thinking of the divine mercy as that which directs all God's purposes and actions in relation to His creation, the mercy which has been revealed in Christ, rather than of a number of different manifestations of it. One might wonder, because of the special prominence of several Greek words connected with mercy in chapters 9–11, whether this phrase and also the 'therefore' refer back specially to these chapters; but, as the whole of 1.18–11.36 is concerned with the action of the merciful God and words like 'grace', 'kindness', 'longsuffering' and 'love' occur in the first eight chapters even though the 'mercy' and 'pity' words may be absent, it is more likely that Paul thought of his exhortation as based on the whole course of what he has so far said in the epistle.

The Greek verb represented here by 'exhort' can bear a range of meanings from 'beseech' or 'implore' to 'invite' and 'request'. It can also mean 'comfort'. But its most characteristic New Testament sense is 'exhort' as used to denote the earnest appeal, based on the gospel, to those who are already Christians to live consistently with the gospel which they have received. When used in this sense as a technical term for Christian exhortation, it expresses urgency and earnestness but also the note of authority – the authoritative summons to obedience issued in the name of the gospel.

to present. The Greek word is quite probably used here as a cultic technical term with the sense 'offer (a sacrifice)', though it is never so used elsewhere in the Greek Bible. That would explain the omission of 'to God', which otherwise would seem to be required in association with the verb either as well as, or instead of, with 'well-pleasing'.

yourselves is literally 'your bodies', that is, yourselves in the whole of your concrete life. The Christian is to present himself in his whole life to God **as a sacrifice.** Already God's by right of creation and by right of redemption, he has yet to become God's by virtue of his own free surrender of himself. And this surrender has, of course, to be again and again renewed.

living, holy and well-pleasing to God. In our translation, as in the original, all three epithets follow their noun. The placing of 'living' before the noun in the AV, RV, RSV, and NEB has the effect of giving it special emphasis, as though Paul's main concern were to indicate that this sacrifice is living, and the other two epithets were added rather as an afterthought. This has encouraged for English readers the tendency to assume that the point of 'living' must be that, unlike an animal victim, this sacrifice is not to be killed. But this widespread explanation of 'living' seems rather unlikely. For one thing, it seems too obvious a point to be judged worth making; for another, the animal victims were anyway always alive when they were offered. But, when all three epithets are recognized as being on a level, it is more natural to take 'living' in a sense more akin to the other two adjectives. We take it that Paul means that the Christian himself freely offered to God is to be living in a deep theological sense, living in 'newness of life' (6.4). Among the other numerous occurrences of 'live' and 'life' in Romans we may refer to, for example, 1.17; 5.17; 6.10, 11, 13, 22; 8.6, 10, 13.

By describing the sacrifice as 'holy' Paul is doubtless first drawing attention to the fact that the Christian who is being offered to God belongs now to God, not to himself. But, while the basic meaning of 'holy' is set apart for God, belonging to God, it also gets an ethical content from the character of God. Since He is the God He has revealed Himself to be, to belong to Him involves the obligation to strive to be and do what is in accord with His character. The other epithet, 'well-pleasing to God', designates the sacrifice as a true and proper sacrifice, one which is desired by God and which He will accept.

which is your understanding worship is best taken as referring to the whole of 'to present yourselves as a sacrifice, living, holy and well-pleasing to God'. The constantly repeated offering of ourselves in all our concrete living as a sacrifice to God is the true action of worshipping. While this certainly must mean that the true worship must include the whole of the Christian's life from day to day and that no cultic worship can be acceptable to God unaccompanied by obedience of life (compare such Old Testament passages as Isa 1.10–17; 58.1–11; Amos 5.21–24), it would be unjustifiable to argue from this that there is no room left for a Christian cultic worship as such. Provided that such worship in the narrower sense is always practised as part of the wider worship embracing the whole of the Christian's living and is not thought of as something acceptable to God apart from obedience of life, there is nothing here to deny it its place in the life of the faithful. What Paul is here saying is, in fact, perfectly consonant with the view that such a cultic worship ought to be the focus-point of that whole wider worship which is the continually repeated self-surrender of the Christian in obedience of life.

The Greek adjective (derived from the noun which can signify both 'reason' and 'word'), which we have represented by 'understanding', was much used by philosophers from the late fourth century on. It belonged also to the terminology of ancient mysticism. It was used in Hellenistic Judaism, though it does not occur in the Septuagint. Recently 'spiritual' has often been favoured as a translation of it here, and the view has been maintained that the point Paul intended to make was that the offering of themselves as a sacrifice was spiritual worship in the sense of being inward as opposed to a matter of external rites. But it is surely much more likely that his point was that it was rational, as being consistent with a proper understanding of the truth of the gospel, so an understanding, intelligent worship. The offering of the self is an offering of one's whole self in the course of one's concrete living, a matter not only of interior thoughts, feelings and aspirations, but also of outward words and deeds, of obedience of life. This is the sort of worship which may properly be called 'understanding', because it is the sort of worship which true knowledge of the gospel demands and makes possible.

2. And stop allowing yourselves to be conformed to this age, but continue to let yourselves be transformed by the renewing of your mind. Very many interpreters have claimed that a significant distinction is to be discerned here between the Greek verbs represented by 'conform' and 'transform', the former referring – so it is argued – to outward form only and so indicating something external and superficial, the latter referring to inward being and so indicating a profound transformation. But the difficulties besetting this contention are such that we should be most unwise to accept it. By rendering the second person plural passive present imperatives (in the former case preceded by a negative particle) by 'stop allowing yourselves to be conformed' and 'continue to let yourselves be transformed', respectively, we have tried to bring out both the sense of the passive imperatives and also, in each case, the significance of the use of the present imperative. Christians still live in 'this age'. But, if they understand what God has done for them in Christ, they know that they belong, by virtue of God's merciful decision, to His new order, and therefore cannot be content to go on allowing themselves to be continually stamped afresh with the stamp of this age that is passing away. On the basis of the gospel, in the light of 'the mercies of God', there is only one possibility that is properly open to them, and that is to resist this process of being continually moulded and fashioned according to the pattern of this present age with its conventions and its standards of values. The good news, to which the imperative 'stop allowing yourselves to be conformed' bears witness, is that they are no longer the helpless victims of tyrannizing forces, but are able to resist this pressure which comes both from without and from within, because God's merciful action in Christ has provided the basis of resistance. In the situation in which he is placed by the gospel the Christian may and must, and – by the enabling of the Holy Spirit – can, resist the pressures to conformity with this age. And this command is something which he needs to hear again and again. It must ever be a great part of the content of Christian exhortation, so long as the Church is 'militant here in earth'. For the pressures to conformity are always present, and always strong and insidious – so that the Christian often yields quite unconsciously. And the implication of the present tense (that what is being forbidden is something which is actually happening) is always true. The Christian has always to confess that to a painfully large extent his life is conformed to this age. Instead of going on contentedly and complacently allowing himself to be stamped afresh and moulded by the fashion of this world, he is now to yield himself to a different pressure, to the direction of the Spirit of God. He is to allow himself to be transformed continually, remoulded, remade, so that his life here and now may more and more clearly exhibit signs and tokens of the coming order of God, that order which has already come – in Christ. And it is **by the renewing of your mind** that this transformation is effected. It is as the Holy Spirit renews the fallen mind, loosening the bonds of its egocentricity so that it begins to think truly objectively instead of egocentrically, that a man's whole life is transformed.

so that you may prove what is the will of God, that which is good and well-pleasing and perfect concludes the two introductory verses with an indication of purpose. The verb represented by 'prove' can mean either 'prove', 'test', or 'approve (as a result of testing)'. Here, followed as it is by an indirect question, it is better understood in the former sense, though Paul, of course, implies that the discernment of the will of God will be followed by obedient acceptance of it. This final clause, on the one hand, implies that the mind, so far from being an unfallen element of human nature, needs to be renewed, if it is to be able to recognize and embrace the will of God (it is thus a warning against the illusion that conscience, as such and apart from its renewal by the Spirit and instruction by the discipline of the gospel, is a thoroughly reliable guide to moral conduct); and, on the other hand, it indicates the dignity of the individual Christian called on as he is to exercise a responsible freedom, and is the decisive refutation of every impudent sacerdotalism that would reduce the Christian layman to a kind of second class citizenship in the Church. To know that it is God's intention that the ordinary Christian man should be so transformed by the renewing of his mind as to be able himself responsibly, in the light of the gospel and within the fellowship of the faithful, to 'prove what is the will of God, that which is good and well-pleasing and perfect', is to know that one dare not patronize one's fellow-Christians.

The addition of the words 'that which is good and well-pleasing and perfect' may at first sight seem rather unnecessary. But the addition of 'that which is good' could have been prompted by the knowledge that among the Roman Christians there were likely to be those who were inclined to value the more spectacular charismatic gifts more highly than the ethical fruit of the Spirit and those who were impatient of moral restraints and prone to mistake licence for the freedom of the Spirit. For those whose background was Gentile paganism the temptation to think of the Christian religion in terms of an unethical mystical communion must have been strong. A reminder that God wills the morally good would be salutary for such people. Perhaps the most likely explanation of Paul's addition of 'well-pleasing (to God)' here is that, having, in order to counter any tendencies toward an unethical mysticism, defined the will of God as 'that which is good', he felt it to be necessary also to guard against a possible misunderstanding of what is meant by goodness. By 'well-pleasing' he underlines the fact that the goodness which is in question is no anthropocentric goodness but a goodness determined by the revelation of God's will, a matter of obedience to God's commandments. On 'perfect' the best commentary is Mk 12.30f (compare Deut 6.5; Lev 19.18): 'thou shalt love the Lord thy God with all thy heart, and with all thy soul, and with all thy mind, and with all thy strength. . . . Thou shalt love thy neighbour as thyself'. God's will, that which God requires of us, is perfect, complete, absolute; for He claims us *wholly* for Himself and for our neighbours. Thus the last of the three terms interprets the other two; for it makes it clear that 'the will of God' is not something manageable and achievable, as the rich young ruler foolishly imagined ('Master, all these things have I observed from my youth'), but the absolute demand of God, which Christ alone has fulfilled. It is this absolute demand of God by which He claims us wholly for Himself and for our neighbours, which those who are being transformed by the renewing of their minds recognize and gladly embrace as it meets them in all the concrete circumstances of their lives, and to which they know themselves altogether committed, although in this life they can never perfectly fulfil it.

VII. 2. THE BELIEVER AS A MEMBER OF THE CONGREGATION IN HIS RELATIONS WITH HIS FELLOW-MEMBERS
(12.3-8)

This first section of particular ethical exhortation is addressed to the members of the Christian community as recipients of various gifts. Each one is to esteem himself soberly in relation to his fellow-believers in the light of the gospel and to give himself wholeheartedly to the particular service to which the God-given gift he has received constitutes his divine vocation.

³For by virtue of the grace which has been given me I bid every single one of you not to think of himself more highly than he ought to think, but so to think of himself as to think soberly, each one according to the measure of faith which God has imparted to him. ⁴For even as we have in one body many members but all the members do not have the same function, ⁵so we, though we are many, are one body in Christ, and severally members of one another. ⁶But, having gifts differing according to the grace which has been given us, if *we have the gift of* prophecy, *then let us prophesy* in accordance with the standard of faith, ⁷or, if *the gift of* practical service, *let us exercise it* in practical service, or, if one is a teacher, *let him exercise his gift* in teaching, ⁸or, if one is an exhorter, *let him exercise his gift* in exhorting; *let him* who distributes *exercise his gift* without ulterior motive, *him* who presides *his* with diligence, *him* who shows mercy *his* with cheerfulness.

3. For by virtue of the grace which has been given me I bid every single one of you. As Paul starts his particular exhortation, he is conscious that he is drawing out the implications and detailed applications of what he has already set forth in principle in vv. 1–2. He proceeds to give a solemn command by virtue of the grace, the undeserved favour, which has been shown him by God – he is thinking, no doubt, particularly of the undeserved favour God has shown him in calling him to be an apostle. And this command is addressed to every single member – the phrase is very emphatic.

What is commanded is **not to think of himself more highly than**

he ought to think, but so to think of himself as to think soberly, each according to the measure of faith which God has imparted to him. The puzzling thing here is the phrase the 'measure of faith'. The Greek word translated 'measure' can have a variety of meanings. So also can the word translated 'faith'. And – to add to the difficulties – the genitive ('of faith') could be either a partitive genitive or a genitive of apposition. It is obvious that a considerable number of different combinations are at least theoretically possible. It will be enough here to indicate the two most generally favoured interpretations and to explain why we think both of them should be rejected in favour of another. The two interpretations are: (i) 'measure (in the sense of measured quantity) of faith (in the sense of the special miracle-working faith referred to in, for example, 1 Cor 12.9; 13.2)'; and (ii) 'measure (in the sense of measured quantity) of faith (in its most characteristic Pauline sense of basic faith or trust in God)'. Both of these interpretations take the genitive as partitive. But (i) is open to the objection that Paul is here explicitly addressing all the members of the Christian community in Rome, whereas he clearly regarded the special miracle-working faith as something possessed not by all, but only by some, Christians (compare 1 Cor 12.8–11). There is an even more telling objection against both (i) and (ii), namely, that the implication would be that a Christian is to think of himself more highly than he thinks of his fellow-Christian who has a smaller quantity of faith (according to (i), of the special miracle-working kind; according to (ii), of the basic Christian kind) than he has. It is surely extremely unlikely that Paul intended to imply this; for such an intention would scarcely be consistent with his apparent purpose in vv. 4ff to encourage the Christians in Rome to conduct themselves in such a way as to maintain their brotherly unity unimpaired. A congregation, the members of which were carefully calculating their relative importance according to the amount of faith (of either sort) which they possessed, would have little chance of being a happy one.

Much to be preferred, surely, is the interpretation which takes 'measure' in the sense of a means of measurement or standard, 'faith' in its basic Christian sense, and the genitive as a genitive of apposition, so that the sense of the verse is that every member of the church, instead of thinking of himself more highly than he ought, is so to think of himself as to think soberly, measuring himself by the standard which God has given him in his faith, that is, by a standard which forces him to concentrate his attention on those things in which he is on precisely the same level as his fellow-Christians rather than on those things in which he may be either superior or inferior to them – for the standard Paul has in mind consists, we take it, not in the relative strength or otherwise of the particular Christian's faith but in the simple fact of its existence, that is, in the fact of his admission of his dependence on, and commitment to, Jesus Christ. When Christians measure themselves by themselves (or by their fellow-Christians or their pagan neighbours), they display their lack of understanding (compare 2 Cor 10.12), and are sure to have too high (or else too low) an opinion of themselves; but, when they measure themselves by the standard which God has given them in their faith, they then – and only then – achieve a sober and true estimate of themselves as, equally with their fellows, both sinners revealed in their true colours by the judgment of the Cross and also the objects of God's undeserved and triumphant mercy in Jesus Christ. And, when we look back to vv. 1–2, which set forth the theme of the whole division, 12.1–15.13, what else does the renewing of the mind mean but to be enabled ever more and more consistently to measure oneself and all things by the standard which God has given one in one's faith and so to become ever more and more able to 'prove what is the will of God, that which is good and well-pleasing and perfect'? And how well the above interpretation of 'measure of faith' fits the following verses will appear in the exegesis which follows.

We conclude then that 'measure of faith' means a standard (by which to measure, estimate, himself), namely, (his) faith; but at the same time note that this does not mean that Paul is bidding the believer to estimate himself according to his fluctuating subjective feelings and personal opinions but that he is bidding him to estimate himself according to his God-given relation to Christ. True though it most certainly is that Christian faith is the individual's free, personal, response (made in the freedom which is restored by God's gift of His Spirit) to God's action in Christ, it must always be remembered that the most important and, indeed, the controlling, determinative, element in faith is not the believing subject but the believed-in Object; and to estimate oneself according to the standard which consists of one's faith in Christ is in the last analysis, to recognize that Christ Himself in whom God's judgment and mercy are revealed is the One by whom alone one must measure oneself and also one's fellow-men.

4–5. For even as we have in one body many members but all the members do not have the same function, so we, though we are many, are one body in Christ, and severally members of one another. Those who do measure themselves by the standard which God has given them in their faith will not fail to discern the one body; they will recognize that they do not exist for themselves but are members of one another and that their fellow-Christians, whether their gifts are more, or less, impressive than their own, are equally with themselves members of the one body. The figure of the body as a unity made up of various members is one that occurs frequently in ancient literature. Since Paul had at an earlier date given expression to the idea of Christians' being the body of Christ (1 Cor 12.27; compare 1 Cor 6.15), it is, of course, quite possible that this idea of the body of Christ was not far from his thoughts, when he dictated this passage. But it is hardly safe to assume this, and much less to assume that the first readers or hearers of the epistle in Rome would have picked up any such reference or that he would himself have expected them to do so, seeing that there has been no reference in this epistle to Christians', or the church's, being the body of Christ (the use of 'the body of Christ' in 7.4 is quite different). We take it then that what we have here is basically a simile, in spite of the form of v. 5, and that the point which Paul is making is simply that Christians, like the various members of a single body, although they differ from one another and have various functions, are all necessary to each other and equally under an obligation to serve one another, because they all belong together in a single whole. There is just one particular which distinguishes Paul's application of the figure of the body and the limbs here in Romans from its use in ancient pagan literature, but that one particular is, of course, all-important. The words 'in Christ' here in v. 5 indicate that the unity of those whom Paul is addressing, unlike the unity of the various communities which ancient authors liken to a body, is a matter neither of nature nor of human contriving but of the grace of God. Whatever other unity the Christians in Rome may have had, the unity to which Paul is appealing is the unity which they have by virtue of what God has done for them in Christ.

6-8. These verses indicate the unselfconscious, business-like, sober way in which Christians who do measure themselves by the standard which God has given them in their faith are to give themselves to the fulfilment of the tasks apportioned to them by the gifts which they have received, using their particular gifts to the full in the service of God and of one another, undistracted by futile calculations of precedence. **But, having gifts differing according to the grace which has been given us.** The word 'gift' is here used to denote a special gift or endowment bestowed by God on a particular believer to be used in His service and the service of the Church and of men generally. Paul's most extensive teaching about such gifts is to be found in 1 Corinthians 12–14. He connected them closely with the Spirit – so much so that he occasionally used the neuter plural of the Greek adjective which means 'spiritual' by itself to denote them (for example, in 1 Cor 14.1). It is the Holy Spirit who mediates them. Paul apparently thought that every Christian had at least one such gift (this is implied here, since the subject of 'having' must be identical with the subject of the previous sentence). Neither the list which follows nor that in 1 Corinthians 12 is to be regarded as in any way exhaustive. The wide variety of the gifts is grounded in the same grace shown to all; for God's grace, His undeserved love in action, while it is one and the same for all, is free and sovereign, and it is according to this royal freedom of His grace that He bestows different gifts on different persons. The gifts are given for the fulfilment of different functions, and, according to Paul (compare 1 Cor 12.31), they differ in value, in importance. But the reception of a greater gift does not carry with it any right to regard oneself, or to be regarded by others, as personally superior to one's fellow-Christian who has only received a lesser gift. While the gifts differ in dignity, the persons of the recipients are – by the measure of faith – of equal dignity, being alike objects of the same judgment and mercy; and the believer, in so far as he is truly a believer, will never forget that his gift is God's free gift, in no way something merited by himself.

if *we have the gift of* prophecy, *then let us prophesy* in accordance

with the standard of faith. Paul takes prophecy as his first example of a gift. The high place he assigned to it among the spiritual gifts is indicated by 1 Cor 14.1, 39. While any Christian might from time to time be inspired to prophesy, there were some who were so frequently inspired that they were regarded as *being* prophets and forming a distinct group of persons. Their number included some women (Acts 21.9). The prophet was distinguished from the teacher by the immediacy of his inspiration: his utterance was the result of a particular revelation. It might be a prediction about the future of the community or of an individual, or an announcement of something which God required to be done. It was a characteristic of prophecy that it was directed to a particular concrete situation. Though he was dependent on special revelations, the prophet's mind – unlike that of the speaker in tongues – was fully engaged; and his message was addressed to the church's understanding. By it the church was instructed, edified, exhorted, comforted, or rebuked. But Paul recognized the need for prophetic utterances to be received with discrimination. He gives instruction in 1 Cor 14.29 that, while the prophets are prophesying, the rest of the church is to 'discern'; and in 1 Cor 12.10 the gift of 'discernings of spirits' is significantly mentioned immediately after the gift of prophecy. For there was the possibility of false prophecy; there was also the possibility of true prophecy's being adulterated by additions derived from some source other than the Holy Spirit's inspiration. Hence the need also to exhort the prophets themselves to prophesy in accordance with the standard of faith. Many commentators understand by 'faith' here a special charismatic faith – in fact, something hardly to be distinguished from prophetic inspiration. According to this view, Paul is warning the prophets against the temptation to add something of their own devising, the temptation, when they come to the limit of their inspiration, to go on speaking. According to others, 'faith' is to be understood in the sense of 'the faith', the body of truth believed. But the simplest and most satisfactory interpretation (especially if our explanation of v. 3 was correct) is that 'faith' here denotes basic Christian faith: the prophets are to prophesy in agreement with the standard which they possess in their apprehension of, and response to, the grace of God in Jesus Christ – they are to be careful not to utter (under the impression that they are inspired) anything which is incompatible with their believing in Christ.

or, if *the gift of* **practical service,** *let us exercise it* **in practical service.** The Greek abstract noun represented by 'practical service' (the RV renders it 'ministry') and the cognate verb can have, in the New Testament, when used theologically, either a wider or a narrower connotation. Thus they are used, on the one hand, quite generally to denote service rendered to God, to Christ, to the church (for example, of the ministry of an apostle in 11.13); they are used, on the other hand, in a specific sense with reference to practical service rendered to those who in some way are specially needy (for example, Mt 25.44; Acts 6.1, 2; Rom 15.25). According to some commentators the noun is here used in its general sense; but so general an item as this would be seems hardly apposite in such a list as we have here. It is surely preferable to understand it in its narrower sense as denoting a range of activities similar to that which came to be the province of the deacon. The point of '*let us exercise it* in practical service', as also of the parallel exhortations in v. 7b and v. 8a, is that one is to use the spiritual gift one has received for the purpose for which it has been given, giving oneself wholeheartedly to the fulfilment of the task to which one's particular endowment is one's divine vocation, and not wilfully to insist on trying to render a service for which God has not called one.

or, if one is a teacher, *let him exercise his gift* **in teaching.** The distinction between 'teacher' and 'prophet' is clear enough. Whereas the prophet of the early Church was immediately inspired, the content of his message being a particular and direct revelation, the teacher based his teaching upon the Old Testament Scriptures, the tradition of Jesus and the catechetical material current in the Christian community. In 1 Cor 12.28 teachers are mentioned in the third place in the list (after apostles and prophets). In Eph 4.11 they are closely associated with pastors (the two nouns sharing the same article), teachers and pastors apparently being regarded as one group.

or, if one is an exhorter, *let him exercise his gift* **in exhorting.** While the immediate purpose of teaching was to instruct, to impart information, to explain, the immediate purpose of exhortation was to help Christians to live out their obedience to the gospel. It was the pastoral application of the gospel to a particular congregation, both to the congregation as a whole and also to the members of it severally. Naturally the same person must often have fulfilled both functions in the early Church; in the modern Church the parish minister has normally to fulfil them both.

let him who distributes *exercise his gift* without ulterior motive, him who presides *his* with diligence, *him* who shows mercy *his* with cheerfulness. It is possible that '*him* who distributes' denotes the person who is charged with the distribution of the church's alms, but perhaps rather more likely that it denotes the one who distributes his own property. On the former assumption, the special gift would consist in the spiritual capacity which makes the particular person suitable for the task of dispensing the church's charity, and the point of 'without ulterior motive' would be that persons responsible for dispensing the church's substance to the needy are to do so faithfully without fraud or favour, or possibly without ambitious hankering after some higher office in the church. On the latter assumption, the gift would lie not just in the possession of the wealth which makes the distributing materially possible but in the spiritual capacity for generosity, and the point of 'without ulterior motive' would be to exclude all such things as desire to win a reputation for generosity and to encourage the giver to direct his attention simply to the other person's need and its relief. It is to be noted that this and the two following exhortations are concerned with the spirit and manner in which particular gifts are to be exercised.

Many have seen in '*him* who presides' a reference to one who presides generally over the life of the congregation. But, since he 'who presides' is here placed between him 'who distributes' and him 'who shows mercy', it seems more likely that the reference is to the person who is in charge of the charitable work of the congregation (on this view the last three functions mentioned in v. 8 are all closely related). Another suggestion which has been made which would also connect the person referred to with the church's charitable work is that the Greek word we have translated 'preside' should here be understood in its sense of 'support', 'succour' or 'protect' (a cognate noun was used to denote the patron of resident aliens in Athens, and in 16.2 the feminine form of that noun is used by Paul of Phoebe). We could then think of a member of the church, who by virtue of his social status was in a position to be, on behalf of the church, a friend and protector to those members of the community who were not able to defend themselves, and who recognized in his relatively strong position a divine vocation. The words '*his* with diligence' present no problem of interpretation, whichever of the possible explanations of '*him* who presides' we adopt.

By '*him* who shows mercy' is probably meant the person whose special function is, on behalf of the congregation, to tend the sick, relieve the poor, or care for the aged and disabled. The assumption that Paul refers to those who (on behalf of the church) have direct, personal contact with the needy and afflicted is confirmed by the following '*his* with cheerfulness'. A particularly cheerful and agreeable disposition may well be evidence of the presence of the special gift that marks a person out for this particular service; but it is also true that an inward cheerfulness in ministering will in any case come naturally to one who knows the secret that in those needy and suffering people whom he is called to tend the Lord is Himself present (compare Mt 25.31ff), for he will recognize in them Christ's gracious gift to him and to the congregation, in whose name he ministers, of an opportunity to love and thank Him who can never be loved and thanked enough. The fact that a few verses later on we get an injunction to contribute to the necessities of the saints (v. 13) suggests that here in v. 8 Paul is thinking of service which reaches beyond the limits of the Christian fellowship. It need hardly be added that the designation of some people specially as those who show mercy in no way implies that the rest of the members of a church are free from the obligation to show mercy personally as they are able; Paul here speaks of those who, having a special aptitude, are appointed by the church to concentrate upon this work in its name.

It is instructive to notice that out of the seven gifts referred to in vv. 6–8 no less than four ('*the gift of* practical service', '*him* who distributes', '*him* who presides' and '*him* who shows mercy') most probably have to do with the practical assistance of those who are in one way or another specially in need of help and sympathy. This fact by itself is a clear and eloquent indication of the importance of the place of diakonia in the life of the church as Paul understood it. If this work bulked so large in the thought and activity of the primitive Church in spite of its poverty, it can hardly be right for it to bulk less large in the life of the relatively so affluent churches of the west in the last years of the twentieth century, when more than half the world's population is underfed, inadequately provided with medical services, and in very many other ways underprivileged, and at the same time ease of communications has made the whole world one neighbourhood. At a time when in many churches the need for the renewal of the diaconate is beginning to be felt and recognized, the careful study of these verses is particularly rewarding; for not only do they afford interesting glimpses of the diaconal work of the early Church, they also open up vistas into the future, suggesting varied tasks which a renewed diaconate and a whole Church, reinvigorated in its understanding of its diaconal responsibility by the existence in its midst of such a renewed diaconate, might undertake, and indicating clearly the truly Christian spirit in which they ought to be undertaken.[1]

VII. 3. A SERIES OF LOOSELY CONNECTED ITEMS OF EXHORTATION
(12.9–21)

Whereas the different instructions contained in vv. 6–8 were addressed to the recipients of the different gifts respectively, those which follow apply equally to all the members of the church. The various items of exhortation, though all deriving from what was said in vv. 1–2, and though they could all more or less easily be brought under some such general heading as 'love in action' or 'the marks of love', are but loosely connected; and it is a mistake to look too anxiously for precise connexions of thought or for a logical sequence in these verses. With v. 14 the construction changes, and this change seems to mark something of a new beginning. In vv. 9–13 Paul has been concerned mainly at any rate

---

[1]Reference may be made to World Council studies 2, *The Ministry of Deacons*, Geneva, 1965: J. I. McCord and T. H. L. Parker (ed.), *Service in Christ: essays presented to Karl Barth on his 80th birthday*, London, 1966.

with the relations of Christians with their fellow-Christians. In vv. 14–21 he is at any rate mainly concerned with the relations of Christians with those outside the Church.

⁹**Let *your* love be genuine. Abhor what is evil, cleave to what is good. ¹⁰In *your* love for the brethren show one another affectionate kindness. Prefer one another in honour. ¹¹Be not slack in zeal. Be aglow with the Spirit. Serve the Lord. ¹²Rejoice in hope. In affliction endure. Persevere in prayer. ¹³Help to relieve the necessities of the saints. Pursue the opportunities you get to be hospitable.**

¹⁴**Bless those who persecute you; bless and do not curse. ¹⁵Rejoice with those who rejoice, weep with those who weep. ¹⁶Agree together one with another. Do not be haughty but readily associate with the humble. Do not esteem yourselves wise. ¹⁷Return evil for evil to no one. In the sight of all men take thought for those things which are good. ¹⁸If it is possible, in so far as it depends on you, be at peace with all men. ¹⁹Do not avenge yourselves, beloved, but give place to the wrath *of God;* for it is written, 'Vengeance belongs to me, I will repay, says the Lord'. ²⁰But, if thine enemy is hungry, feed him; if he is thirsty, give him to drink: for by so doing thou shalt heap coals of fire upon his head. ²¹Be thou not overcome by evil, but overcome evil by good.**

9. Let *your* love be genuine. Up to this point in Romans the noun 'love' has been used only with reference to the divine love (5.5, 8; 8.35, 39); it is now used of the love which the Christian owes his fellow-man (compare 13.8–10). Paul does not give any absolutely clear indication whether, when he uses 'love' (Greek: *agape*) here, he is thinking of love of fellow-Christians only or of love which embraces those outside the Church as well; but, in view of v. 10a, it seems more probable that he intends the wider sense, for 'In *your* love for the brethren show one another affectionate kindness' will have more point, if the love referred to in the previous verse is not just the same thing as love-for-the-brethren (the last four words are just one word in the Greek – *philadelphia*), the specially intimate affection which is proper between Christians, but an all-embracing love. Paul exhorts the Roman Christians to let their love be 'genuine', the real thing, no counterfeit. The fact that Paul twice uses the Greek word represented here by 'genuine' with reference to love (here and in 2 Cor 6.6) suggests that he was aware of the danger in this connexion of deceit and – even more serious – self-deceit. Calvin's comment is to the point: 'It is difficult to express how ingenious almost all men are in counterfeiting a love which they do not really possess. They deceive not only others, but also themselves, while they persuade themselves that they have a true love for those whom they not only treat with neglect, but also in fact reject'. The recognition that the man who has made himself believe he is loving when he is not is a far greater danger both to others and to himself than the man who, knowing that he is not, pretends to be loving, is of vital importance.

Abhor what is evil, cleave to what is good. The fact that this is general does not at all make it not worth saying. The attempt to connect these two injunctions specially closely with v. 9a by, for example, interpreting them as meaning that Christian love is to abhor the evil in the person loved and only attach itself to the good in him is surely mistaken. Paul's point is to insist that the Christian is to be utterly committed in his opposition to what is morally wrong and in his support of what is morally good.

10. In *your* love for the brethren show one another affectionate kindness enjoins the tender and intimate affection as between members of the same family which is appropriate between members of the Church. The use of 'brother' with reference to adherents of the same religion was, in the ancient world, not peculiar to Christians, but its use among Christians had its own special quality derived from the gospel.

Prefer one another in honour seems, on the whole, the most probable interpretation of four Greek words which are patient of two other interpretations: 'anticipate one another in showing honour' and 'surpass one another in showing honour'. If our interpretation (it is that of the AV, RV, and many commentators) is correct, Paul's intention can hardly be that each Roman Christian should pretend that his or her fellow-Christian is always better or wiser than himself or herself. That would be nonsense. The clue to a satisfactory explanation is to remember that the gospel has revealed a fact of transcendent importance in connexion with love of the neighbour, namely, that the Son of man Himself is mysteriously present in the other person in his human need. It is surely because Christ is present for me in my fellow-Christian (as indeed in all my fellow-men) that I must honour him above myself. That has nothing to do with pretending.

11–12a. Be not slack in zeal. Be aglow with the Spirit. The first and second parts of the verse form a pair (compare v. 9b and c, v. 10a and b, vv. 11c and 12a, v. 12b and c, v. 13a and b). In lives which are being transformed by the renewing of the mind there is no room for slackness or sloth. In the other member of the pair it is possible to understand the Greek word we have represented by 'Spirit' as referring to the human spirit (the injunction being to ardour of spirit), and some have so interpreted Paul's meaning; but an ardent temperament is by no means necessarily good. It is surely much more likely that Paul has in mind the fire which God's Spirit kindles.

The next pair is **Serve the Lord. Rejoice in hope.** The variant, which gives 'time' instead of 'Lord', has been favoured by a number of modern scholars as being the more difficult reading and also because 'Serve the Lord' seems rather too general to suit this series. But the variant may well be explained as an accidental error (the two Greek words have four letters in common); and Paul may well have thought that the words he had just used ('aglow with the Spirit') were liable to very serious misunderstanding on the part of those who tended to regard exciting and showy ecstasies as the most precious evidences of the Spirit. If so, it was altogether appropriate to add immediately a sobering reminder of the true nature of this Spirit-given fervour. The real proof of the presence of this fire of the Spirit would be not effervescent religious excitement but renewed energy and determination in the humble and obedient service of the Lord Jesus. (It should perhaps also be said, at least as a parenthesis, that there are very serious objections to any suggestion that Paul may have used the Greek phrase 'serve the time' in a good sense, whether eschatological or of any other sort.) The second member of this pair (the verse-division obscures the pairing) requires little explanation. On its correlation of joy and hope 5.2–5; 8.16–25 and 1 Pet 1.3–9 provide the necessary commentary.

12b–c. In affliction endure. Persevere in prayer. From 'hope' to 'endurance' is for Paul a very natural transition (compare 5.2–4; 8.24f; 1 Cor 13.7; 1 Th 1.3). Endurance is necessary, because an inevitable accompaniment of the Christian's existence in this world is affliction, tribulation (compare, for example, Jn 16.33; Acts 14.22). This affliction stems from the world's resistance to Christ. The world hates Him: therefore his followers must expect to be hated too. In the face of this affliction the Christian is to endure, to hold out steadfastly, in the knowledge that the final issue is not uncertain. This he will do not in his own strength, but in the strength which God supplies; for it is God who is the source of endurance (compare 15.5). Coupled with 'In affliction endure' is 'Persevere in prayer'. Distressed by the pressure from without, by the affliction of the world's unrelenting hostility, and always in danger of succumbing to the inward anguish, which is its natural result, the Christian should indeed have recourse continually to prayer. Only in his reliance upon 'the God *who is the source* of patient endurance' (15.5) has he hope of holding out to the end. But it is precisely this thing, which is altogether vital and necessary if he is to endure, which he is specially tempted whether through sloth or discouragement or self-confidence to give up: hence the special frequency with which the Greek verb represented here by 'persevere' is used in the New Testament in connexion with prayer (Acts 1.14; 2.42; 6.4; Col 4.2: compare Eph 6.18, and also Lk 18.1; 1 Th 5.17).

13. Help to relieve the necessities of the saints. The Christian who is being transformed by the renewing of the mind will not doubt his obligation to help in relieving the destitution of his fellow-Christians. But the fact that, whereas in Paul's time a large proportion of the Christian community must have been very poor, at the present time western Christians share the affluence of their nations to a great extent, and in the poor countries the Christians are often among the less poor members of their communities, would seem to indicate that less emphasis needs to be placed today on the special claim of the saints and more on the greatest depths of human distress irrespective of whether Christian or otherwise.

The second member of the last pair is **Pursue the opportunities you get to be hospitable.** In the first century the need for Christian hospitality for individual Christians from other places, though perhaps hardly as great and pressing a problem as it has become in our western European cities with their large numbers of immigrants and foreign workers of various sorts, must have been very considerable, and this would be especially so in Rome. And, in the absence of special church buildings, there was the further need for hospitality to be shown to the church in a particular place as a whole for its meetings for worship and other purposes. There is a hint of the possibilities of disappointment, abuse and exasperation which such hospitality involved in 1 Pet 4.9.

14. Bless those who persecute you; bless and do not curse looks as if it may reflect the influence of the traditional dominical saying, which we have in two different forms in Mt 5.44 and Lk 6.27f, and traces of which are perhaps also to be discerned in 1 Cor 4.12, and possibly Jas 3.9–12; 1 Pet 2.23. Not only to refrain from desiring that harm should come to those who are persecuting us, but to desire good for them and to show that this desire is no mere pretence by actually praying for God's blessing upon them – this is clearly opposed to what is natural to us. Calvin comments finely: 'Although there is hardly any one who has made such advance in the law of the Lord that he fulfils this precept, no one can boast that he is the child of God, or glory in the name of a Christian, who has not partially undertaken this course, and does not struggle daily to resist the will to do the opposite'.

15. Rejoice with those who rejoice, weep with those who weep is often understood to refer to relations of Christians with one another; but the verse contains nothing which forbids us to assume that Paul is thinking just as much, or even perhaps more particularly (in view of v. 14), of Christians' relations with those who are outside the Church. Very probably Paul's meaning is that the Christian is to take his stand beside his fellow-man (whoever he may be), to have time and room for him in those experiences in which he is most truly himself, in his real human joy and his real human sorrow, and to strive to be both with him and for him, altogether and without reserve, yet without compromising with his evil or sharing, or even pretending to share, the presuppositions of this age which is passing away, even as God Himself is in Christ both 'with us' (Mt 1.23) and 'for us' (8.31) all.

16. Agree together one with another. This is not just a domestic matter within the Church; for agreement among themselves is something which Christians owe the world, since their agreement (or disagreement) affects it (compare Jn 17.20–23). Men – and this includes Christians – can, of course agree together in error and in wrong-doing. The agreement which Paul enjoins is agreement in true faith in Christ and in loyal obedience to Him. And this agreement must be genuine or it is worthless. There is nothing in these words of Paul to give any encouragement to the notion that a unity which is merely disagreement disguised by ambiguity to look like agreement can in any way benefit either the Church or the world, or that shuffling of any sort or carelessness about truth can ever promote Christian love or the glory of God.

Do not be haughty is perhaps placed here because haughtiness is specially destructive of the Church's unity and a most effective hindrance to its mission to the world. **but readily associate with the humble** forms a natural partner with the preceding prohibition. Paul is enjoining a friendly and unselfconscious association both with ordinary unimportant people and with the outcasts of society that is free from any suggestion of patronizing or condescension (the AV 'condescend to men of low estate' has come to be a most unfortunate translation because of the bad sense which 'condescend' tends to have today). Such an attitude, so contrary to the nature of the worldly man, comes naturally to those who are being transformed by the renewing of the mind, and it is always a sign of the worldliness of the Church when its 'leaders' no longer associate as readily and freely with humble people both inside and outside the Church as with those who are socially superior, and when such humble people no longer feel free to speak with them as man to man.

Do not esteem yourselves wise. In the original there is a catchword link between this sentence and the rest of v. 16; but Paul probably inserted this echo of Prov 3.7 at this point because he recognized that the attitude of the Christian who is self-sufficient in his confidence in his own wisdom is particularly destructive of the harmony to which he has just referred.

17. Return evil for evil to no one. The close similarity between this and 1 Th 5.15 and 1 Pet 3.9 suggests that we have here the fixed formulation of the catechetical tradition. Compare Prov 20.22; 24.29, and, for the general spirit, Exod 23.4f; 2 Chron 28.8–15, and, of course, Mt 5.38f, 44; Lk 6.29, 35.

In the sight of all men take thought for those things which are good. This is surely a more likely interpretation of the Greek than is the NEB translation ('Let your aims be such as all men count honourable'), which connects the phrase we have represented by 'in the sight of all men' closely with the word we have rendered 'those things which are good'; for Paul was well aware of the darkening of men's minds (compare 1.21) and their inability to recognize and approve the will of God unless they are renewed (compare 12.2). It is unlikely that he intended to suggest that the common opinion of men is to be the arbiter of what is good. His meaning is rather that Christians are to take thought for, aim at, seek, in the sight of all men, those things which (whether men recognize it or not) are good (in the sight of God).

18. If it is possible, in so far as it depends on you, be at peace with all men. Compare Mt 5.9. Those who are the ambassadors of God's peace (compare 2 Cor 5.18–20) must necessarily be peaceably disposed toward all men. Paul is careful, however, to qualify his precept by the words 'if it is possible' and 'in so far as it depends on you', no doubt with the sort of reservation in mind that Calvin makes explicit: 'We are not to strive to attain the favour of men in such a way that we refuse to incur the hatred of any for the sake of Christ, as often as this may be necessary', and '. . . good nature should not degenerate into compliance, so that for the sake of preserving peace we are complaisant to men's sins'.

19–21. It was perhaps because he recognized that **Do not avenge yourselves** was a very hard injunction even for Christians – though the idea that vengeance should be avoided was not altogether strange even to the ancient pagan world – that Paul added the affectionate **brethren** at this point. **but give place to the wrath of God; for it is written, 'Vengeance belongs to me, I will repay, says the Lord'.** Instead of avenging themselves they are to make way for the wrath of God. In support of his command Paul quotes the first part of Deut 32.35 (in a form nearer to the Aramaic version than to either the Greek or the Hebrew). Already in the Old Testament vengeance is forbidden (for example, Lev 19.18a; Prov 20.22; 24.29; 2 Chron 28.8–15), and Judaism gave the same reason for this prohibition as is given here, namely, that vengeance is God's prerogative. But, while the influence of the Old Testament and of Judaism is apparent in these verses, Paul's words must, of course, be understood in the light of all that has already been said in the epistle. In this context (compare 'all men' in v. 17 and again in v. 18) there is no question of limitation to one's fellow-members of the religious community: the prohibition of revenge is freed from the limitations and restrictions which adhered to it in Judaism, and is universal in its application. To 'give place to the wrath' is to make way for that wrath 'which alone is righteous, and alone is worthy of the name of wrath' (Bengel), the wrath of God which was revealed in its full awfulness in Gethsemane and on Golgotha as the wrath of the altogether holy and loving God. To make way for this wrath is to recognize that one deserves oneself to be wholly consumed by it, but the Son of God Himself has borne it for one: it is therefore to have the vengeful sword dashed from one's hands. If one is to continue to live by grace, then one cannot do other than make way for this wrath – to do otherwise would be to cease to live by grace. To give place to the wrath is to leave vengeance to God in the knowledge that He is the God who smites in order to heal. When we recall what God has done for us 'when we were enemies' (5.10), we cannot but hope that His mercy will finally embrace those who now are our enemies.

But, if thine enemy is hungry, feed him; if he is thirsty, give him to drink (the first part of the quotation of Prov 25.21–22a) has the effect of sharpening what has just been said: it is not enough merely to refrain from seeking to inflict injury in return for injury, we are also to do positive good to those who have injured us. For to fail to do to our enemies the good they stand in need of, when it is in our power to do it, is a kind of indirect retaliation. **for by so doing thou shalt heap coals of fire upon his head** completes the quotation. Some of the Greek Fathers see in 'coals of fire' a reference to future divine punishment and understand the thought to be that one's doing good to one's enemy will cause his punishment, in the event of his not repenting, to be the greater (though it is only fair to add – something which those who refer to this interpretation sometimes omit to add – that the same Fathers also say that one is not to do good to one's enemy with this intention). But Origen, Pelagius, and Augustine, as well as the majority of later commentators prefer to take the 'coals of fire' to signify the burning pangs of shame and contrition. That, as far as Paul's meaning is concerned, this latter interpretation is to be preferred is abundantly clear; for it is congruous with the context in Romans, while the former interpretation is quite incompatible with it. We take the sense of v. 20b, then, to be that by thus ministering to one's enemy's need one will inflict upon him such an inward sense of shame as will either lead him to real contrition and to being no more an enemy but a friend or else, if he refuses to be reconciled, will remain with him as the pain of a bad conscience.

Be thou not overcome by evil, but overcome evil by good. To retaliate is to be overcome both by the evil of one's enemy and also by the evil of one's own heart which responds to the other's evil. Instead of allowing himself to be overcome of evil, the Christian is to overcome the evil by the good. It is, of course, much to be hoped that his victory will include the transformation of the persecutor into a friend, but it will not necessarily do so. He who in the fullest sense has overcome the world (Jn 16.33) has not yet turned the hatred of all His persecutors into love. The Christian's victory over the evil consists in his refusal to become a party to the promotion of evil by returning evil for evil and so becoming himself like the evil man who has injured him, in his accepting injury without resentment, without allowing his love to be turned into hate or even only weakened. Though he may not succeed in making the enemy cease to be an enemy in the sense of one who hates, he can refuse to allow him to be an enemy at all in the sense of one who is hated. By so doing he will be sharing in the victory of the gospel over the world and setting up signs which point to the reality of God's love for sinners; he will be living as one who is being transformed by the renewing of the mind.

VII. 4. THE BELIEVER'S OBLIGATION TO THE STATE (13.1–7)

With regard to the relation of 13.1–7 to its context it has been urged that there is a lack of connexion between this section and its immediate context; that it interrupts the continuity which may be discerned between 12.21 and 13.8; that there are positive incongruities between this section and its context, among which the contrast between the apparent absence of any eschatological reserve in this section and what is said in 12.2 and 13.11–14, the seemingly quite non-christological character of this section, and the contrast between the idea of the state with its use of force and the theme of love in 12.9–21 and 13.8–10 may be specially mentioned. Not surprisingly those who feel most strongly that the relation between 13.1–7 and its context is problematical tend to feel the need to postulate some special circumstances in the Christian community in Rome which may have led Paul to insert this section. But the difficulties seem to us to have been exaggerated. Would it not be fair to suggest that it would actually have been rather surprising, if in such a relatively full section of exhortation as 12.1–15.13 Paul had had nothing to say on a subject which must have been of great importance to Christians of the first century just as it is to Christians today? And the assumption that this passage is empty of christological substance must be challenged. It is, of course, true that Christ is not mentioned at all in these seven verses, and that the words Paul uses could have been used by a Rabbi or a philosopher; but, in the absence of clear evidence to the contrary, the presumption should surely be that, when Paul uses the word 'God', he uses it in a fully Christian sense and expects his readers so to understand it. We take it therefore that the God, of whom these verses speak, is the God whose authority and love are one with the authority (8.34) and love (8.39) of Jesus Christ. For Paul, to say that the civil authorities are 'ministers' and 'servants' of God is necessarily to imply that they are in some way linked with God's holy and merciful purpose in Christ and in some way subserve it. Moreover, if we are to enter fully into Paul's meaning here, we must understand these verses in the light of the central affirmation of Paul's, and of the early Church's, faith, the affirmation 'Jesus is Lord'. It is clear from (among other things) the way in which Paul applies to Christ a number of Old Testament passages in which 'Lord' represents the divine Name (see (i), p. 258) that in calling Christ 'Lord' he was ascribing to Him the authority and Lordship of God Himself. But, according to the Scriptures, that authority included authority over the kingdoms of men (compare, for example, Isa 10.5ff; 45.1ff; Dan 4.17, 25, 32; 5.21). A christological understanding of the state (in the sense of an understanding of it as in some way serving God's purpose in Christ and lying within the scope of Christ's lordship) is thus implicit in this passage.

It will be convenient to refer at this point to the question whether Paul thought that the civil authorities of this world had actually been affected by Christ's death, resurrection and ascension. It has been maintained that, while Christ was indeed Lord over history, the actual events of His death, resurrection and ascension have in no way altered His universal Lordship outside the Church, and that His already accomplished victory is, outside the Church, not only unknown but actually without consequence. But, while it is true that outwardly the civil authorities as such have indeed not been affected, it may nevertheless be true to say that an objective change in their situation has been brought about. The issue by a competent authority of a warrant for a man's arrest effects a radical alteration of his situation, even though he and his associates may at the time know nothing about it and may for a while carry on in just the same way as before. And, though it is true that the governments of this world were, even before the death, resurrection and ascension of Christ, subject to divine control, and that they are now no more submissive than they were before, yet the fact that God's claim over them, as over all other things visible and invisible, has been decisively and finally asserted, means that they fulfil their functions now under the judgment, mercy and promise of God in a way that was not so before.

¹Let every person be subject to the governing authorities. For no authority exists as such except by God's appointment, and the authorities which are have been ordained by God. ²So he who refuses to be subject to the authority is opposing God's ordering: and those who oppose that shall bring judgment on themselves. ³For those engaged in government are not a *cause for* fear to the good work but to the evil. Dost thou wish not to fear the authority? Do what is good, and thou shalt receive praise from it; ⁴for it is God's minister to thee for good. But, if thou doest evil, fear; for it is not to no purpose that it is armed with the sword; for it is God's minister, an agent of punishment for wrath to him who does evil. ⁵Wherefore there is a necessity to be subject not just by reason of the wrath but also by reason of conscience. ⁶For it is for this reason that you do actually pay tribute: for, when they busy themselves earnestly with this very matter, they are God's servants. ⁷Render to all that which it is your obligation to render them, to him to whom you owe tribute tribute, to him to whom you owe indirect tax indirect tax, to him to whom you owe fear fear, to him to whom you owe honour honour.

1. Let every person be subject to the governing authorities. In its
context 'every person' is 'every Christian (in Rome)'. The phrase is
emphatic. No Christian is to imagine himself exempt from the
obligation indicated. It is clear and agreed that by 'authorities' the
civil authorities are meant. That there is a double reference, to the
civil authorities and also to angelic powers thought of as standing
behind, and acting through, the civil authorities, has been
suggested (the Greek word represented here by 'authority' is used
with reference to invisible angelic powers in 1 Cor 15.24; Eph 1.21;
3.10; 6.12; Col 1.16; 2.10, 15; 1 Pet 3.22 (in the first and last of these
verses it is represented in the RV by 'authority', in the other verses
by 'power')). But, on the whole, it seems more probable that in
using 'authorities' here Paul had in mind simply the civil
authorities as such. The Greek word we have represented here by
'governing' means 'superior'. The sense it bears is hardly 'superior
(to other authorities)', Paul referring to the higher grades of civil
authorities, but 'superior (to the Christians in Rome)', that is,
having authority over them.

The most interesting expression here is 'be subject'. It is clearly a
key word in this section. It is often assumed that the Greek verb
translated 'be subject' means 'obey'. Thus Sanday and Headlam
entitled this section 'On Obedience to Rulers', and stated in their
introductory summary to it: 'The civil power . . . must be obeyed.
Obedience to it is a Christian duty . . . '; Barrett has used the
phrase 'obedience to magistrates'; and the United Bible Societies'
Greek New Testament (3rd ed., 1975) has headed this section
'Obedience to Rulers'. But the Greek verb used is not the obvious
verb to use to express the meaning 'obey': there are in fact three
other Greek verbs, all of which occur in the New Testament,
which do mean precisely that. It seems likely that Paul has
deliberately chosen to use this particular verb here because he felt
it suited his intention better than one of those other verbs. In the
occurrence of this verb in Eph 5.21 ('subjecting yourselves one to
another in the fear of Christ') the meaning 'obey' is quite clearly
excluded; for here it denotes a reciprocal obligation, and
obedience cannot be reciprocal. A comparison of that verse with
Rom 12.10 ('Prefer one another in honour') and Phil 2.3 ('each
counting other better than (or 'superior to') himself') suggests that
what is meant is the recognition that one's fellow-Christian has a

greater claim on one than one has on oneself, and the conduct which flows from such a recognition. It seems virtually certain that in the present verse what Paul is enjoining is no uncritical obedience to whatever command the civil authority may decide to give but the recognition that one has been placed below the authority by God and that it therefore has a greater claim on one than one has on oneself, and such responsible conduct in relation to it as results from such a recognition.

Paul has in mind, of course, an authoritarian state, in which the Christian's 'subjection' to the authorities is limited to respecting them, obeying them so far as such obedience does not conflict with God's laws, and seriously and responsibly disobeying them when it does, paying them direct and indirect taxes willingly, since no government can function without resources, and – a very important element which is not mentioned here but may be supplied from 1 Timothy 2 – praying persistently for them. In such a state he is bound to do what he can for its maintenance as a just state; but there is no question of the ordinary citizen's having a responsible share in governing.

The proper exposition of Paul's words involves for the Christian living in a democracy the translation of them into the terms of a different political order. Such a Christian can, and therefore must, do much more for the maintenance of the state as a just state. His 'subjection' will include voting in parliamentary elections responsibly, in the fear of Christ and in love to his neighbour, and, since such responsible voting is only possible on the basis of adequate knowledge, making sure that he is as fully and reliably informed as possible about political issues, and striving tirelessly in the ways constitutionally open to him to support just policies and to oppose unjust.[1]

For no authority exists as such except by God's appointment states a reason for the injunction which has just been given. It expresses a truth already familiar to the Jews (compare, for example, 2 Sam 12.8; Jer 27.5f; Dan 2.21, 37f; 4.17, 25, 32; 5.21;

[1] I have tried to draw out in some detail the implications for the Christian living in a modern democracy of what the New Testament says in this connexion in 'The Christian's Political Responsibility according to the New Testament', in *Scottish Journal of Theology* 15 (1962), pp. 176–92 (reprinted in C. E. B. Cranfield, *The Service of God*, London, 1965, pp. 49–66; now in *The Bible and Christian Life*, 1985, pp. 48–68).

Wisd 6.3), namely, that it is God who sets up (and overthrows) rulers, and that no one actually exercises ruling authority unless God has, at least for the time being, set him up.

and the authorities which are have been ordained by God could be understood as a general statement, the positive equivalent of the preceding sentence. But it is perhaps more likely that it is a particular statement about the actual authorities with which Paul and the Roman Christians had to do, namely, the Roman Emperor and his representatives. Pagan though the imperial government was, it was yet to be acknowledged as a divinely appointed authority.

2. So he who refuses to be subject to the authority is opposing God's ordering; and those who oppose that shall bring judgment on themselves. Since the civil authority is ordained by God, to fail to render it the appropriate subjection and, instead, to set oneself against it is to be guilty of rebellion against God's ordering. (Note that the Greek verbs represented by 'be subject' in vv. 1 and 5 and 'refuse to be subject' in the present verse and the noun represented by 'ordering' are all different compounds of the same simple verb or, in the last case, of a cognate noun, while 'ordained' represents the perfect passive participle of the simple verb.) The 'judgment' referred to is probably a divine judgment and not merely the civil authority's reaction.

3–4. For those engaged in government are not a *cause for* **fear to the good work but to the evil. Dost thou wish not to fear the authority? Do what is good, and thou shalt receive praise from it; for it is God's minister to thee for good. But, if thou doest evil, fear; for it is not to no purpose that it is armed with the sword; for it is God's minister, an agent of punishment for wrath to him who does evil.** These two verses are puzzling. The difficulty is that Paul seems to take no account of the possibility of the government's being unjust and punishing the good work and praising the evil. There seem to be three possible explanations: (i) Paul is so taken up with his own good experiences of the Roman authority that he is oblivious of the possibility that it might do what is unjust. But Paul himself had had other experiences (see Acts 16.22f, 37; 2 Cor 11.25ff). And could he ever forget that it was this same authority which had condemned and executed his Lord? (ii) Paul, though fully aware of this possibility, is here, as Calvin suggests, speaking only 'of the true and natural duty of the magistrate', from which however 'those who hold power often depart'. But it is hard to see how the giving of such a one-sided picture could be compatible with a serious pastoral purpose. Moreover, it would be in striking contrast to the realism of 8.35–39. (iii) Paul means that consciously or unconsciously, willingly or unwillingly, in one way or another, the power will praise the good work and punish the evil. The promise of v.3 is absolute: the Christian, in so far as he is obeying the gospel, may be sure that the power will honour him. It may indeed intend to punish him, but its intended punishment will then turn out to be praise. It may take his life, but in so doing it will but confer a crown of glory. On the other hand, if he does evil, it must needs punish him – though it may be by shameful honours or a false security. This third explanation, though admittedly difficult, seems preferable to the other two.

The two clauses in v. 4 which begin 'for it is God's minister' indicate the grounds of the promise in v. 3 and the warning in v. 4. The reason why the ruler cannot help but praise the good work and punish the evil is that he is (whether he knows it or not, whether willingly or unwillingly) God's servant (compare Isa 10.5–15). The purposes to which he ultimately gives effect are, in spite of all contrary appearances (and we certainly must not, even for a moment, deny or belittle them!), not his own, but God's. The civil authority is 'God's minister' for the believer's good ('to thee for good'). The ruler helps him toward 'the good' which God has in store for him, toward salvation, if he is a just ruler, by providing him with encouragement to do good and discouragement from doing evil (which even the Christian needs in so far as he is still also an unbeliever), and by curbing the worst excesses of other men's sinfulness and providing them with selfish reasons for acting justly; while, if he is unjust, he still, by God's over-ruling and in spite of his own intentions, must needs help (for the troubles which he will contrive for the faithful Christian will be such troubles as, so far from hindering his salvation, actually assist it). The civil authority is also God's servant, inasmuch as it is 'an agent of punishment for wrath to him who does evil', through which a partial, relative, provisional manifestation of God's wrath against sin takes place. In this connexion the mention of the sword is, in our opinion, more probably to be understood as a reference to the authority's possession of military power than to the power of capital punishment – a reminder that it is in a position to quell resistance.

5. Wherefore there is a necessity to be subject not just by reason of the wrath but also by reason of conscience. It follows from what has been said in vv. 1b–4 that the Christian must be subject not only for fear of wrath but also by reason of conscience. We have already had occasion to say something about the Greek noun represented by 'conscience', in connexion with 2.15 and 9.1. It is perhaps best here to understand it to mean simply 'knowledge'. The knowledge in question would be the knowledge that the ruler is, whether consciously or unconsciously, willingly or unwillingly, God's minister. Whereas the pagan fulfils his obligation to the state (if he does) for fear of punishment and perhaps also because he realizes that the state is, on the whole, beneficial to society, the Christian has a further, and all-important, reason for fulfilling his obligation to it, namely, his knowledge of the secret of the relation in which it stands to God and to Christ.

6. For it is for this reason that you do actually pay tribute. The Christians in Rome do, as a matter of fact, pay taxes, and the real ground of their doing so is their knowledge of the place of civil authority in the divine purpose. **for, when they busy themselves earnestly with this very matter, they are God's servants** is a reminder that it is as God's servants, and therefore as those whose claims must not be rejected or evaded, that the authorities demand the payment of taxes and dues.

7. Render to all that which it is your obligation to render them, to him to whom you owe tribute tribute, to him to whom you owe indirect tax indirect tax, to him to whom you owe fear fear, to him to whom you owe honour honour sums up the section. That there is some connexion between this verse and the saying attributed to Jesus in Mk 12.17 (compare Mt 22.21; Lk 20.25) seems extremely likely. It seems quite probable – though it is of course not certain – that Paul is here consciously echoing a dominical saying known to him from tradition. Common to this verse and to Mk 12.17 is the strong emphasis on the thought of obligation, of paying or paying back what is a debt owed.

It is generally taken for granted that 'fear' in this verse denotes a greater, and 'honour' a lesser, degree of respect, and that by 'him to whom you owe fear' is meant the magistrate who is entitled to the greater degree of respect. While it is possible – maybe we ought even to say 'probable' – that this interpretation is right, there are certain difficulties about it which should at least be mentioned.

(i) Paul has just said: 'For those engaged in government are not a *cause for* fear to the good work but to the evil. Dost thou wish not to fear the authority? Do what is good ... But, if thou doest evil, fear ...'. Is there not at least a certain awkwardness or harshness in Paul's using 'fear' in the sense of 'respect' in a general positive exhortation to the Christians in Rome concerning their duty with regard to the authorities three verses after this very emphatic use of the noun and verb 'fear' with reference to that fear of the authorities from which they are to be free?

(ii) If there is a real possibility of a connexion between this verse and the saying which we have in Mk 12.17, then it would seem natural at least to raise the question whether perhaps (as in the saying) there is in this verse a reference to the debt which is owed to God. Could it be that Paul intended by 'him to whom you owe fear' not the human authority but God?

(iii) A comparison with 1 Pet 2.17, which is probably also connected with the saying to which we have just referred, is very suggestive. Here, as in the Jesus-saying, the debt to God is mentioned distinctly as well as the debt to the Emperor, and there is an interesting similarity of structure between the 1 Peter verse and the present verse.

(iv) It is noteworthy that in 1 Pet 2.17 the wording of Prov 24.21 has been significantly altered. Proverbs has 'My son, fear thou the LORD and the king'; but in 1 Peter two different verbs have been used, presumably in order to avoid using the same verb to denote what is owed to the Emperor and what is owed to God. God is to be feared and the Emperor honoured. The alteration, whether original in 1 Peter or already made in the primitive catechetical tradition of the Church, suggests that there was in the Church a feeling that 'fear' was particularly due to God and 'honour' rather than 'fear' appropriate to the Emperor.

(v) A survey of the occurrences of the verb and the noun 'fear' in the New Testament confirms the suspicion that 'fear' is not characteristically used of what is due to earthly rulers. Nowhere in the New Testament is there a general exhortation to 'fear' a civil authority, and, apart from v. 3, which is concerned with wrong-doers, and the verse which is presently under discussion, the noun 'fear' is not used in connexion with rulers.

While it will probably be felt that the generally accepted interpretation of v. 7 should still be supported, the suggestion that by 'him to whom you owe fear' Paul meant God should not, in our judgment, be cavalierly dismissed.

VII. 5. THE DEBT OF LOVE
(13.8–10)

Having dealt in 13.1–7 with the Christian's fulfilment of his political responsibility, which, as Calvin puts it, 'constitutes not the least part of love', Paul now goes on to sum up his particular ethical exhortation in the all-embracing commandment of love.

⁸Leave no debt outstanding to anyone, except the debt of love to one another; for he who loves the other has fulfilled the law. ⁹For 'Thou shalt not commit adultery', 'Thou shalt not kill', 'Thou shalt not steal', 'Thou shalt not covet', and whatever other commandment there is, it is all summed up in this word, 'Thou shalt love thy neighbour as thyself'. ¹⁰Love does not do the neighbour wrong: love is therefore the fulfilling of the law.

8. Leave no debt outstanding to anyone repeats in negative form the positive injunction of v. 7, 'Render to all that which it is your obligation to render them', and so forms a neat transition from the preceding paragraph. Christians are to leave no debts, no obligations to their fellow-men undischarged.

except the debt of love to one another. Two questions need settling here: the former concerns the meaning of the Greek expression represented by 'except', and the latter the scope of 'one another'. With regard to the former, it has been maintained by some that the expression should here be translated 'but' (it occasionally has this meaning: for example 14.14; Mt 12.4; 1 Cor 7.17), and that the whole of v. 8a means 'Owe no man anything, but you ought to love one another' (so Barrett). But this involves supplying in the second half of a sentence a verb used in the first half, and supplying it not just in a different sense but also in a different mood; and, while the supplying of the same verb in a different sense would be a quite feasible word-play (compare 14.13, where the same verb is used in different senses in the two parts of the verse), the combination of change of sense and change of mood, where the verb is not repeated, is surely so harsh as to be extremely improbable. We therefore take the Greek expression in its ordinary sense of 'except', and understand the point of these words to be, not, of course, that this is a debt which we have no obligation to discharge, but that, unlike those debts which we can pay up fully and be done with, this is an unlimited debt which we can never adequately discharge even for the present moment and which, however hard we try to discharge it, is moreover always mounting up afresh. So we must ever be trying our best to discharge it and yet always be owing it. With regard to the other question, 'one another' has sometimes been understood as implying that the love referred to is limited to fellow-Christians. But it is much more likely that, having just said 'Leave no debt outstanding to anyone', Paul meant 'the debt of love to one another' in an all-embracing sense. The universal negative with which the sentence begins (it is more emphatic in the original Greek than in our translation) is naturally understood to control the reference of the following words. There is no one who is not included in 'one another'.

for he who loves the other has fulfilled the law. The suggestion that the Greek should be construed as meaning, 'for he who loves has fulfilled the other law', must surely be firmly rejected. There has been no clear reference to any law in the preceding sentences – the word 'law' has not been used since 10.5. To explain that by 'the other law' Paul means the Old Testament law as opposed to the civil law of Rome suggested by the first words of this verse understood in close connexion with vv. 1–7 is surely intolerably forced. There is little doubt that we must take 'the other' as the object of 'loves'. It must mean not just 'another' (AV) or 'someone other than himself' (Barrett), but 'the other', that is, the one who at a particular moment confronts him as his neighbour in the New Testament sense – and so *all* those who from time to time present to him God's claim to his service. A man has not fulfilled the law by the mere fact that he loves *an*other, some*one* other than himself (most men surely do this, though more or less inadequately, at least at some time in their lives). The definite article before 'other' is important – it has a generalizing effect. Fulfilment of the law involves not just loving someone other than oneself, but loving *each* person whom God presents to one as one's neighbour by the circumstance of his being someone whom one *is in a position to* affect for good or ill. The 'neighbour' in the New Testament sense is not someone arbitrarily chosen by us: he is given to us by God.

The initial 'for' indicates that what is said is in some way a reason for, or an explanation of, what is said in v. 8a. Two possible interpretations present themselves: (i) verse 8b may be understood as stating a reason for loving one another: to do so is to fulfil the law. Paul would hardly mean to imply that some people do as a matter of fact fulfil the law in the sense of obeying it fully (for that would be inconsistent with what he says elsewhere in Romans (for example 3.20)), but simply that to try to love is to be set in the direction of obedience to the law. (ii) verse 8b may be understood as explaining why the debt of love can never be fully discharged: it stands to reason that it cannot be fully discharged, because, if there were people who were in the fullest sense loving their neighbours, they would have done what we have seen to be impossible for fallen men – they would have perfectly fulfilled the law. Of these interpretations (ii) would seem to be preferable. It fits what seems to be the movement of Paul's thought better, and, if it is accepted, the use of the perfect tense 'has fulfilled' presents no difficulty.

9. For 'Thou shalt not commit adultery', 'Thou shalt not kill', 'Thou shalt not steal', 'Thou shalt not covet', and whatever other commandment there is, it is all summed up in this word, 'Thou shalt love thy neighbour as thyself'. In a confirmation of v.8b Paul goes on to indicate that the particular commandments of the 'second table' of the Decalogue are all summed up in the commandment to love one's neighbour as oneself (Lev 19.18). He specifies only four, indicating by 'and whatever other commandment there is' that he is only giving some instances. While in Lev 19.18 the neighbour is clearly the fellow-Israelite, as the first part of the verse indicates, for Jesus the term had a universal range, as is shown by Lk 10.25–37. There is no adequate ground for thinking that its scope was less wide for Paul than for Jesus. It has sometimes been argued that the commandment to love one's neighbour as oneself legitimizes, and indeed actually requires, self-love. The significance of 'as thyself' is rather that God addresses His command to us as the men that we actually are, the sinners who do, as a matter of fact, love ourselves, and claims us as such for love to our neighbours. And this form of the commandment indicates that the love for our neighbour which is required of us is a love which is altogether real and sincere – as real and sincere as our sinful self-love, about the reality and sincerity of which there is no shadow of doubt.

10. The negative formulation of **Love does not do the neighbour wrong** is due to the negative form of the commandments to which Paul has just referred. But, as in the commandments themselves, so here a positive content is also implied. It is anyway a foolish mistake to despise the negative formulation; for it will always be necessary (in addition to the positive) as a touchstone of the reality of love. How often is Christian love brought into disrepute, because those who are loud in their praise of it and confident of their possession of it persist in actually injuring their neighbours!

love is therefore the fulfilling of the law. To draw the conclusion from this that we can afford to forget the Ten Commandments and all the rest of the law and just make do with the general commandment to love (or, as those who are inclined to draw this conclusion, would probably prefer to call it, the principle of love) would be altogether mistaken. For, while we most certainly need the summary to save us from missing the wood for the trees and from understanding the particular commandments in a rigid, literalistic, unimaginative, pedantic, or loveless way, we are equally in need of the particular commandments, into which the law breaks down the general obligation of love, to save us from resting content with vague, and often hypocritical, sentiments, which – in ourselves and quite often even in others – we all are prone to mistake for Christian love.

VII. 6. THE ESCHATOLOGICAL MOTIVATION OF CHRISTIAN OBEDIENCE
(13.11–14)

Paul has already referred to the eschatological context in which Christian obedience is set in 12.2 ('stop allowing yourselves to be conformed to this age, but continue to let yourselves be transformed by the renewing of your mind'). Throughout chapters 12 and 13 it is assumed. Now at the end of the more general part of his ethical exhortation Paul takes up again the reference of 12.2, and makes explicit the eschatological motivation of Christian obedience.

[11]And this, knowing the time, that now it is high time for you to awake out of sleep; for now salvation is nearer to us than when we became believers. [12]The night is far advanced, and the day is close at hand. Let us then lay aside the works of darkness, and let us put on the armour of light. [13]Let us walk honourably as in the day, not in revels and bouts of drunkenness, not in repeated promiscuity and debauchery, not in strife and jealousy. [14]But put on the Lord Jesus Christ, and cease to make provision for the flesh for the satisfaction of its lusts.

11. And this serves to introduce a reference to an additional circumstance which heightens the force of what has been said. This additional circumstance is the fact that those whom Paul addresses are **knowing the time.** The things which Paul has been exhorting his readers to do (probably we should think not just of 13.8–10, but of chapters 12 and 13 as a whole) they must – and they will – strive all the more earnestly to do, because they know the significance of the time. For this appeal to eschatology as an incentive to moral earnestness we may compare, for example, Phil 4.4–7; 1 Th 5.1–11, 23; Heb 10.24f; Jas 5.7–11; 1 Pet 4.7–11, and also such passages in the Gospels as Mt 25.31–46; Mk 13.33–37. Paul's readers know the significance of the time, because, as believers in Christ, they see the present time in the light both of what He has done and of what He is going to do.

that now it is high time for you to awake out of sleep indicates something of the significance of the present time. Sleep is a vivid image for that state which is altogether opposed to that of preparedness for the coming divine action. **for now salvation is**

nearer to us than when we became believers supports the preceding statement. These words certainly imply that Paul was looking forward realistically to a divine event to happen at a particular time, that his future tenses were no mere accommodation of language, that his eschatology was no eschatology of the timeless fact. They imply that he regarded the amount of time which had passed between his own, and his readers', conversion and the moment of writing as of real significance in relation to the Parousia – it was that much nearer than it had been. But do they also imply that he was certain that this amount of time would necessarily prove to be an appreciable fraction of the whole interval between the Ascension and the Parousia? Do they, in fact, imply that he was certain that the Parousia would necessarily occur within, at the most, a few decades? It is sometimes assumed that they do. But there is nothing in this verse by itself – for the moment we confine ourselves to this verse – to compel us to accept such an assumption. It is clear that, if the Parousia is really going to happen at a particular time, each hour that we live must bring us an hour nearer to it, however far off it may be. Moreover, the point of this sentence was to underline the urgency of the need to awake: the time of opportunity for faith and obedience was for Paul and his readers the shorter by this lapse of time. And, with this point in mind, it was surely natural for him not just to think of this lapse of time as a fraction of the interval before the Parousia but also to think of it in relation to the ordinary span of human life. It may further be said that the very transcendent importance of the expected Event itself lends significance to each passing moment and period of time.

12. The night is far advanced, and the day is close at hand. Let us then lay aside the works of darkness, and let us put on the armour of light. The whole verse is characterized by the metaphorical use of 'night', 'day', 'darkness', 'light', for which the reference to awaking from sleep has prepared the way. It is imagery which occurs again and again in the Bible. Here 'the night' clearly denotes the present age (compare 12.2), and 'the day' the coming age of God's final, unambiguous manifestation of His kingdom. We have here a clear instance of the New Testament insistence on the nearness of the End. We may compare 16.20 ('soon'); Mk 13.29 = Mt 24.33; Lk 18.8a (as understood apparently by Luke: compare the latter part of the verse); Jn 16.16ff (if, as is probable the author intended a double reference to be recognized in 'again a little while, and ye shall see me' – both to the Resurrection and to the Parousia); 1 Cor 7.29; Phil 4.5; Heb 10.25; Jas 5.8f; 1 Pet 4.7; 1 Jn 2.18; Rev 22.20.

What is the meaning of this insistence on the nearness of the End – this 'near-expectation'? It is well known that very many scholars regard it as an assured result that the primitive Church was convinced that the End would certainly occur within, at the most, a few decades, and that its conviction has been refuted by the indisputable fact of nineteen hundred years of subsequent history. The true explanation, we believe, is rather that the primitive Church was convinced that the ministry of Jesus had ushered in the last days, the end-time. History's supreme events had taken place in the ministry, death, resurrection and ascension of the Messiah. There was now no question of another chapter's being added which could in any way effectively go back upon what had been written in that final chapter. All that subsequent history could add, whether it should last for few years or for many, must be of the nature of an epilogue. It could only be something added after the conclusion of the final chapter, an interval provided by God's patience to give men time to hear the gospel and to make the decision of faith. However long such an interval should last, it would in a real sense have the essential character of 'short time', its continuance dependent solely on God's patience. Such a near-expectation is not the same thing as certainty that the End would necessarily come within, at the most, a few decades. Some Christians apparently did misunderstand it in this sense (see Jn 21.23; 2 Pet 3.3ff); but there is – so far as we can see – no compelling evidence at all that the Church as a whole cherished such an illusory confidence. To say this is not, of course, to deny that the primitive Church reckoned absolutely seriously with the *possibility* that the Parousia might occur very soon. Nor is it to deny that there is this significant difference between the near-expectation of the apostle Paul and that of Christians today: we – unlike him – *know* that the Parousia has *not* occurred within nineteen centuries.

The real significance of the near-expectation expressed in the statement, 'The night is far advanced, and the day is close at hand', is that the time which is left is time in which watching for Christ's second coming with alert minds – with proper eagerness and a proper sense of urgency, and with all the active and resolute engagement in the tasks of faith and obedience and love which these involve – is the whole duty of Christians. Truly to apprehend this shortness of the time is to be turned in the direction of obedience to the exhortation of 12.1–13.10 – that, surely is why Paul wrote in 13.11: 'And this, knowing the time . . .'

In the exhortation of the latter part of the verse (so also in the following verse) Paul uses the first person plural, associating himself with those he addresses. He recognizes that he too needs to be reminded. The metaphorical use of 'lay aside' and 'put on', which occurs often in New Testament moral teaching, is a very obvious one. By 'the works of darkness' Paul no doubt means the works which belong to, and are characteristic of, the night of this present age, but the thought may perhaps also be present to his mind that the things he is going to mention in the latter part of v. 13 are such as are commonly indulged in in the dark but that even pagans might shrink from engaging in in broad daylight. The substitution of 'armour' for 'works' in the second clause reflects Paul's consciousness that the Christian life is necessarily a warfare. The Greek word, used in 6.13 in the sense of instruments, here no doubt has its special sense of armour, including both defensive and offensive arms. The meaning of 'the armour of light' will be clarified by v. 14, just as that of 'the works of darkness' is clarified by the list in v. 13.

13. Let us walk honourably as in the day. The last four words are puzzling. They can be understood in various ways, thus: (i) with reference to the relative respectability of what men do in broad daylight, as opposed to the revelries and debaucheries of the night-time; (ii) with reference to the Coming Age and with an 'if' understood ('as if in the day', 'as if the day were already here'), the day being thought of as not yet come; (iii) with reference to the Coming Age, the day being thought of as in some sense at any rate already here for Christians; (iv) 'day' being used, quite independently of its use in the previous verse, as a metaphor for the state of enlightenment and regeneration in which the Christian is at present, contrasted with the condition of paganism. The fact that they involve taking 'day' in a quite different sense from that in which it is used in the previous verse would seem to tell against both (i) and (iv), though (iv) is widely supported. While (ii) fits the context ('the day is close at hand') more smoothly, (iii) is probably to be preferred, on the ground that it is more forceful and more in line with Paul's manner of exhortation generally. The element of unreality involved in (ii) tells against it. It is not Paul's custom to appeal to Christians to behave as they would if something were true, which in fact is not true. When in 6.11 he exhorts the Christians in Rome to recognize that they are dead to sin but alive to God in Christ, he means, not that they are to pretend that this is so, but that they are to recognize this as the *truth* which the gospel reveals. We take it then that Paul's meaning here probably is that he and his readers are to walk honourably as those who in Christ belong already to God's new order, whose lives are already illumined by the brightness of the coming day.

not in revels and bouts of drunkenness, not in repeated promiscuity and debauchery, not in strife and jealousy provides examples of the works of darkness which are to be shunned. There are three pairs of nouns in the original, and the relation between the two nouns in each pair is very close: each pair may, in fact, be understood as suggesting one composite idea (for example, drunken revelries) rather than two distinct ideas. The nouns of the first and second pairs are plurals, suggesting frequent repetition. Those of the third pair are in the singular. Jealous strife and brawling often resulted from the drunken revels and the debauchery to which they led. With regard to the connexion between drunkenness and the other things mentioned in this list, Chrysostom comments (and his words recall poignant memories to one who for some months during the Second World War shared pastoral responsibility for a large concentration of venereal disease patients): 'For nothing so kindles lust and sets wrath ablaze as drunkenness and tippling', returning later to the subject with the appeal, 'Wherefore, I exhort you, flee from fornication and the mother thereof, drunkenness'.

14. But put on the Lord Jesus Christ interprets 'let us put on the armour of light'. Paul has used the expression 'put on Christ' in connexion with baptism in Gal 3.27, and comparison of Gal 3.27 with Rom 6.2ff makes it clear that, as we have to reckon with several different senses in which the believer may be spoken of as dying with Christ and being raised with Christ, so too we must distinguish different senses in which the believer may be said to put on Christ. He has already put on Christ in his submission to baptism and his reception through the sacrament of God's pledge that – in what is the fundamental sense – he has already been clothed in Christ by virtue of God's gracious decision to see him in Christ. So in Gal 3.27 Paul uses an indicative. But here in the present verse he uses the imperative, since putting on Christ has here its moral sense (answering to sense (iii) of our dying and being raised with Him in our note on 6.2). To put on the Lord Jesus Christ means here to embrace again and again, in faith and confidence, in grateful loyalty and obedience, Him to whom we already belong.

and cease to make provision for the flesh for the satisfaction of its lusts. For the meaning of 'flesh' here compare 7.18, 25; 8.3–9, 12f. It signifies the whole of our human nature in its fallenness. The list of 'the works of the flesh' in Gal 5.19ff makes it clear that the term is wider in its scope than 'flesh' is apt to be in much modern English piety, covering such things as 'strife' and 'jealousy'. That those who now walk not according to the flesh but according to the Spirit (8.4) should deliberately make provision for the satisfaction of the flesh's desires would plainly be ridiculous.

VII. 7. THE 'STRONG' AND THE 'WEAK'
(14.1–15.13)

What exactly the problem is with which Paul is concerned in this section is not at all easy to decide, and various explanations have been suggested. Some, at least, of them must be mentioned here.

(i) It is often assumed that the people referred to as 'weak in faith' or simply 'weak' must be legalists who think to earn a status of righteousness before God by their own works, imagining that their abstention from meat and wine and observance of special days constitute a claim on God, people who have not yet learned to accept justification as God's free gift. But, were this really the case, Paul would surely not have regarded them as genuine believers, as he clearly does, and would have taken a different line with them from that which he has taken in this section – though a less vehement polemic than that in Galatians might be understandable on the ground that the 'weak' of this section are clearly not aggressive like the Judaizers of Galatians.

(ii) It has been suggested that the disagreement between the weak and the strong of this passage is about the question of 'things sacrificed to idols', with which Paul is concerned in 1 Corinthians 8 and 10. It is clear at once that there are an impressive number of contacts between the present section and those two chapters. Moreover, it is easy to understand how some Christians, knowing that the meat to be purchased in the butchers' shops of a pagan city would normally have been involved in sacrifice to a pagan deity, would decide to become vegetarian as the only way of being sure that they were not being accomplices in idolatry. The abstention from wine (14.21) is also explicable along these lines, since libations were offered from the firstfruits of the wine. But the explanation of this section as being mainly concerned with the problem of 'things sacrificed to idols' should also, we think, be rejected; for, first, it is scarcely credible, in view of its prominence in 1 Corinthians 8 and 10, that Paul should never once have used the Greek word for 'sacrifices to idols' in this passage, had he had this problem in mind (and there are, moreover, other indications in 1 Corinthians 8 and 10 of the nature of the question at issue besides the use of this word; secondly, the mention of the observance of days can hardly be brought within the framework of this explanation; and, thirdly, there is no indication in this section that Paul saw any harm at all in the practice of the strong in itself, apart from its effect on the weak, but in 1 Cor 10.20–22 there is a warning against a danger to which the Corinthian 'wise' were exposed, the reality of which was quite independent of the presence of weak brethren with their scruples. While it is clear that Paul saw the tension between the strong and the weak with which he was concerned in Rom 14.1–15.13 as involving the same issues of the respect due to one's fellow-Christian's conscience and the absolute obligation to refrain from insisting on exercising the liberty allowed one by one's own faith at the risk of wrecking a fellow-Christian's faith, which were raised by the question of 'things sacrificed to idols' (hence the very close similarities between this section and 1 Corinthians 8 and 10), it seems unlikely that it was the problem of the 'things sacrificed to idols' that Paul had specially in mind here.

(iii) It has been suggested that the twofold abstinence was a manifestation within primitive Christianity of ideas and practices which were characteristic of various religious-philosophical movements in antiquity and which persisted with remarkable vitality down the centuries. If such were the provenance of the vegetarianism of the weak, the use of such expressions as 'ritually unclean' in 14.14 and 'clean' in 14.20 would be understandable, since the adherents of these movements regarded the killing of living creatures for food as unnatural and defiling. Abstention from wine on the ground that it was inimical to the higher and more refined uses of human reason and to the reception of divine communications was less widespread than the abstention from flesh, but not uncommon. There is wide support for this suggestion in one or another of its possible variations. A disadvantage of it is that a plausible explanation of the third feature, the observing of special days (14.5f) is not to be had along these lines, but has to be sought elsewhere.

(iv) A further possibility is that the weakness of the weak consisted in a continuing concern with literal obedience of the ceremonial part of the Old Testament law, though one that was very different from that of the Judaizers of Galatians. The Judaizers of Galatians were legalists who imagined that they could put God under an obligation by their obedience and insisted on the literal fulfilment of the ceremonial part of the law as necessary for salvation. With such legalism Paul could not compromise. But the possibility which we have in mind here is that the weak, while neither thinking they were putting God in their debt by their obedience nor yet deliberately trying to force all other Christians to conform to their pattern, felt that, as far as they themselves were concerned, they could not with a clear conscience give up the observance of such requirements of the law as the distinction between clean and unclean foods, the avoidance of blood, the keeping of the Sabbath and other special days.

In our view it is not possible to decide with absolute certainty between (iii) and (iv); but we regard (iv) as the more probable. In support of it the following points may be mentioned: (a) It agrees well with 15.7–13, which strongly suggests that the division between the weak and the strong was also, at any rate to a large extent, one between Jewish and Gentile Christians. (b) It agrees well with the use of 'ritually unclean' in 14.14 and of 'clean' in 14.20. Specially suggestive is a comparison of Mk 7.19, which would seem to imply that the question whether Christians ought to observe the distinction between clean and unclean foods was still, or had been quite recently, a live issue in the church for which Mark was writing. That Christians in a pagan city, wishing to be sure of avoiding meat which was in one way or another unclean according to the Old Testament ritual law, should decide simply to abstain altogether from meat would scarcely be surprising. There was a notable biblical precedent for such a course in Dan 1.8, 12, 16: and Barrett's statement that, in view of the fact that there was a large Jewish colony in Rome, 'it must be regarded as certain that suitable meat could be obtained by anyone who wished to do so' does not take account of the possibility that Jewish Christians may not have been able to rely on the willingness of their unbelieving fellow-Jews to accommodate them (moreover, the pressing problem may well have been the meat which their strong fellow-Christians were liable to offer them). (c) It agrees well with the mention of observance of days in 14.5f. (d) It accords with the implication of the whole section that the weak in faith are also characterized by a certain weakness of character, a liability to yield to social pressure and allow themselves to be blown off the course which their own faith has set them. The attachment to the ceremonial requirements of the law which suggestion (iv) presupposes in the weak is not the stubborn self-righteous legalism of the Galatians Judaizers but a feeling, which, while it goes very deep, is ill-defined and difficult to defend by argument. (e) It accords too with what is said about the spiritual ruin to which the weak can easily be brought; for to have a deeply held conviction but be unable to marshal clear-cut arguments in its defence is to be very vulnerable as regards one's personal integrity. (f) It also accords well with Paul's sympathetic attitude to the weak and the fact that the main thrust of his exhortation is directed to the strong, to persuade them to go out of their way to 'please' the weak and to refrain from doing anything likely to 'grieve' them.

The mention of abstinence from wine (14.21) is not so easily accommodated in the framework provided by suggestion (iv) as are the references to not eating meat and to observing days. The Old Testament law nowhere forbids the drinking of wine, except to priests on duty (Lev 10.9) and to Nazirites (Num 6.2f). But perhaps (as is argued in the comment on 14.21) the reference to abstinence from wine should be understood as hypothetical rather than as indicating an actual characteristic of the weak.

In our view, then, the most probable explanation of the nature of the disagreement between the weak and the strong, to which this section refers, is that, whereas the strong had recognized that, now that He who is the goal and substance and innermost meaning of the Old Testament law has come, the ceremonial part of it no longer requires to be literally obeyed, the weak felt strongly that a continuing concern with the literal obedience of the ceremonial law was an integral element of their response of faith to Jesus Christ, though their attitude was fundamentally different from that of the Judaizers of Galatians in that they did not think to put God under an obligation by their attempted obedience but only to express their faith.

¹Him who is weak in faith receive, *but* not in order to pass judgments on his scruples. ²One man has faith to eat any food, but he who is weak eats *only* vegetables. ³Let not him who eats despise him who does not eat, and let not him who does not eat pass judgment on him who eats, for God has received him. ⁴Who art thou that passest judgment on Another's house-slave? It is his own Lord whose concern it is whether he stands or falls; and he shall stand, for his Lord has the power to make him stand. ⁵One man esteems one day more than another, another man esteems every day *alike*. Let each be settled in his own mind. ⁶He who observes the day observes it to the Lord. And he who eats eats to the Lord, for he gives thanks to God; while he who abstains from eating abstains to the Lord, and gives thanks to God *for his meatless meal.* ⁷For none of us lives to himself, and none dies to himself; ⁸for, if we live, it is to the Lord that we live, and, if we die, it is to the Lord that we die. Whether we live, then, or die, it is to the Lord that we belong ⁹For it was for this purpose that Christ died and lived *again*, namely, that he might become Lord both of the dead and of the living. ¹⁰But thou – why dost thou pass judgment on thy brother? Or thou on the other side – why

dost thou despise thy brother? For we shall all of us stand before the judgment-seat of God. ¹¹For it is written: 'As I live, saith the Lord, to me shall every knee bend, And every tongue shall acclaim God'. ¹²So [then] each one of us shall give account of himself [to God].

¹³So let us pass judgment on one another no more; but decide rather not to put a stumbling-block or an occasion of falling in your brother's way. ¹⁴I know and am persuaded in the Lord Jesus that nothing is ritually unclean objectively; but if a man reckons something to be unclean, for him it is unclean. ¹⁵For, if thy brother is grieved on account of *thy* food, thou walkest no longer in accordance with love. Do not by thy food destroy him for whom Christ died. ¹⁶So let not your good thing be reviled. ¹⁷For the kingdom of God is not eating and drinking, but righteousness and peace and joy in the Holy Spirit; ¹⁸for he who therein serves Christ is well-pleasing to God and deserves men's approval. ¹⁹So then let us pursue what makes for peace and what makes for mutual edification. ²⁰Do not for the sake of *a particular* food destroy God's work. All things are indeed clean, but for the man who eats in such a way as results in the presence of a stumbling-block, it (*that is, his eating*) is evil. ²¹It is a good thing to abstain from eating meat or drinking wine or *doing* anything else by which thy brother stumbles. ²²The faith which thou hast keep to thyself before God. Blessed is the man who does not condemn himself over what he approves. ²³But he who is troubled by doubts is condemned if he eats, because *he does* not *do so* from faith: and whatever is not from faith is sin.

¹But we who are strong have an obligation to carry the infirmities of the weak and not to please ourselves. ²Let each one of us please his neighbour for his good with a view to his edification. ³For even Christ did not please himself; but, as scripture says, 'The reproaches of them that reproached thee fell upon me'. ⁴For whatsoever things were written of old *in the scriptures* were written for our instruction, in order that with patient endurance and *strengthened* by the comfort which the scriptures give we might hold hope fast. ⁵May the God *who is the source* of patient endurance and of comfort grant you to agree together among yourselves according to Christ Jesus, ⁶in order that you may glorify the God and Father of our Lord Jesus Christ with one heart and one mouth.

⁷Wherefore receive one another, because Christ also received you, to the glory of God. ⁸For I declare that Christ has become the

minister of the circumcision for the sake of God's faithfulness, in order to establish the promises made to the fathers, ⁹but the Gentiles glorify God for his mercy, even as it is written in scripture, 'Wherefore I will praise thee among the Gentiles and sing hymns to thy name'; ¹⁰and again it says, 'Rejoice, you Gentiles, together with his people'; ¹¹and again, 'Praise the Lord, all you Gentiles, and let all the peoples praise him'. ¹²And again Isaiah says, 'There shall be the scion of Jesse, and he who rises to rule the Gentiles: on him shall the Gentiles hope'.

¹³May the God of hope fill you with all joy and peace in believing, so that you may abound in hope by the power of the Holy Spirit.

1. Him who is weak in faith. The weakness in faith to which this chapter refers is not weakness in basic Christian faith but weakness in assurance that one's faith permits one to do certain things. That the use of the term 'weak' to be seen here and in 1 Corinthians 8 originated with those who disagreed with the persons so described is virtually certain. The weak will hardly have referred to themselves as 'the weak (in faith)'. Paul shares the assurance of the strong (so in 15.1 – 'we who are strong' – he numbers himself among them), and so accepts, and makes use of, their application of the terms 'strong' and 'weak', as having at least a limited validity, while he disapproves of their unbrotherly insistence on expressing their inward freedom outwardly to the full, quite regardless of the effects on others. **receive** is the fundamental imperative of this passage. It is the church as a whole which is addressed (it is the second person plural which is used and no particularizing vocative is inserted), the implication being that the Christian community in Rome as a whole is strong and that the weak are a minority – most probably a fairly small minority. They are to accept the weak in faith, to receive them into their fellowship, recognizing them frankly and unreservedly as brothers in Christ. This 'receive' must surely include both official recognition by the community and also brotherly acceptance in everyday intercourse. *but* **not in order to pass judgments on his scruples** introduces a qualification. The last five words represent two Greek plural nouns, one in the accusative, and the other in the genitive. They are patient of a very wide variety of interpretations, as can easily be seen from a comparison of different English

341

versions of the New Testament. This is so, because both nouns can bear several different meanings and the genitive can be understood either as objective or as adjectival. But the context would seem to tell in favour of taking the first noun in the sense 'judging', 'passing judgment on', and this would necessitate understanding the genitive as objective. In the context the most likely meaning for the second noun would seem to be 'scruple'. They are not to stultify their brotherly acceptance of the man who is weak in faith by proceeding to pass judgment on his scruples.

2. One man has faith to eat any food, but he who is weak eats *only* vegetables. The Greek verb meaning 'believe', 'have faith', is here used in a sense corresponding to the special use of the cognate noun in v. 1, so 'have the assurance that one's faith permits one (to)'.

3. Let not him who eats despise him who does not eat, and let not him who does not eat pass judgment on him who eats. The choice of 'despise' and 'pass judgment on' is significant; for in the situation which Paul envisages, in which the eaters (that is, those who eat all things) are the great majority, the non-eaters (that is, those who abstain from meat) a small minority, the eaters would be liable to despise the non-eaters as not worth taking seriously, while the non-eaters would be prone to adopt a censorious attitude to the eaters. **for God has received him** states the all-important reason why the non-eater must not pass judgment on the eater: God Himself has received the eater into His fellowship. For a believer to presume to pass judgment on one whom God has thus received clearly cannot be right. At this particular point (as also in v. 4) Paul directs his exhortation to the weak: he will presently bring the full weight of his exhortation to bear on the strong.

4. Who art thou that passest judgment on Another's house-slave? The one who does not eat, who is passing judgment on his fellow-Christian who does eat, is challenged to consider who he himself is who thus presumes to pass judgment on someone who, like himself, is Christ's (or God's) household-slave and therefore answerable only to Him (as according to ordinary human law a household-slave was answerable solely to his own master). **It is his own Lord whose concern it is whether he stands or falls.** Very often the Greek we have so translated is taken to mean that it is his own Lord (and not his fellow-Christian) who decides whether he stands or falls in God's judgment (whether present or future); but the first three words of the Greek are more probably explained as a dative of advantage or disadvantage, as our translation assumes. Christ (or God Himself) is concerned, His interest is at stake, in the question whether the strong Christian continues in faith or falls away from it. **and he shall stand** is a confident affirmation made on the basis of the preceding statement of the divine concern. **for his Lord has the power to make him stand** is added in confirmation of the promise just made: the certainty of the promise rests not on the strong Christian's ability to stand but on the Lord's ability to make him stand.

5–6. One man esteems one day more than another, another man esteems every day *alike.* Paul introduces another example of the disagreement between the strong and the weak. It is most likely that this had to do with the observance of the special days of the Old Testament ceremonial law (possibly also with the change from Sabbath to Lord's Day). **Let each be settled in his own mind** is a rule applying equally to every member of the church. In this area of disagreement, in which equally sincere Christians may feel constrained by their faith to take, and follow out in practice, opposite decisions, each is to seek to be as settled as possible in his mind, using his own powers of reasoning which have at least begun to be renewed by the gospel to form his own judgment as to what course of action obedience to the gospel requires of him, in responsible independence, neither ignoring, nor yet showing undue deference to, the opinions of his fellows. This is not an injunction to cultivate a closed mind, which refuses all further discussion, but an injunction to resist the temptation (to which those whom Paul calls 'weak' were no doubt particularly liable) to luxuriate in indecision and vacillation and to allow himself to be so preoccupied with balancing again and again the opposing arguments in what are anyway not the essential issues, that he is quite incapacitated for resolute and courageous action. It is a reminder to each member that, whether his faith leads him to adopt the practice of the strong or the practice of the weak, it can, and must be allowed to, set him free for an obedience which (according to his own particular way of faith) is firm, decisive, resolute, courageous, joyful.

He who observes the day observes it to the Lord. That is, he observes it with the intention and desire of serving the Lord by so doing. The variant reading which adds 'and he who observes not the day, to the Lord he observes it not' (compare AV) is no doubt due to a natural feeling that a pair of sentences referring to the question of special days is required to balance the pair of sentences concerned with eating and not eating; but the person responsible for the addition did not properly grasp Paul's thought, for the two positive sentences do not correspond, since the former refers to a weak Christian, while the latter refers to a strong one. **And he who eats eats to the Lord, for he gives thanks to God.** This statement concerning the strong Christian who eats all things is coupled with the preceding statement about the weak Christian who observes days, in order to make the point that both alike do what they do with the intention of serving the Lord. That the strong Christian does so is shown by the fact that he renders thanks to God for what he eats. The point Paul wishes to make here has now been made: but it seems that he felt that in what he had just said he had given the strong an advantage over the weak, since it had been only with regard to the former that he had mentioned the giving of thanks to God, and so, in order to restore the balance, added **while he who abstains from eating abstains to the Lord, and gives thanks to God** *for his meatless meal.*

7–9. For none of us lives to himself, and none dies to himself; for, if we live, it is to the Lord that we live, and, if we die, it is to the Lord that we die. That both weak and strong alike, as they follow their different ways, do what they do as service of the Lord, is necessarily true, since no Christian at all (the first person plural must here be limited to Christians) lives or dies 'to himself', that is, with no other object in view than his own gratification; for, in fact, all Christians live 'to the Lord', that is, they live with the object of pleasing Christ, they seek to use their lives in His service, and, when it comes to dying, they glorify Him by committing themselves to His keeping. **Whether we live, then, or die, it is to the Lord that we belong** sums up the underlying theological truth. The reason why we live and die 'to the Lord' is that we belong to Him both in life and in death. Our belonging to Him is explained in the following sentence: **For it was for this purpose that Christ died and lived** *again,* **namely, that he might become Lord both of the dead and of the living.** Paul's intention is not to connect Christ's being Lord of the dead and His being Lord of the living with His death and resurrection, respectively. Christ's death and resurrection are not to be separated in this way: His being Lord of the dead and His being Lord of the living depend equally on both His death and His resurrection.

10–12. Paul takes up again the thought of v. 3 with the reproachful questions, **But thou – why dost thou pass judgment on thy brother? Or thou on the other side – why dost thou despise thy brother?** In the light of the fact (affirmed in v. 6 and supported by the weighty argument of vv. 7–9) that the strong and the weak alike follow their differing ways with the intention of serving Christ, how can the weak Christian presume to set himself up to judge his strong brother, or the strong Christian dare to despise his weak brother?

As a powerful dissuasive from all such judging and despising of one's brothers Paul adds: **For we shall all of us stand before the judgment-seat of God.** This statement he supports by a scriptural quotation (apart from the opening formula, it is from Isa 45.23): **For it is written: 'As I live, saith the Lord: to me shall every knee bend, and every tongue shall acclaim God'.** To this is added a hortatory conclusion drawing out the meaning of the foregoing quotation: **So [then] each one of us shall give account of himself [to God].** Since some important witnesses to the text omit 'to God', its originality is slightly in doubt; but intrinsic probability is strongly in its favour, for, without it, the sentence is unsatisfactory as a conclusion to this paragraph. Each element of the sentence would seem to carry emphasis. Each one of us (that is, each individual Christian) will indeed have to give account: none will be exempted. He will have to give account of himself: his fellow-Christian, who may be very ready now to interfere with him where he has no right to interfere, will not be able to answer in his stead then. And it will be to God, not to men, that he will have to give his account of himself.

13. **So let us pass judgment on one another no more** begins the new paragraph by summing up succinctly the exhortation of the preceding one. It is best understood as addressed to both strong and weak alike. **but decide rather not to put a stumbling-block or an occasion of falling in your brother's way** is directed to the strong. In this second part of the verse Paul turns to a fresh aspect of the subject under discussion, namely, the effect one's conduct may have on one's brother, in particular, the effect which the exercise by the strong of the liberty he himself possesses may have on the weak. The possibility that here and also in v. 20f Paul may be indebted to the tradition of Jesus' teaching (compare Mt 18.6–7; Mk 9.42; Lk 17.1–2) should be recognized. (There is a word-play in the Greek, which the RV preserves ('judge'–'judge') at the cost of not bringing out the intended sense clearly.)

14. I know and am persuaded in the Lord Jesus is strikingly emphatic and gives great weight to what follows. By the words 'in the Lord Jesus' Paul may perhaps have meant simply that what he was about to say was an insight derived from his fellowship with the risen and exalted Christ or – more generally – that it was consonant with God's self-revelation in Jesus Christ as a whole, that is, with the gospel, or that his certainty of its truth rested on the authority of the risen and exalted Christ; but we certainly cannot rule out the possibility that he had in mind some specific teaching of the historic Jesus (the use here of the personal name 'Jesus' could be, as has been suggested, a pointer to the presence of such a reference), and the evidence of Mk 7.15–23 and Mt 15.10–11, 15–20, has, of course to be considered.

The truth, his acceptance of which Paul has stated so emphatically, is: **that nothing is ritually unclean objectively.** Paul is thinking of the resources of the created world which are available for men's use. The point Paul is making in the first half of this verse is essentially the same as that made in Mk 7.15a. He is indicating his own agreement with the basic position of the strong, namely, that the fact that Christ's work has now been accomplished has radically transformed the situation with regard to the ceremonial part of the Old Testament law: now it is no longer obligatory to obey it literally (one is to obey it by believing in Him to whom it bears witness and understanding Him in the light it throws upon His person and work). But, while for the believer who has grasped this truth the foods which the ceremonial law had pronounced unclean are no longer unclean, there are other believers who have not yet clearly understood this, and for them, not yet having been given this inward liberty, to neglect the literal obedience of the ritual law is wrong. The meats, which had been forbidden, though not objectively unclean, are, for them, subjectively unclean. It is their situation which is indicated by the words, **but if a man reckons something to be unclean, for him it is unclean.**

15. For, if thy brother is grieved on account of *thy* food, thou walkest no longer in accordance with love is connected, not with v. 14 (which is a parenthesis introduced in order to make clear both Paul's own acceptance of the basic assumption of the strong and at the same time the fact that there is an important qualification of that assumption which must not be forgotten), but with v. 13b. The weak in faith will be grievously hurt, he will have the integrity of his faith (that is, faith in its deepest sense) and obedience destroyed, and his salvation put at risk, if he is led by his strong fellow-Christian's insistence on exercising the liberty, which he (the strong Christian) truly has, into doing something for which he as yet does not possess the inward liberty. The strong will therefore not be acting in accordance with Christian love, if his weak brother is thus seriously hurt on account of the food which he (the strong Christian) eats. It is to be noted that once again Paul drives home the earnestness of his exhortation by changing to the use of the second person singular in this verse and also in vv. 20–22. **Do not by thy food destroy him for whom Christ died** drives home the truth that to bring about the ruin of one's brother by insisting on exercising outwardly one's own inner freedom with regard to the ritual law would be to trample on the sacrifice of Christ.

16. So let not your good thing be reviled. With regard to this three closely related questions require to be answered: (i) Is this verse addressed only to the strong, or is it addressed to both strong and weak? (ii) To what does 'your good thing' refer? (iii) Whom does Paul have in mind as likely to do the reviling to which he refers? Of these (ii) has been continuously debated since patristic times, and opinion is still divided about it. On the one hand, the answer is often given that liberty from the ceremonial observances is meant. On the other hand, various suggestions of a more comprehensive reference have often been made, such as Christ's doctrine generally, 'the kingdom of God', 'salvation', 'faith'. If to (i) the answer 'to both the strong and the weak' is given, then (ii) is settled at the same time, and very probably (iii) also; for, if the verse is addressed to both the strong and the weak, 'your good thing' clearly cannot refer to the inner freedom enjoyed only by the strong but must refer to something common to both parties, and it is almost, if not quite, certain that the people Paul has in mind as liable to turn to reviling or speaking evil must be people outside the church. If, however, the answer 'to the strong alone' is given to question (i), questions (ii) and (iii) remain open to discussion.

In view of the thrust of the exhortation in this whole passage it seems much more probable that the answer to (i) must be 'to the strong only'. With regard to (ii), it is often assumed that, if only the strong are addressed, 'your good thing' must denote the freedom enjoyed by them. But, though the explanation that Paul is here warning the strong against bringing reproach upon the 'good thing' which consists of their inner freedom by selfishly insisting on exercising it outwardly to the hurt of their weak brothers is certainly possible, we are inclined to think that it is more probable that he is here warning the strong against an even more serious danger, namely, that of bringing reproach on that 'good thing', which belongs not only to them but also to their weak fellow-Christians, that is, the gospel itself. The presence among Christians of such selfishness as would willingly risk causing a weak brother's spiritual ruin (compare v. 15b) for the sake of a plateful of meat would surely bring into disrepute not just the liberty of the strong but also the very gospel itself. With regard to (iii), if the verse is addressed to both strong and weak, or if (as has been argued above) it is addressed only to the strong but 'your good thing' refers to the gospel, it is highly likely that the people whom Paul has in mind as possible revilers are people outside the church.

17. For the kingdom of God is not eating and drinking, but righteousness and peace and joy in the Holy Spirit. The verse appeals to the nature of the kingdom of God as proof of the terrible absurdity of the strong Christian's readiness to bring about his weak brother's spiritual ruin for the sake of such a triviality as the use of a particular food and thereby to cause the gospel to be reviled by unbelievers. The kingdom of God (Paul is here thinking of it in its present reality) is not a matter of eating and drinking. It is not one's insistence on expressing one's freedom to eat a particular food which attests the presence of God's kingdom (nor is one in the slightest degree worse off in relation to it for having forgone the expression of one's freedom for one's brother's sake): its presence is attested rather by the presence of 'righteousness and peace and joy in the Holy Spirit'. By 'righteousness' Paul probably means the status of righteousness before God which is God's gift, by 'peace' the state of having been reconciled to God, by 'joy in the Holy Spirit' that joy which is the Spirit's work in the believer and so altogether different from any joy which is merely the temporary result of the satisfaction of one's own selfish desires. Where these things are really present and understood in the life of the church, there the wickedness and the absurdity of destroying a brother for the sake of eating a particular food will be clearly recognized.

18. for he who therein serves Christ is well-pleasing to God and deserves men's approval is best taken closely with v. 17 and as underlining what was said there. Puzzling is 'therein'. Of the various explanations of it which have been offered (it has, for example, been explained as meaning 'in the Holy Spirit', 'in this way' in the sense of recognizing the truth expressed in v. 17 as a whole, 'in this matter') the most probable, in our view, is that the reference is to the three things, righteousness, peace, joy in the Holy Spirit, the singular 'this' ('therein' represents the Greek 'in this') being used because the three things are thought of as forming a single whole. The Christian who serves Christ in this combination of righteousness, peace and joy in the Holy Spirit is well-pleasing to God and, far from causing men to revile the gospel by his selfish conduct, will deserve men's approval—even though he may not always receive it.

19. So then let us pursue what makes for peace and what makes for mutual edification is the practical conclusion drawn from what has just been said. Here 'peace' probably means peace with one's fellow-Christians. The addition of 'and what makes for mutual edification' should probably be understood as serving to fill out and clarify the significance which 'what makes for peace' has in this context rather than as introducing a reference to any further things. What is required is an altogether earnest seeking to promote among brethren such a true peace (based on the fundamental peace with God which God Himself has established in Christ) as must manifest itself in mutual upbuilding. There is a rich biblical background to Paul's use of the word 'edification'.

Here it will perhaps suffice to say that Paul's thought seems to be that God Himself, His apostles and other ministers, and also all the members of the Church, are engaged both in the building of the Church as such and also in the building up, in faith and obedience, of each several member. It is true that the building up of the Church and the building up of the individual members are two aspects of the same process, but the process will hardly be understood in its true wholeness, if either aspect has attention concentrated on it in such a way that the other is lost sight of. That, in so far as the building up is a human activity, it is not just intended to be in one direction, is brought out in this verse (compare 1 Th 5.11).

20. Do not for the sake of *a particular* food destroy God's work. In view of the context, it is more probable that by 'God's work' Paul means God's work in the weak brother, the new man He has begun to make, than the Church which God is building up. **All things are indeed clean** takes up what appears to be a slogan of the strong. As with the statement 'nothing is ritually unclean objectively' in v. 14, we have to understand this in a restricted sense as referring not to such things as men's thoughts, desires and actions, but only to the resources of the created world which are available and appropriate for human consumption. Paul first concedes the truth of this clause, but then qualifies it by the sentence he adds. **but for the man who eats in such a way as results in the presence of a stumbling-block, it (*that is, his eating*) is evil** is a qualification which the strong are liable to overlook. 'the man who eats in such a way as results in the presence of a stumbling-block' has often been understood to be the weak Christian who, under pressure from his strong fellow-Christians who do not share his scruples, eats with a bad conscience, and this interpretation is still favoured by some. But, in view of the context in which Paul's exhortation is directed mainly toward the strong, and especially in view of what follows, it seems better to take the reference to be to the strong Christian who by insisting on eating his meat causes his weak brother to stumble.

21. It is a good thing to abstain from eating meat or drinking wine or *doing* anything else by which thy brother stumbles is an authoritative pronouncement commending as definitely good, in contrast with the evil just mentioned, the unselfish course of action which is open to the strong. That Paul should put here 'to abstain from eating meat' is not at all surprising in view of v. 2 and what has been said since v. 2. The strong Christian who 'has the faith to eat any food' has more room in which to manoeuvre than the weak Christian who 'eats *only* vegetables'. He has the inner freedom not only to eat flesh but also equally to refrain from eating it. So for him to refrain for his weak brother's sake is assuredly good. Paul's continuing with the words 'or drinking wine' is less easy to understand. It is usually taken as definite evidence that the weak, or at any rate some of them, abstained from wine. But it is to be observed that, whereas both abstinence from meat and observance of days are mentioned near the beginning of the section and in a way which makes it quite clear that these are actual practices of the weak, abstinence from wine is not mentioned until the end of chapter 14 and the reference is then to abstinence on the part of the strong, not – except indirectly – to abstinence on the part of the weak. Moreover, 'or drinking wine' is the second of a series of three terms, the third of which is quite indefinite and general. In view of these facts, the possibility that not drinking wine is mentioned simply as an hypothetical example cannot be ruled out. We are indeed inclined to think that this is the most probable explanation of these words. The choice of abstinence from wine as an example could perhaps have been suggested by the use in v. 17 of the stereotyped phrase 'eating and drinking'. The third term of the series, 'or *doing* anything else by which thy brother stumbles', serves both to indicate the comprehensiveness of the pronouncement's scope and also at the same time to underline the requirement of Christian love, already formulated in vv. 13 and 15, that one should be ready to forgo the outward expression of the inner freedom one has received with regard to the sort of matters which Paul has in mind in this section, whenever, by insisting on expressing it outwardly, one would be running the risk of causing the spiritual ruin of a fellow-Christian, by leading him to do something for which he has not received the necessary inner freedom and so cannot do without violating his personal integrity as a believer.

22. The faith which thou hast keep to thyself before God. That 'faith' is here used in its special sense of confidence that one's faith allows one to do a particular thing (see on vv. 1 and 2) is clear –

Paul would not be likely to exhort Christians to make a secret of their faith in the basic sense of faith in God. To be free from the sort of scruples which trouble the weak is in itself a precious gift. The inward freedom does not have to be expressed outwardly in order to be enjoyed: one may enjoy it in one's own inner life – a secret known only to oneself and God. And, if a weak brother is going to be hurt by one's giving outward expression to one's freedom, then one should be content with the inward experience of it, of which God is the only witness.

Blessed is the man who does not condemn himself over what he approves is difficult and has been variously explained. One obvious possibility – it makes a good connexion with what precedes – is to take the sentence to be a declaration of the blessedness of the strong Christian who, heedful of the truths which vv. 21 and 22a set forth, avoids judging or condemning himself (in the sense of bringing God's judgment upon himself) by what he approves (that is, by allowing himself to insist on the outward exercise of his liberty, to the ruin of his weak fellow-Christian). But it would seem, on the whole, preferable to take the words as intended to describe the strong Christian as being truly possessed of the inner freedom to do those things which he approves and therefore untroubled by the scruples which afflict the weak Christian. That the scope of this statement (that is, of v. 22b) is limited to the sort of matter which is at issue between the weak and the strong referred to in this section should go without saying. It is certainly not to be taken as a general statement that Christians who have no doubt about the rightness of what they do are blessed; for that would be merely an assertion of the blessedness of those Christians who have insensitive consciences.

23. But he who is troubled by doubts is condemned if he eats follows naturally upon the previous sentence as we have just explained it. The weak Christian, who has not received that particular inner liberty which his strong brother has received and so is doubtful about the rightness of the action he proposes, is here contrasted with the strong Christian who (as described in the previous sentence) is not troubled by such doubts. And this weak Christian stands condemned, if he eats meat. **because *he does* not do so from faith** indicates why this is so: it is because he has eaten meat without having received the inner freedom to do so, without having full confidence that his faith (in the basic New Testament sense of the word) allows him to do so.

and whatever is not from faith is sin. This sentence has been variously interpreted. But a sober exegesis must surely insist (i) that the statement refers only to the matters which have been under discussion in chapter 14, the matters at issue between the weak and the strong, a statement of universal application being quite inapposite here (it would break the continuity between 14.23a and 15.1); (ii) that 'faith' must be given here the same special sense as it has elsewhere in chapter 14, namely, that of confidence that one's faith permits one to do a particular thing, an inward liberty with regard to it. If these two points are accepted, then there can be no question of understanding Paul to be enunciating a general doctrine about works done before justification or by unbelievers. It should also be said that 'sin' is here used in a different way from that in which Paul characteristically uses it. Here it describes the conduct of the Christian who does a particular action in spite of the fact that he has not received the inner freedom to do it, in contrast with the conduct of the Christian who has received the freedom to do what he is doing. It is thus used in a *relative* way, whereas Paul characteristically thinks of sin as a power from which even the most sincere believer is, in this life, never completely free (compare, especially, 7.14–25).

1–3 may be said to sum up Paul's exhortation to the strong. **But we who are strong have an obligation to carry the infirmities of the weak.** The actual term 'strong' is used here for the first time in this section; and the natural inference to be drawn from 'we who are strong' is that Paul includes himself in their number. Under the gospel the strong, those who, because of the inner freedom which has been given to them, have plenty of room in which to manoeuvre, have an inescapable obligation to help to carry the infirmities, disabilities, embarrassments and encumbrances of their brothers who are having to live without that inner freedom which they themselves enjoy. Their response to this obligation will be a test of the reality of their faith (in the sense of basic Christian faith); for what is required of them is utterly opposed to the tendency of our fallen human nature, which – so far from being to help those weaker than oneself with their burdens – is for the strong to seek to compel the weak to shoulder the burdens of the strong as well as their own. That Paul is still thinking specially of the problem with which he has been concerned in chapter 14 may be taken as certain, though the possibility that already in 15.1 he is beginning to widen the scope of his exhortation, so as to be no longer exclusively concerned with this problem, should perhaps be reckoned with. **and not to please ourselves** serves to clarify what has just been said. This helping to carry the burden of the infirmities which weigh down the weak will involve not pleasing oneself, that is, not pleasing oneself regardless of the effects which one's pleasing oneself would have on others. What Paul is forbidding in particular is that strong Christians should please themselves by insisting on exercising outwardly and to the full that inner freedom which they have been given, when to do so would be to hurt a weak brother's faith.

Let each one of us please his neighbour puts the matter positively. Every strong Christian is to learn to please his neighbour instead of pleasing himself regardless of his neighbour's interest. He is to be considerate, to take due account of the position in which his brother is placed. Compare the use of 'please' in 1 Cor 10.33. But, since not all pleasing of one's fellow-men is good, Paul adds the necessary qualification **for his good with a view to his edification.** The neighbour is very likely to be ready to be pleased by flattery and by the condonement of his wrong-doing; but the pleasing of the neighbour which is here commanded is such a pleasing as has regard to his true good, to his salvation, a pleasing which is directed toward his edification, a pleasing of one's neighbour which is no mere man-pleasing but has regard to God.

For even Christ did not please himself. Paul appeals to Christ's example. The statement 'did not please himself' sums up with eloquent reticence both the meaning of the Incarnation and the character of Christ's earthly life. **but, as scripture says, 'The reproaches of them that reproached thee fell upon me'.** People are often very surprised that, instead of giving an example or examples from the story of Christ's earthly life, Paul should just quote the Old Testament. But Paul's use of the Old Testament here is understandable, when one recognizes how important it was for him that Jesus Christ is the true meaning and substance of the Old Testament and how important for the early Church as a whole to be assured that the scandal of the Passion was an essential element in God's eternal plan, which the scriptures attest. The quotation is from Ps 69.9. In the psalm it is the righteous sufferer who speaks, and the second person singular pronoun refers to God: the reproaches levelled against God have fallen upon this righteous sufferer. As in the psalm, so in this verse of Romans (in spite of some opinions to the contrary) 'thee' must refer to God. Paul thinks of Christ as addressing God and saying that the reproaches with which men reproached God have fallen on Him (Christ). The purpose of the quotation is to indicate the lengths to which Christ went in His not pleasing Himself. If He, for men's sakes, was willing to bear, as one element of His sufferings, the concentration of all men's hatred of God, of all their futile, inanely contemptuous, insolence against God, how absurdly ungrateful should we be, if we could not bring ourselves to renounce our self-gratification in so unimportant a matter as the exercising of our freedom with regard to what we eat or whether we observe special days – for the sake of our brothers for whom He suffered so much!

4. For whatsoever things were written of old *in the scriptures* were written for our instruction, in order that with patient endurance and *strengthened* by the comfort which the scriptures give we might hold hope fast justifies the use, for the purpose of exhortation, of the christologically understood Old Testament passage just quoted. For the general thought of the first half of the verse compare 4.23–24. The second half brings out what Paul sees as the aim of this instruction, that Christians may hold fast their hope. At first sight it might seem rather surprising that Paul should single out hope as the one thing to be mentioned just here; but, in view of the importance of hope in Romans (see 4.18; 5.2, 4f; 8.17–30; 12.12; 15.12f: also 13.11–14) and in the rest of the New Testament, it is not really surprising. To speak of Christians as holding fast their hope is, in fact, a very appropriate way of indicating their continuing to live as Christians.

5–6 is a prayer-wish. For this form compare vv. 13 and 33; 1 Th 5.23; 2 Th 3.5, 16a; 2 Tim 1.16, 18; Heb 13.20–21. Though formally a wish and not a prayer (since in it God is not directly addressed), it is closely akin to prayer. **May the God *who is the source* of patient endurance and of comfort grant you to agree together among yourselves according to Christ Jesus.** From here on for the rest of the section Paul addresses all the Christians of Rome alike and together. It is not easy to decide whether in the present context the agreement referred to must include agreement over those questions about which the weak and the strong are still sincerely disagreeing. At first sight the advantage might seem to lie with the view that it must, and that, in view of 14.14a and the 'we who are strong' of 15.1, Paul's desire must really be – though his sensitiveness prevents him from stating it unambiguously – that the weak may be enabled to be fully convinced of the rightness of the position of the strong. But Paul's whole treatment of his subject throughout this section surely tells strongly against this view. And in this verse his addition of the words 'according to Christ Jesus' suggests that he has not presumed to decide already in his own mind the exact content of the agreement he desires to be given, but is humble enough to leave that decision to Christ the Lord. Such an agreement among the Christians of Rome as is according to the will of Christ Jesus is desired and prayed for; and this may, or may not, include identity of conviction on the matters at issue between the weak and the strong, but must certainly mean a common sincere determination to seek to obey the Lord Jesus Christ together with the mutual respect and sympathy befitting brethen.

in order that you may glorify the God and Father of our Lord Jesus Christ with one heart and one mouth indicates the goal of the desired agreement. Such united praise of God will make impossible the despising and the passing judgment to which 14.3 referred and the heartlessness which can willingly cause a brother to be grieved (14.15) and for a mere food's sake destroy the work of God (14.20).

7. Wherefore introduces the concluding paragraph of the section. The conclusion to be drawn by the Christians of Rome from what has been said in 14.1–15.6 is summed up in the command: **receive one another, because Christ also received you, to the glory of God.** For the meaning of 'receive', as used here, see on 14.1; but, whereas there the church as a whole is contrasted with the individual who is 'weak in faith', here the church is thought of as composed of the two groups, the strong and the weak. Both are to recognize and accept each other sincerely and without reserve. The reason why they must do this is that Christ has accepted them.

(The well-supported variant 'you' should probably be preferred (so Nestle[26]) to 'us', which may be explained as reflecting the usage of worship: 'you' is more pointed.) Their so accepting each other will redound to God's glory. We follow the RV in connecting 'to the glory of God' with 'receive one another' rather than with the clause about Christ, on the ground that this suits the context much better.

8–12 provide additional support for the command of v. 7. That, we take it, is the reason for the **For** by which these verses are connected with what precedes them. **I declare** introduces a solemn doctrinal pronouncement. **that Christ has become the minister of the circumcision for the sake of God's faithfulness, in order to establish the promises made to the fathers** is the first, and less difficult, part of what Paul declares. Christ has become the servant of the Jewish people ('circumcision' here, as in 3.30 and in one of the two occurrences in 4.12, denotes the Jewish people), inasmuch as He was born a Jew, of the seed of David according to the flesh, lived almost all His life within the confines of Palestine, limiting His personal ministry almost exclusively to Jews, and both was in His earthly life and atoning death and also still is, as the exalted Lord, the Messiah of Israel. This was, and is, in order that God's faithfulness to His covenant might be honoured and that Christ might fulfil the promises made to the patriarchs. It is to be noted that in this first part of his solemn doctrinal declaration Paul has underlined yet once more the special priority and privileges of the Jews, and that there is a special significance in his doing this in the present context, since most, if not all, of the weak will have been Jews, and a good many of the strong will have been Gentiles. It might perhaps be a further encouragement to the strong to show considerateness.

but the Gentiles glorify God for his mercy represents a Greek clause which has given a great deal of trouble to interpreters, and has been variously explained. The translation just given is, in our view, by far the most natural way of understanding the Greek. It has been suggested very plausibly that in vv. 8–9a Paul has left unexpressed two of the thoughts which were actually in his mind, first, expecting Jewish Christians in Rome to recognize (without his pointing it out explicitly) that the implication of what he has said in v. 8 is that they, above all others, ought especially to glorify

God for His faithfulness, and, secondly, omitting to state the parallel thought to v. 8, namely, that Christ has called the Gentiles for the sake of God's mercy, in order to manifest His kindness, and, instead, simply indicating that the Gentiles are glorifying God for His mercy – the present action which is the result of their having recognized the implication of this truth which Paul has omitted to state.

even as it is written in scripture, 'Wherefore I will praise thee among the Gentiles and sing hymns to thy name'. The first of the series of four supporting Old Testament quotations is from Ps 18.49. It is sometimes assumed that the series of quotations is intended simply to support v. 9a; but, in view of the close connexion between vv. 8 and 9a, it seems more likely that it is intended as support for the whole of vv. 8–9a, and that Paul saw in all four quotations the combination of Jews and Gentiles in the believing community foreshadowed. Whether Paul took the first quotation as words of the Jewish king David spoken in his own name (the psalm is one that is ascribed to David) or as a foreshadowing of his own mission as the Jewish apostle of the Gentiles or (and this is perhaps most likely) as messianic, a promise of the proclamation of the praise of God by the exalted Messiah of the Jews speaking by the mouths of His evangelists, he is surely likely to have seen in this psalm-word support not only for v. 9a but also for v. 8. **and again it says, 'Rejoice, you Gentiles, together with his people'.** The quotation of Deut 32.43, as an express summons to the Gentiles to rejoice together with God's own people, may clearly be regarded as support for the declaration of vv. 8–9a as a whole, and for the command in v. 7. **and again, 'Praise the Lord, all you Gentiles, and let all the peoples praise him'.** The third supporting quotation (Ps 117.1), with its repetition of 'all', stresses the fact that no people is to be excluded from this common praise of God. **And again Isaiah says, 'There shall be the scion of Jesse, and he who rises to rule the Gentiles: on him shall the Gentiles hope'.** The last quotation is from Isa 11.10. The word we have represented by 'scion' ordinarily means 'root', but in Isa 11.10 both it and the Hebrew word it renders probably denote a shoot springing from the root, a scion. In the quotation of the promise that Gentiles shall hope in the coming scion of Jesse, the Messiah of the Jews, a promise now already being fulfilled in the lives of the Gentile Christians in Rome, there is an implicit appeal to the strong (many of them Gentile Christians) to receive (compare v. 7), and show considerateness to, those weak brothers (most, if not all, of them Jewish Christians), according them special honour for the sake of their Kinsman, the Messiah of the Jews, who is the Gentiles' only true hope.

13. May the God of hope fill you with all joy and peace in believing, so that you may abound in hope by the power of the Holy Spirit. This prayer-wish concludes the section. Its fulfilment would carry with it, as Barth notes, the success of all the exhortation of this section and, indeed, from 12.1 onward. There is real point in the inclusion of the phrase 'in believing'; for it serves to qualify 'joy' and 'peace'. There are sorts of joy and peace which Paul certainly does not desire for the Christians of Rome: what he does desire is all the joy and peace which result from true faith in Christ. The double reference to hope in this verse is specially significant. An essential characteristic of the believer, as this epistle has very clearly shown, hope is perhaps also that characteristic which has at all periods most strikingly distinguished the authentic Christian from his pagan neighbours. The last phrase, 'by the power of the Holy Spirit', indicates the fact that the existence in men of this hope is no human possibility but the creation of the Spirit of God. Compare chapter 8, in which Paul has shown that it is because the life promised for those who are righteous by faith is a life characterized by the indwelling of the Holy Spirit that it is also a life characterized by hope.

VIII

CONCLUSION TO THE EPISTLE
(15.14–16.27)

In 15.14–29 Paul takes up again the subject with which he was concerned in 1.8–16a, namely, that of his interest in, and his intention to visit, the Christians in Rome. He emphasizes his confidence in their Christian maturity, so as to prevent possible misinterpretation of the boldness which he is conscious of having shown in part of his letter. His words of explanation in v. 15 lead naturally into some statements in vv. 16–21 about his ministry as apostle of the Gentiles. It is the demands which this ministry as he has understood it have made upon him which have so far hindered him from visiting Rome (v. 22). The unfinished sentence which forms vv. 23 and 24a contains the first mention in the epistle of Spain and of Paul's purpose to go there; and the latter part of v. 24 discloses his hope that on his way thither he may at last visit the Christians who are in Rome and, having enjoyed their fellowship for a while, be assisted by them in the accomplishment of his Spanish plans. But, before he can come to them, he must go to Jerusalem in connexion with the collection which the churches of Macedonia and Achaia have made on behalf of the poor of the church in Jerusalem (vv. 25–29). Verses 30–33 consist of his request for the Roman Christians' earnest prayers for himself and for the success of his visit to Jerusalem and a prayer-wish for the Christians in Rome.

On the question of the relation of chapter 16 to the rest of the epistle the reader may be referred to pp. ix–xi.

The first two verses of chapter 16 are Paul's commendation of Phoebe, the bearer of his letter. Verses 3–15 are a series of greetings to named individuals and other, unnamed, Christians associated with some of these in church life and also to two other easily identifiable groups of Christians (vv. 10b and 11b). Verse 16 bids the Roman Christians greet one another with a holy kiss, and assures them of the greetings of all the churches of Christ.

In vv. 17–20a we have a piece of pastoral counsel, warning them to be on their guard against plausible false teachers and encouraging them to continue to live up to their good reputation. Verse 20b is Paul's customary concluding greeting written in his own hand. It is followed by a postscript consisting of greetings from persons who are with Paul, including (v. 22) that of Tertius whose hand it has been which has actually written the letter. Verses 25–27, though unlikely (we think) to be Pauline, form (when the Greek is correctly construed) a not unfitting doxological appendage to the epistle.

[14]**But, as to myself, I too am persuaded, my brothers, concerning you, that you yourselves are full of honesty, being filled with all knowledge, able also to admonish one another.** [15]**But in part** *of my letter* **I have written to you rather boldly, as putting you again in remembrance because of the grace given me from God** [16]**to be a minister of Christ Jesus unto the Gentiles, serving God's message of good news with a holy service, in order that the offering consisting of the Gentiles may be acceptable, having been sanctified by the Holy Spirit.** [17]**This glorying then I have in Christ Jesus with regard to what pertains to God;** [18]**for I am not going to dare to speak of anything of the things which Christ has not wrought through me to bring about obedience of the Gentiles, by word and deed,** [19]**in the power of signs and wonders, in the power of the Spirit, so that from Jerusalem and round even to Illyricum I have fulfilled the message of good news of Christ.** [20]**But I made it my earnest endeavour so to preach the good news not where Christ had already been named, that I might not build upon another man's foundation,** [21]**but, as it is written, 'They shall see, to whom it has not been announced concerning him, and those who have not heard shall understand'.** [22]**Wherefore I have also been hindered these many times from coming to you:** [23]**But now, no longer having room in these regions and having for enough years desired to come to you** [24]**whenever I should go to Spain (for I hope to see you on my way and to be set forward by you on my journey thither, having first in some measure had my fill of your company) –** [25]**but now I am going to Jerusalem to minister to the saints.** [26]**For Macedonia and Achaia have resolved to make a contribution for the**

poor among the saints in Jerusalem. [27]They have resolved to do this, and, indeed, they are under an obligation to them; for, if the Gentiles have partaken of their spiritual good things, then they are under an obligation to render them service in the things necessary for their bodily welfare. [28]So, when I have completed this task and sealed for them this fruit, I shall set out for Spain by way of you*r city*. [29]And I know that, when I do come to you, it will be with the fullness of Christ's blessing that I shall come.

[30]I exhort you [, brethren,] by our Lord Jesus Christ and by the love of the Spirit to join earnestly with me in prayers on my behalf to God, [31]that I may be delivered from the disobedient in Judaea and that my ministry to Jerusalem may be acceptable to the saints, [32]so that, if it be God's will, my coming to you may be a matter of joy and I may find full refreshment in your fellowship.

[33]May the God of peace be with you all. Amen.

[1]I commend to you Phoebe, our sister who is [also] a deacon of the church in Cenchreae, [2]that you may give her a welcome in the Lord that is worthy of the saints, and assist her in any matter in which she may need your help; for she herself has been a source of assistance to many, myself included.

[3]Greet Prisca and Aquila, my fellow-workers in Christ Jesus, [4]who risked their necks to save my life and to whom not only I but all the churches of the Gentiles are grateful, [5]and the church in their house. Greet my beloved Epaenetus, who is Asia's firstfruits for Christ. [6]Greet Mary who laboured much for you. [7]Greet Andronicus and Junia, my kinsfolk and fellow-prisoners, who are outstanding among the apostles and who also were in Christ before me. [8]Greet Ampliatus, my beloved in the Lord. [9]Greet Urbanus, our fellow-worker in Christ, and my beloved Stachys. [10]Greet Apelles who has been proved in Christ. Greet the *brethren* among the members of the household of Aristobulus. [11]Greet Herodion my kinsman. Greet those from the household of Narcissus who are in the Lord. [12]Greet Tryphaena and Tryphosa who labour in the Lord. Greet Persis the beloved, who has laboured much in the Lord. [13]Greet Rufus, the elect in the Lord, and his mother who is also a mother to me. [14]Greet Asyncritus, Phlegon, Hermes, Patrobas, Hermas, and the brethren who are with them. [15]Greet Philologus and Julia, Nereus and his sister, and Olympas, and all the saints who are with them. [16]Greet one another with a holy kiss. All the churches of Christ greet you.

¹⁷I exhort you, brethren, to mark those who cause divisions and occasions of stumbling in opposition to the teaching you have learned. Avoid them; ¹⁸for such people serve not our Lord Christ but their own bellies, and deceive the hearts of the simple by their high-sounding plausibility. ¹⁹For your obedience is known to all, and for this I rejoice over you. But I want you to be wise unto that which is good, but kept pure from what is evil. ²⁰And the God of peace shall crush Satan under your feet soon.

The grace of our Lord Jesus be with you.

²¹Timothy, my fellow-worker, greets you, and *so do* Lucius and Jason and Sosipater, my kinsmen. ²²I, Tertius, who have written this letter, greet you in the Lord. ²³Gaius, my host (and, indeed, the whole church's), greets you. Erastus, the city treasurer, and brother Quartus greet you.

²⁵To him who is able to confirm you in accord with my gospel and the proclamation of Jesus Christ, *which is* according to the revelation of the mystery which has been hidden in silence for ages from before creation ²⁶but has now been manifested and, in accordance with the command of the eternal God, has been clarified through the prophetic scriptures for the purpose of bringing about obedience of faith among all the Gentiles, – ²⁷to the only wise God, through Jesus Christ, to him be glory for ever and ever. Amen.

14. But, as to myself, I too am persuaded, my brothers, concerning you, that you yourselves are full of honesty, being filled with all knowledge, able also to admonish one another is often regarded as an attempt at blandishment. But it is difficult to believe that Paul is likely to have thought that the Christians in Rome, if they were not favourably disposed to him after reading or hearing fourteen and a half chapters of his epistle, could be won over at this stage by a flattering sentence. It seems more probable that he felt that, in addressing the particular exhortation of 12.1–15.13 to a church which he had not himself founded and which he had so far never even visited, he had taken a liberty (compare what is said on the following verse), with reference to which, while, in view of his commission as apostle of the Gentiles, there was no need of any apology, some explanation would be appropriate. Nothing which he had said in 12.1–15.13 had been intended as a calling in question of the spiritual adulthood of the Christians in Rome.

Paul recognized – something which the clergy have too often been apt to forget – that it is courteous to assume that one's fellow-Christians are moderately mature until they have given positive evidence of their immaturity. What we have here is Christian courtesy, not flattery. The words 'as to myself, . . . too' emphasize Paul's personal commitment to the conviction expressed, and 'yourselves' underlines his acknowledgment of the Roman Christians' adulthood as Christians. It is his right and his duty to expect them to be frank in their dealings and to have a firm grasp of the truth of the gospel, and so to be capable of admonishing one another.

15–16. But in part *of my letter* I have written to you rather boldly. In the preceding main division of the letter (12.1–15.13) he has indeed taken a certain liberty in that he has addressed quite particular exhortation to a church which he has not himself founded nor even visited. The words **as putting you again in remembrance** express the thought that in his exhortation he has been appealing to knowledge already possessed by the Roman Christians. **because of the grace given me from God to be a minister of Christ Jesus unto the Gentiles, serving God's message of good news with a holy service** indicates the basis of Paul's authority to put the Roman Christians in remembrance. It is that he has received a commission from God which is altogether God's gracious gift, something which he has in no way merited.

Important for the understanding of the nature of this commission as Paul views it is the Greek word represented here by 'minister'. It was used in 13.6 in connexion with the civil authorities. That in the present passage it has some sort of sacral or cultic sense is strongly suggested by 'serving . . . with a holy service' and more than one expression in the latter part of v. 16. But it does not follow that the generally accepted view that Paul is thinking of himself as exercising a priestly ministry is necessarily to be upheld. The fact that the verb and the abstract noun, which are cognate with the Greek personal noun used here, while they are quite often used in the Septuagint Old Testament with reference to priests, are specially frequently used in connexion with the Levites suggests the possibility that Paul was thinking of himself as fulfilling the function of a Levite rather than that of a priest. The dependent 'of Christ Jesus' would, in fact, be surprising, if 'minister' were used in the sense of 'priest': much more natural in that case would be 'of God'. But, if Paul used the word translated 'minister' with the intention of signifying the Levite who assisted the priest, then the genitive 'of Christ Jesus' presents no difficulty at all: Paul's commission is to be an attendant of the Priest Jesus Christ, having a ministry which is altogether subordinate and auxiliary to His. That this explanation of 'minister' should be accepted is, in our judgment, highly probable. The words which follow 'Christ Jesus' indicate the activity in which Paul's ministry consists. It is directed towards the Gentiles and is 'a holy service' of the gospel message.

in order that the offering consisting of the Gentiles may be acceptable, having been sanctified by the Holy Spirit indicates the divine purpose behind the commission. As the purpose of the due fulfilment by the Levites of their subordinate and auxiliary role in the cultus was that the sacrifices offered by the priests might be acceptable to God, so Paul's preaching of the gospel to the Gentiles is a service subordinate and auxiliary to Christ's priestly service of offering them to God as a sacrifice, and the preaching of the gospel is a necessary service if that sacrifice is to be truly well-pleasing to God, including in itself the willing and intelligent response of their gratitude for all that God has done for them in Christ. 'sanctified by the Holy Spirit' fills out the meaning of 'acceptable'. The sacrifice offered to God by Christ, which Paul has here in mind, consists of the Gentile Christians who have been sanctified by the gift of the Spirit.

17. This glorying then I have in Christ Jesus with regard to what pertains to God. Paul is asserting that the glorying which he has allowed himself in v. 16 is a legitimate glorying, since it is a glorying in Christ concerned with what truly pertains to God, being a glorying in the results of his mission viewed not as his achievements (so to have understood them would indeed have been to glory in man), but as the works of Christ in obedience to the will of God.

18–19a. for I am not going to dare to speak of anything of the things which Christ has not wrought through me to bring about obedience of the Gentiles, by word and deed, in the power of signs and wonders, in the power of the Spirit explains how it is that the glorying contained in v. 16 is really, as v. 17 has claimed that it is, a

365

glorying 'in Christ Jesus with regard to what pertains to God'. It is because Paul has no intention of presuming to refer to anything other than what Christ has wrought through him. What Paul has done as the minister of Christ Jesus has not only been a subordinate service subsidiary to Christ's own priestly work, it has also been something which Christ has actually Himself effected, working through His minister. It is probable that 'word' here includes words spoken and written, and 'deed' things done and suffered, conduct generally, while the two following phrases characterize Paul's ministry as powerfully confirmed by accompanying miracles and also accomplished as a whole in the power of the Holy Spirit.

19b. so that from Jerusalem and round even to Illyricum I have fulfilled the message of good news of Christ. The point of 'so that' is probably that the progress of the gospel here described is the result of the work of Christ through Paul referred to in vv. 18–19a. Jerusalem is probably mentioned as being the starting-point of the Christian mission generally and in a real sense Paul's own spiritual base as well as that of the Jewish Christian mission (compare vv. 25–31, especially v. 27). An evangelistic activity by Paul in Jerusalem is not implied. The word represented by 'round' may be understood as referring to the fact that the area covered in his preaching can be described as a great arc. Whether 'even to' is used inclusively or exclusively is not clear, and 'Illyricum' could conceivably denote a part of the province of Macedonia inhabited by people of Illyrian race, though it is more natural to take it to mean the Roman province of Illyricum. We are nowhere else informed of Paul's having gone 'even to Illyricum' in any of the senses the phrase could bear; but it is not at all impossible that he reached the border of the province of Illyricum or that he crossed it (if he followed the Via Egnatia to its western end at Dyrrhachium (Durazzo or Durrës), he would have been close enough to the border to be able to say without too great exaggeration that he had gone 'even to (the province of) Illyricum'; for Lissus (Lesh), which was within it, was only about forty miles away), and to have approached or entered a part of Macedonia that might be referred to as Illyrian he would have had to go less far. The period of time indicated by the last few words of v. 1 and the first part of v. 2 of Acts 20 may well have been long enough to allow such a journey. That the function of the phrase is to indicate the north-western limit of the area Paul has covered is clear.

Still to be considered are the words 'I have fulfilled the message of good news of Christ'. There has recently been a good deal of support for the view that Paul's meaning is that he has completed, as far as the area indicated is concerned, all the preaching of the gospel which must be done before the Parousia (compare Mk 13.10). This explanation fits well, of course, the widespread assumption that it is an 'assured result' of modern New Testament scholarship that the primitive Church was sure that the End would come within a few years; but it would seem that Paul has himself given in the next two verses a fairly clear clue to his meaning, and, in view of their contents, we understand his claim to have fulfilled the gospel of Christ to be a claim to have completed that trail-blazing, pioneer preaching of it, which he believed it was his own special apostolic mission to accomplish.

20–21. But I made it my earnest endeavour so to preach the good news not where Christ had already been named, that I might not build upon another man's foundation, but, as it is written, 'They shall see, to whom it has not been announced concerning him, and those who have not heard shall understand'. This qualifies the claim made in v. 19b: Paul's statement that he has completed the gospel in the area mentioned is not to be taken in an absolute sense but in relation to what he understands to be his own particular function in the service of the gospel, namely, that of a pioneer preacher. The decisive ground of his eagerness is neither to avoid possible rivalry nor yet to cover as wide an area as possible, but his understanding of the nature of the particular commission entrusted to him by God, confirmation of which he sees in the scriptural words he is about to quote. The passive of the verb 'to name' is here more probably used with some such solemn sense as 'be named in worship' or 'be acknowledged and confessed' or 'be proclaimed (as Lord)' than as signifying merely 'be known'.

Some have felt that there is an inconsistency between v. 20 and Paul's intention of visiting Rome, and it has been suggested that the breaking-off of the sentence at the end of v. 24 may be the result of his embarrassment on account of his consciousness of it. But that there is inconsistency between this verse and Paul's visiting Rome is only to be maintained on the assumption that Paul thought of the particular commission which he believed God had entrusted to him in a singularly rigid, unimaginative and legalistic way, quite out of keeping with all we know about him. And v. 20f is anyway not a statement of an absolute rule to be followed irrespectively of all other considerations, but a statement of Paul's own earnest desire and endeavour, grounded in his understanding of God's special assignment to him, to act as a pioneer missionary rather than as one who builds upon foundations already laid by another. There is no suggestion here that he felt himself under an absolute obligation to refrain from ever visiting a church which had been founded by someone else; and Rome was after all a very special case.

The Old Testament quotation is from Isa 52.15 (Paul follows almost exactly the Septuagint which brings out more clearly the reference to the Servant of the Lord than does the Hebrew text). Paul sees the words of the prophet as a promise which is even now being fulfilled by the spreading of the knowledge of Christ, the true Servant of Yahweh, to those who have not yet heard of Him, accomplished by his own mission.

22. Wherefore I have also been hindered these many times from coming to you. In 1.13 no indication was given as to what had hindered: here an indication is given. What has hindered Paul from fulfilling his purpose to visit Rome so far has been the demands of his missionary labours. The 'Wherefore' is more naturally taken as referring back to the missionary activity described in v. 19b (to which v. 20f was, as we understood it, a necessary qualification) than as referring to the principle (stated in v. 20f) of not preaching where Christ has already been named.

23–24a. The sentence which begins with **But now** is broken off, there being no main verb expressing what Paul is about to do.

no longer having room in these regions is no doubt to be understood in close connexion with v. 19b, and, if we were right in our interpretation of that half-verse, Paul's meaning here is simply that his presence is no longer required in the regions in which he has laboured up till now, since in them the pioneer work of evangelism which is his special task has already been accomplished. Those who take 'fulfilled the message of good news' to denote the completion of the preaching which has to be done before the Parousia are naturally inclined to explain these words accordingly. But to say, as Barrett does, that 'Since the eastern end of the Mediterranean had been dealt with and Paul had "no more scope in these parts" there remained for missionary work the north coast of Africa (from Alexandria to the province of Africa), Gaul, and Spain', is surely to attribute to Paul a notion which it is altogether unlikely that he could ever have entertained. There might be a certain superficial plausibility in maintaining that the early Church thought of only a token preaching to all nations as having to be accomplished before the Parousia; but, when once we begin to speak in terms of lists of countries remaining to be evangelized, the obligation to ask about the probable extent of Paul's geographical knowledge can scarcely be evaded. To think of him as oblivious of the existence of territories figuring prominently in the Old Testament is surely impossible. He himself uses elsewhere the name 'Scythian'. It is hardly conceivable that any intelligent Roman citizen of Paul's time could be ignorant of the existence of Parthia or of Britain, the southern part of which had been conquered by Claudius's troops only a few years before the epistle was written, or of Germany, where a Roman army had been destroyed in the reign of Augustus and from which the adopted son of the Emperor Tiberius had taken his surname of 'Germanicus'. One who had travelled as much as Paul and mixed with different sorts of people would surely have heard of India (it is quite often mentioned by Greek and Latin authors) and other far-distant lands, the products of which found their way to Rome (it is interesting that the Greek word translated 'silk' in Rev 18.12 is derived from an ancient name for the Chinese). The notion that Paul thought, when he dictated vv. 19b and 23a, that he had completed all the preaching to the Gentiles which needed to be accomplished before the Parousia, as far as the east was concerned, and was hoping himself to deal with the west, should surely be abandoned.

and having for enough years desired to come to you whenever I should go to Spain. This is the first mention of Paul's intention to go to Spain (he made no mention of it in 1.8–16a) and the only other reference to Spain in the New Testament is in v. 28, apart from 'thither' later in v. 24. Whether Paul ever did get to Spain is uncertain (as far as the interpretation of Romans is concerned, the question is not really of any great importance: what is relevant is simply that at the time of writing it he was hoping to go there); but 1 Clement 5.7 would seem to be fairly strong evidence in favour of the view that he did get there, since 'the limits of the west' can scarcely refer to anywhere other than Spain in a document written in Rome and it is difficult to believe that firm information about the end of Paul's life was not readily available in the Roman church in the last decade of the first century, when people who had known him must surely still have been alive.

That Paul should have decided to embark on the evangelization of Spain is in no way surprising. Many centuries before Christ the Phoenicians of Tyre had colonized Cadiz. Later Phocaean colonists had settled in Spain, and they had been followed by colonists from their own colony of Marseilles. Later still (in the third century B.C.) Carthage had conquered large territories in Spain, and New Carthage (Cartagena) had been founded. Towards the end of the third century B.C. the Carthaginians had been driven out by Scipio Africanus, and Rome had held territory in Spain from that time onward, though it was not till the time of Augustus that the whole Iberian peninsula had been subjugated by the Romans and organized in three provinces. By Paul's time a good deal of Spain was thoroughly romanized, though some parts (particularly the north-west) were much less civilized. It is likely that there were by this time some Jewish settlements, and Paul may well have hoped that these would afford him some openings.

24b. (for I hope to see you on my way and to be set forward by you on my journey thither, having first in some measure had my fill of your company) is a parenthetic explanation of the substance of the preceding incomplete sentence. Paul hopes to visit the Roman Christians in the course of his journey to Spain and to receive from them active help towards the carrying out of his proposed mission. Exactly how much in this way of help and support for his Spanish mission Paul hoped to receive from the Christians of Rome we cannot tell; but it seems extremely likely that he hoped for considerably more than a mere- farewell accompanied with prayers and good wishes. He may well have hoped, for example, that Roman Christians with a knowledge of Spain might be commissioned to accompany him thither. The last clause indicates his wish to enjoy, before being sent onward on his travels by them , at any rate some measure of fellowship with them – though it cannot be enough to be all the fellowship that he would like to have with them.

25. – but now I am going to Jerusalem to minister to the saints. Before Paul can direct his course towards Rome he must go to Jerusalem (compare Acts 19.21; 20.3, 16, etc.) with the collection which the Gentile churches have made on behalf of the poor among the Jerusalem Christians. With regard to the Greek word here rendered by 'minister' see on 12.7 ('practical service'). An earlier collection for the Jerusalem church is mentioned in Acts 11.27–30; 12.25. For the collection to which the present verse refers compare Acts 24.17; 1 Cor 16.1–4; 2 Corinthians 8–9, and also Gal 2.10a. That Paul regarded this collection as of great importance is clear from the rest of this chapter and the passages cited above from 1 and 2 Corinthians. No doubt he thought of it as likely to contribute to the cause of unity between the Gentile and Jewish parts of the Church (compare vv. 27 and 31b) as well as being an appropriate response to human need on the part of Christians in a position to make such a response, an act of love – in this case, of brotherly love. But Barrett's 'politic expedient' is misleading even as an expressly partial description of it. That 'it was intended to play a vital part among the events of the last days' (Barrett) is true in the sense that every action which is truly an act of Christian love fulfils a vital part in the history (as seen by God) of that period which (whether short or long) is determined by the fact that it began with the Incarnation and is to end with the Parousia (compare on 13.12); but there is no good reason, as far as we can see, for thinking it true, if it was meant to imply that Paul was confidently expecting his collection to be among the events of the last few years before the Parousia.

26. For Macedonia and Achaia have resolved to make a contribution for the poor among the saints in Jerusalem explains the previous verse. The use of 'resolve' indicates that the offering was the result of a decision freely and responsibly taken by the churches concerned. There is no need to see any inconsistency between this emphasis and the evidence in 1 Cor 16.1–4 and 2 Corinthians 8–9 of Paul's own eager and energetic promotion of the collection; for a Christian's decision to do what is right is no less his own free personal decision because he has been enabled to recognize, and strengthened to do, his duty by the faithful exhortation of another Christian. The suggestion that the collection was actually a levy imposed on Paul's churches by the Jerusalem church authorities, and that Paul is deliberately playing this aspect down and seeking to represent the offering of his churches as a purely voluntary gift of love, we find unconvincing.

27. They have resolved to do this underlines the freedom and independence of the decision of the Macedonian and Achaian churches. But now another aspect of the matter, which is also important, is brought out by **and, indeed, they are under an obligation to them.** The Gentile churches are indebted to these poor ones, because they are indebted to the Jerusalem church as a whole in the way the next sentence makes clear. **for, if the Gentiles have partaken of their spiritual good things, then they are under an obligation to render them service in the things necessary for their bodily welfare.** Since the Gentile Christians have received the gospel message itself and the whole tradition of the works and words of Jesus, and indeed all the spiritual blessings which have come to them by the Gentile mission, through the mediation of the original Jerusalem church, they are clearly under an obligation to afford what material help they can to the specially needy among the members of the Jerusalem church, though such material aid could never repay their debt.

28. So, when I have completed this task and sealed for them this fruit, I shall set out for Spain by way of your *city* sums up Paul's statement of his plans. That the 'fruit' referred to is to be identified with the total of the collection is scarcely to be doubted. Paul's use of 'seal' here has been variously explained. Most probably the reference is to the confirmation (whether by the act of handing over or by words spoken) of the collection's significance as the token of the Gentile churches' love and gratitude to the Jerusalem church or as the fruit of the spiritual blessings which have been mediated by the Jerusalem church to the Gentiles.

29. And I know that, when I do come to you, it will be with the fullness of Christ's blessing that I shall come expresses Paul's firm confidence that, when at last he does come to the Christians in Rome, he will come with Christ's sure blessing.

30–32. I exhort you [, brethren,] is the beginning of a new paragraph, in which Paul expresses his desire for the prayers of the

Roman Christians. **by our Lord Jesus Christ and by the love of the Spirit** indicates the authority invoked and the ground of appeal in Paul's urgent request. The phrase 'the love of the Spirit' means 'the love which the Spirit works', that love between Christians which is the effect of the Holy Spirit's indwelling. **to join earnestly with me in prayers on my behalf to God** probably gives the sense of the original. Some interpreters' insistence that the idea of wrestling is contained in the Greek verb which is used is not borne out by Greek usage, and the suggestion that Paul had in mind Gen 32.22–32 seems unlikely in view of the fact that in the Septuagint version of that passage two quite different verbs, having no connexion with the verb used here, are used in vv. 24, 25 and 28. What Paul is entreating them to do is simply to pray for him and with him, not half-heartedly or casually, but with earnestness, urgency and persistence.

Paul knows well that he is the object of fierce hostility on the part of the unbelieving Jews and that a special concentration of this hostility must be expected in Judaea and particularly in Jerusalem itself – hence **that I may be delivered from the disobedient in Judaea.** The clause **and that my ministry to Jerusalem may be acceptable to the saints** is claimed by some as evidence of serious tension between Paul and the Jerusalem church. Some tension there doubtless was; but any one who has had any considerable experience not just in organizing a church's collection of money for charitable purposes but also in the actual passing on of it to those in need will know full well that its being acceptable is no foregone conclusion, and will be more likely to recognize in these words evidence of Paul's spiritual and human sensitivity and freedom from self-centred complacency than to draw from them any confident conclusions about the tension between the Jerusalem church and Paul.

so that, if it be God's will, my coming to you may be a matter of joy and I may find full refreshment in your fellowship expresses the more distant hope which the fulfilment of the twofold prayer indicated in v. 31 will make possible of realization. Both deliverance from the dangers threatening him from the side of the unbelieving Jews and also the peace of mind resulting from the truly brotherly acceptance of the Gentile churches' gifts by the Jerusalem church are necessary to Paul, if his coming to Rome is really to be fraught with joy and he is to find full refreshment there in Christian fellowship.

33. May the God of peace be with you all. Amen. A prayer-wish concludes this part of the final division. Here 'peace' probably signifies the sum of all true blessings including final salvation. By calling God 'the God of peace' Paul is characterizing Him as the Source and Giver of all true blessings, the God who is both willing and able to help and save to the uttermost. The sense is well brought out in P. Doddridge's paraphrase of Heb 13.20f ('Father of peace, and God of love') by the words 'We own Thy power to save'.

1–2. I commend to you Phoebe begins the commendation of the woman who was, we may presume, the bearer of the letter. That she was a Gentile Christian may be inferred from her name; for a Jewess would scarcely have had a name deriving from pagan mythology. With such a name she may well have been a freedwoman. **our sister** indicates her membership of the Christian community. Paul continues: **who is [also] a deacon of the church in Cenchreae.** Cenchreae was the eastern port of Corinth. While it is perhaps just conceivable that the word *diakonos* should be understood here as a quite general reference to her service of the congregation, it is very much more natural to take it to refer to a definite office. We regard it as virtually certain that Phoebe is being described as 'a (or possibly 'the') deacon' of the church in question, and that this occurrence of *diakonos* is to be classified with its occurrences in Phil 1.1 and 1 Tim 3.8 and 12. And, while it is true that the functions of a *diakonos* are not expressly indicated in Phil 1.1 or in 1 Tim 3.8ff or in the present two verses, there is nothing in any of these passages in any way inconsonant with the inherent probability that a specialized use of *diakonos* in New Testament times will have corresponded to the clearly attested specialized use of the cognate verb and abstract noun with reference to the practical service of the needy, and there are some features, for example, what is said about Phoebe in v. 2b, which would seem to afford it some support. (Compare what was said on 12.7a and 8b.) It is interesting that this is the first time that the word 'church' has occurred in Romans.

that you may give her a welcome in the Lord that is worthy of the saints, and assist her in any matter in which she may need your help. Paul wants the Christians in Rome to welcome Phoebe 'in the

Lord', that is, as Christians receiving a fellow-Christian, beloved for the Lord's sake, and loyally to afford her whatever assistance she may stand in need of. **for she herself has been a source of assistance to many, myself included** is a further reason why they should readily help her. The choice of the particular Greek word which we have rendered by 'a source of assistance' might perhaps suggest that she was possessed of some wealth and independence.

3–5a. Greet Prisca and Aquila is the first of a series of greetings which extends without a break to the end of v. 15 (so long a list of greetings, though without a parallel elsewhere in the New Testament, makes quite good sense in connexion with v. 1f, since it would have served to give Phoebe an immediate introduction to a large number of individuals in the Christian community in Rome). The two are always mentioned together in the New Testament, the wife's name being given in its diminutive form of 'Priscilla' in Acts but its proper form of 'Prisca' in the epistles. Aquila is described in Acts 18.2 as 'a certain Jew . . . , a man of Pontus by race', and, unless fairly strong grounds can be shown for thinking otherwise, the probability that his wife also was Jewish must be reckoned very high. Apparently the couple had been established in Rome, since their presence in Corinth is explained as due to the edict of Claudius by which Jews had been expelled from Rome. As Aquila was a tentmaker like Paul, as well as being a Christian, Paul made his home with them in Corinth. When, after eighteen months in Corinth, Paul set out for Syria, they accompanied him as far as Ephesus. It was from Ephesus that they sent their greetings and the greetings of the church 'in their house' to the church in Corinth (1 Cor 16.19). That Prisca and Aquila should be back in Rome at the time of the writing of the epistle is in no way surprising, as the edict of Claudius had lapsed, and those who had been expelled probably lost no time in returning. The interesting fact that in the New Testament this particular wife's name is more often than not placed before her husband's is probably to be explained as due either to her having been converted before him or to her having played an even more prominent part in the life and work of the church than he had.

Paul's description of Prisca and Aquila as **my fellow-workers in Christ Jesus** illustrates the emphasis on working which is characteristic of this greetings-list (compare vv. 6, 9, 12a and b).

For Paul, being a Christian involves being set to work, participating actively and responsibly in the work of the gospel. With feeling Paul adds **who risked their necks to save my life and to whom not only I but all the churches of the Gentiles are grateful.** It may have been during the disturbance at Ephesus related in Acts 19.23–40 that they risked their lives to save Paul's life, but we cannot be certain.

With **and the church in their house** compare 1 Cor 16.19 (also referring to Prisca and Aquila); Col 4.15; Philem 2. Grammatically the Greek phrase rendered by 'the church in their house' could certainly mean the church consisting simply of the Christian members of their household ('household' denoting not just the family in our sense of the word 'family' but also their slaves, employees, and other dependants); but it is not to be doubted that what is meant is rather the community of Christians regularly meeting in their house, including, in addition to the Christian members of the household or *familia*, other Christians for whom it was convenient to meet for worship in their house. There were of course no buildings specially appropriated to church purposes at this time.

5b. Greet my beloved Epaenetus, who is Asia's firstfruits for Christ. He is not mentioned anywhere else in the New Testament. His name makes it likely he was a Gentile. Apparently he was the first convert or one of the first converts of the province of Asia (compare 1 Cor 16.15). The description of him as Paul's 'beloved' should not be taken to imply that he was more beloved than those who are not so described. Paul seems to have tried to attach some expression of kindly commendation to all the individuals he mentions. He has managed to keep this up (apart from v. 10b) right to the end of v. 13; but with v. 14 he simply lists names.

6. Greet Mary who laboured much for you. Elsewhere in English versions of the New Testament 'Mary' represents either a transliteration of the Hebrew 'Miriam' or a Hellenized form of that name: in this instance it is possible that the name is Roman, 'Maria', the feminine form of 'Marius'. Whether the woman referred to was a Jewish Christian or a Gentile is therefore uncertain. Note again the reference to working.

7. Greet Andronicus and Junia, my kinsfolk and fellow-prisoners, who are outstanding among the apostles and who also were in Christ

before me. That the the fourth Greek word of the verse should be accentuated as the accusative of the common Roman female name Junia is hardly to be doubted. The persistence of the accentuation which makes it the accusative of an hypothetical masculine name Junias (for example, in Nestle[26]) seems to rest on nothing more solid than conventional prejudice (compare Lietzmann's confident assertion that the possibility of the name's being a woman's is ruled out by the context). There seems to be no clear evidence of the supposed masculine name's having existed. Most probably Andronicus and Junia were husband and wife. By 'kinsfolk' Paul almost certainly means just fellow-Jews (compare vv. 11 and 21). We have no knowledge of a time when Paul and Andronicus and Junia were prisoners together, though it is not impossible that there was such an occasion (Paul had already been 'in prisons' more abundantly than his adversaries, according to 2 Cor 11.23). It would, however, be not unnatural for him to call them his fellow-prisoners, if they, like him, had been prisoners for Christ's sake, though not actually together with him.

It is grammatically possible to take the Greek rendered by 'among the apostles' to mean 'in the eyes of the apostles': 'apostle' could then have its narrower sense. But it is much more probable that the phrase has the sense 'among the apostles', which is the way in which it was taken by the patristic commentators. On this interpretation 'the apostles' must be given a wider sense as denoting those itinerant missionaries who were recognized by the churches as constituting a distinct group among the participants in the work of spreading the gospel (compare, for example, Acts 14.4, 14; 1 Cor 12.28; Eph 4.11; 1 Th 2.7). That Paul should not only include a woman among the apostles but actually describe her, together with Andronicus, as outstanding among them, is highly significant evidence (along with the importance he accords in this chapter to Phoebe, Prisca, Mary, Tryphaena, Tryphosa, Persis, the mother of Rufus, Julia and the sister of Nereus) of the falsity of the widespread and stubbornly persistent notion that Paul had a low view of women and something to which the Church as a whole has so far failed to pay proper attention. The last words of the verse indicate that Andronicus and Junia were converted before Paul.

8–15 contains the rest of Paul's special greetings to individuals and groups. **Greet Ampliatus, my beloved in the Lord. Greet Urbanus, our fellow-worker in Christ, and my beloved Stachys.** The first two are common slave names, the third is a rare Greek name, but is found in an inscription as the name of a slave in the imperial household. There would seem to be a real possibility that the earlier of two people bearing the name Ampliatus who are commemorated in a burial-chamber in the Catacomb of Domitilla is the person here greeted by Paul. **Greet Apelles who has been proved in Christ.** Did Paul happen to know that under some particular trial this man had proved himself a faithful Christian? Or did he simply want to vary his commendatory expressions? – any true Christian of some maturity could be so described. **Greet the** *brethren* **among the members of the household of Aristobulus.** The suggestion seems quite likely that this Aristobulus is the grandson of Herod the Great and brother of Agrippa I, who apparently lived in Rome as a private person and was a friend of the Emperor Claudius; that after his death his household was united with the imperial household, though still keeping their identity as a group according to the custom obtaining in such circumstances; and that Paul is greeting the Christians among them. **Greet Herodion my kinsman. Greet those from the household of Narcissus who are in the Lord.** Maybe there were Christians among the members of the household of the notorious Narcissus, who had been an influential favourite of the Emperor Claudius but had been forced to commit suicide shortly after that emperor's death: this household had most probably passed into the ownership of Nero. In the next verse three more women are greeted, the first and second possibly twin sisters, the third – to judge from her name – probably a slave or freedwoman: **Greet Tryphaena and Tryphosa who labour in the Lord. Greet Persis the beloved, who has laboured much in the Lord.** With reference to **Greet Rufus, the elect in the Lord, and his mother who is also a mother to me** it is natural to wonder whether the Rufus named is the same man who is mentioned in Mk 15.21, which seems to imply that someone called Rufus was well known among those for whom the evangelist was writing. But that the name is a common one has to be admitted. We may presume that on some occasion Rufus's mother had befriended Paul in a motherly way, and that Paul is here gracefully acknowledging the fact. **Greet Asyncritus,**

Phlegon, Hermes, Patrobas, Hermas, and the brethren who are with them. Greet Philologus and Julia, Nereus and his sister, and Olympas, and all the saints who are with them. These are apparently greetings to two different groups of Christians meeting for purposes of church life. Compare v. 5a. All the five men named in the former greeting are likely – to judge from their names – to have been slaves or freedmen.

16. Greet one another with a holy kiss. Having completed his greetings to particular individuals and the groups associated with some of them, Paul now makes a general request to the Christians in Rome to greet one another with a holy kiss. Compare 1 Cor 16.20; 2 Cor 13.12; 1 Th 5.26; 1 Pet 5.14. The earliest clear reference to the kiss as a regular part of the Church's worship is in Justin, *I Apol.* 65 (about A.D.155), according to which it was given between the intercessory prayers and the offertory. It is not impossible that Paul's injunction itself presupposes the likelihood that the Christians in Rome would already be accustomed to exchange a kiss in preparation for their celebration of the Holy Supper (the way the injunction is given suggests that he did not expect it to cause any surprise).

All the churches of Christ greet you might seem to have a special appropriateness, addressed to the Christians of Rome, the imperial capital.

17–20a. The abruptness of the introduction of these verses at this point has, in our judgment, been greatly exaggerated. It is not true that they interrupt the series of greetings; for the greetings which follow are of a different sort, being not Paul's greetings but messages of greeting from those who are with Paul, and are a postscript added after Paul's autograph attestation of the letter (v. 20b). Nor is it true that there is nothing in the context to explain the introduction of these verses at this point; for the injunction to greet one another with a holy kiss contains in itself an implicit warning against those things which are liable to destroy the church's peace and against the unholy kisses of those who would attach themselves to the church's fellowship while remaining all the time alien from it in doctrine or life. And the mention of 'All the churches' indicates that Paul's mind was not so concentrated on the Christians in Rome as to exclude all thought of other churches well known to him, and, if he began to think about those other churches, it would be but natural for him to remember the troubles which had afflicted them, and from which the Christian community in Rome was unlikely to be exempt.

I exhort you, brethren, to mark those who cause divisions and occasions of stumbling in opposition to the teaching you have learned. Here 'mark' means 'mark (so as to beware of)': contrast its use in Phil 3.17. The words 'in opposition to the teaching you have received' are important. Sometimes divisions have to be caused for the sake of the truth (see, for example, Gal 1.8f; and note that Jesus Himself was a cause of division – compare, for example, Mt 10.34–36); and in certain circumstances the truth itself is a stumbling-block (see, for example, 9.32b–33; Lk 7.23). **Avoid them** clarifies and strengthens 'mark': the Roman Christians are not only to mark such people in the sense of recognizing them for the danger which they are: they are actually to avoid them, to keep out of their way.

for such people serve not our Lord Christ but their own bellies, and deceive the hearts of the simple by their high-sounding plausibility is clearly intended to explain why it is that the people to whom Paul has just referred constitute so serious a danger. The first part declares that they are no servants of Christ, who is Paul's and the Roman Christians' Lord, but instead of serving Him serve their own belly. Barrett takes the reference to be to 'their preoccupation with food laws'; but, while this interpretation goes back to the early Church and has some modern supporters, it does not seem very likely. If 'bellies' is really to be taken quite literally, a much more natural explanation, in view of 14.15–21, would surely be that Paul has in mind the selfish insistence of the 'strong' of 14.1–15.13 on eating meat even at the cost of the spiritual ruin of their 'weak' brothers (see, especially, 14.17f, where the strong are reminded that the kingdom of God is not a matter of eating and drinking, and their selfish and frivolous conduct is contrasted with the proper service of Christ). But it seems more probable that the expression 'serve one's own belly' is here used in a less narrowly literal sense. Perhaps the most likely explanation is that 'serve one's own belly' is here used to denote serving oneself, being the willing slave of one's egotism, that walking according to the flesh and having one's life determined by the flesh, to which 8.4 and 5 refer. In the second part Paul states that these people (whoever they are) take in the unsuspecting by their fair-sounding speech.

What then can be said about the identity of these people, against whom this warning is issued? Some have assumed that they must be Judaizers, others have seen a reference to antinomians. One might think of the selfish among the 'strong' of 14.1–15.13, or wonder whether possibly Paul had in mind people of 'gnosticizing' tendencies, or people who made much of their possession of the Spirit and were inclined to value exciting and showy gifts unduly, to the detriment of charity and brotherliness. But the probability that there were in the early Church, as there are in the Church today, people eager to cause divisions and to set stumbling-blocks in the way of their fellows not because of any more or less seriously held theological or practical convictions but simply out of a desire to gratify their own self-importance, should certainly not be overlooked. To imagine that one can, on the basis of vv. 17 and 18 or of any other evidence afforded by the epistle, single out one group of trouble-makers, either already present in the church in Rome or as yet only constituting a possible danger from outside, as the people whom Paul has in mind, seems to us quite unrealistic. If Paul had one particular group in mind, we cannot be at all certain which it was. But he may well have had more than one group in mind, or he may have been warning in a quite general way against a danger which he knew would always threaten the churches but could present itself in many different forms.

For your obedience is known to all, and for this I rejoice over you supports the exhortation of v. 17f: the Roman Christians have a reputation to live up to. **But I want you to be wise unto that which is good, but kept pure from what is evil** expresses Paul's desire that the Roman Christians may be wise for the purpose of what is good and therefore constant in their obedience (which he has just mentioned), but preserved in their integrity over against what is evil and so proof against the specious approaches of those against whom he has just warned them. **And the God of peace shall crush Satan under your feet soon** is a promise of the final consummation (that the reference is to the people mentioned in v. 17f, regarded as servants of Satan, seems to us quite unlikely). But this does not mean that we should see in the 'soon' a proof that Paul was sure that the Parousia would occur within, at the most, a few decades. (On this important matter see on 13.12 and on 15.19 and 23.)

20b. The grace of our Lord Jesus be with you is Paul's autograph authentication of his letter. It was customary for the sender of a letter, when the laborious task of actually writing the text had been fulfilled by someone else, to add a concluding greeting in his own hand. This served to authenticate the letter as a signature does today. The ordinary concluding greeting was 'Farewell'. Just as Paul did with the opening letter formula, so he also transformed the closing greeting into a vehicle of specifically Christian and theological content. The Pauline closing greeting occurs in varying forms, but in every closing greeting in the Pauline corpus the word 'grace' occurs. On the word 'grace' see on 1.7.

21–23 is a postscript. **Timothy, my fellow-worker, greets you, and** *so do* **Lucius and Jason and Sosipater, my kinsmen.** Four friends of Paul who are with him send their greetings to the Christians in Rome. For Timothy, who had certainly earned the description 'my fellow-worker', reference may be made to 1 Cor 4.17; 16.10f; 2 Cor 1.1, 19; Phil 1.1; 2.19–24; Col 1.1; I Th 1.1; 3.2, 6; 2 Th 1.1; Philem 1; also Acts 16.1–3; 17.14f; 18.5; 19.22; 20.4f; and, of course, 1 and 2 Timothy. The only other occurrence in the New Testament of the name 'Lucius' is in Acts 13.1; but it is not very likely that the Lucius mentioned here is the same as the one referred to in Acts. Some have identified this Lucius with Luke (Col 4.14; Philem 24; 2 Tim 4.11). It is true that the Greek represented by 'Luke' is a possible equivalent of 'Lucius', and also that Acts 20.5ff implies that the author of the 'we' passages of Acts was with Paul at the appropriate time. But a definite decision about this suggestion seems to be impossible. Jason could be the same person as is mentioned in Acts 17.5–7, 9. Sosipater could well be the same person as the Sopater of Acts 20.4 ('Sopater' would be a quite likely shortened form of 'Sosipater').

I, Tertius, who have written this letter, greet you in the Lord. On the part played by Tertius see p. xi. It could be that Tertius had some connexion with Rome and would be known to some of the Christians there.

Gaius, my host (and, indeed, the whole church's), greets you. The natural conclusion to draw from 'my host' would seem to be that Paul was actually staying with Gaius at the time of writing. 'Gaius' is an extremely common Roman *praenomen* (that is, first or personal name as opposed to the *gens* or clan and family

names). It has been suggested that this could be the same person as
is designated 'Titius Justus' in Acts 18.7, and who received Paul
and – it is probably implied – the Corinthian believers into his
house, when they were driven out of the neighbouring synagogue.
Titius Justus could have had 'Gaius' as his *praenomen*. But no
more can be said than that this identification is possible. Whether
'the whole church's' is meant to indicate that the local church met
in his house or that he gave hospitality to any Christians passing
through Corinth, the implication would probably be that he was,
at least, fairly wealthy. **Erastus, the city treasurer, and brother
Quartus greet you** completes the postscript. It seems impossible to
decide with any degree of certainty whether this Erastus and the
Erastus of Acts 19.22 and 2 Tim 4.20 are the same person. It is
interesting to find a highly placed official of such an important city
as Corinth a member of the Christian community at this date.
About Quartus nothing is known beyond this mention of him. By
'brother' (the Greek is literally 'the brother') is surely meant
simply 'fellow-Christian'.

That v. 24 is secondary may be regarded as certain. It is rightly
omitted by the RV, and other modern versions.

**25–27. To him who is able to confirm you in accord with my gospel
and the proclamation of Jesus Christ, *which is* according to the
revelation of the mystery which has been hidden in silence for ages
from before creation but has now been manifested and, in
accordance with the command of the eternal God, has been clarified
through the prophetic scriptures for the purpose of bringing about
obedience of faith among all the Gentiles, – to the only wise God,
through Jesus Christ, to him be glory for ever and ever. Amen.** These
verses (on which see pp. ix-xi), though certainly not part of Paul's
letter to the Christians in Rome, form a not unsuitable
doxological appendix to it. Glory is ascribed to the One who is
able to confirm the readers in their commitment to the gospel
preached by Paul and other Christian preachers, that is, the
proclamation of Jesus Christ. The further explanatory material
introduced by (in our translation) '*which is*' and continuing down
to the end of v. 26 characterizes still more closely the content of the
proclamation. The apostolic preaching of Jesus Christ is a matter
of God's revelation of His secret which has been hidden in silence
for ages from before the creation of the universe but has now been

manifested. It is only in the present time of the earthly ministry of Jesus Christ and the on-going proclamation of Him by the Church that God's secret has been manifested. The contrast indicated by the 'but' at the beginning of v. 26 is the contrast between the ages before Christ's incarnation and the period which began with it. It was in the gospel events, the life, death, resurrection and ascension of Jesus Christ, that the mystery was manifested decisively, but there is a continuing manifestation (wholly dependent on the manifestation in the gospel events) in the on-going proclamation of that once for all manifestation.

The words 'and, in accordance with the command of the eternal God, has been clarified through the prophetic scriptures for the purpose of bringing about obedience of faith among all the Gentiles' form a third member of the series begun with 'which has been hidden in silence for ages' and 'but has now been manifested'. The manifestation, which has taken place in the gospel events and their subsequent proclamation, and is contrasted with the hiddenness of the mystery in the past, is a manifestation which is properly understood in its true significance only in the light of its Old Testament foreshadowing and attestation. It is when the manifestation of the mystery is understood as the fulfilment of God's promises made in the Old Testament (compare 1.2), as attested, interpreted, clarified, by the Old Testament (compare, for example, 3.21; 9.33; 10.4–9, 11, 13), that it is truly understood as the gospel of God for all mankind. 'in accordance with the command of the eternal God' indicates that it is in accordance with God's will and appointment that this attestation and clarification have been effected; and 'for the purpose of bringing about obedience of faith among all the Gentiles' indicates God's purpose in so ordering things.

In v. 27 'to him' represents a dative singular masculine relative pronoun in Greek. This would ordinarily give us the meaning 'to whom', and the natural reference would be to Jesus Christ, just mentioned. If this was intended, the author of the doxology would have slipped from an ascription of glory to God into an ascription of glory to Christ. We have assumed that it is rather more likely that he has used a relative pronoun as an equivalent to a demonstrative, intended to pick up the preceding datives – hence our translation 'to him', referring to God.

INDEX OF SUBJECTS